More praise for *Intimate Nature*

"Writings by contributors as various as tribal elders and writers Ursula K. Le Guin, Tess Gallagher, and Alice Walker seem to convey a new ethic of relating to animals in a way that is less aggressive and more respectfully attuned to the nuances not only of different species, but of individual animals."

—*The Seattle Times*

"The editors—Linda Hogan, Deena Metzger, Brenda Peterson—have ardently and successfully conjoined panels of individual texture and vibrancy into another, larger work, a quilt remarkably harmonious despite, or because of, the differing qualities each piece brings to the work as a whole. Unique as each poem, story, and essay is, all begin at the same place, a place of being and relating, and that has everything to do with empathy, and empathy has so much to do with being female. . . . And luckily for us, [these] women . . . have the additional gift of communicating to the rest of us the beauty, intelligence, and inestimable value of our animal kin."

—*The Bloomsbury Review*

"Reading [these] fascinating accounts of close encounters with whales, dolphins, orangutans, bears, wolves, elephants, chimpanzees, birds, and horses can, in the editors' words, help begin to 'return us to a sacred relationship with the natural world.' "

—*Publishers Weekly*

"An impressive and thought-provoking anthology . . . A groundbreaking collection . . . A vast range of viewpoints . . . This book is the first of its kind."

—*Boulder Planet*

"[An] enchanting read."

—*Seattle Magazine*

Please turn the page for more reviews. . . .

Intimate
NATURE

The Bond Between Women and Animals

Edited by

LINDA HOGAN,

DEENA METZGER,

and **BRENDA PETERSON**

FAWCETT BOOKS
THE BALLANTINE PUBLISHING GROUP • NEW YORK

A Fawcett Book
Published by The Ballantine Publishing Group

CONTENTS

ACKNOWLEDGMENTS

The authors would like to gratefully acknowledge all the women in this book who have contributed to changing the way we see, protect, conserve, and understand animals. We would also like to give special thanks to those who have helped bring this book to life: Marlene Blessing for creating the original title *Stories of An Intimate Nature*; Becca Robinson for her extraordinary organization, insights, and editorial assistance; and Jenny Robinson for helping us make our initial deadline. Thanks also to Toni Frohoff, Stacy Young, and Karen Campbell for editorial help with final galleys. We are also abidingly grateful to our editors, Joanne Wyckoff and Andrea Schulz, who believed in this project and had the vision to help us every step of the way.

A nimals have been with us from the beginning of our existence in this world. They have been here since the first sacred times of the gods and creation, from places with names as diverse as Turtle Island, Eden, Gondwana. They have shared with us this land, water, and air. They have suffered with us, as accomplices of accused witches, as sacrificial offerings. They have suffered for us, as bearers of fur and other parts we have wanted or needed, as subjects in the desolate laboratories of our scientific and medical worlds. They have been consumed by us and have, by this nourishment, become our very bodies, bone and blood.

We have also experienced animals as sacred beings in a spiritual relationship dating back to the first petroglyphs and paintings in caves: Women and animals have existed together in the interior world of the soul. It is no coincidence that the word *anima* bespeaks the human soul in its feminine form. The source word for soul and animal is "anima"—breath. And the Jungian term for the feminine is "anima." Animals have been the source of our connection with the world all along, and of that connection is born spiritual power, feminine presence, and human survival.

We have also lived with animals as cocreators of this world. Most creation stories name animals as the first beings to exist in this present Earth-time, as creators or as partners in the creation of this world. For most peoples, including the early indigenous Europeans, it was not a singular god who created the world; the whole of creation was shaped by the animals. Turtle. Frog. Panther. Coyote. Dolphin. Fox. Their names are many. They arrived here before us. They have been intermediaries between humans and gods. And through their teachings and their own sometimes chosen relationships with the human people, they have taught us hunting, healing, and medicine ways. From them we have even learned about love and the depths of community and familial bonding. We have followed them to the plants that heal us and they have helped infuse this shared world with beauty and magic and grace. We are animated by animals. Their lives have transformed our lives. They are so powerful a presence that even when they aren't here, we imagine them or try to summon them in spirit as we have done in embodied animal flesh.

In recent years, according to Earth-time, humans have lost their more intimate relationships with animals as peers, teachers, and kindred allies. For centuries now, male priests, doctors, and scientists have declared animals a territory to be approached with objectivity and detachment. And in these last centuries we have become increasingly separated from animals and the natural world. We've been taught to see them as creatures who have no soul, no capacity for pain, emotion, intelligence, or worth. In Claude Bernard's *Physiology*, he states that "A man of science no longer hears the cry of animals, the blood that flows . . . he sees only his idea."

Most of the women represented in this book are daughters of this Western worldview that privileges the human above all else and denigrates the rest of our sister creatures. In more recent times, however, there has been a renewed interest in and respect for the older traditions; we have taken a fresh look at the value of animals, plants, and other lives evolving alongside ours. Now, even in science, we find that our futures depend upon reaching out beyond our own species' estrangement and loneliness to connect with the physical presences in the world around us.

We are witnessing a return to respect for the natural world and the authority of wildness. We have begun to remember what was encoded in our blood, our DNA, in centuries past. There has been a return to the belief that everything is alive, that all matter is resonant with energy. This old tribal intelligence is newly called the Gaia hypothesis, and it again turns toward a world that is, in all its matter, alive. While the Gaia story is a theory born of older, tribal knowledge, its reappearance has given us a renewed concept of the creation. The Deep Ecology movement, too, has emerged as a new science, a perspective that turns us again toward the ancient respect for the life of animals as beings worthy in their own right, within their own necessary environment, and not only for how they can be used by us. It is a step away from a worldview that, often, only sees the sacred in the abstract. The animal rights movement has helped to turn many thinkers back toward a sense of sacred nature as well, and to reconsider the role of human compassion for nonhuman life-forms. While it has seemed extreme to some, it provides a necessary balance to the views that have governed science, medicine, and philosophy for so many years.

Women have been vital in reestablishing the relationships with animals and the rest of nature. There have been writers, our mother writers, such as Rachel Carson, the author of *Silent Spring*, who have insisted that every piece of this world of life is an interconnected whole, organic and endangered. Susan Griffin's revolutionary work, *Woman and Nature: The Roaring Inside Her,* helped to reveal how animals and women have been identified and defined inside a male imagination. Groundbreaking field studies by women scientists have also changed the way the world sees animals. Living in the field for decades alongside wild animals, such scientists as Jane Goodall, Birute Galdikas, Cynthia Moss, Katy Payne, Alexandra Morton, Helena Symonds, and Dian Fossey have shown us the intimate natures of animal families. Often matriarchies, these animal societies have much to teach us about nurturing the next generation, mating choices, family history, and group survival.

These writers and researchers, together with those ancient indigenous intellectual and religious traditions, began to mend what has been broken by a system of careless thought. They increased our awareness of the physical and spiritual relationship we need to establish with the earth, teaching us that we are woven together with the rest of the world equally and beautifully. It is both heartening and hopeful that some of these women descend from those Western thinkers who have been responsible for breaking the web of our being. This offers us hope for a future in which we all will survive and thrive.

Perhaps these women have been transformative because our approach to relationship has been different from that of men. What women have brought into the equation is a respect for feeling and empathy as tools to create intimate bonds of connection. Perhaps it is our own bodies that remind us that we, too, are animal, kin to those we work with, live with, love, and swallow. Perhaps it is because, like animals, we have so often been cherished at the same time we have been hated. Historically we have been identified with animals; it was once thought that a woman was "basically an infertile man with an animal soul." Whatever the reasons, we have seen the world differently than our sons and fathers and lovers, and in that different view we have felt that we are not such different kinds of people than the other animals.

It has been women, primarily, who have spoken out most often against the suffering and pain of animals, and it has mostly been women who have had the courage to admit their love for the other lives around us. As forbidden a concept as it has seemed in scientific scrutiny, love for other species must always be part of the equation.

It has been the women in science, largely, who have revised ideas about what is considered knowledge and fashioned a new approach to this knowledge. Researchers such as Birute Galdikas, who waited twelve years to be accepted into orangutan society as an adopted "grandmother," and Denise Herzing, who has studied the same pod of wild dolphins for over a decade, documenting their generations, show us, in Herzing's words, that "All observation is intimate." In their work, these women integrate receptivity as well as objectivity. When these women watch animals, they also engage their hearts in what Jane Goodall calls "compassion . . . a heightened moral responsibility for beings who are so like ourselves." Goodall also said that when she helped an animal in the wild, she was told by her male peers that she was not objective and was interfering with nature. "You call it interference, I call it help," she told them. And Goodall's "help" has since been admired internationally not only as compassion but as the best of science.

This strong sense of compassion that many women bring to the study, celebration, and love of animals has been world-changing and visionary. We can say now that the old guard of detached science is being replaced with the new guardians, many of them the women in this book.

The passion to know nature continues to motivate us as scientists and writers as we study animals, form bonds with them, and write about them. Intimacy and relationship with other animals has become one of the places we inhabit, like land, home, air, or water. In turn, we are inhabited by it, our work and lives shaped by the relationships forged by it. Because of our work, we are replacing the hard, objective eye of the past with one of a softer sight, replacing a concept of anthropomorphism with one of empathy.

At the center of empathy and compassionate understanding lies the ability to see the other as true peer, to recognize intelligence and communication in all forms, no matter how unlike ourselves these forms might be. It is this gift of empathy and connection, embodied in the relationship between us and other species, that enables us to thrive now and into the future.

Because we share with them the same life force, to know the animal other as worthy, alive, and even as a beloved peer is to be truly in relationship with the powerful forces of creation itself. To acknowledge and even cherish the intelligence in other forms of life is to sustain our own futures. To honor intimacy across the seeming boundaries of species is to return the sacred to the world. We are all the same world inside different skins, and with different intelligences.

We glimpse these unique other intelligences when women such as acoustic scientist Katy Payne studies humpback whales. In their enormous voyages around our planet, humpbacks are vulnerable and endangered by our activities.

In her scientific testimony to protest ocean sound testing (ATOC), Katy Payne (who also discovered the language of elephants) said of whale songs: They are "the most wonderful form of nonhuman culture we know. They are highly structured, but fluid and ever-evolving, using structures and devices we find in human song and poetry. Beautiful and moving to listen to, they are a powerful part of the bridge between ourselves and the rest of nature." It is through the work of such scientists as Payne that we now have the knowledge that whales, while taking in new information, change their songs over time in an ongoing story of transformation and creation.

Contained here are writings that open new pathways of understanding, stories of an intimate nature, the shared worlds of woman and animal, the words and languages that are bridges between species. There are testimonies about how the relationships between species form and how they open us to new knowledge. The book includes indigenous activists and thinkers such as Hawaiian native Haunani Kay-Trask and Guatemalan native Rigoberta Menchu, who have both been part of the struggles for survival of their own people, as well as the environment.

This is a book of changing stories, ongoing transformation and creation, by women who are struggling to protect and look after the world. It reports the changing story of our lives in this time of history as well as those of our sister creatures.

Women's caretaking and leadership impulses are finding deep and resonant voice in words that return us to a sacred relationship with the natural world. Because of the work so many women are doing in the field, in the study, in the heart, we are all coming to new insights about our vulnerable planet. We are being changed as a species; we are taking greater care; we are confirming what we have already known or suspected—each species is valuable beyond measure and compare, and the world thrives by our keeping each life, and even each death, in its own place of inhabitance.

The women in this anthology are describing a new creation, the creation of emotional and physical bridges, lifelines between species, that take us to new ways of being human in our shared world.

Every contributor here evinces this reciprocity. In these pages are women who study animals, live with, and among, them, women who have been present at animal births, women who have hand-raised lions and rhinos in the wild, women who have mourned animal deaths. Speaking against the loss of animals, which is a human loss as well, these women are no longer only arguing animal intelligence or animal emotion, but are engaged with the responsibilities of kinship as they set before us the words that will shape a living future. Their work offers a new understanding, and places before our eyes a new vision rising out of the ashes of old beliefs. As these writers cross the threshold between species, they keep open a way to survival by shaping animal alliances that are organic, fertile, alive.

The animals are speaking to us, through us, and with us. They are coming to us, not only in our dreams but in our lives. Perhaps in these moments of their disappearance and endangerment, they are offering themselves in ways unknown in the past, in the words of women, and we are beginning to remember and understand their lives and their many languages. And we rejoice in their great beauty and intelligences. The renewed reconciliation between the human family and our sister creatures is a hopeful sign for a shared future. We see this book as not only a lament and a passionate wake-up call, but as a celebration of the shared lives of animals and women.

ANIMALS AND PEOPLE:
"THE HUMAN HEART IN CONFLICT WITH ITSELF"

Pattiann Rogers

Some of us like to photograph them. Some
of us like to paint pictures of them. Some of us
like to sculpt them and make statues and carvings
of them. Some of us like to compose music
about them and sing about them. And some of us
like to write about them.

                     Some of us like to go out
and catch them and kill them and eat them. Some
of us like to hunt them and shoot them and eat them.
Some of us like to raise them, care for them and eat
them. Some of us just like to eat them.

                         And some of us
name them and name their seasons and name their hours,
and some of us, in our curiosity, open them up
and study them with our tools and name their parts.
We capture them, mark them and release them,
and then we track them and spy on them and enter
their lives and affect their lives and abandon
their lives. We breed them and manipulate them
and alter them. Some of us experiment
upon them.

           We put them on tethers and leashes,
in shackles and harnesses, in cages and boxes,
inside fences and walls. We put them in yokes

and muzzles. We want them to carry us and pull us
and haul for us.

And we want some of them
to be our companions, some of them to ride on our fingers
and some to ride sitting on our wrists or on our shoulders
and some to ride in our arms, ride clutching our necks.
We want them to walk at our heels.

We want them to trust
us and come to us, take our offerings, eat from our hands.
We want to participate in their beauty. We want to assume
their beauty and so possess them. We want to be kind
to them and so possess them with our kindness and so
partake of their beauty in that way.

And we want them
to learn our language. We try to teach them our language.
We speak to them. We put *our* words in *their* mouths.
We want *them* to speak. We want to know what they see
when they look at us.

We use their heads and their bladders
for balls, their guts and their hides and their bones
to make music. We skin them and wear them for coats,
their scalps for hats. We rob them, their milk
and their honey, their feathers and their eggs.
We make money from them.

We construct icons of them.
We make images of them and put their images on our clothes
and on our necklaces and rings and on our walls
and in our religious places. We preserve their dead
bodies and parts of their dead bodies and display
them in our homes and buildings.

We name mountains
and rivers and cities and streets and organizations
and gangs and causes after them. We name years and time
and constellations of stars after them. We make mascots
of them, naming our athletic teams after them. Sometimes
we name ourselves after them.

We make toys of them
and rhymes of them for our children. We mold them
and shape them and distort them to fit our myths
and our stories and our dramas. We like to dress up
like them and masquerade as them. We like to imitate them
and try to move as they move and make the sounds they make,
hoping, by these means, to enter and become the black
mysteries of their being.

Sometimes we dress them
in our clothes and teach them tricks and laugh at them
and marvel at them. And we make parades of them
and festivals of them. We want them to entertain us
and amaze us and frighten us and reassure us
and calm us and rescue us from boredom.

We pit them
against one another and watch them fight one another,
and we gamble on them. We want to compete with them
ourselves, challenging them, testing our wits and talents
against their wits and talents, in forests and on plains,
in the ring. We want to be able to run like them and leap
like them and swim like them and fly like them and fight
like them and endure like them.

We want their total
absorption in the moment. We want their unwavering devotion
to life. We want their oblivion.

Some of us give thanks
and bless those we kill and eat, and ask for pardon,
and this is beautiful as long as they are the ones dying
and we are the ones eating.

And as long as we are not
seriously threatened, as long as we and our children
aren't hungry and aren't cold, we say, with a certain
degree of superiority, that we are no better
than any of them, that any of them deserve to live
just as much as we do.

And after we have proclaimed
this thought, and by so doing subtly pointed out

that we are allowing them to live, we direct them
and manage them and herd them and train them and follow
them and map them and collect them and make specimens
of them and butcher them and move them here and move
them there and we place them on lists and we take
them off of lists and we stare at them and stare
at them and stare at them.

        We track them in our sleep.
They become the form of our sleep. We dream of them.
We seek them with accusation. We seek them
with supplication.

        And in the ultimate imposition,
as Thoreau said, we make them bear the burden
of our thoughts. We make them carry the burden
of our metaphors and the burden of our desires and our guilt
and carry the equal burden of our curiosity and concern.
We make them bear our sins and our prayers and our hopes
into the desert, into the sky, into the stars.
We say we kill them for God.

        We adore them and we curse
them. We caress them and we ravish them. We want them
to acknowledge us and be with us. We want them to disappear
and be autonomous. We abhor their viciousness and lack
of pity, as we abhor our own viciousness and lack of pity.
We love them and we reproach them, just as we love
and reproach ourselves.

        We will never, we cannot,
leave them alone, even the tiniest one, ever, because we know
we are one with them. Their blood is our blood. Their breath
is our breath, their beginning our beginning, their fate
our fate.

        Thus we deny them. Thus we yearn
for them. They are among us and within us and of us,
inextricably woven with the form and manner of our being,
with our understanding and our imaginations.
They are the grit and the salt and the lullaby
of our language.

We have a need to believe they are there,
and always will be, whether we witness them or not.
We need to know they are there, a vigorous life maintaining
itself without our presence, without our assistance,
without our attention. We need to know, we *must* know,
that we come from such stock so continuously and tenaciously
and religiously devoted to life.

We know we are one with them,
and we are frantic to understand how to actualize that union.
We attempt to actualize that union in our many stumbling,
ignorant and destructive ways, in our many confused
and noble and praiseworthy ways.

For how can we possess dignity
if we allow them no dignity? Who will recognize our beauty
if we do not revel in their beauty? How can we hope
to receive honor if we give no honor? How can we believe
in grace if we cannot bestow grace?

We want what we cannot
have. We want to give life at the same moment
we are taking it, nurture life at the same moment we light
the fire and raise the knife. We want to live, to provide,
and not be instruments of destruction, instruments
of death. We want to reconcile our "egoistic concerns"
with our "universal compassion." We want the lion
and the lamb to exist in amity, the lion and the lamb
within finally to dwell together, to lie down together
in peace and praise at last.

I: FIRST PEOPLE

"*When the salmon are gone,*" writes Liz Woody, "*that is the end of life as we know it.*" The words of indigenous women are words of necessity, words that come from a close proximity to the land, from unbroken treaties between human beings and the animal people. We depend on the animals for our survival, both cultural and physical. Our way of seeing animals is different from the Western worldview. It comes from people whose lives, languages, and ways of being in the world are intimately connected with the animal world, where humans remain caretakers and guardians of the other species by which we live. The animals are not only our food source, but the center of many languages, including those of prayer, ceremony, and spiritual relationship. Here, native women turn these words toward the animals to reveal the shared histories of animals and native peoples, the lives held in common. These words come from women who remember the relationships because the bonds have only recently been broken, and in many places and for many peoples the connection remains intact.

Leslie Silko

You will know
when you walk
in bear country
By the silence
flowing swiftly between the juniper trees
by the sundown colors of sandrock
all around you.

You may smell damp earth
scratched away
from yucca roots
You may hear snorts and growls
slow and massive sounds
from caves
in the cliffs high above you.

It is difficult to explain
how they call you
All but a few who went to them
left behind families
       grandparents
       and sons
       a good life.

The problem is
you will never want to return
Their beauty will overcome your memory
like winter sun
melting ice shadows from snow
And you will remain with them
locked forever inside yourself
        your eyes will see you
        dark shaggy and thick.

We can send bear priests
loping after you
their medicine bags
bouncing against their chests
Naked legs painted black
bear claw necklaces
rattling against
their capes of blue spruce.

They will follow your trail
into the narrow canyon
through the blue-gray mountain sage
to the clearing
where you stopped to look back
and saw only bear tracks
behind you.

When they call
faint memories
will writhe around your heart
and startle you with their distance.
But the others will listen
because bear priests
sing beautiful songs
They must
if they are ever to call you back.

They will try to bring you
step by step
back to the place you stopped
and found only bear prints in the sand
where your feet had been.

Whose voice is this?
You may wonder
hearing this story when
after all
you are alone
hiking in these canyons and hills
while your wife and sons are waiting
back at the car for you.

But you have been listening to me
for some time now
from the very beginning in fact
and you are alone in this canyon of stillness
not even cedar birds flutter.
See, the sun is going down now
the sandrock is washed in its colors
Don't be afraid
        we love you
        we've been calling you
        all this time
Go ahead
turn around
see the shape
of your footprints
in the sand.

Linda Hogan

It is a warm autumn day and we are driving east to release a golden eagle. We drive out past the farmlands with gold stalks of last year's corn bristling up from the flat fields, past hills showing the signs of a recent snow; moisture, a scattering of white. The front range of mountains is soft in the west behind us, the fields furrowed and lined where the mowers have been.

The eagle is quiet in a carrier in the back of the car. We drive with it past old, worn-looking houses, over railroad tracks, past trees twisted by years of shaping wind. We travel past a marsh of old, rattling cattails, and blue sky laying itself down on a snaking irrigation canal. There are rolls of hay and grain silos. Antlers of deer and elk are nailed on the barns as if to say they are worshiped. And beneath all this is the black, rich earth.

As we reach the place where the eagle came from, something inside the car changes; something strong and different is in the air. We stop talking, as if to listen. As soon as I feel it, Sigrid, the caretaker of injured raptors, feels it, too. She says of the eagle, "He knows he's home."

This feeling is a language larger than human, conveyed to us by the eagle we are transporting, the eagle we have held in our hands. Wordless, it seems to be a language spoken from and to the body. It enters skin, stomach, and heart. Feeling it, I can't help but think of the limits of our human language, what we can't speak, what we have no words for. It is clear there is a vocabulary of senses, a grammar beyond that of human making.

The eagle is still. He is waiting, listening. Looking back at him, I see what I can only call a look of wonder on his face, his beak slightly open, his eyes alert. The excitement and tension is strong and palpable, as if it had long been beyond the eagle's belief that he would ever return to this place. The changed climate in the car is so powerful that I am anxious; I want to pull over right away and let him go, but we drive farther, checking every small detail of the terrain, the currents of air, to make certain the tawny dark-eyed eagle will have the best chance for flight and survival. He needs a hill to rise from, a wide-trunked tree in the distance where he can sit in a branch and groom while he looks over the land and sky and decides what he will do. From past experience with birds, we know this; we have watched them do this many times before, an eagle, hawk, or owl sitting, taking in the world's terrain, even the parts of it we, with our limited human vision, can't see. He will look at the land and remember it, remembering the alive currents of air as they sweep the grasses as surely as we remember the contours of our own homelands.

Finally, finding the right place, we pull over and take him out of the carrier. With grief and joy mixed together in our hearts, we say good-bye and set him free, placing him on the ground. He looks around for only a moment and then, in a muscular rise, his long wings open, strong and wide, he pulls upward. This bird doesn't stop in a tree to wait and watch. He flies, the light on him gold and brown. His dark eyes watch us. He circles back one last time the way so many birds do, as if to say good-bye. And then he travels away until he is only a spot in the sky and soon he disappears altogether from our sight, although with his keener vision, we know that he still sees us where we stand on the autumn earth wondering, as I will always wonder, what was communicated by the bird to us, how it was spoken, how taken in.

MAGIC WORDS (ESKIMO)
In the very earliest time,
when both people and animals lived on earth,
a person could become an animal if he wanted to
and an animal could become a human being.
Sometimes they were people
and sometimes animals
and there was no difference.
All spoke the same language.
That was the time when words were like magic.
The human mind had mysterious powers.
A word spoken by chance
might have strange consequences.
It would suddenly come alive
and what people wanted to happen could happen—
all you had to do was say it.
Nobody could explain this:
That's the way it was.

This is how many stories begin: Long ago, when animals and human beings were the same kind of people, they understood each other. When the world was young, the animals, people, and birds lived together peacefully and in friendship. In these early days of the world, in some locations, animals and humans were equals and, it was said, they spoke a common language, across species bounds. Perhaps they spoke in the way the eagle's language was communicated to two women on that day of its return home. Maybe there is a language deeper than, or beyond, mere human words.

According to many of the old stories, too, the animals are our elders, our ancestors, our sisters. In many reaches of this Earth, they were the first people created. They were here before humans were even imagined or dreamed of, before humans were sung of or breathed into existence by a creator. In the beginning, according to an Iroquois creation account, the only people in the world were animals. When a divine woman fell from the sky, the animals saved her from drowning. They created the land. For the Seminole, after a bird pecked a hole into this world, Panther was the first person to enter this place we now inhabit. Humans came later, imperfect and not quite whole, and sometimes even a little comical in our frailties.

In some places, it was said, animals changed into human form, or humans became animals. "We have respect for the animals," says an Alaska Koyukon elder. "We don't keep them in cages or torture them, because we know the background of animals from the Distant Time. We know that the animal has a spirit—it used to be human—and we know all the things it did. It's not just an animal; it's lots more than that."

In this distant time, "Raven found our forebears in a clamshell on a beach and let them enter a world that was populated by animals and birds that were of 'great power and stature.' " In the distant time, there was a kind of divine flux. At some times, in some ways, there was no line between the species. As we now know from recent science, this is still the case. We all consist of the same spirit of creation, although the terms of expression have changed; we now say we contain the same atomic matter as the rest of life, the same DNA as all life-forms. Our lives are a fluid interchange with all other lives. But the time I am thinking of was before the Christian "fall" of humankind from grace, before Adam was created and before he named and took power over the animals.

In a Tewa Pueblo narrative from the Southwest, people and animals lived together beneath a lake in darkness. The first Mothers—powerful women—sent one man to find the way to the surface world, the one we now inhabit. When he reached this world he saw the wolves, mountain lions, and coyotes. On seeing him, they ran to him and wounded him, then they told him, "We are your friends," and healed him, showing him the special abilities they possessed, their abilities to harm and their equal abilities to heal. When the Tewa man returned to the Mothers he said to them, "We have been accepted."

When I was younger, before I knew the presence of the eagles who would later become my teachers, I had heard stories of the times when humans and animals spoke with one another, but even while I concerned myself always with the lives of animals, caretaking the wounded ones, visiting the healthy, I never gave the old stories as much thought as they deserve. They were just stories, as if stories didn't matter. I didn't think then, as I do now, that a story is a container of knowledge. It is not only how we know about the world, but story is also how we find ourselves and our place of location within this world, as species, as Indian people, as women. According to the people who are from the oldest traditions, the relationship between the animal people and the humans is one of most significance. And this relationship is defined in story. Story is a power that describes our world, our human being, sets out the rules and intricate laws of human beings in relationship with all the rest. And for traditional-thinking native peoples, these rules of conduct and taboos are in place to keep a world alive, to ensure that all life will continue.

> Once the world was occupied by a species called Ikxareyavs, "First People," who had magical powers. At a certain moment, it was realized that Human Beings were about to come spontaneously into existence. At this point, the First People announced their own transformation—into mountains or rocks, into disembodied spirits, and above all into the species of plants and animals that now exist in the world. . . . At the same time, it is ordained how the new species, the Human Beings, will live.
>
> —MAMIE OFFIELD, *KAROK*

As a young person, I didn't notice the similarity of stories the world over, that the Dineh people say we are relatives of the animals, and that the aboriginal people of Australia say we are only one of many kinds of people. Nor did the old stories fit in with my American education. Even though I was a halfhearted student at best, this education taught that what my own, indigenous people once knew were the stories of superstitious and primitive people, not to be believed, not to be taken in a serious light. But we live inside a story, all of us do, and not only does a story prescribe our behavior, it also holds the unfathomed and beautiful depths of a people, fostering and nurturing the very life of the future.

The traditional native complex of laws and religion creates a way of seeing the world that doesn't allow for species loss, whether animal, plant, or insect. It has also been in the indigenous traditions, the place of ancient stories and ways of telling, that I have found the relationship between humans and other species of animals most clearly articulated. Or, I might better say that the stories have found me. In this half-century-old Chickasaw woman they have found a ground in which to grow; they have found their place.

What finally turned me back toward the older traditions of my own and other Native peoples was the inhumanity of the Western world, the places—both inside and out—where that culture's knowledge and language don't go, and the despair, even desperation, it has spawned. We live, I see now, by different stories, the Western mind and the indigenous. In the older, more mature cultures where people still live within the kinship circle of animals and human beings there is connection with animals, not only as food, but as "powers," a word which can be taken to mean states of being, gifts, or capabilities.

I've found, too, that the ancient intellectual traditions are not merely about systems of belief, as some would say. Belief is not a strong enough word. They are more than that: They are part of lived experience, the ongoing experience of people rooted in centuries-old knowledge that is held deep and strong, knowledge about the natural law of Earth, from the beginning of creation, and the magnificent terrestrial intelligence still at work, an intelligence now newly called ecology by the Western science that tells us what our oldest tribal stories maintain—the human animal is a relatively new creation here; animal and plant presences were here before us; and we are truly the younger sisters and brothers of the other animal species, not quite as well developed as we thought we were. It is through our relationships with animals and plants that we maintain a way of living, a cultural ethics shaped from an ancient understanding of the world, and this is remembered in stories that are the deepest reflections of our shared lives on Earth.

That we held, and still hold, treaties with the animals and plant species is a known part of tribal culture. The relationship between human people and animals is still alive and resonant in the world, the ancient tellings carried on by a constellation of stories, songs, and ceremonies, all shaped by *lived* knowledge of the world and its many interwoven, unending relationships. These stories and ceremonies keep open the bridge between one kind of intelligence and another, one species and another.

Until recent years, the Western mind has believed that the Native accounts of creation were simple, primitive. But these were times of creation in all cultures, were times of what we'd now call extraordinary and unlikely happenings, ours no more extraordinary than a sky god saying, "Let there be." In retrospect the Native stories are not more far-fetched than the notion of evolution where fish were transformed into birds, where we people traversed the same shifting space between species from ape to human. Of course, in recent years, the more conservative creationists insist upon the biblical account of how a man was made of clay in a beautiful garden, life breathed into him by a maker from the sky, a woman created of his rib. A story no less or more unusual.

What to make of our older stories and truths and teachings has been a problem for nontribal thinkers. For them, the stories of people and animals are considered magical or mythic. If nothing else, they are considered metaphoric, and "not real." But it would seem that the real difficulty lies in the difference between the tribal cultures' systems of knowledge and thought and those of the conquering people.

Systems of thought create our perception and influence every aspect of how the world is experienced by members of a race or culture. We are educated into our ways of thinking and perceiving, our spiritual and mental orientations. And this "entrainment," as physicist David Bohm called it, of the Western mind has resulted in a way of living in the world that has broken the trust between human and animal. Because the habit of a way of being in the world, of staking our claim to the world, has taken us to a point of devastating loss, we need to rethink not only the stories of a culture but where the stories take their people, and to what ends.

In this light, the old stories of the human relationships with animals can't be discounted. They are not primitive; they are primal. They reflect insights that came from considerable and elaborate systems of knowledge, intellectual traditions and ways of living that were tried, tested, and found true over many thousands of years and on all continents.

But perhaps the truest story is with the animals themselves because we have found our exemplary ways through them, both in the older world and in the present time, both physically and spiritually. According to the traditions of a Seneca animal society, there were medicine animals in ancient times that entered into relationships with the people. The animals themselves taught ceremonies that were to be performed in their names, saying they would provide help for humans if this relationship were kept. We have followed them, not only in the way the early European voyagers and prenavigators did, by following the migrations of whales in order to know their location, or by releasing birds from cages on their sailing vessels and following them toward land, but in ways more subtle and even more sustaining. In a discussion of the wolf dance of the Northwest, artists Bill Holm and William Reid said that "It is often done by a woman or a group of women. The dance is supposed to come from the wolves. There are different versions of its origin and different songs, but the words say something like, 'Your name is widely known among the wolves. You are honored by the wolves.' "

In another recent account, a Northern Cheyenne ceremonialist said that after years spent recovering from removals and genocide, indigenous peoples are learning their lost songs back from the wolves who retained them during the grief-filled times, as if the wolves, even though threatened in their own numbers, have had compassion for the people.

Sometimes animals literally show us the way back, as in the case of a Lakota woman named Lucy Swan. As a child, Lucy Swan was kidnapped and taken into Canada. She escaped and was led home by a coyote, who then told her to always be kind to the coyotes, to make sure that they, its own people, had food.

Ceremonies, too, have often been taught by the animals, in vision and in waking consciousness. It seems we have always found our way across unknown lands, physical and spiritual, with the assistance of the animals. Our cultures are shaped around them and we are judged by the way in which we treat them. For us, the animals are understood to be our equals. They are still our teachers. They are our helpers and healers. They have been our guardians and we have been theirs. We have asked for, and sometimes been given, if we lived well enough, carefully enough, their extraordinary powers of endurance and vision, which we have added to our own knowledge, powers, and gifts when we are not strong enough for the tasks required of us. We have deep obligations to them. Without the other animals, we are made less.

In our histories, both traditional people and our contemporary intellectuals tell us that these relationships between humans and animals are not rare occurrences, not the product of undeveloped minds, but have come from centuries of intimate experience between the animals and humans; it is knowledge from those who have learned directly from the world, whose knowledge came from the world itself. And in the present time, something important is being overlooked if we ignore the intelligence of those who successfully maintained this world on all continents for many thousands of years.

So as we look at stories of the human bond with other species that exists in tribal societies, we see stories of a primary radiance. They keep clear a relationship that is both ancient and practical. They are stories of a world of unending relationship and this is the very essence of creation and life. And these are stories, as much as anything, about humanity, the beauty of humankind, and about our human role here, the role that was considered by so many first peoples to be that of helping to maintain harmony and peace.

These are stories of eternity, reminding us how the human participates in this world of one piece. It is through such accounts and such relationships and stories that we take back the soul, the anima, which has stepped away from our bodies and hidden in fear from what it has witnessed and endured. It is through such relationships that we return to a respect and love for life and other species.

We first people are people whose elaborate and elegant systems of knowledge were systematically taken apart by those who did not understand them. Our sciences, agriculture, spiritual traditions, and hunting practices were dismantled by government policies and religious organizations. And yet, in places, this knowledge endured in spite of the fact that it was forbidden by those who, because of their own disconnection from nature, did not believe in the complexity of the relationships between humans and the other species by which we live. They did not adhere to religions of participation, because it would not have been possible to have such traditions and still have had uncontrolled development, settlement, and genocide. Nor does it pass by me lightly that we have ourselves been likened and compared to animals historically, that we—our histories, the names of our forebears—are filed in metal cabinets and storage boxes under the agency of the U.S. Department of the Interior along with wildlife, fish, and forest. Or that George Washington once said we were like wolves, to be driven off our lands to make room for settlement and civilization.

Not only this, but our ceremonies, the means through which we've maintained the balance with and within the world, were forbidden by U.S. law until 1978. Native people in America were the only inhabitants without freedom of religion because our religion, of the earth, so frightened the newcomers. They were as afraid of this as they were of the animal wilderness all around them. The loss of kinship with the natural world, and the knowledge about that world, while clearly more painful to us because of the genocide that accompanied it, became a loss to all because of what was discarded and banished and forbidden. Now what was banished is exactly the knowledge Western science is arriving at and looking toward for confirmation and promise for the future. We are all now asking the essential questions about how humans participate in context with the rest of creation. The old stories that were thought by the invaders to be simple, childlike expressions of belief have turned out to be a key to a new understanding by science.

The hidden gift at the bottom of all this history and policy might be that some of us have not lost the connection, have not taken the biblical "fall" of humankind away from animals and other life-forms.

Perhaps it was the day of the eagle release that I realized, finally, how much lies beyond human knowing. What I have learned from my years of being in the presence of animals is how limited my knowledge and intelligence are, and yet I understood a common language.

For eight years, working with animals became the center of my life, the pivot point at which I learned to think, and because of this work I took a fresh look at the traditions of the past. I offered animals my time and care, bathing them, feeding them, cleaning their cages, removing the carcasses of their prey. It was hard work, dirty work, but in exchange, they offered me peace and healing, a kind of knowledge that is still finding its way into words. I knew I was in the presence of intelligence, and I had to learn new kinds of behavior to be with them, a slowness, a stillness and inner silence that is no longer common in our fast-moving lives, a careful watching to see if their health had improved or lessened.

But mostly what I learned turned me back toward the traditions of my ancestors and those of other tribal people to help me define the possibilities of the future and of the relationship between animals and ourselves.

The stories that are songs of agreement and safekeeping, and the ceremonies that are their intimate companions, tell us not only how to keep the world alive, they tell us how to put ourselves back together again. In the language of ceremony, a person is placed—bodily, socially, geographically, spiritually, and cosmologically—in the natural world extending all the way out into the universe. This placing includes the calling in of the animal presence from all directions.

The ceremonial language and the images it evokes allow a human to see herself in relation to what's around, in, and outside of the seemingly singular human body. A ceremony enacts the recalled participation with nature. It reorients us, locates us in our human place, according to the natural laws of the world. But what happens when this world, when natural law itself, has gone out of balance?

When I place myself within the four directions today, I see that to the north is the land of waters and blue-white belugas, now toxic with mercury and other environmental poisons. Where the caribou people have lived for many thousands of years is a land now planned for oil development.

To the south are the beautiful and imperiled sea turtles that come up from the green light of ocean to lay eggs in the sand, the animals of the dense green rain forest, and the tribes of people who are being destroyed along with the animals and plants they have depended upon since the distant time.

West of here are the salmon people who once offered themselves to the humans, and who are given to journeys of creation that would be impossible for humans. Their numbers are now so greatly diminished by pollution and dams that the dams are being removed. We are having to undo what's been done. And even farther west, in the Pacific, are the graceful and quiet monk seals of the waters of Hawaii, their eyes dark and liquid, endangered.

In the east, the Florida panther, who is a first person in this world, is sick and unable to reproduce. There are also the vanished snail darters whose lives were traded for real estate property owned, in part, by the same politicians who made the decisions to let this species die when the Tellicho Dam was constructed.

We are hoping for, in need of, a ceremony that will heal this. In a changed world, we are in need of an ancient way of being.

It is, perhaps, the darkest pain of the contemporary human that we are losing everything of true worth from this world. In all the four directions, the animals are leaving. Through our failed humanity they are vanishing, and along with them we are losing something of utmost importance: the human traits of love, empathy, and compassion. As we lose the animals, it is not only clear that our own health will soon follow, but some part of our inner selves knows that we are losing what brings us to love and human fullness. Our connection with them has been perhaps the closest thing we have had to a sort of grace.

As women we have especially tried to protect them, for maintaining life seems to be our feminine work. And we know, remember, that when we return to our relationships with the animals, it is not just the animals that we begin to restore, but our own place within the dynamic of life. The human soul, too, in its feminine form, as anima, is restored along with the other life-forms. With it, we find the deepest meaning of what it is to be human, and how we are meant to live in this godly world.

There is such intelligence to creation, such power of generation that humans have had few spare ways to understand it, express it, or connect with it except through religion and art and more recently, science, which now seems to border on a thin "cutting" edge with a sometimes hard objectivity on one side, the mystical and the miraculous on the other.

The diverse disciplines of science now speak to us of the great animal and terrestrial brilliance that surrounds us. They reveal to us that eels turn silver to mate, that far out in the deep ocean squid larger than we had imagined create their own light in the darkness, that birds fly by the magnetic feel of Earth, by the arrangements of stars, even by the sounds of fish beneath water; that whales stun squid into motionlessness by the sounds they make; that elephants speak over hundred-mile distances in ranges the human ear can't hear. All this speaks about intelligences beyond ours, and as we learn this world, we are coming to realize how mighty and wise is the intelligence all around us, even beneath us. What we are now learning about animals returns us to a world so powerfully beyond our contemporary imaginations that we have almost missed it, even though such things have been contained in ancient stories, informed by animals themselves in a world of dynamic interchanges. We have been in the midst of the holy and amazing all along, the sacred, the lives and journeys of animals. There are ways of knowing and being in the world that have not been available to our own human intelligence, that have only recently entered our own perceptual maps, territories, and records. And together all the different intelligences equal a whole. This, I think, is the telling thing.

The belief that the Western way has been the best seems to me to be the shape of a madness that has been turned around and stated as logic and rationality, and it is this confusion that characterizes the culture that now dominates. Where is the logic, we Indian women are asking, in the extinction of species, in deforestation that takes away our air, in emptying the sustaining oceans. What's being lost is almost everything, including our own lives.

In an Anishnabe prayer, it is said, "We know that in all creation, only the human family has strayed from the sacred way." This, by our own evidence, appears to be true. The constructed world of our own human intelligence in a Western system has not been a fit large enough or deep enough; it has betrayed us. So have the Western systems of education and medicine and agriculture. It seems that all we can say for certain is that we have been deceived by what we thought was knowledge and by the many systems that have been born of this inadequate knowledge.

Daily, new information about our world and universe is seen, taken in, understood. But it is still new, unassimilated knowledge. The science of ecology, which is an ancient science for tribal people, is still only a recent field of study in the Western science tradition, too new to yet grasp the significances and connections. In terms of the animals upon which we depend, we can't afford to live and act on such small and broken parts of knowledge as are left to us.

At the time of first contact on this continent, Europe was a devastated place. The animals, land, and people of that continent were plundered and destroyed. Both humans and animals were tortured and killed for the amusement of a bloodthirsty people. The voyagers to other continents robbed those "new worlds" of their lives, taking back animals and indigenous people. There are accounts of four hundred tigers killed in a single day. In other accounts, five thousand animals and humans were tortured and killed in one day. These included not only lions, hippos, elephants, bison, crocodiles, bears, and giraffes, but humans as well.

Ironically, looking at the "bestiaries," stories and illustrations of animals at those times, the animals were seen as everything except what they were: they were mystical, they were fantastical, they were representations of Christ and symbolic of meanings of Christianity. Human properties were ascribed to them. Kings were lions. There was an enormous split between the idea of animal and the reality of how they were treated. The imagined, mystical presence and supposed meaning of animals was worshiped even as the true body, the physical matter, of the animal itself was made to suffer, was destroyed and hated.

This distorted tradition continues into the present time as we listen to the music of the rain forest and its animals and endangered peoples at the very time those lives are being extinguished. Animals as well as colonized peoples have been used to enrich the nonindigenous, or Western, human world at the price of their own diminishment. In this world, animals reside primarily inside human constructs: parks, zoos, fences, even inside the human mind as we reimagine and totemize them. They have been reviled or sentimentalized or eroticized but seldom known by us. They have lived for human convenience. We have become the boundary, the cage, the walls of captivity for all the rest. We define the borders where they may reside, where they may even, if we desire it, be permitted into our small, square plots of land, our houses. We stand between destruction and creation, between life and death, for other species and ultimately for ourselves.

And yet, for tribal cultures, animals are still seen as kith and kin, as other nations of people who have different intelligences from ours. There are still terms between the species; we know this is true. Traditionally minded people still give animals the respect and acknowledgment and relief from suffering that we promised them at our creation, before the time we made separate ways between human cultures and animal societies. We have been their caretakers, protectors, their apprentices. They have been our allies, our food, the sustainers of our lives, our equals.

It is not now the case that all of us who are tribal people are living in a traditional way. We, too, have suffered the loss of our relationships with animals and plants by force and conquest, and we have become dependent on the same forces that have caused such devastation, but still we can look to the roots of Native tradition for the intelligence that once sustained our lives and hope to understand it again. Those of us who came from this land can see before our eyes and in our own bodies that what has happened to this land and the animals is the same thing as what has happened to us.

Looking back, I think so often of that moment the eagle was returned to his homeland, of what was communicated in the car that day, what was known by the bird who had vision many hundreds of times more acute than ours, and I think of what was felt by us. It was a language, an opening between species, where something was spoken and communicated, not by words as we think of them, but by feel, by body, by pure life. It was a felt intelligence. It was something we no longer have words for, but it was clear that there was an intelligence surrounding ours on all sides, in all directions, and deeper than what we have yet measured or mapped. We are—all of us—returning to the traditional thinking that speaks of the natural laws of the world and of a wisdom that we are once again articulating. We are looking with new eyes at the old world around us, at what is equal to us, and we are looking, too, with old eyes at the changed world.

> i stand here humbly
> with extended arms, for the spirit of the air
> has brought down game for me!
> —IGPAKUHAK, *WE ANIMALS*

Last year a group of tribal elders and thinkers came together here to talk about our relationship with animals. Alex White Plume, a Lakota man who was one of the originators of the buffalo restoration programs on tribal lands, said that as the buffalo were returning so were the native grasses, insects, and birds. The people, too, returned to the traditions, stories, and the language, which itself reflects ecological relationships not contained by English. When taking back tradition, Alex said that the people looked again for their human place in the world. As we brought the animals back, he said, "We found that we, too, are just common people, like the squirrel and sparrow."

At the same gathering, Sarah James, a Gwichin woman from interior Alaska, and the spokesperson for the caribou, said, "It was given to us by the creator to take care of the Earth. Every time we speak, we speak for tree, water, fish. We are trying to save the Caribou. I learn oil and gas rule the world, but we're not going to compromise to save the Caribou; they are the reason we are here today. We put ourselves in a humble position, no greater than bird or duck or plant. We're as humble as they are. I look at the mountain as if my life depends on it—for food, medicine—not just to see how beautiful it is. The animals can't speak for themselves, so we speak for them."

To be common people, humble people, how freeing that is. How much it offers us, placing us back in the participatory relationship with the world. It offers us the animal underpinnings of our own minds and bodies, and it is those we must rely on to bring us back to our humanity and compassion, to restore ourselves to our place. As in the Tewa story, it lets us say, "We have been accepted." Let us act in a way that permits us all to answer, to say, "Your name is honored among the wolves," and to speak with the Grandmother eagle, one of the many shapes god takes.

WHO SPEAKS FOR WOLF

Paula Underwood

LONG AGO
  Our People grew in number so that where we were
    was no longer enough
  Many young men
    were sent out from among us
      to seek a new place
        where the People might be who-they-were
  They searched
    and they returned
      each with a place selected
      each determined his place was best

AND SO IT WAS
  That the People had a decision to make:
    which of the many was most appropriate

NOW, AT THAT TIME
  There was one among the People
    to whom Wolf was brother
  He was so much Wolf's brother
    that he would sing their song to them
      and they would answer him
  He was so much Wolf's brother
    that their young
      would sometimes follow him through the forest
      and it seemed they meant to learn from him

So it was, at this time
   That the People gave That One a special name
   They called him WOLF'S BROTHER
      and if any sought to learn about Wolf
      if any were curious
         or wanted to learn to sing Wolf's song
            they would sit beside him
               and describe their curiosity
                  hoping for a reply

As I have said
   The People sought a new place in the forest
   They listened closely to each of the young men
      as they spoke of hills and trees
            of clearings and running water
            of deer and squirrel and berries
   They listened to hear which place
      might be drier in rain
      more protected in winter
   and where our Three Sisters
         Corn, Beans, and Squash
               might find a place to their liking
   They listened
      and they chose
   Before they chose
      they listened to each young man
   Before they chose
      they listened to each among them
            he who understood the flow of waters
            she who understood Long House construction
            he who understood the storms of winter
            she who understood Three Sisters
      to each of these they listened
         until they reached agreement
         and the Eldest among them
               finally rose and said:
                  "So be it—
                     for so it is"

"But wait"
   Someone cautioned—
      "Where is Wolf's Brother?
         who, then, speaks for wolf?"

BUT
    THE PEOPLE WERE DECIDED
      and their mind was firm
      and the first people were sent
         to choose a site for the first Long House
         to clear a space for our Three Sisters
         to mold the land so that water
            would run away from our dwelling
              so that all would be secure within

AND THEN WOLF'S BROTHER RETURNED
  He asked about the New Place
    and said at once that we must choose another
    "You have chosen the Center Place
        for a great community of Wolf"
  But we answered him
    that many had already gone
    and that it could not wisely be changed
    and that surely Wolf could make way for us
      as we sometimes make way for Wolf
  But Wolf's Brother counseled—
    "I think that you will find
      that it is too small a place for both
      and that it will require more work then—
         than change would presently require"

BUT THE PEOPLE CLOSED THEIR EARS
    and would not reconsider
  When the New Place was ready
    all the People rose up as one
      and took those things they found of value
      and looked at last upon their new home

NOW CONSIDER HOW IT WAS FOR THEM
  This New Place
    had cool summers and winter protection
    and fast-moving streams
    and forests around us
      filled with deer and squirrel
    there was room even for our Three Beloved Sisters

AND THE PEOPLE SAW THAT THIS WAS GOOD
  and did not see
    wolf watching from the shadows!

BUT AS TIME PASSED
   They began to see—
      for someone would bring deer or squirrel
         and hang him from a tree
         and go for something to contain the meat
         but would return
                  to find nothing hanging from the tree
                     AND WOLF BEYOND
AT FIRST
   This seemed to us an appropriate exchange—
      some food for a place to live

BUT
   It soon became apparent that it was more than this—
      for Wolf would sometimes walk between the dwellings
         that we had fashioned for ourselves
                  and the women grew concerned
                     for the safety of the little ones
   Thinking of this
      they devised for awhile an agreement with Wolf
            whereby the women would gather together
                  at the edge of our village
                  and put out food for Wolf and his brothers

BUT IT WAS SOON APPARENT
   That this meant too much food
      and also Wolf grew bolder
         coming in to look for food
                  so that it was worse than before
   WE HAD NO WISH TO TAME WOLF

AND SO
   Hearing the wailing of the women
      the men devised a system
         whereby some ones among them
                  were always alert to drive off Wolf

AND WOLF WAS SOON HIS OLD UNTAMED SELF

BUT
   They soon discovered
      that this required so much energy
         that there was little left for winter preparations

and the Long Cold began to look longer and colder
with each passing day

THEN
The men counseled together
to choose a different course

THEY SAW
That neither providing Wolf with food
nor driving him off
gave the People a life that was pleasing

THEY SAW
That Wolf and the People
could not live comfortably together
in such a small space

THEY SAW
That it was possible
to hunt down this Wolf People
until they were no more

BUT THEY ALSO SAW
That this would require much energy over many years

THEY SAW, TOO,
That such a task would change the People:
they would become Wolf Killers
A People who took life only to sustain their own
would become a People who took life
rather than move a little

IT DID NOT SEEM TO THEM
THAT THEY WANTED TO BECOME SUCH A PEOPLE

AT LAST
One of the Eldest of the People
spoke what was in every mind:
"It would seem
that Wolf's Brother's vision
was sharper than our own

To live here indeed requires more work now
than change would have made necessary"

NOW THIS WOULD BE A SIMPLE TELLING
OF A PEOPLE WHO DECIDED TO MOVE
ONCE WINTER WAS PAST

EXCEPT
THAT FROM THIS
THE PEOPLE LEARNED A GREAT LESSON

IT IS A LESSON
WE HAVE NEVER FORGOTTEN

FOR
At the end of their Council
one of the Eldest rose again and said:
"Let us learn from this
so that not again
need the People build only to move
Let us not again think we will gain energy
only to lose more than we gain
We have learned to choose a place
where winter storms are less
rather than rebuild
We have learned to choose a place
where water does not stand
rather than sustain sickness

LET US NOW LEARN TO CONSIDER WOLF!"

AND SO IT WAS
That the People devised among themselves
a way of asking each other questions
whenever a decision was to be made
on a New Place or a New Way
We sought to perceive the flow of energy
through each new possibility
and how much was enough
and how much was too much

UNTIL AT LAST
Someone would rise

and ask the old, old question
to remind us of things
we do not yet see clearly enough to remember

"TELL ME NOW MY BROTHERS
TELL ME NOW MY SISTERS
WHO SPEAKS FOR WOLF?"

THE NAHUAL

Rigoberta Menchú

*"That night he spent howling like a coyote while he slept as a
person."*
"To become animal, without ceasing to be a person."
*"Animal and person coexist in them through the will of their
progenitors at birth."*
—MIGUEL ANGEL ASTURIAS, *MEN OF MAIZE*

Every child is born with a *nahual*. The *nahual* is like a shadow, his protective spirit who will go through life with him. The *nahual* is the representative of the earth, the animal world, the sun and water, and in this way the child communicates with nature. The *nahual* is our double, something very important to us. We conjure up an image of what our *nahual* is like. It is usually an animal. The child is taught that if he kills an animal, that animal's human double will be very angry with him because he is killing his *nahual*. Every animal has its human counterpart and if you hurt him, you hurt the animal too.

Our days are divided into dogs, cats, bulls, birds, etc. There is a *nahual* for every day. If a child is born on a Wednesday, his *nahual* is a sheep. The day of his birth decides his *nahual*. So for a Wednesday child, every Wednesday is special. Parents know what a child's behavior will be from the day of the week he is born. Tuesday is a bad day to be born because the child will grow up bad-tempered. That is because Tuesday's *nahual* is a bull and bulls are always angry. The child whose *nahual* is a cat will like fighting with his brothers and sisters.

We have ten sacred days, as our ancestors have always had. These ten days have their *nahual*. They can be dogs, cats, horses, bulls, but they can also be wild animals, like lions. Trees can be *nahuals* too: trees chosen by our ancestors many centuries ago. A *nahual* is not always only one animal. With dogs, for example, nine dogs represent a *nahual*. Or in the case of horses, three. It can vary a lot. You don't know how many in fact, or rather, only the parents know the number of animals which go to make the *nahuals* of these ten special days. For us the meekest days are Wednesday, Monday, Saturday and Sunday. Their *nahuals* are sheep, or birds or animals which don't harm other animals.

All this is explained to young people before they get married so that when they have children they know which animal represents each day. One very important thing they have to remember is not to tell the child what his *nahual* is until he is grown up. We are only told what our *nahual* is when our personalities are formed and our parents see what our behavior is normally. Otherwise a child might take advantage of his *nahual*. For example, if his *nahual* is a bull, he might like fighting and could say; 'I behave like this because I'm such and such an animal and you must put up with me'. If a child doesn't know his *nahual* he cannot use it as an excuse. He may be compared to the animal, but that is not identifying him with his *nahual*. Younger children don't know the *nahual* of their elder brothers and sisters. They are only told all this when they are mature enough and this could be at any age between ten and twelve. When this happens the animal which is his *nahual* is given to him as a present. If it is a lion, however, it is replaced by something else. Only our parents, or perhaps other members of the community who were there when we were born, know the day of our birth. People from other villages don't know and they are only told if they become close friends.

A day only has a special meaning if a child is born on it. If no baby is born on any one Tuesday, it is of no interest to anyone. That is, there is no celebration. We often come to love the animal which is our *nahual* even before we know what it is. Although we love all the natural world, we are often drawn to one particular animal more than to others. We grow to love it. Then one day we are told that it is our *nahual*. All the kingdoms which exist on this earth are related to man. Man is part of the natural world. There is not one world for man and one for animals, they are part of the same one and lead parallel lives. We can see this in our surnames. Many of us have surnames which are the names of animals. *Quej*, meaning horse, for example.

We Indians have always hidden our identity and kept our secrets to ourselves. This is why we are discriminated against. We often find it hard to talk about ourselves because we know we must hide so much in order to preserve our Indian culture and prevent it being taken away from us. So I can only tell you very general things about the *nahual*. I can't tell you what my *nahual* is because that is one of our secrets.

WHY I LOVE WITH ADMIRATION
EVERY SALMON I SEE

Elizabeth Woody

My maternal grandmother's people's name, Wyampum, means "The Echo of Falling Water." I was born into the Wyampum, and the salmon are part of our genetic makeup and personal history. Salmon are not only the symbols on our traditional baskets, but for centuries they have been our lives.

The civilizations of the Northwest that preceded the Euro-Americans were sustained by an elaborate system of rules, embodied by the phrase *tee-cha-meengsh-mee sin-wit na-me ad-wa-ta-man-wit* (At the time of creation the Creator placed us in this land and gave us the voice of this land and that is our law). These unwritten laws sustained the environment and its people to ensure the renewal of abundance, especially the seasonal return of the spawning salmon, the *nusoox*.

Salmon was a key element in the spiritual framework of my people. It was one of those things without which life wouldn't be possible. Salmon may be as old as three million years. Their journey to the Pacific and home is a saga. They mate only once, and the future generations depend on this pair's strength and tenacity. The abundance surrounding salmon in the biosphere gives us comfort and identity.

Wyam, the most significant fishery, was located on the Middle Columbia River, with fishing sites passed along through inheritance. My grandfather and great uncles fished at Celilo Falls, a fishing village for over fourteen thousand years. They fished (dip-netting) from immense platforms built above the white water on the "fishing rocks" above the falls. The first salmon of the season was honored by ceremony, and a salmon feast was held to give thanks for the return of the salmon.

Now this place is flooded by the Dalles Dam. Wyam, the longest continuously inhabited site of human habitation in the Northwest, possibly in the United States, was destroyed by the Army Corps of Engineers on March 10, 1957, when the massive steel and concrete gates of the Dalles Dam closed and choked the downstream surge of the Columbia River. But in the past, during the summer season, one could stand at Wyam and smell salmon mingled with the water of Celilo Falls.

The Salmon Feasts celebrated and thanked the salmon. When the salmon first arrived, our thoughts were given with prayer. For us, this gratitude was restorative and regenerative. We lived because of the return of the salmon to this place. We would gather in the Longhouse for worship and communal feasts in what the Columbia River Inter-Tribal Fish Commission called "a beautiful and dignified ceremonial response to the Creator in appreciation for the willingness of Nature to serve humankind."*

In my memory, during the singing at a Salmon Feast, the children and able-bodied adults danced in a circular pattern around the floor. Men on the south side, women on the north, they began to move in a circle with the drumming and the songs. In Indian dress, they showed respect to the Creator, people lifting up and down with the bend of their knees, swinging their cupped hands to their hearts. Older people sat and swung their right hands to signify how the good of the songs was gathered into their hearts.

In the kitchen several women cooked the meal, then brought out trays filled with food. Salmon (*nusoox*), venison, edible roots, berries. The women who cooked the salmon and gathered the roots and berries brought only their kindest thoughts to the gathering. When they brought out the food, they carried it with care, with a ceremonial attitude. The tribal men who hunted and fished were also of this mind.

We sat at the tables while the prayers were sung. The people waited with a cup of water and a plate with the salmon, roots, and venison beside each of them. Then the people picked up a sample of each food and ate. The water was called for and the communion was finished. The people ate their meal in a feeling of friendship and community wholeness. The food was holy. We were peaceful in mind and heart. My uncle, Lewis Pitt, says, "We travel from the river to the mountains with these foods."

But now this communal scene I recall from my childhood and young adulthood is threatened and may not continue. The women and men who nurture the people and the Earth's systems through ceremony have a new concern. They are missing a vital piece of the circle—the wild runs of the *nusoox*—and in this time we face, prayer and gratitude and song may not be enough to regenerate and restore them.

The salmon are so drastically diminished that in 1995 there was a

*Columbia River Inter-Tribal Fish Commission Annual Report, 1994, Portland, Oregon, p. 15.

moratorium on the ceremonial harvest in the Columbia River because of the scarcity of the salmon. Historically, between five and eleven million fish swam through the portion of the Columbia River watershed that is now above the Bonneville Dam. But in 1995 only twelve thousand passed the dam, returning to their original spawning grounds.

These are elements essential to the salmon: clean gravel for the eggs; oxygen-rich, chemical-free waterways, cool from the shade of the forests; clear passages to and from the oceans. These elements are now nonexistent in many places. Dams block the fish, while soil from riverbanks stripped of trees runs into the river and chokes the oxygen from it. And the Columbia River is currently the most polluted and radioactive waterway in the world.

The salmon who do manage to return are underfed and not as strong as those in the past. They absorb many chemicals and pollution from the ocean and the river. Even loaded with pollutants, the decaying salmon that have spawned leave nutrients from the ocean in the forest soils. But now salmon are often caught out in the ocean, and when they do not return, the land is not enriched with their nutrients. Each of us is weakened by the breaking of this cycle between land and sea.

As Congresswoman Elizabeth Furse says, "Salmon are a defining symbol of our region; a warp thread in the cultural, economic, and ecological fabric of the Northwest. And like canaries in a coal mine, salmon are a barometer for the health of our forests, rivers, and range-lands. We have two choices: We can opt for minimal and incremental action that won't unduly disrupt the status quo, but will doom our salmon to extinction. Or we can swallow hard, and make sacrifices to bring back the salmon."

Living beings, like salmon and other foods, are an integral and significant aspect in our lives. It is part of our human dignity, freedom, and faith to care for them. The Indian people say, "When the salmon are gone, that is the end of life as we know it." And in my lifetime, they have come close to disappearing.

Today, the tribes in the Northwest have asked others for help in saving the salmon species from extinction. Concern for the land, we think, is part of the human being's makeup, and even the new Northwesterners are talking about salmon as a part of our human souls. People are coming together in agreement that it is time to do the right thing, to take down the dams and leave the trees standing, before it is too late. Now many kinds of people grieve and worry; in this late twentieth-century crisis, concern is voiced about the salmon. They, too, believe the government had not made the right decisions when they built the dams and cut down the forests. And now others are experiencing the dispossession of lifeways and land and health in much the same way as tribal people did, centuries before.

In the Columbia River Plateau, every being possesses a song that contributes to the light of this earth. We need to give voice. We need to trust that together we will participate in a solution or plan to nourish healthy forests and salmon. In this life, we are connected. The land and all the life upon it is united. This is simple enough. Culture, both ancient and new, will be altered by any species' absence. With extreme sadness, I acknowledge that some of my relatives, the salmon, are gone, but even distressed over the loss, I remain open to the possibility of hope and of restoring them.

Luanne Jamieson, a woman from the Haudenosaunee people (Iroquois), demonstrated a dance in Cuernavaca for the Nahuatl people. She said of the Women's Dance that it enabled the women to massage the earth with their feet, because being a great mother, the earth is tired. The earth needs the dancing. Her heart is a mother's heart that feels strong with the gratitude and love of her children. The song Luanne Jamieson danced to was simple and direct, thanking the earth.

As a woman, I believe my spirit and heart can comprehend that which the mind cannot. I sense how one can interact with all aspects of life.

Recently, in a stream near Multnomah Falls, I saw small smolt leaping at dusk like little slivers of light and I remembered that there were days when my grandmother needed to be near a river. My grandpa would load us into the car with a paper sack of food, and we would drive to the river to watch it, listen to it, smell it. My grandmother would laugh and point out the fish jumping. I would drift with the swirls of the river, the waves over boulders, the way the tree branches dipped in the river, rose in swells. All of it was deliberate. Life here had its own intelligence.

We need animals as helpers, my grandmother explained to me, as allies. We are essentially weak and isolated as human beings. We do not know how to be truly alive in the present. The song around salmon is the river's voice and the way the fish fight to live is our fight as well. Once my friend, Spokane writer Gloria Bird, and I were talking about the worship songs. I told her that my grandmother had translated one song to me that I loved, and it was about light. Gloria said, "It could have been the river's light. We spent so much time by the river, the sun on the river gave us songs." Thinking back to my experience of the river as a living being, I see this may be true, and that every being has a song that helps the earth.

Biodiversity is not a law of man, but the law of the land.

My people's passionate adherence to a time-honed cultural life system goes beyond our own lives. Science is not separate from religion in our cultural worldview. Our stories and ceremonies contain knowledge in all aspects of natural processes akin to the language people describe in quantum physics. With the past and future in mind, we endure, and the earth is more productive. The individuals in each generation have a responsibility for the next, bringing forward the past, enacted in the present. And we understood, before the science of ecology, that fish are not only fish, they are part of a river or body of water, part of all the rest.

Dreams are significant to the Columbia River Plateau people. As a child, I had a recurring nightmare that stopped before I understood it. It was a strange, difficult dream. I was in an open field with all sorts of animals, our pets, the deer, bear, cougars, and birds. I could not count them or see them all, but we were happy. The trees were all around us in a circle. Then the earth started to shake. The trees fell and snapped, the animals disappeared under a rolling road. The road came over me and I was the only one left. My uncle would wake me. While he held me, I would say, "They are all gone."

It was the loneliness and silence without the animal lives that hurt the most. I did not know then about endangered species or imperiled forests or the sacredness of a circle. The silence that I feared in this nightmare is the absence of their multiple songs and the absence of my own song. I was a child and I was afraid. But now, as a grown woman, I comfort myself by writing about the known relationships that were long ago understood, established, and celebrated in a culture, our culture, that bonds animals with people, salmon with humans, water, ocean, and tree.

PRAYER

Beth Brant

I can't remember the first time I saw you, Great Blue. It seems as though that moment should be imprinted on the cells of my brain that record memory. The other times, the hundreds of times you have crossed my path of vision, sent messages to my heart, are always the first time. The quick intake of my breath, then silence, as I watch you glide across the marsh, or flap your wings for a take-off of indescribable grace; the patient watch on your particular hunting place, or the speed of your beak spearing a fish, a frog, and the easy way it slides down your long, lovely throat.

I have watched you through binoculars, asking a quick forgiveness for this ineffably human way of looking at you.

I have seen you in Michigan, in many provinces of Canada, in California. I have watched you with my lover, with my grandchildren, with special friends. I have met your cousins—Egret, Sandhill Crane, Bittern, Green Heron, Night Heron, Little Blue Heron, Least Bittern. I have watched you build nests, have seen your babies. I have gathered your feathers from the waters where they drifted as you traveled on your journeys. These make a bundle on my altar where I pray.

You have come to me in ordinary times, extraordinary times. Before my surgery in 1987, I saw you. Before my surgery in 1994, I saw many of you. When I was separated from my beloved, two of you flew close over my head as I sat weeping. I am not arrogant enough to believe that you chose to show yourself to relieve my human pain, but I do believe that your presence was a gift, is the gift that keeps me spiritually bound to life.

I am Turtle Clan. That deliberate creature who is comfortable in water and on land. That being who wears a shell for protection and camouflage. But you, Great Blue, are the means by which I fly and dream. You are the way to worship. You are the physical manifestation of my love—

34

you and I become one-in-my-body as my orgasms call forth the spirit of you. You are *there*, in the sky, on the land, stepping through the reeds. You are in me. You are Creator's mark.

Once I saw you dead beside a road. As I prayed over you and plucked some of your feathers, that moment became a story. I clumsily attempt to explain the mystery of my relationship with you. Nothing can explain you. Nothing can describe the way the sun turns your feathers blue as you gaze into the waters. No human being can relate the strength of your neck as it folds into yourself when you reach flight. I cannot tell the story of seeing your eyes meet mine—you were unafraid, but my heart was beating so fast in awe, in fear, in gratitude. I am humble and small in your presence, Great Blue.

Your story is in the air, in sound, in your yellow legs gently walking through the shallow waters. Your story resides in each stick you bring to the dead treetops to make your nest. It lives in the curve of your great wings; it shapes itself in the pale brown ovals of the eggs you lay in your huge stick house. Your story tells itself in the open mouths of your chicks. Your story goes on ceaselessly as you fly to find food, fly home to bring food to those open beaks. You relive your story through generations.

I am blessed to see you. I am blessed to hear your infrequent squawks. I am blessed to come onto your territory and visit with you. You have taught me that it is possible to soar without benefit of wings. That it is possible to live. That it is possible to love. That hope endures with each silent minute searching for sustenance. That faith can be as tangible as a bundle of feathers that lie on my altar. That a story is always in the beating of a heart. That I cry in wonder of you.

You have lived on this Earth and in the skies for centuries beyond imagining. You have completed transformations and resurrections that have brought you into the *here* where I reside. You once lived on an Earth that had no humans. What was your thought the first time you encountered one of my kind?

You do nothing that is not perfect and beautiful. Even your chicks, in their newborn awkwardness, give promise of glory: the large beaks that seem too big for the delicate neck to hold; the down that sheds and leaves bare patches soon to be filled in by the colors that will become you—gray, brown, blue. Everything about you is a covenant with the rest of creation.

You have become a Clan. Peoples have worshiped you. Peoples have longed to uncover the secrets they think you are hiding beneath your feathers. Peoples have wished in their human souls to *be* you. You are that glimpse into what is possible. Flight. Moving your great wings over trees, over expanses of water, and over those of my kind who look up in awe as we point—"Look, look."

You sojourn in my dreams.

During the winter months there was that one day in late January when I heard your familiar voice and looked up, into the gray, cold sky, and saw you flying overhead—alone. I wondered what had kept you behind in this cold place. Your body was almost etched into the air, a solitary being. I felt the immense solitude of your journey. I heard a kind of music in my heart. I smelled the air—snow, cold, perhaps the hint of thaw. I cried, "Thank you, thank you." I lifted my arms as if to embrace you. A portrait of a woman gone mad from winter—standing in her backyard, turning in circles, shouting her thanks, arms reaching for possibility. I fell in the snow; sparrows eating from the birdfeeder flew away in distress as I laughed and ate snow. I laughed, pulling myself up, returning to the warm kitchen.

You have brought me so much. What can I bring you? Assurances that your territories will not be polluted and blasphemed by the corruptness of man? Promises I cannot keep? I *will* bring you this: As each of our grandchildren come into the age of seeing with their hearts, I will point you out to them. I will say your name with reverence. I will draw in my breath as we watch you fly. They in turn will know what prayer is— the hushed moment of discovery. The quiet flame of regeneration. They will love you and treasure the completeness that is you. They will honor you in their lives. This I promise you.

Nia:wen.

THE DOG THAT RUNS IN THE ROUGH SEAS

Haunani-Kay Trask

I.

Aloha mai. Aloha kākou.

I greet you as a descendant of Papahānaumoku—she who gives birth to islands—and Wākea—sky father—who created our home of Hawai'i Nei. My ancestors descend from great genealogical lines of Native islanders who settled the vast Pacific millennia before the invasion of the Americas. We were a voyaging people, and we remain tied to the sea today.

Like Native peoples everywhere, our lives were regulated in traditional times by the natural rhythms of our universe: the land, the waters, the heavens, the animals, and the gods, who were themselves manifested in nature. We understood our dependency on the islands, our mother, and we cared for her most religiously. Strict regulation of our social and cultural and environmental relationships gave us a bountiful existence, one that was both orderly and pleasurable.

Our *ali'i* (chiefs) and *kahuna* (priests) created an intricate system of laws, or *kapu*, that ensured protection of all we believed important, and beyond that, all we held to be sacred. Prohibitions were placed on harvesting the young and the wasteful killing of plant and animal. The behavior of common folk and chiefs alike was strictly regulated, as was the time for combat and for worship, for separation and for congregation. *Kapu* meant both restriction and sanctity: our most sacred chiefs suffered the most restrictive conditions.

Both the natural and the human world were divine. Thus, Hina, goddess of the moon, was simultaneously the mother of Kamapua'a, the pig god; wife of Wākea; and wife and sister of other deities. Our great male gods of Lono, Kāne, Kanaloa, and Ku took both plant and animal form. And there were also specific gods like Pele, of the volcano, and Na-makaokaha'i, her lizard, or *mo'o* sister, and their seven Hi'iaka sisters who inhabited the forests and the flowers of the vast lands of Puna and Ka'ū. All gods were visible: in cloud formations, in trees, in gushing water, in the mist from the mountains, in the steam from the volcano, in the fish and mammals of the sea. Such manifestations of divinity are still known as *kino lau*. Pele may appear, for example, as the fire of the volcano, the volcano goddess herself, a young girl, and occasionally, an old woman. The food of the land, banana and coconut and breadfruit are *kino lau* of the gods, Kanaloa and Kāne. And the food gourd is a symbol of Lono, a major deity of fertility who was celebrated in the Makahiki, a four-month period when war was prohibited and feasting and athletic games were enjoyed.

Our gods were intertwined with our chiefly lines. Thus our *ali'i* often referred to themselves as gods, taking a given deity, such as Lono, as part of their chiefly lineage. Our people understood their chiefs as gods who walked upon the earth. Everywhere in traditional Hawaiian life, the sacred was visible in the mundane. Everywhere, divinity was near, to be sensed, heard, and felt. Such was our Native way of life: sentient beings in a divinely sentient world.

Then foreigners arrived, and our spiritual and physical worlds collapsed. Gifting us with disease and iron and profit and Christianity, the foreigner introduced the profane, the destructive, and the sacrilegious. Less than a century after contact, most of our people, including our leaders, had died out. When our numbers had dwindled, the United States invaded. Landing Marines at the port of Honolulu in 1893, the U.S. minister, in concert with white American sugar planters, overthrew our reigning *ali'i*, Lili'uokalani, securing those same white businessmen in her place. When Hawai'i was annexed by the United States in 1898, fewer than forty thousand Hawaiians remained of the estimated one million who had lived in our islands at contact in 1778. An outpost of American empire ruled by white sugar planters had been secured.

Today, Hawaiians are a shadowy version of what we once were, struggling to reclaim our lands and some form of self-government. But the effort at reconnection is hampered by the political status of our country as part of the United States, by our language as a minority tongue, and by the transformation of our spiritually profound culture into a commercialized artifact for the ever-present tourist.

In such a predatory, anti-Hawaiian world, we have made our Native culture a focus of protest, of civil and human rights assertions. We are in the process of reclaiming our dignity through indigenous practice. And when cultural protest and assertion have met the corrosive effects of

American values, some of our Native people have deformed our beliefs to justify abuse and wrongdoing.

Within a colonized world, "tradition" can be easily invoked, not only by parasitic foreigners (like anthropologists and archaeologists) in an effort to disparage Native values, but by our own people for profit-making and electoral gain. Native culture becomes a political commodity traded for special status.

In Hawai'i, tourism is the most visible place where such perversion occurs. Everything from Hawaiian *hula* (dance) and *ōlelo* (language) to *aloha 'āina* (our indigenous love of the land) is manipulated to support tourism. Everywhere, one can hear the tireless advertisement that "giving" is Hawaiian. *Aloha*, a traditional value of generosity and love, is used to peddle vacations, cars, hotel rooms, city events, and anything else politicians and businessmen wish to sell. Tourism employees are trained to practice *aloha* on the job, to offer *aloha* freely to tourists, all 6.5 million of them. The din of this constant promotion has the same effect as elevator music: Most residents, including Hawaiians, don't protest the grotesque commercialization of our culture because they have become inured to it.

Faced with a degraded world, some opportunistic Hawaiians have falsified our culture to conceal *hewa*—wrong behavior. These offenders assert "Native practice" to escape sanction for illegal behavior. The culprit appeals to tradition or indigenous status or both to exempt himself from punishment. False traditions suddenly make an appearance. An argument is heard, for example, that taking endangered turtles is defensible for Hawaiians because this was practiced before *haole* (white people) arrived, or simply because the takers are Native.

In most cases, the "tradition" in question can readily be unmasked as false. Occasionally, when specific historical evidence is lacking, an appeal is made to the "common" practice in ancient times. The question is usually one of indigenous custom. In Hawaiian culture generally, there was no killing of the pregnant, nursing, and young; and no killing of man or animal during certain times of the year.

But with the coming of foreigners, every part of our existence was undermined and politicized, including the definition of who and what qualifies as Hawaiian. Two hundred years after Western contact, Native ways, as our islands themselves, have been irreparably altered. Like radiation in our waters, colonialism has seeped into our beings, damaging us forever. Cultural practices of husbanding the earth, her bounty, and her Native people have all but vanished in the wake of aggressive foreigners. And those of us who struggle to protect our beloved Hawai'i are painfully confronted not only by the predations of capitalism but by the twisted behaviors of our own colonized people.

II.

In 1989, a Hawaiian named Daniel Kaneholani (ironically, this name is a variant of Kanehoalani, god of the heavens), a fisherman from the island of Kaua'i, shot and killed a female monk seal with a bullet between her eyes. Weighing several hundred pounds, the seal had hauled out onto a beach at Anahola to bask in the sun. After killing the seal, Kaneholani decapitated it. He then slit the seal's back and removed two long sections of meat, offering pieces to bystanders. Kaneholani stored the remainder of the seal in a friend's freezer.

Kaneholani was apprehended and charged with violating the Endangered Species Act by killing and eating a Hawaiian monk seal, a protected animal. He was found guilty and sentenced to prison.

Kaneholani's attorney, also a Hawaiian man, argued that the Endangered Species Act provision exempting "Alaskan natives" from the prohibition against hunting endangered animals for subsistence violated the equal protection rights of Native Hawaiians, who should have an aboriginal right to hunt monk seals. The court concluded the exception for "Alaskan natives" was a rational (i.e., permissible) one given the reliance of Native Alaskans on certain endangered or threatened species for subsistence purposes.

By contrast, there was no evidence that Native Hawaiians relied on monk seals for subsistence purposes. Kaneholani's trial, as well as the opposition his actions generated in the Hawaiian community, revolved around questions of traditional knowledge and practice. The Office of Hawaiian Affairs sent a letter to Kaneholani's attorney, advising him that cultural experts agreed Hawaiians did not hunt or eat monk seals in ancient times. Linguistic evidence indicated seals were so rare in Hawai'i there was no common Native name for the animal. Moreover, no monk seal bones have ever been uncovered in any archaeological site in Hawai'i.

Although short-lived, the controversy split the Hawaiian community. Many of our people felt the killing of the seal, especially as it might have been a nursing female, was *hewa*—wrong. Given that the seal is a protected mammal, and that efforts to bring the seal back from near extinction have been ongoing since the 1980s, no excuse existed for Kaneholani, whose defense seemed outrageously opportunistic. Questioning whether Kaneholani had ever participated in Native resistance of any kind, critics argued that his "rights" defense was only an effort to save him from prison.

Intertwined with this issue was another, almost unarticulated feeling that his killing of the endangered seal was particularly male. Taking a female animal of reproductive age, whether nursing or not, is egregiously against our Hawaiian ethic of *mālama 'āina*, or *aloha 'āina*, that is, of nourishing our islands. Many of our women felt that only a man, one who is biologically incapable of bringing life into the world, and also one so damaged by colonialism that he would kill an endangered mammal, could have shot and dismembered the seal. There was the feeling that only a man would defend such action in the American court system, fabricating abhorrent traditions to save his client. Hawaiian women attorneys privately raged against both Kaneholani and his lawyer for their reprehensible legal strategy, arguing that Hawaiian women would never have defended such actions.

Despite the flash of outrage, the controversy disappeared from newspapers almost as quickly as it appeared. Public interest subsided in the Native issues that the killing raised. Scientists and others involved in the protection of the monk seal continued their programs to prevent extinction. And the political conflict surrounding "traditional" Hawaiian behavior moved on to other arenas. Monk seals, meanwhile, slipped quietly from public notice.

III.

Small, sleek, and shy, the monk seal came to live in our Hawaiian archipelago millennia before we arrived. Scientists say our seal is related to the Caribbean and Mediterranean monk seals, but the former is now considered extinct and the latter is about to become so. The oldest of all living fin-footed mammals is nearing the end of its time on Earth.

The only name for the monk seal we have inherited from our ancients is *ilio-holo-i-ka-uaua*—"the dog that runs in the rough seas." The absence of a specific Hawaiian designation for the monk seal is telling. Genealogically related to the land and wholly dependent upon her, our ancestors developed a detailed taxonomy for all living things. A single type of fish, for example, had several names at each stage of maturity. The delicious mullet, generally known as *'ama'ama*, is called *pua 'ama 'ama* when it is finger length; *kahaha* when hand length; *'ama'ama* when eight inches long; and *'anae* when twelve inches or more. The same was true for plants and humans. And we had descriptive names for each mountain and valley, for each constellation, for the appearances and disappearances of rains and clouds in certain places. Indeed, we named each and every thing in our Native world because we were intimately connected to all parts of it.

But it seems our ancestors knew little about the monk seal. Perhaps, as we slowly settled our main islands, our sly friend gradually slipped away and took up residence in the waters surrounding the small unpeopled islets and atolls at the farthest reaches of our far archipelago.

After millennia of Hawaiian occupation and at the close of the eighteenth century, Westerners pushed into the Pacific, pillaging the seas and lands for profit. Sealing and whaling, along with other brutal pastimes, extinguished many species. Monk seals were killed for their oil and meat, and possibly for their fur. One ship, the *Gambia*, returned to Honolulu in 1859 with a reported take of 1,500 skins. By the late 1800s, sightings of monk seals were already rare. As with the great dying of our Native people, the coming of the *haole* nearly destroyed the seal. But where we fell in mass epidemics recorded by historians, our Native animals and plants passed almost without comment.

Like a raging infestation, Westerners spread to every part of our region, extending their empires across the vast ocean to Asia and the rest of the island Pacific. Everything Native was at risk of extinction. By the dawn of the twentieth century, indigenous populations had collapsed while their territories were taken by foreigners. Hawai'i was part of the United States; Tahiti and other archipelagoes belonged to France; and farther south and east, Britannia ruled.

With the *haole* came the *haole* way of life or, as many indigenous peoples experienced it, the *haole* way of death. The whites were killers. Nothing was sacred or *kapu*; not the unborn or the breeding, not the young or the old. No restrictions or considerations barred the way. And when the demand for oil lamps and whalebone corsets and feather hats declined, there was always the thrill of sport killing. As the Spanish hunted Natives in the Americas and hung their body parts on porches, so English seamen took whales, seals, sharks, turtles, and other living things, taunting and dismembering them for entertainment. Just before Captain James Cook stumbled onto Hawai'i, his surgeon, William Anderson, recorded in his journal that the men of the ship noticed molting seals which, in his own words, were "so tame that we kill'd what number we chose." While at Christmas Island in 1777, Cook's seamen reported the great fun they had in tormenting sharks by tying their tails together, or strapping them to boards so they couldn't dive. Turtles, too, were tortured on the reefs by grabbing their fins, making them unable to swim. When the crew tired of their fun, they killed the turtles. On one good outing, they killed, by their own gleeful count, forty-two turtles in half an hour.

This kind of pillaging was not unique to England or Spain but was characteristic of European, and later American, cultural behavior. Indeed, even President Theodore Roosevelt, although known as a killer himself (that is, a great sportsman), was stunned by the bloody marauding of American seafarers in the far Pacific. Hoping to prevent extinction of monk seals and other sea animals, Roosevelt designated the Northwestern Hawaiian Islands, with the exception of Midway atoll, as the Hawaiian Islands Reservation, rendering the area a protected sanctuary. In 1940, the islands were renamed the Hawaiian Islands National Wildlife Refuge. Their management was turned over to the U.S. Fish and Wildlife Service.

The Northwest Islands stretch more than one thousand miles leeward of the main islands of our Hawaiian chain. Kaua'i, one of our eight largest islands, is about five million years old. Kure, the oldest of the Northwest Islands, is over thirty million years old. Most of the leeward islands are sand dunes perhaps only a few feet above sea level. As ancient volcanoes eroded into the sea, these atolls were all that remained. Today, they provide hauling-out areas where seals rest and nurse their young. Except where the military has occupied the area, the Northwest Islands are uninhabited.

As a result of Roosevelt's protection, the monk seal appeared to recover during the first half of the twentieth century. But between the late 1950s and the late 1970s, there was an approximate decline of 50 percent in the total number of seals. Scientists believe the decline attributable to human disturbance, mostly by the military but also by fishermen. At mid-century, the Second World War was partially fought in the Pacific, which witnessed great incursions by both American and Japanese warships and fighter planes. While all living things, particularly animals, are stressed by war, the mere appearance of humans disturbs monk seals. Thus the presence of U.S. Navy and Coast Guard personnel at Kure atoll resulted in female seals abandoning their pupping locations in the early 1970s.

Female monk seals give birth on shore, close to shallow, protected waters. Mothers gorge themselves until they weigh near six hundred pounds, then find a suitable birth site where both mother and pup will remain for about six weeks. After the weaning period, the emaciated mother returns to the sea to hunt, and the pup begins life as a weanling, perhaps the most dangerous time of its life. For a year, the pup will learn to feed and navigate alone.

To survive this fragile period, the monk seal requires protected areas. However, because of the disastrous effects of human disturbance beginning in the 1970s, pup survival on Kure atoll was reduced, resulting in the eventual reproductive failure of the Kure population. The monk seal was subsequently designated as depleted under the Marine Mammal Protection Act of 1972, and endangered under the U.S. Endangered Species Act of 1973.

Efforts to save the monk seal intensified in the early 1980s. The National Marine Fisheries Service completed work on recovery plans, monitoring, and rehabilitation programs. All beach areas and ocean waters out to a depth of ten fathoms around most of the Northwest Islands were designated as protected critical habitat. And a program to save undersized, weaned female pups was begun.

But a new threat appeared late in the decade. The pelagic longline fishery in Hawaiian waters grew fourfold, from 37 vessels in 1987 to over

140 in 1990. Dangerous interactions between seals and humans increased. By January 1991, seals were observed at French Frigate Shoals with injuries, including embedded fishhooks.

In the early 1990s, other warnings of a renewed crisis came with alarming speed: a serious drop in birthrates, an increasing loss of females, and an overall decline in the total number of monk seals. Apart from direct human disturbance, other causes of this decline include a possible peak in carrying capacity at certain atolls, the killing of female seals during what is called "mobbing" by sexually aroused male seals, poisoning by ciguatoxins (poisons in normally edible tropical fish), and the loss of prey. Of course, all of these causes are *indirectly* the result of human actions. The undoubted reason for the decline of monk seals, as for the population collapse of indigenous peoples, is intrusion by predatory humans. The balance of relations has been altered by human forces opposed to it. And that imbalance has set in motion other interactions now proceeding after their own fashion.

IV.

On the front page of our daily newspaper, dated February 6, 1996, is a large color photograph of a monk seal, entangled in nets with a three-inch fishhook puncturing its jaw. Distressed, the seal had hauled out at a busy beach in Honolulu. And two National Marine Fisheries employees are pictured attempting to remove the hook without injuring the seal or themselves.

One of the men in the photo is Tim Ragen, a scientist I interviewed while conducting research on our monk seal. He appears flushed and strained, trying to save a singular animal of a doomed species. Because of his efforts, the seal survives, but the article mentions that only 1,300 seals remain in the world.

During our interview, I asked Mr. Ragen if anything could be done to revive the monk seal. He answered that there are some signs of recovery in certain populations on a few of the atolls in the Northwestern Islands. He mentioned that other species, like the Northern elephant seal and the Guadalupe fur seals, have come back from the brink of extinction. Possibly, he hinted, such recovery may occur for the Hawaiian monk seal.

Despite his reassuring comparisons, Mr. Ragen didn't seem a believer, nor did his voice sizzle with conviction. I asked whether he thought humans should be kept away from monk seals, including military men, fishermen, tourists, even Native Hawaiians. All of us human beings.

He paused, staring at his desk, framing his thoughts. Without looking up, he replied: The only way to save some ecosystems is to make them off-limits to everyone, completely.

I think of our ancient *kapu* system, where careful restrictions preserved the land and her bounty. Scientists such as Tim Ragen try to enforce a modern *kapu*. But predation rather than conservation drives the engine of the world now.

I look again at the photograph. I think of the state of the earth, our mother; of our people, her children; of myself, her Native daughter. I think of the only monk seal I have ever seen, in captivity, of course. Like myself, like our people and lands, in captivity.

Nature in captivity, in human captivity. A perversion of the natural order. I think of what we must do, as a species. I doubt we have the will to do it. But some of us already use our lives in trying to stop predation, to restore the natural order. What else can we do? What else could we choose to do?

Heartened by this tender resolution, I look out from my writing table to the comforting wetlands beyond. The sky is a blowing mass of darkening clouds. Beyond the fertile lava crevices of the Ko'olau mountains, a dying sun fades away. Just now, great billows of rain refresh the earth, releasing the cool smelling mud of mango and breadfruit trees. A cleansed moment. A nourishing feeling. I lean back and ponder the coming beauty of night.

NOTES

1. Technical information on the current status of the Hawaiian monk seal can be found in an administrative report by Timothy J. Ragen, published in April 1993, and available from the National Marine Fisheries Service in Honolulu. The report is titled *Status of the Hawaiian Monk Seal in 1992*.
2. Information on the treatment of seals, turtles, sharks, and other animals as well as indigenous peoples in the Pacific during Cook's voyages is available in *The Journals of Captain James Cook*, edited by J. C. Beaglehole (London: Cambridge University Press, 1967), Part One, p. 258; and Part Two, p. 772.
3. Information on the decline of the Hawaiian population, as well as other Pacific Islander populations, can be found in David Stannard, *Before the Horror: The Population of Hawai'i on the Eve of Western Contact* (Honolulu: Social Science Research Institute, University of Hawai'i, 1989).
4. Population collapse in the Americas as a result of Spanish, British, and American conquest is painstakingly analyzed in David Stannard, *American Holocaust: The Conquest of the New World* (New York: Oxford University Press, 1992).

CARIBOU

Mary Lockwood

Some of my memories get crowded like the tangle of caribou legs seen from the eyes of a ground squirrel. They hurry up on each other, big hooves thumping on soft tundra, cutting the stems of grass and berry bushes. Antlers clatter together, shattering the dam of forgetfulness.

I saw somebody far down the gravel beach. The perspective made the person look little. He was yelling, running fast, looking back and throwing a finger like a harpoon toward the distant Indian Head Cliffs. What could make him so frantic? All I could see was a mirage of waving tan and white specks warping from Norton Sound heat waves along the coastline.

Suddenly, the drowsy dogs tied up among the big driftwood logs on the rocky beach exploded in a snarling fervor. People from our summer camp dropped things and ran up the tundra banks to look anxiously up the beach.

I scampered to a taut larger form, who yelled "Caribou!" and nearly ran over me as he dashed to get the guns in the cabin. The electrified air of an unexpected hunt jolted the dogs to a new degree of frenzy. I clasped my hands over my ears and ran into the cabin.

The sound of clattering gray stones flying from striking hooves pierced the air. I ran to the window where Dad looked out to check his gill net and heard the hissing spray of ocean water as some of the big animals, driven to migrate, pushed along the sea. In all my young life, I had never before witnessed the tremendous power of pure, strong movement. The snorting, bawling creatures did not hesitate to continue, though this close contact with people spelled their doom.

My parents were not going to let the caribou go on without some harvest.

"Let them go past!"

"Ah ka! How big and plenty they are!"

They whooped and waved their arms to spook the huge animals on-ward, toward the town and their doom. Positioning themselves on the tundra bank, away from the tied dogs, breathing and sweating profusely, they found a resting post for their shooting arms.

As the caribou skittered away from the dogs, I noticed they pushed their young into the middle of their protective pod. Time slowed as I nar-rowed my eyes to concentrate on a flash of white among the jostling herd. There was a smaller caribou of pure white—an albino! I had heard of these creatures of fortune before, and seeing one made me yell and hop in front of the window.

The caribou surged as the rifles began firing. Several fell immedi-ately, their knobby knees buckling, tossing a quick prayer for a speedy ending into the air with their final moos. Their great heads tilted for a proud show of beautiful antlers as they gave up their spirits and quickly fell into the blood pooling on the rocky beach. One struggled to get up, managing to hop on front legs, dragging a hind that would not respond. A quick aim and crack from a rifle knocked it down.

I was crying, torn between the magnificence of the caribou and the horror of the slaughter and noise. The air remained repercussive from the barking of dogs, clattering of stones, whoops of victory.

I went outside, hurrying to see a caribou up close, I suppose. The madness was tangible.

A CARIBOU THAT GOT AWAY

The remaining caribou herd thundered down the beach, some dashing frantically between the tundra and the main herd as if their trauma had to be shared by those who survived the massacre.

As the blood drained from the caribou where they lay, we heard faraway barks and yells and crackling shots. Looking down the long stretch of beach, we remembered the sounds we made just a little while ago and the last wild movements of these animal bodies now devoid of spirit.

I winced at those cruel, distant sounds. How I wished the caribou could just trample forever unharmed over the vast Arctic!

"They came."

I marveled at their heraldic pace with their heads held back and long, elegant noses high, letting the sea air come far into their sinuses to tingle the bone bases of their antlers.

I remembered those high steps, leaping the length of a house with one bound, with a hop and spring of tendons that never grew tired, carrying all that inert mass I saw, all that heavy, heavy fur Mom was now peeling from the red muscle of a body that we would eat later on.

I remembered the spirit and vitality in the black globes of their eyes, so intelligent, courageous, and determined to move with one more bounding step, though their eyes blazed with white flashes of fear, though their caribou people fell right next to them.

"Why?"

I wanted to grab someone by the shoulders and shake an answer out of them.

"Why do we have to kill such gallantry? Because I can see—we are *not* superior! *They* are! They are free, they have family ties and caribou order in the midst of shootings and chaos. Unlike us! The caribou are superior!"

I agonized, no longer listening to reprimands. The caribou needed mourning, and in a little girl way I mourned there at the beach with no roof to block my imploring to our Maker.

I found a place where no one could see me. The high hot sun moved and stretched the afternoon shadows. I wanted to look toward town. I saw the dark stubby stands of pine and yellow meadows beside a tiny thick forest. The blue mountains were distant and aloof below a pale wide sky. The shallow ocean sparkled and lapped at the gray rocky shore. Old dry piles of driftwood rested upon the stones. A most beautiful, reassuring sight.

Breaking through the idyllic scene came a desperate young caribou, shocked into confusion—but getting away, tearing branches of willows with his antlers, leaping and staggering toward our cabin. Snorting with a twist of his head, gasping in great sobs, his eyes were full of dust and tears.

I stood up to be as noticeable as I could, making that lone caribou see me.

"Boo!" I shouted. "Don't come this way!" I waved my arms. "Turn around! Get away! Just one more scare! Just one more scare, and never, never come here again!" I pleaded.

The caribou saw me and reared off at a right angle to the safety of the forest and tundra.

Older folks came running. Their two-legged gait seemed slow and cumbersome compared to the leaping bound of four strong hooves.

Glaring at them, I hissed between my teeth, "Let it go."

In two meaningful seconds, I silently conveyed my disgust. Just as wordlessly, they turned away.

Since then, I have been allergic to caribou meat.

CLAN EYES

Susan Arkeketa

When a child is born to the people of the Otoes, she is born to her father's clan. To follow the way of his clan and all that it means—family, song, names, and tradition.

When a child is born to the people of the Muscogee, she is born to her mother's clan. To follow the way of the clan and all that it means—family, song, names, and tradition.

The marriage of my mother and father bore me and my sisters into the worlds of the buffalo and tiger. Two different worlds and ways of life. I have heard many times the saying that Native people live in two worlds, the white and the Indian. I live in three worlds: the buffalo, the tiger, and the white. In these clan worlds, I have a place and a purpose.

Sometimes I see through the eyes of my father's clan—the buffalo clan. Spring is the season of the buffalo. It is the time to take care of the people.

"The buffalo is our brother," my grandfather explained to me at a powwow in Oklahoma about a year before he died in 1979.

"Take care of your brother, respect him," he continued as we watched the dancers and singers. It was the last time he told me about my clan.

Through my clan eyes, I know who my relations are and the names of our brothers and sisters. I know not to marry within the clan. The buffalo provides me an identity that is centuries old. The people are named through their clan. My father is named after his grandfather. Years ago, my nephew—my father's grandson—took his name also.

The people know me through my clan, through my brother.

Sometimes I see through the eyes of my mother's clan—the tiger clan.

"Be strong, we are tigers," my grandmother once said.

The clan has a story as do the other clans of the Muscogee people. We follow the clan of our mothers. The clan mothers are strong and generous.

Through my clan eyes, I know who my relations are and the names of our brothers and sisters. I know not to marry within the clan. The tiger provides me an identity that is centuries old. I am a tiger and so are my daughters. The tiger will live in our family through the daughters.

I know my grandchildren will be tigers, to carry on the tradition.

The Creator placed me in three worlds: the buffalo, the tiger, and the white. Through my clan eyes I have a way of life. I always have a place among the people, my children and grandchildren will always have a place as have all the generations before our time.

Through the eyes of the buffalo and the tiger, I will teach my daughters to continue the clan way of life.

THE LAST WOLF

Mary Tall Mountain

the last wolf hurried toward me
through the ruined city
and I heard his baying echoes
down the steep smashed warrens
of Montgomery Street and past
the few ruby-crowned highrises
left standing
their lighted elevators useless

passing the flicking red and green
of traffic signals
baying his way eastward
in the mystery of his wild loping gait
closer the sounds in the deadly night
through clutter and rubble of quiet blocks

I heard his voice ascending the hill
and at last his low whine as he came
floor by empty floor to the room
where I sat
in my narrow bed looking west, waiting
I heard him snuffle at the door and
I watched
he trotted across the floor

he laid his long gray muzzle
on the spare white spread
and his eyes burned yellow
        his small dotted eyebrows quivered

Yes, I said.
I know what they have done.

SHE HAD SOME HORSES

Joy Harjo

She had some horses.

She had horses who were bodies of sand.
She had horses who were maps drawn of blood.
She had horses who were skins of ocean water.
She had horses who were the blue air of sky.
She had horses who were fur and teeth.
She had horses who were clay and would break.
She had horses who were splintered red cliff.

She had some horses.

She had horses with long, pointed breasts.
She had horses with full, brown thighs.
She had horses who laughed too much.
She had horses who threw rocks at glass houses.
She had horses who licked razor blades.

She had some horses.

She had horses who danced in their mothers' arms.
She had horses who thought they were the sun, and their
bodies shone and burned like stars.
She had horses who waltzed nightly on the moon.
She had horses who were much too shy, and kept quiet
in stalls of their own making.

She had some horses.

She had horses who liked Creek stomp dance songs.
She had horses who cried in their beer.
She had horses who spit at male queens who made
them afraid of themselves.
She had horses who said they weren't afraid.
She had horses who lied.
She had horses who told the truth, who were stripped bare
of their tongues.

She had some horses.

She had horses who called themselves, "horse."
She had horses who called themselves, "spirit," and kept
their voices secret and to themselves.
She had horses who had no names.
She had horses who had books of names.

She had some horses.

She had horses who whispered in the dark, who were afraid to speak.
She had horses who screamed out of fear of the silence, who
carried knives to protect themselves from ghosts.
She had horses who waited for destruction.
She had horses who waited for resurrection.

She had some horses.

She had horses who got down on their knees for any savior.
She had horses who thought their high price had saved them.
She had horses who tried to save her, who climbed in her
bed at night and prayed as they raped her.

She had some horses.

She had some horses she loved.
She had some horses she hated.
These were the same horses.

II: DEEP SCIENCE

Living in the Field

*T*wo decades ago, the field of primatology was a male bastion with studies centering on male-dominated hierarchies and skills. Because there
were so few women in the field of animal behavior, the conclusions we
drew about animals were as biased as the prejudices about our own
species. For example, humans were believed to be the only toolmakers
among animals—until Jane Goodall's field research proved that chimpanzees also constructed tools in the wild for foraging and feeding. About
Goodall's revolutionary discovery, primatologist Alison Jolly at Princeton
University said, "She essentially redefined what it is to be a human
being. ... Everyone knew that things would never be the same again."

As we move into the twenty-first century, the number of women scientists and researchers in the field of animal study has increased so dramatically that among primatologists, 50 percent are now women. Such
famous researchers as Jane Goodall, Dian Fossey, and Birute Galdikas—
the "Trimates" chosen for primate studies by Dr. Louis B. Leakey—have
already redefined what it is to be a human as well as a nonhuman primate.
But less-well-known women researchers, many included here, have la-
bored for decades living alongside wild animals.

As more women study animals, we realize how important females
are in animal societies—from the matriarchal elephants, orcas, dolphins,
and lions to the sisterhood of hyenas and the female bonding among bonobos that assures a less violent society.

Is there a female style in science? By listening closely, calling upon
empathy as well as acute observation, engaging "hard" science with intuition and compassion, these women researchers have made sure that we
will never see the world or other animals in quite the same way.

AKMAD

Birute M. F. Galdikas

And the end of all our exploring
Will be to arrive where we started
And know the place for the first time.

—T. S. ELIOT

Akmad and I were alone by the edge of the great forest of Borneo, the second largest continuous stretch of tropical rain forest in the world. Akmad had just given birth, and her gentle, elongated orangutan face with its delicately etched features looked tired. The light of the late afternoon sun shone eerily through Akmad's long auburn hair, silhouetting her form in an incandescent halo.

I wanted to photograph the tiny, wrinkled, nude face of Akmad's newborn infant. I moved forward on my knees and elbows and focused on the baby's elfin face pressed to her mother's bosom. Moving my hand gently, I shifted the little infant. Her bright orange hair, newly dry from the fluids of birth, was soft and fluffy and contrasted with the deep, almost mahogany red of her mother's longer, coarser coat. Despite my touch, the infant rested quietly in her mother's arms. Akmad's liquid brown eyes remained expressionless. She seemed unaware of my hand on her newborn. Her arm brushed carelessly across my leg as she reached for a pineapple, almost as if I didn't exist. The magical soft light, peculiar to dusk in Borneo, etched the scene in gold, a moment transfixed in time.

Other orangutans began to emerge from the trees and descend to the ironwood causeway that runs from Camp Leakey, my research base deep in the forest, to the Sekonyer Kanan River six hundred feet away. Mr. Achyar, the camp feeder, appeared pushing a cart of food. In his forties and very slight, like a shadow, he walked with the slow, deliberate gait typical of older Indonesians. His Green Bay Packers T-shirt, faded from the equatorial sun and countless sudsy beatings in the name of cleanliness, was a reminder that the outside world intruded even here in Borneo.

Mr. Achyar stooped low as he passed by us, twisting sideways politely, his right arm and shoulder bent forward in a pose reminiscent of a figure on an ancient Egyptian mural. His bow reflected the courtesy typical of traditional Dayaks. Paradoxically, these most gentle and courteous of any people were once fierce headhunters, the "wild men of Borneo."

The spell continued as Mr. Achyar began chanting. He called the orangutans in a singsong voice, like a supplicant in an ancient ritual, the names of ex-captive orangutans like the names of spirits. His voice rose over the trees, "Pola, Kusasi, Hani, Kuspati, Siswoyo."

Mr. Achyar had been feeding the mature ex-captive orangutans at Camp Leakey for seven years. Of all my Dayak assistants, he was the one most trusted by the orangutans. Many Indonesians called him a *pawong*, a person who has the power to call wild animals to him. He had no children of his own and had developed a special relationship with the orangutans, referring to them as his children. His devotion to them was obvious as he moved among them in a careful, solicitous way, making certain each received an equal share of rice, bananas, and pineapple. Although Mr. Achyar was slim and slightly stooped, in this particular orangutan hierarchy he was the dominant male. Gigantic wild male orangutans who occasionally came to camp, attracted by orangutan females, deferred to him.

Dusk ends suddenly in the tropics, and I felt hurried. I twirled the focusing mechanism on my Nikon, clicking rapidly. I wanted to record this moment, to celebrate this as yet unnamed female infant on the day of her birth.

To take a clearer picture, I moved back from Akmad and her baby and crouched nine or ten feet away. A piece of dry fern had caught in the infant's hair, obscuring her face. Mr. Achyar was nearby cutting pineapples into quarters. He was closer to Akmad than I. Speaking in the hushed voice that the moment dictated, I asked him to take the fern from the infant's hair. Nestled on her mother's side, the baby was dozing peacefully, her miniature fingers clenched tightly around strands of her mother's hair.

Mr. Achyar gently approached Akmad and slowly reached over to remove the fern. Akmad seemed oblivious to his approach. My fingers closed around the lens, preparing for another shot. The golden light still held.

Never, not in a millennium, could Mr. Achyar or I have anticipated Akmad's reaction to his simple gesture. His fingers never touched the infant's head. Without warning, Akmad recoiled. Baring her teeth, she exploded. Her hair went erect, tripling her size, and she lunged at Mr. Achyar, her fangs glistening, the soft expression on her face gone. Not large for an adult female orangutan, Akmad weighed about seventy pounds. Yet leveraged, taut muscles provide even female orangutans with the strength of perhaps five men. An orangutan female's teeth can rip off a person's scalp or arm. Had Mr. Achyar not been so agile, he would have been badly mangled. However, he leaped back in one motion. Akmad did not pursue her attack. Her point made, she simply sat down and picked up the pineapple she had been eating. Her face was once again expressionless.

Shocked, Mr. Achyar stared at Akmad as if his own child had turned on him. "Not once, not ever before," he gasped in bewilderment. "I have never been attacked by an orangutan before. They are all my children and my friends." He sighed, "Akmad is the gentlest of them all. I never expected her to attack me."

I moved over to Akmad and gazed at the infant nestled against her. Without hesitating, I reached out and pulled the fern from her infant's hair. Akmad did not even blink to acknowledge me. Her eyes were focused elsewhere, somewhere in the distance. She was back in the universe orangutans inhabit.

Emboldened, I carefully moved the infant into a better position for a photograph in the fading light. As I gently tugged at her, the infant squealed. Akmad's opaque, inner-directed gaze did not change. I glanced at Mr. Achyar, who was watching me intently. The wonder on his face was palpable. I, too, was amazed. Up to that moment I had never imagined the degree to which Akmad accepted me.

When I arrived in Kalimantan, or Indonesian Borneo, fifteen years earlier in 1971, my goal was to study wild orangutans in their natural habitat. But almost immediately I became involved in the rescue and rehabilitation of wildborn orangutans who had been captured by humans—to keep as pets or to sell to zoos, circuses, laboratories. I have always felt strongly that saving orangutans is as important as studying them. By working to return captive orangutans to the wild, I was trying to eliminate the captive orangutan trade in the area and so protect the wild orangutans. My work rescuing and rehabilitating ex-captive, wildborn orangutans has always been distinct from my main work, studying wild orangutans. Over the years these separate endeavors sometimes rivaled and sometimes reinforced one another but never became blurred.

Akmad was one of the first of many ex-captives I rescued from captivity and returned to the forest. Although she had been independent for some years, she occasionally left the trees and came to camp for the feeding we provided daily.

I had not realized until that moment how much I identified with Akmad and how deeply our lives were linked. Akmad started her life as a wild orangutan and now had returned to the forest. But part of her passage through life was totally different from the experience of orangutans who spend their entire lives in the great forest of Borneo. Akmad had been kidnapped by humans in her youth. When we rescued her, she had elected to live in my camp for a time, as my adopted orangutan "daughter." But gradually she had returned to the forest and the freedom that were her natural rights.

Like Akmad, I, too, followed a life path that differed radically from those of my family, my childhood companions, and my university friends and acquaintances. I left the experiences and culture of my youth to live as an adult in Kalimantan. Yet my life in Kalimantan gave me a deeper understanding of the life and youth I left behind. Like Akmad, I had been touched by two worlds, that of humans and that of orangutans. I gained experience in the forest, learned from the orangutans and from the Dayaks, who are the aboriginal people of Borneo, and then, like the T. S. Eliot poem, came back to where I started. I rediscovered the woods where I played as a child in Canada, the forests of my Lithuanian forebears, and ultimately the tropical rain forests where our ancestors evolved—our Garden of Eden.

The choices that had been forced on Akmad paralleled the paths that I had chosen consciously and voluntarily. Akmad and I were kindred spirits.

I first saw "Akmad" only a month after I arrived in Borneo, at the door of our hut, clinging to the arm of our assistant, Mr. Hamzah. As he brought her in, Mr. Hamzah lifted his arm and unrolled her like a paper towel spilling onto the floor. She stood up, still holding on to his arm above her. Her long face was serene, the fluid brown of her eyes veiled by thick lashes. My first thought was, "Why, she looks just like a Parisienne! A lady from Paris!"

The weeks that followed confirmed this initial impression; Akmad was a lady. She had a gentle way about her. She never ran, she always walked. She never grabbed, she always reached. Even her squeal had a daintiness that the vocalization of other orangutans lacked.

How human she appeared, like an orange gnome, with her intelligent, quietly inquisitive face. Like all orangutans, Akmad was covered with dark orange hair. Although coarser and thicker than ours, the distribution is similar. Her face, her palms, and the soles of her feet were hairless, while her small naked ears, almost identical in shape to human ears, protruded from the hair on her head. When Akmad stood up, however, her long arms dangled to her knees while her legs were proportionately shorter than ours and slightly bowed. What distinguished Akmad's body most from a human shape was her rotund belly that made her look perpetually pregnant, although at the time she was far too young to bear offspring. Had Akmad been an infant, her eyes and mouth would have been encircled by patches of whitish skin. Akmad's face was already dark, although not as black as it would become once she reached adulthood.

The look on Akmad's face was aware but self-contained. Whatever emotions she might have been feeling, her soft brown eyes revealed nothing. Orangutans, in general, are even-tempered and serene compared to their volatile African cousins, chimpanzees. Even among members of her own tranquil species, Akmad stood out as being exceptionally calm. We named her after an official of the Indonesian Institute of Sciences, Ms. Sjamsiah Akmad, who had been kind and helpful when we first arrived in Jakarta.

At this time Akmad was about six years old, the orangutan equivalent of a young girl. Her sweetness was all the more impressive given her history, for she had been kidnapped under what must have been brutal circumstances.

Several weeks after we arrived in Borneo, we heard from local people that nearby loggers had captured a young orangutan and were holding her in a rough cage at their camp just outside the Tanjung Puting Reserve, where we were based. Killing, capturing, or selling a wild orangutan was illegal in Indonesia, but the law was rarely enforced. I was determined to change this.

My husband in those early years was Rod Brindamour (known locally as "Mr. Rod"). A take-charge kind of person, Rod always seemed to display the self-assurance and determination essential to official transactions. While I went to the forest to observe wild orangutans, Rod set out with Mr. Hamzah and a young official from the Forestry Department to confiscate the orphaned orangutan, much as a North American social worker might remove a child from a home where she was being neglected or abused.

In Indonesia there is a phrase *"negara hukum,"* meaning that Indonesia is a "country of laws." It is also a country where power, position, and connections command respect. At this time, Forestry Department officials were empowered to enforce forestry laws directly, without assistance from the police. Many of these laws, such as those protecting orangutans, stemmed from Dutch colonial days; they were not grounded in local norms and customs. But the head of the Forestry Department in Kalimantan, Mr. Widajat, had taken us under his wing and made it clear that he expected his officers to be helpful to us. Any Indonesian under his command would feel compelled to assist us, regardless of personal attitude.

Mr. Hamzah and Rod arrived at the logging camp, the reluctant local forestry officer in tow. Even at this late stage, the official queried doubtfully, "Are you sure that I must confiscate this orangutan?"

Without hesitation Rod declared, "You must."

The officer summoned up his most official manner and announced, "It is against the law to keep an orangutan without special permission." Akmad was released into Rod's custody.

Rod did not learn the exact circumstances under which Akmad had been orphaned, but the only way to capture a wild orangutan is to kill a mother and abduct her infant or juvenile. Akmad's mother must have been killed by the loggers. Firearms are under tight control in Indonesia, available only to the army and police, but the guards at the logging camp probably had guns to protect the cut timber and to provide fresh meat. Most often the guards hunted deer and wild pigs. But the logging operations had cut wide paths through the forest, forcing orangutans into the open where they became "fair game."

An equally unpleasant possibility was that Akmad's mother had been murdered for the express purpose of acquiring a young orangutan for sale abroad. To local entrepreneurs, baby orangutans meant easy cash. They could buy an orangutan from loggers or from Dayak hunters for a hundred dollars (several months' wages in Borneo at the time), then sell the prize to a sea captain or sailor with connections abroad for two or three times that amount. The infant orangutan would then be crated, stowed below deck, and often kept for days without food or water until the ship was outside Indonesian waters. For every five baby orangutans smuggled out of the country, at least three died en route. But the potential profit made the risks worthwhile. In Hong Kong or Singapore, an orangutan sold for five thousand dollars or more. The ape trade was an open secret in those days. Asian zoos were still buying wild orangutans, as were private collectors in both Asia and the West.

There are no photographic records of an orangutan kidnapping. But missionaries who work in the interior of Borneo have seen and described what happens. Once a mother-infant pair is spotted, the rest apparently is very easy. When a mother orangutan is threatened, her infant or juvenile invariably rushes to her side and clings tightly to her body. This slows the mother down, making her an easy target. Spotting a group of humans, Akmad's mother probably vocalized and dropped branches on them in a display of fear. Hearing her kiss-squeaks and hoots, Akmad rushed to her mother. One or two well-placed shots, and the mother would have crashed to the ground, clutching for branches, screaming as she fell. If the shots hadn't killed her, the fall might have. Rather than fleeing, Akmad would have clung to her dead mother's body until she was pried loose. She might have tried to bite her attackers, but at twenty or twenty-five pounds she could not have put up much resistance. The final horror, as reported by missionaries, might have been when Akmad, secured with a rope or chain, watched as her mother was skinned, gutted, and prepared for consumption. In some cases the mother's flesh is cut up and laid out to dry, for "orangutan jerky," and the infant is kept and fattened up for a stew.

At about age fifteen, Akmad found a mate and became pregnant. She gave birth when she was about sixteen. Before her first infant, "Arnold," was born, a large four-year-old female we named "Carey" came to camp. Recently orphaned and apparently lonely, Carey tried to get a human to adopt her. By now I had my own son, Binti, and could not be a surrogate to a clinging, demanding orphan orangutan. No other person in camp volunteered for the job.

Rejected by humans, Carey tried orangutans. Her first target was "Sobiarso," a fluffy, engaging adolescent who captivated visitors with her energy and charm. Following one of the "I'm-a-poor-orphan" advances, I saw the usually very sweet Sobiarso smash Carey onto the boards of the causeway, then run away to escape further advances. Carey looked ruffled but unhurt by this fierce rejection. I also saw Carey attempt to cling to a subadult male. He pried her off his body as if she were a disgusting parasite.

Finally Carey turned to Akmad. Despite a period of initial rejection (I once counted as Akmad peeled Carey off her body seventy times in a mere thirty minutes), Carey persisted. In a resigned fashion, perhaps with as much anguish and doubt as I had felt toward my orphaned orangutan babies, Akmad finally accepted the young female. Orangutans learn by imitation, just as we humans do. Akmad was mothered by a stranger of another species; now she became a mother to a stranger of her own species.

Once Carey sensed Akmad's good nature (and her no doubt abundant maternal hormones), the die was cast. For the rest of her pregnancy, Akmad carried Carey everywhere, even allowing her to suckle. An orangutan pregnancy lasts eight months, and Carey had been suckling for several months by the time Arnold was born. Akmad gave birth in a nest on a low-lying branch in a tree near the edge of camp. I climbed as high as I could into a nearby tree to watch. Akmad seemed tired after the birth and stayed in the nest for a long time. Usually the mother consumes the placenta, but in this case Carey, not Akmad, devoured the afterbirth. Carey's face and hands were smeared with Arnold's life blood. In my mind, this became symbolic of their whole relationship.

I began to worry about how Akmad would cope. Ordinarily, an

orangutan does not give birth until her previous offspring is large enough to be independent. As I discovered after many years of research, the average birth span for wild orangutans is almost eight years. Nobody has reported twin orangutan infants in the wild. Nor has anyone reported a wild female adopting another female's infant. I wondered what price Akmad would pay for taking care of two babies.

I don't think I have ever seen a more harried mother—human or orangutan—than Akmad. She would come into camp, the usually neat-looking hair framing her forehead in disarray, pouches under her eyes, and her normally benign expression strained. My eyes would shoot down to her breasts, where Carey and Arnold both sucked fiercely, their bodies swinging below her nipples as she walked. Both infants grew and thrived; it was Akmad who carried the burden. Often I would watch her climbing ever so slowly to the forest canopy 150 feet up, one infant on her shoulder and the other clinging to her side.

As Arnold grew, he seemed remarkably independent for his age. Infant orangutans rarely leave their mother's body for the first year of their life, and usually stay within touching distance for another year after that. Even at five years they do not let their mother out of their sight. But at age three, Arnold sometimes lagged far behind as Akmad moved on the ground in the seasonally dried-up swamps near camp. Perhaps he was imitating his older stepsister, Carey, or perhaps his mother carried him less often to avoid having to lug Carey as well. One thing was certain: Arnold was the one who paid the price of the adoption, not Carey.

When Arnold was a little over four years old, he vanished. The day after he disappeared, Akmad came to camp to feed in the late afternoon. I was watching her when she suddenly dropped her bananas. She climbed into the tallest tree overlooking the bridge and began a series of actions that, in the orangutan lexicon, expressed severe annoyance and distress. She started with kiss-squeaks of irritation, followed by a series of low, prolonged grunts. Her eyes fixed on something in the distance with an almost maniacal stare. Then she started breaking branches. With enormous anger she hurled them toward the distant object. This display went on for over an hour. Not once did Akmad allow her eyes to stray from that single point of concentration.

I walked around trying to see what was upsetting Akmad so much. In the distance a crested serpent eagle sat with a snake in its talons. But this was not an uncommon sight in Kalimantan, and the bird was behind Akmad, not in front of her. I was mystified. Ex-captive orangutans were slowly congregating toward the end of the bridge where Mr. Achyar was dispensing the day's meal, rice and bananas. The other orangutans were busy eating; everything seemed normal. I kept looking for the object of

Akmad's violent display. All I could see was a glimpse of a large forest pig in the distance.

Akmad abruptly moved off into the treetops near camp. She had eaten nothing. Gradually the other orangutans left, one by one. The bridge, minutes earlier the scene of frenzied activity, once again became an oasis of calm. Only the sound of cracking branches betrayed the presence of orangutans building night nests nearby. Mr. Achyar walked toward me, silently pushing the cart with the remains of the evening meal.

"Mr. Achyar," I said, breaking the silence, "what happened to Arnold?" I paused, studying his face. "Do you know what happened to Arnold?"

Mr. Achyar answered sadly, "I believe he was eaten by the pig, *Ibu*." He used the term of respect for women in Indonesia.

"Are you sure?" I asked, not wanting to believe his words.

"I am sure," he replied, his face hardened by an inner pain I was feeling as well. "I didn't see it, but why else would Arnold be gone?" Mr. Achyar paused.

"I am sure," he repeated. "*Permissi, Ibu,*" he said slowly, and then he picked up the handles of the cart and continued moving down the bridge toward camp.

I was left alone with my thoughts and the darkening sky. Mr. Achyar was right; nothing else could explain Akmad's uncharacteristic behavior. I knew. I remembered the last time I had seen Arnold, way behind Carey and Akmad, in a vulnerable position on the ground with no large trees nearby. A bearded pig, with his enormous jaws and massive teeth, could have swallowed Arnold (who had weighed less than twenty pounds) almost whole.

Carey's persistent demands on Akmad had led, indirectly, to Arnold's death. I couldn't blame Carey; she had only sought a mother to replace the one killed by humans when she herself was captured. But nonetheless Arnold was dead, sacrificed to Akmad's intense efforts to rear her own offspring plus an unrelated foster child. Having nurtured so many orphaned infant orangutans myself, I understood Akmad's behavior. There is something so compelling, so insistent, about their demands that is it difficult *not* to sacrifice one's comfort and personal life in their behalf. How many times had I given them my food, let them come between me and my husband, almost crowding us off our mattress? Ultimately, Arnold was the victim of the illegal trade in wild orangutans that produced Carey and other orphans like her. I told myself that I had chosen to take part in their rescue, but perhaps I had merely succumbed to my maternal instincts. Were Akmad and I so different? That evening, as on many occasions, I thought not.

Now Akmad had given birth again, and I was photographing her new-born infant. Akmad was free; she had an infant who was free. In a moment of absolute clarity I realized the intensity of the bond that I had forged with Akmad. She had singled me out for this unique historic honor: I was a female of another species, but as her bonded mother I had been granted the privilege of sharing her newborn infant. I was probably the first human being in history who was truly an orangutan infant's grandmother.

The light shifted, putting an end to my musing. The otherworldly glow that illuminated the causeway and gave the line of forest trees in the distance an almost surreal beauty vanished. Akmad's eyes went upward. The machinelike rhythm of the evening cicadas and the fading light were signals as old as time. Slowly she scanned the distant forest. It was time to nest. Without even a glance in my direction, she ambled away.

It had taken me more than a decade of living with orangutans, day by day in their great forest home, to understand finally that orangutans are not just simpler versions of ourselves. All those years that orangutans had walked by me, seemingly oblivious, I had despaired of ever reaching them. For a split second, Akmad had allowed me a clear glimpse of her universe. And yet, without knowing it, I already had been allowed into that world years before. What I had taken as indifference and rejection was the orangutan expression of acceptance. I had measured orangutans by human standards of sociability, and had misunderstood. In that moment everything I had been through—the heat, the mud, the humidity, the torrential rains, the fire ants, the leeches, the cobras, pythons, and pit vipers, the fevers, the deaths, the frustrations—became insignificant. I knew that my journey, my personal odyssey into the uncharted depths of the rain forest and the orangutan mind, started years earlier, had truly begun.

Orangutans reflect, to some degree, the innocence we humans left behind in Eden, before our social organization, bipedalism, and toolmaking gave us "dominion over" the planet. Thus, understanding orangutans gives us a clouded, partial glimpse into what we were before we became fully human. Such a partial glimpse is the best we can hope for until time machines are invented that will actually take us back to face our ancestors in the flesh, to smell their sweat and to hear their voices.

I had understood orangutans intuitively without realizing that I understood them. Now, that intuition crystalized. By giving Akmad her freedom and encouraging her independence, I had forged the deepest possible bond, that of a female and her adult daughter. Reintegrating ex-captives into the wild orangutan population had been my ultimate goal. I wanted them to forget the time they had spent in captivity, the period when they depended on humans. But being human, I could not avoid a twinge of loss when they disappeared into the forest. It was a feeling not unlike that mothers feel when a child leaves for college: success and relief, mixed with nostalgia. Yet the distance was so much greater. In returning to the forest, the ex-captive orangutans were crossing back over the line that has divided our two species for millennia. Their life with us would become a remembered dream, I imagined, sometimes joyful and sometimes terrifying. Irrationally, I had joined the mothers who complain, "They never call, they never write." But now I saw that Akmad remembered, in her own, and very special, orangutan way.

I continued sitting on the causeway long after darkness fell, thinking about what name I should give Akmad's newborn. The name had to begin with "A"; this was to keep members of Akmad's and other family groups easily identifiable. I thought of my human family back in North America, so far from the forests of Southeast Asia. I thought of my sister. Her beautiful, kind face appeared before me: in her gentleness she was much like Akmad. I didn't have the time to write to her as often as I would like, but I thought of her often. Aldona.... I named the tiny orangutan infant "Aldona."

A year passed before I had close contact with Akmad again. I was sitting on the bridge, the same bridge where I had photographed her newborn infant. It was feeding time. Unexpectedly Akmad materialized from the forest. She came straight over to me, sat down, and leaned into me as she ate. She stayed there, leaning lightly against my side, for more than fifteen minutes. When she finished eating her dark brown eyes flickered over my face, as if I held only momentary interest for her. Then she stood up, adjusted her infant with my sister's name, Aldona, on her head as though the one-year-old were an oversize Easter bonnet, and moved away.

The buzz of the evening cicadas evaporated into the humidity as Akmad slowly made her nest in the nearby canopy. I felt blessed. Twice that year Akmad had acknowledged, however briefly, the relationship we had shared more than fifteen years earlier. Now I understood how for orangutans, honed by countless generations of living mostly alone in the canopy of the dank, dark forest, volumes could reside in a glance. Orangutans do not need to endlessly test and reaffirm their relationships, as chimpanzees, gorillas, and especially humans do. It had taken me fifteen years to understand that for orangutans, a bond once forged is forever.

BONOBO SOCIETY:
AMICABLE, AMOROUS AND RUN BY FEMALES

Natalie Angier

Nature's raucous bestiary rarely serves up good role models for human behavior, unless you happen to work on the trading floor of the New York Stock Exchange. But there is one creature that stands out from the chest-thumping masses as an example of amicability, sensitivity and, well, humaneness: a little-known ape called the bonobo, or, less accurately, the pygmy chimpanzee.

Before bonobos can be fully appreciated, however, two human prejudices must be overcome. The first is, fellows, the female bonobo is the dominant sex, though the dominance is so mild and unobnoxious that some researchers view bonobo society as a matter of "co-dominance," or equality between the sexes. Fancy that.

The second hurdle is human squeamishness about what in the 80s were called P.D.A.'s, or public displays of affection, in this case very graphic ones. Bonobos lubricate the gears of social harmony with sex, in all possible permutations and combinations: males with females, males with males, females with females, and even infants with adults. The sexual acts include intercourse, genital-to-genital rubbing, oral sex, mutual masturbation and even a practice that people once thought they had a patent on: French kissing.

Bonobos use sex to appease, to bond, to make up after a fight, to ease tensions, to cement alliances. Humans generally wait until after a nice meal to make love; bonobos do it beforehand, to alleviate the stress and competitiveness often seen among animals when they encounter a source of food.

Lest this all sound like a nonstop Caligulean orgy, Frans de Waal, a primatologist at Emory University in Atlanta who is the author of *Bonobo: The Forgotten Ape*, emphasizes otherwise. "Sex is there, it's pervasive, it's critical, and bonobo society would collapse without it," he said in an interview. "But it's not what people think it is. It's not driven by orgasm or seeking release. Nor is it often reproductively driven. Sex for a bonobo is casual, it's quick and once you're used to watching it, it begins to look like any other social interaction."

In *Bonobo*, Dr. de Waal draws upon his own research as well as that of many other primatologists to sketch a portrait of a species much less familiar to most people than are the other great apes—the gorilla, the orangutan and the so-called common chimpanzee. The bonobo, found in the dense equatorial rain forests of Zaire, was not officially discovered until 1929, long after the other apes had been described.

Even today there are only about 100 in zoos around the country, compared with the many thousands of chimpanzees in captivity. Bonobos are closely related to chimpanzees, but they have a more graceful and slender build, with smaller heads, slimmer necks, longer legs and less burly upper torsos. When standing or walking upright, bonobos have straighter backs than do the chimpanzees, and so assume a more human-like posture.

Far more dramatic than their physical differences are their behavioral distinctions. Bonobos are much less aggressive and hot-tempered than are chimpanzees, and are not nearly as prone to physical violence. They are less obsessed with power and status than are their chimpanzee cousins, and more consumed with Eros.

As Dr. de Waal puts it in his book, "The chimpanzee resolves sexual issues with power; the bonobo resolves power issues with sex." Or more coyly, chimpanzees are from Mars, bonobos are from Venus.

All of which has relevance for understanding the roots of human nature. Dr. de Waal seeks to correct the image of humanity's ancestors as invariably chimpanzee-like, driven by aggression, hierarchical machinations, hunting, warfare and male dominance. He points out that bonobos are as genetically close to humans as are chimpanzees, and that both are astonishingly similar to mankind, sharing at least 98 percent of humans' DNA. "The take-home message is, there's more flexibility in our lineage than we thought," Dr. de Waal said. "Bonobos are just as close to us as are chimpanzees, so we can't push them aside."

Indeed, humans appear to possess at least some bonobo-like characteristics, particularly the extracurricular use of sex beyond that needed for reproduction, and perhaps a more robust capacity for cooperation than some die-hard social Darwinists might care to admit.

One unusual aspect of bonobo society is the ability of females to form strong alliances with other unrelated females. In most primates, the males leave their birthplaces on reaching maturity as a means of avoiding incest, and so the females that form the social core are knit together by kinship. Among bonobos, females disperse at adolescence, and have to insinuate themselves into a group of strangers. They make friends with sexual overtures, and are particularly solicitous of the resident females.

The constructed sisterhood appears to give females a slight edge over resident males, who, though they may be related to one another, do not tend to act as an organized alliance. For example, the females usually have priority when it comes to eating, and they will stick up for one another should the bigger and more muscular male try to act aggressively.

Dr. de Waal said that many men grow indignant when they learn of the bonobo's social structure. "After one of my talks, a famous German professor jumped up and said, 'What is wrong with these males?' " he recalled. Yet Dr. de Waal said the bonobo males might not have reason to rebel. "They seem to be in a perfectly good situation," he said. "The females have sex with them all the time, and they don't have to fight over it so much among themselves. I'm not sure they've lost anything, except for their dominance."

Denise Herzing

The air is still, and the ocean surface is as smooth as glass. Only a few dorsal fins and short breaths break the surface. But below, the picture is quite different. Little Gash, a young adult female dolphin, zooms up behind me. As I direct the underwater video and sound gear her way, Knuckles, a young adult male, comes into view. He is pursuing her rapidly, his body arched and neck stretched, making an S-shaped posture typical of a courting male. He turns belly up, underneath but behind her, echolocating continuously on her genital area. Perhaps he is receiving acoustic as well as chemical information about her receptivity.

Little Gash darts here and there, but Knuckles is persistent. Eventually he parallels her every move, belly to belly, occasionally caressing her with his pectoral fins. Finally, after a few soft whistles, they mate. Little Gash is then approached by two other males who have been observing; they also mate with her. Surprisingly, the oldest male in the coalition, Stubby, does not pursue her. The mating system may appear promiscuous to us, but is it really—or do individuals have preferred partners over their years of acquaintance? Most likely there are many subtleties of their sexual and social lives we have yet to unravel.

When last I observed Little Gash being pursued by a similar coalition of males, her reaction was far from cooperative. She aggressively confronted one male, while the other two kept close to her pursuer. Swimming upside down, Little Gash repeatedly charged the male, Cat Scratches, who remained upright. At first glance it seemed a ballet, but to a trained eye it had a different meaning. The inverted posture, combined with an open mouth and butting of the body against the other, is an expression of aggression. The same ballet, performed by mature males, often escalates into a stationary face-off with additional signals, including an arched back, jaw-snapping and loud 'squawks' directed towards rival males.

Little Gash's behaviour escalated only to the extent of directing a few tail slaps at Cat Scratches' face. Eventually, it appeared her message—'Not interested, but try another time'—was received. I had seen Little Gash perform this sequence years earlier, when she was a juvenile, but then it was in the context of play with her juvenile friends.

Observing dolphins is like observing icebergs. What you see on the surface is only a small percentage of what is underneath. That's one reason I chose the Bahamas to work in. Here, the warm, crystal-clear waters make it possible for a person to observe, under water, for extended periods of time. The shallow sandbanks are home to a resident school of Atlantic spotted dolphins *Stenella frontalis* (formerly known as *S. plagiodon*), a species which is relatively unstudied, unlike the pantropical spotted dolphin *S. attenuata* (though the tens of thousands of pantropicals killed in purse-seine tuna nets in the Eastern Tropical Pacific have provided biologists with a depressingly steady supply of carcasses).

The members of the Bahamas school of Atlantic spotteds have grown accustomed to humans in the water, giving me an incredible opportunity to observe them in their natural environment and, like elephant and primate researchers, to observe and record them foraging, mating and otherwise socialising.

It was in the summer of 1985 that I first began observing the spotted dolphins. Since then, I have spent five months of each year living at sea, documenting individuals, behaviours and vocalisations. The more I observe this group, the more I realise how limited we are by our terrestrial senses. For this reason I have employed high-tech equipment to decipher many of their signals. The use of underwater video with sound input has been invaluable in capturing moments that are too quick to note by eye. Dolphins move fast under water and their communication and behaviour is complex and rapid. In addition, some of their acoustics are above our hearing range. To capture and catalogue their vocalisations, I use a high-speed digital sound-processing board in my computer, which can produce sonagrams of different calls for comparison.

For a variety of reasons, we tend to think of dolphins as primarily acoustic communicators. First, sound travels very effectively under water—up to four and a half times as fast as it does in air. Second, dolphins utilise frequencies 10 times as high as we do, and have highly developed acoustic areas of the brain. But they also have excellent vision, taste and touch. Together with sound these create a rich repertoire of signals vital for the development and maintenance of the long-term bonds and associations characteristic of close-knit dolphin society.

Spotted dolphins live in groups for protection from predators and possibly to aid in co-operative foraging. Because of the apparent importance of their social bonds, I have chosen a framework for studying the Atlantic spotteds which incorporates not only the physical signals but also the social context in which they are used. This entails identifying individuals—by their spots, and marks on the dorsal fin and flukes—following relationships and association patterns over the years, and analysing their communication signals throughout their life history and within a social context—a 20-year project at a minimum.

What we know so far is that Atlantic spotteds live in groups of 50–60 animals. Most of an individual's time is spent in a smaller subgroup during the day, although it appears that these subgroups remain within acoustic range of each other for much of the time. During the day, the dolphins spend their time resting, socialising and foraging. Research on pantropical spotted dolphins shows that they are 'crepuscular' feeders, feeding mainly at dawn and dusk. And indeed, the Atlantic spotteds in my study area do move off the sandbanks in the late afternoon to feed on squid in deeper waters. But, like other behaviours, their foraging strategies are flexible, and they also hunt on the banks during the day for bottom-dwelling fish such as lizardfish, flounders, razorfish, garden eels and shoaling reef fish such as needlefish and ballyhoo.

Calves learn to forage when they are as young as six months. To help them, mothers, as well as older juveniles, will often chase up a flounder for the young calf to catch. But during this time, the mother is still providing most of her offspring's food. In fact, the calf suckles throughout its first three years. When her calf is very young, the mother will turn and present herself to it. Later, the calf will turn to suckle underneath its mother, signaling before it turns with only a few soft chirps.

When first born, spotted dolphins have no spots at all—they look just like small bottle-nosed dolphins. This makes them convenient subjects to study, because their spotting increases with age through predictable stages. First there is the 'two-tone' stage, from about two weeks to three years (newborns of less than two weeks look much the same, but noticeably more awkward) followed by the juvenile or 'speckled' stage, from four to eight years; then the young adulthood or 'mottled' stage, marked by a rapid increase in spotting, from nine to fifteen years; and finally the mature adult, or 'fused' stage, at age fifteen and above, in which many of the spots are joined together.

Over the first three to five years, sometimes until well into the speckled stage, young spotted dolphins are tightly associated with their mothers. The mother/calf subgroup is one of the tightest units of dolphin society, and much revolves around it. Luna and Apollo are a mother/calf pair I've observed frequently over the past six years, since Apollo was born. By the time he was three years, he had developed a few dark spots on his side, which helped us identify him and record his behaviour as he learnt how to manage his sound-production and, by observation and interaction with Luna, how to forage on the bottom.

Luna may have had several offspring before Apollo, and appears to be on a fairly consistent three-year calving cycle. Gestation takes almost a full year, and lactation two to three years, and so a three-year cycle is probably the absolute minimum for this population of dolphins. A female can conceive while still lactating, and so she is likely to expend a great deal of energy during her reproductive years, which probably last until she is about 40. We still don't know what age individuals live to in this group, but pantropical spotteds have been known to live well into their forties.

In 1988, three years after Apollo was born, Luna had a female calf, Diamond; in 1991 she had a male calf, Latitude, and in 1994 she had Laser. After the birth of each new offspring, the previous one begins to associate with other juveniles, though all a mother's offspring will still sometimes join her and the new sibling. In Luna's case, I noticed that another young adult, Little Gash, also spent a significant time with each of the new offspring. In 1985, when I began the study, Little Gash was already a fairly independent juvenile, and it had never been clear to me who her mother was. But after noticing her associations with Luna's recent offspring, I began to suspect that she, too, was one of Luna's calves.

Results from cataloguing dolphin sounds in the computer have lent weight to my suspicions. One of the few things known about dolphin vocalisations is that each individual has a unique signature whistle, the equivalent of a human name. A dolphin may use this whistle to broadcast its identity, initiate contact with other individuals, and possibly to label a family unit. In fact, in some populations of bottle-nosed dolphins *Tursiops truncatus* it appears that a calf's signature whistle may be a derivative of its mother's. When I compared the signature whistles of Luna and Little Gash, they were almost identical.

Apart from vocal signals, there are many other communication techniques that a calf has to learn. In the early years it will remain in physical contact with its mother for much of the time, and she may guide it with her body to indicate a change of direction. A brush of the pectoral fin is used when the pair reunite or when the calf is preparing to depart briefly. Visual cues can also be initiated by the mother at a distance; she may rotate her pectoral fin, for example, which means, 'Come over and get a pec rub'.

Calves also explore social signals in the context of play with juveniles. Chases, head-to-head confrontations, raking of teeth against each others' bodies and slamming against each other are all explored in the form of friendly competition. These same signals, if used by older dolphins, carry specific information about aggression, courtship and affiliation. Just as they learn the socially appropriate time to use acoustic signals, youngsters have to test and learn appropriate uses of other social signals.

One of the quickest ways of doing this is through mimicry. The young dolphin has the advantage of being surrounded by juveniles of varying ages who act as demonstrators. The southern stingray is a preferred plaything. I recall watching Apollo learn the fine art of herding a stingray by mimicking the agility and moves of the older juveniles. He first tried a circle around the 'prey', but his movements were not quick or clear enough to be effective. The older juveniles then returned to demonstrate the correct manoeuvres.

A juvenile's success at this stage seems to depend on how well it has accepted independence from its mother, and how it has related to other youngsters while still with her. Apollo and then Diamond each mixed successfully with other juveniles of their own age when their mother, Luna, gave birth to another sibling. But Pictures, a female calf of Nippy's, did not fare so well. She stayed with Nippy a full five years, until Nippy had another calf, and tended to be very dependent on her mother during that time, never venturing off with other juveniles. Pictures has not been sighted since the birth of her sibling, and probably did not survive the transition, possibly due to her failure to form bonds with others as a calf.

Though not entirely independent from the larger group, juvenile subgroups (comprising four- to eight-year-old 'speckleds') do spend time on their own foraging expeditions, with only an older juvenile present as babysitter, or an adult supervising from a distance. Many of the shark scars we observe are caused at this age. This may be due to juveniles spending increased time off the shallow sandbanks looking for food, or to them having less protection. It's easy to see how a predator might sneak up on a young dolphin. Juveniles, especially, can be stubborn and disobedient when out of range of immediate discipline. The first signal that a supervising adult uses to recontact the juveniles is its own signature whistle. If that fails, a tail slap is used, sometimes repeatedly, and often inverted to emphasise the urgency of regrouping. Finally, if they fail to heed any of these calls the adult will physically round up the juveniles.

Association patterns change dramatically between the juvenile and the 'mottled' young adulthood phase (nine to fifteen years old). Females who conceive during adolescence are more likely to associate with other pregnant females than with previously close, nonpregnant associates. This may be out of energetic necessity, because pregnancy requires more foraging.

This change became clear to me after watching three tightly associated females—Little Gash, Rosemole and Mugsy—reach sexual maturity at about 12 years old. Little Gash was the only one of the three not to get pregnant one year, but the subsequent year she was frequently observed with male subgroups, actively engaged in courtship behaviour. Meanwhile Rosemole had successfully given birth to a female, Rosebud. At the end of the next research season, Mugsy was also visibly pregnant, but she must have lost her calf through miscarriage or soon after birth because when I first saw her during a field season, she was swimming with a nursery group of three mother/infant pairs, as if she had a phantom calf in tow.

Males, too, go through social changes during young adulthood. Strongly associated males keep their bonds, but seem to become more fluid in their association patterns. Aggressive conflicts within large groups of young adult males are routine, presumably a means of working out dominance and mating strategies. Such conflicts can escalate into serious aggression if not resolved quickly. Rapid chases, quick jaw snaps, tail slaps, and increasing rates of repetitive aggressive vocalisations all serve to get the message through. It is in these male subgroups that conflicts are worked out, and when females are present, the coalitions of males work co-operatively.

Working out who has fathered which calf is very difficult. Yet spotted dolphins must have strategies to avoid interbreeding. Hints of one possible strategy emerged in 1988, when a previously unknown group of dolphins appeared in the area resulting in a certain amount of emigration and immigration between the groups. And this summer, another group of spotteds has appeared, and all the adults have been heavily engaged in mating and courtship. Where these groups come from, and whether or not there are transient as well as resident groups of dolphins in this larger population, are questions for which we hope to have answers in the future.

The final transition to adulthood occurs at about 15 years of age, when an individual's spots have become fused. When compared with other intensively studied mammals, spotted dolphins seem to have no clear overall hierarchy, no alpha males or females. Age and experience seem to count more than gender when it comes to certain roles. Old males do often take on a defensive/protective role around newborns. But they also take a significant role, along with old females, in the care of the young calves. And it is not just young adult females, but males too, that take on babysitting tasks with juvenile subgroups.

Probably my greatest insights about dolphin behaviour have come from following individuals through the age classes and observing their changing roles in the society. But there are many inherent problems in documenting and deciphering signals under water. A starting point is to correlate basic types of behaviour and nonacoustic signals with the sounds recorded on my equipment. But it's not always easy even to identify the animal that a sound is coming from. (Unlike dolphins, humans have no ability to discriminate the direction of a sound source under water.) A signature whistle is often accompanied by the expulsion of air from the blowhole, and so if you happen to be facing that particular individual, you can be reasonably confident of the sound source. And when dolphins are young, and extremely excitable, they often lose control of their sound apparatus, creating an erratic vocalisation that is accompanied by rapid, excited swimming. Signature information is often contained within this sound, and can be readily correlated with the relevant individual.

Sometimes, though, a signature whistle may come, not from a nearby individual, but from a supervising mother or babysitter in the distance. In fact, this is a world where, because of the salinity, temperature and density of the water, individuals can stay in contact acoustically for miles. Spotted dolphins appear to use the shallow sandbanks for this purpose, in the manner of an underwater phone line. Individuals often descend the six metres or so to the white sand bottom, lie still and apparently make no sound at all; at other times, they will emit sounds on the bottom when no other dolphin is in sight.

The problem of studying visual and acoustic signals is compounded by the fact that one signal from an individual can have different functions depending on who else is interacting, what their relationship is, what their ages are, and what main events are under way. Only when I include all these relevant factors do I start to make sense of the spotted dolphins' rich but subtle communication.

The problem which will always remain is that, as a land mammal, I am totally out of my element and can only get a small glimpse of their lives under water. When the seas pick up and a squall moves in, the dolphins disappear. Where they go during large storms I have no idea—possibly to the leeward side of an island, though the nearest one is far away, and in any case, they are animals of the open ocean. I, though, am forced to return to the boat and wait out the storm—trapped on the surface again.

BEYOND SPECIES

Toni G. Frohoff

IN THE PRESENCE OF DOLPHINS

I have laughed underwater many times while swimming in the company of free-ranging dolphins. It's the type of laughter that erupts from my heart. And I have been met with the same shining eye by my dolphin companions as I have during my finest moments of friendship.

As I swim I am surrounded by dolphins—above me, below me, to either side. While some exchange places as they swim, others remain nearby, maintaining eye contact. "I am lost again as I am waking . . ." This phrase, written by Jim Carroll, keeps running through my mind as I recall the feeling of being in the midst of dolphins. The experience is surreal, yet my senses are more alive than ever. The dolphins' bodies around me feel somewhat protective, almost like a huge, flowing hand, supporting and guiding me gently. Their vocalizations come from every direction and I sometimes feel them on and inside of my body as their echolocation explores me. As I swim along, young dolphins occasionally dart in and out of our group, eyeing me most directly as they swim by. Their carefree exuberance is contagious and I know that I am in bliss.

I do not look forward as I swim. I feel safe in the presence of these exquisitely beautiful animals. But am I? As I swim up to the surface to take a breath of air, I look up and find myself staring straight ahead into a living wall of very large barracudas. I wonder why the dolphins have escorted me here. If I were to carefully construct a practical (or cosmic) joke, I could not have done it better myself. At this time in my life, I am unusually nervous when encountering even lone barracudas, who in these parts are very curious.

As I begin to initiate my panicky retreat, my instinct to flee is interrupted. I look around and see that several of the dolphins are still around me; they have remained at my side. They do not appear nervous at all and the barracudas do not seem particularly interested in any of us. Soon, calmed, I swim back toward our boat with my dolphin escorts. This experience has helped me ever since, when studying marine life in the company of extraordinarily curious or large barracudas and sharks. It was my first lesson in relying on the behavior of "predatory" animals rather than their reputation in determining my safety in their presence. I feel as if I was given a great gift—taught an invaluable lesson.

As a scientist, I cannot say whether or not this occurrence was incidental. However, after years of being in the presence of dolphins, I have learned most profoundly that science does not always have the capacity to address some of life's most important wonders. I find solace in the knowledge that I am not simply a scientist—I am also an animal, a member of the genus and species *Homo sapiens*. Therefore, I cannot dismiss the very personal nature of my interactions with these incredibly lovely beings. I cannot forget the many lessons that I have learned from them, inadvertently or otherwise. I cannot, and will not, put aside what my senses tell me is rare and wonderful. How ironic that it is from being in the presence of another species that I have learned how to be more "human."

IN THE PRESENCE OF WHALES

In the birthing lagoons of Baja, Mexico, I watched as a young gray whale approached us. He seemed enthusiastic and playful, bounding over to us in our relatively tiny skiff. As he approached, he looked some of us in the eye by tilting his head to one side, showing us the elongated line of his mouth. Sometimes, the spray from his blowhole as he breathed would wash us as we squealed with soggy delight. He repeatedly came up to the side of our boat to be touched and we even more eagerly reached out our hands toward him.

I have reservations about touching wild animals, but this situation was unique—so direct that I acted on impulse, as if someone had extended a hand to shake mine—and I automatically reciprocated the action. The skin of this whale was shiny, so clean, soft, and sensitive. And most interesting were the occasional "hairs" that arose from the baby's otherwise silky smooth head. These stiff, almost awkward bristles were vestigial reminders of his ancestral relationship to land mammals similar to ourselves.

And then the mother whale came right up to our boat. (She had never been far away.) The feeling I sensed from her was completely different

from that of her calf. At first I thought it was because of her calmer behavior or her great size—at least forty feet. But when her eyes gazed into
mine, I knew that I was sensing something else as well. The depth of her
gaze transcended species. I felt bonded with her as a female; as a daughter,
a mother, and a grandmother, even though I do not have children of my
own. It was as if we related in a way which was truly, and uniquely, feminine. This was the first time that I have been so acutely aware of my gender in relating to a member of another species.

I sensed a great knowing from this whale, an ancient sort of wisdom.
As a mother, she would share the joy of her child with us, but only if we
understood her code of behavior: We would never separate her from her
calf with our boat; we would remain in the boat during the interaction.
We would interact on terms that have evolved, so to speak, for a very long
time, resulting in what I would describe as a sacred trust. How odd that
the friendly gray whale was once also referred to as the "devilfish" by
whalers, named so because of the fierce devotion mothers of this species
exhibited when protecting their young. The same whales who we were
playing with in our little skiff could have been the descendants of those
whales who once smashed larger whaling boats to pieces upon injury of
their calves.

In a great irony, this particular mother whale had notable round
scars on either side of the top of her back which we had deduced were
from an old harpoon injury. Gray whales migrate from the lagoons in
Mexico north to the Bering Sea, where Siberian hunters still kill one hundred or more gray whales per year under a subsistence hunting permit;
they kill the gray whales to feed foxes on their fur farms. We figured that
this same animal accompanying her calf to visit us in the lagoon was
probably hit by one of their harpoons during her migration north and
somehow survived the ordeal. Why she would trust us in the southern
end of her habitat, in San Ignacio Lagoon in Mexico, while having been
pursued and hunted in the north, was a mystery to us. However, the
safety that she felt in this lagoon may be short-lived because of a salt mine
that the Mitsubishi Corporation and the Mexican government have proposed to build in this ancient mating and calving ground.

Accompanying us in our boat was another great female elder.
Alberta, a Makah Indian Elder from Neah Bay in Washington State, was
invited on this trip because of her courageous work to protect gray
whales from being killed in more northern latitudes by members of her
tribe. Almost a century ago, the Makah had killed whales for nutritional
and cultural subsistence. Now, despite a lack of nutritional need, some
members of the Makah Tribe (as well as their Vancouver Island neighbors, the Nuu-Chah-Nulth), have recently announced plans to resume

whaling, only this time using modern technology and an expressed interest in commercial profit.

As a consultant to The Humane Society of the United States, I have worked with several of the Makah people who are in opposition to the whale hunt. Ironically, I, and others working on this issue, have been occasionally criticized for being insensitive to the aboriginal rights of these people. What our critics do not seem to acknowledge, however, is that it is not aboriginal whaling that we are opposing—it is modern, exploitive whaling conducted under the guise of a traditional and necessary harvest. This is at least partly the reason why these elders, some of whom are from great whaling families, have fought the resumption of whaling. How odd that in our efforts to protect whales, many of us have developed an increased sensitivity to the lost voices of the tribal elders as well as that of the whales. When Alberta the Elder touched the mother whale, the whale emitted a tremendous shudder as she exhaled. Everyone on the boat heard and felt it, but I think Alberta was most connected with the whale in that deep breath.

It is easy to romanticize encounters with wildlife. But it is not so easy to discount the tremendous emotional and spiritual effects that they sometimes have on people. As a biological scientist, I see that sharing these effects is still frowned upon. Even though most of us know they exist, we are not supposed to acknowledge them, perhaps because our field of study has not learned how to measure them.

But I take great comfort in my interactions with, and study of, other animals. While we are just beginning to appreciate the diversity of colors and accents among our own species, I like to think that we are increasing our appreciation for the diversity of our extended animal family as well.

OUR QUESTIONABLE RELATIONSHIP WITH CETACEANS

The gregarious nature of cetaceans is fairly unique among wild animals. It is rare indeed for other types of wildlife to interact so closely with people without being fed by them. Anecdotes of free-ranging dolphins initiating sociable contact with people around the world are numerous and have occurred for thousands of years. It is interesting to note, however, that after the classical period, from around A.D. 109 until early in this century, very little was written about sociable dolphin-human interactions. This does not mean that none occurred. With the increase of Western cultures and religions that hierarchically separated humans from other species, little respect remained for anything other than what was human or could be used for human benefit. Consequently, dolphins and other mammals of the sea became more of a commercial resource than a friend to humankind.

We seem to be turning a corner and appreciating cetaceans, once again, as sentient beings. Yet this corner is long indeed. For example, in Japan, people flock to swim with free-ranging dolphins who, ironically, may be legally and intentionally killed by fishermen on another side of the bay.

AT WHAT RISK TO CETACEANS?

Social encounters with cetaceans and other wild animals may affect humans profoundly, but these interactions certainly have serious drawbacks for other species. For example, giving food to free-ranging dolphins is one of the most destructive of all forms of wildlife interaction. Human feeding of dolphins has been associated with alteration of natural foraging patterns, death from contaminated fish, and more than a few accounts of serious injury and death due to human abuse.

Interacting with cetaceans from boats and by swimming with them also presents risks to them. One concern is that the cetacean, by becoming habituated to humans and their vessels, may become increasingly vulnerable to harm from humans. The whales we touch from our boats in Mexico may be increasingly trusting of hunters with harpoons farther north. Also, unless swimmers and boaters are exceptionally experienced with, and responsive to, the dolphins' subtle signals, their presence may interrupt activities (e.g., feeding, mating, and resting) vital to the well-being of the individual cetaceans as well as that of entire populations. Excessive human presence could inadvertently lead to degradation of important areas of natural habitat as well.

In my research, I have consistently found that some people operate their boats very dangerously around dolphins and whales. I was told that one professional boat operator, when criticized by one of his passengers for running down and encircling the dolphins, justified his actions by saying, "Well, there are so many boats out here that the dolphins don't come around as much anymore, and people won't pay unless they get to spend time with the dolphins." Even if boats are operated responsibly, the sheer number of them in an area can be harmful to wildlife. For example, it is not unusual for fifty or more boats to regularly follow orcas that inhabit Washington State waters. While research has not yet determined the effects of this situation on the orcas, the noise from the boats above, let alone below, the water's surface is deafening.

DOLPHINS IN CAPTIVITY

Captive dolphins may be further threatened by human interaction with members of the public. Stresses such as increased chlorination of pools, smaller enclosures, excessive noise and environmental stimuli, inappropriate and even dangerous behavior on the part of human visitors, and artificially manipulated social groups are often inflicted on captive dolphins so that the public may interact with them in petting pools and swim-with-the-dolphin programs. The popular demand for these programs and the amount of money generated from them is so great that many dolphins have been captured from the wild and transported to locations around the world for facilities offering new or expanded versions of these programs.

Some people maintain that the educational benefits of interacting with dolphins in captivity justify the negative consequences. However, I have seen no evidence showing that interactive programs using dolphins are any more educational than those that do not offer interaction. On the contrary, I suspect that viewing dolphins in such unnatural conditions may actually impart an undesirable message to the public—that it is appropriate to forcibly remove wild animals from their natural environment and to exploit them without regard for the environment of which they are an integral part. With regard to the need for conservation education, I have heard it said that the "save the whales" movement was one of the most successful conservation movements in the world, yet this was accomplished without the public seeing large whales in captivity, let alone swimming with, petting, or feeding them.

HUMAN RESPONSIBILITY

Our human preoccupation with what cetaceans can do for us (whether it be recreational or therapeutic) has seriously overshadowed our sense of responsibility for how our interactions might be affecting them. Recently, a newspaper article featuring opportunities to swim with captive dolphins was titled "Delighting in the Dolphins." I was waiting for a subsequent article to be titled "But Are the Dolphins Delighting in Us?"

I think that it is difficult for humans, who are so used to being in control of our environment, to interact with other species on their terms. However, this is what must be done so that we do not hurt the very animals with whom we seek to interact, despite our good intentions. To restrict our own desires and actions in acknowledgment of the needs of another is not one of our species' most striking behaviors. However, as delightful as dolphins and whales are to us, they are wild animals with unique biological and psychological needs, most of which we are just beginning to understand.

Our interactions with cetaceans and other wild animals reflect upon more than the individual animals with whom we interact. The nature of these interactions exemplifies the way in which people interact with the natural environment in general. If we are to learn how to actively respect the natural world, then we need to learn how to respect individuals within the natural environment as well as the environment itself. Each individual organism, population, and species is an integral part of the environment as a functional whole. And what affects the individual also affects the whole. When humans learn to respect individual members of other species as they exist in their natural environments, then that respect may extend to all members of a species, to other species, and to the environments that sustain them.

Currently, we are walking a fine line in our relationship with cetaceans. The same attraction to cetaceans that motivates us to protect them from harm is also what drives us to be close to them, to have them "within reach." However, it is clear that we need to learn how to interact with wild animals in a manner that does not put them at unnecessary risk. Learning to interact with other species on their terms, not ours, may be one of the greatest challenges to interspecies communication as well as environmental preservation. Yet it may also be one of the most rewarding and enriching experiences that humans can have as part of such an immensely diverse natural world.

LOOKING AFTER GOD'S BIRDS

Susan Cerulean

It was twenty years ago, somewhere on the coastal plain of the south-eastern United States, that I first encountered the swallow-tailed kite. I was newly employed as a technician at a biological field station in South Carolina, just out of college, wide-eyed and open-hearted. I loved the ducks that year, especially, and the painted bunting, and went anywhere I thought I could add to my new life list of North American birds.

It was in the Okefenokee Swamp, or maybe on the Edisto River, that I saw that first kite. The name of the river swamp has faded, but in my brain is etched a clear memory of how that bird swung into view and hung over me, like an angel, so starkly black and white, with its wide scissored split of a tail. In my rush and clatter to grab binoculars, I nearly flipped the canoe. The bird drifted on a breeze too subtle to imagine, its breast a centerpoint for the sleek maneuver of wing and tail, as if a kite string actually were attached to the deeply muscled breastbone. As suddenly as it appeared, the bird was gone.

To me, kites are about surprise. Mystery. Being gifted. Except when they nest or gather to migrate, it's hard to specifically "bird" for swallow-tailed kites. You can increase your chances of finding them by looking in the right places. It's best just to *be* in the right places. In this part of the world that means getting out on the water, on the rivers, in the summer months. When I drive up the west coast of Florida, north from Tampa to my home in Tallahassee, climbing the ladder of latitude, I slow at each river crossing, and look skyward: Little Wacasassa, Wacasassa, the broad Suwannee, the Steinhatchee, Spring Warrior Creek, the injured Fenholloway, the Econfina, the mysterious Aucilla, the Wacissa, the St. Marks, and dozens of creeks in between. You still can't be sure of seeing a kite, but that's how I increase my chances.

———

Two years ago, I met Dr. Ken Meyer, a National Park Service biologist, at a research meeting in the Everglades, and learned of his groundbreaking swallow-tailed kite studies. I jumped at the chance to follow up on my early passion with an expert, in the field. Since then, I have followed Meyer through the Big Cypress National Preserve, Golden Gate Estates, and Everglades National Park, learning how to find kite nests, watching them court, coming to tell young from adult, and recognizing preferred habitat.

It was Meyer who told me that in Peter Matthiesson's novel *Killing Mr. Watson*, swallow-tailed kites are referred to as God's birds, because only a heavenly overseer can view the steely-blue back of this bird, reflecting sky back unto itself.

In August 1993, I traveled south to LaBelle, Florida, thirty miles and fifty years from the hustle and condos of Ft. Myers and Naples, right in the heart of the state's cattle country. Meyer took me up in a tiny Cessna, and I saw kites hung like a thousand exotic blossoms on a tight cluster of Australian pine trees. More kites than all but a handful of people will see in their lifetimes. What concerns Meyer most about these birds, who very competently move between North and South America twice a year, is this remarkable gathering.

"As far as we know," he told me, "more than half of the North American population of swallow-tailed kites funnels down through the peninsula of Florida every summer, and briefly stops right here," said Meyer. "Presumably they're getting fat and waiting for favorable winds to migrate south."

Meyer worries about this roost. First of all, it's unprotected. The land that it sits on is owned by an indifferent, powerful corporation not known for its gentle handling of indigenous species. Second, the vast and diverse landscapes where the birds nest and forage are under siege from agricultural development.

"And third," admits Meyer, "we have absolutely no idea where they are going when they leave south Florida. Or what human-induced threats they encounter once they reach their wintering grounds in Central or South America."

Another August, another pilgrimage to visit the kites. I want to see where the kites based at the big roost might be foraging, how they look from the ground. Meyer suggests I drive twenty-five miles east toward Moore

Haven and Lake Okeechobee. There's a wetland nearby called Lake Hicpochee where they've been reported by some West Palm birders. I circle a strip of Highway 78 east of Moore Haven on my map and drive out to look. Labelle's cattle pastures and open savannas give way to intensive agriculture: citrus, vegetables, sugar cane. In fact, the first kite I see, precisely at the spot Meyer predicted, is sharing patrol of an endless field of eight-foot-tall sugar cane with a fat yellow spray plane, both in search of the same insect prey.

What Meyer did not predict was the specter of swallow-tailed kites against the backdrop of Moore Haven itself. Here they are, scores of them, dipping over the Barnett Bank, tilting over Circle K gas. Not high and safely out of reach, but hunting singly and low. Low enough to be worshiped. Low enough to be shot.

It's too early to harvest cane, fishing won't pick up till later this fall. Apparently in August no one is in Moore Haven who doesn't have to be. The town is a tatter of trailers, broken-down motels, boarded-up bait shops, all pressed tight against the dike of Lake Okeechobee by cane fields on three sides. The people are poor here, very poor. A heavy young woman slumps on the white metal steps of a rusted double-wide. Two dark-skinned men bend hard over the closed hood of a pickup truck. Right in their midst, kites clip through the canopy of the Brazilian pepper hedges, scream through the yard of a deserted white trailer. No one notices.

I stop to watch the kites in a tiny fringe of a park. There are long empty slips painted on the asphalt, room enough for hundreds of trucks and boat trailers. It's clearly a major launching point for fishermen, at some other time of the year. A shirtless man with a white visor cap sprays herbicide on the weedy edges of the parking lot, and the banks of the canal. His work is so silent, so lethal. The kites swing overhead, so silent, so living.

Heading south out of Moore Haven on Highway 27, I'm agitated, and angry. The birds are still all around me; I can spot them thousands of feet up against the mounting cumulus. I see one so intent on hunting the median of this hard-working road that it just skips over the cab of a speeding red pickup. I realize that I don't *want* to see the birds here. I want them safely back in the river swamps, out of sight and reach of 99 percent of the human population. They are too visible here, and they seem oblivious to their peril. So ancient is their tie to this lake, these once open prairies, this rich mix of flying insects and small vertebrate prey, they can have no concept of relocating.

There should be worship happening here, I think. In an earlier time, surely the local peoples noted the return of the kites year after year after year. I can imagine a child running in from a dugout canoe, from the flood-plain swamps of Lake Okeechobee, breathless, stumbling, saying "The kites have arrived, they're here!" The child would be hustled back into the heart of the camp and all the elders would begin making preparations to mark the return of the kite: prayer ties all over the village, and special rituals, and drumming. There would be offerings of anole and snake and dragonfly on high poles or platforms around the entrances to the village, all to celebrate the birds and to invite them to bring their energy and their blessings to the native peoples who live here at this place where God's birds gather each summer. The wetlands are drying down, and the fish are fat and concentrated in the alligator holes. This is the time of summer fire, the fulcrum between the summer solstice and the fall equinox, a hot, slow time, a time when you might lie on your back and watch the flight of the kites, one of many natural events that allows you to mark time and the passage of the year on your place on the planet. Earlier peoples must have wondered at the mystery of where the birds go, and how is it that these thousands of birds converge on this one place. I like to imagine that they took the time to reassert the sacredness of this piece of ground that calls the swallow-tailed kite to return again and again, and to give thanks for the abundance of the insect and the anole, the things that feed the bird, just as the bird feeds our spirits.

Nothing like this is happening here today. And I don't trust the kites to the misery of Moore Haven. I want to guard them somehow, but after all, I'm the stranger here. The fact is, I don't trust the kites to myself. My inability to fix all that underlies their security stares me in the face.

As I drive, I'm half-listening to Attorney General Janet Reno talk about the president's crime bill on National Public Radio. She talks about comprehensive prevention programs, how we can't simply lock up the bad guys. I can see how that's true for the kites, too, only in reverse. We can't confine them to big preserves to keep them safe: They won't have it. That's only where some of them live, and only for part of the year. They need the preserves, but they also need Fish Eating Creek to roost, they need this lake and this town to forage, and they need large expanses of Central and South American rain forest to overwinter.

Three weeks later, I am invited along with twenty-five other environmentalists to meet with Florida's lieutenant governor in rare, intimate conversation. We gather in a circle in the plush living room of a remote ranch house near Ocala, four hours south of my home. We speak in turn the concerns of our organizations: Sierra, Audubon, Friends of the Everglades, the Nature Conservancy, 1000 Friends of Florida, and others. My colleagues ask the lieutenant governor to speed the Everglades cleanup, fund more land acquisition, do more for energy conservation. Everyone is eloquent, full of facts, advocating like the lawyers many of them are. My turn draws closer, I don't have any planned remarks. My heart races, I am shivering. All I can think of is kites.

And so I launch into an unrehearsed description of the plight of swallow-tailed kites in Florida. I describe the vulnerable roost, the graceful bird, my desire for my young son to be able to see them all his life, and for all Florida's children to know and revere them. My eyes shine with hot tears. I offer no solutions. My throat closes, I stop. The lieutenant governor responds to me, kindly, vaguely. The room is still. The woman next to me picks up with the Everglades legal suit as if I had never spoken. I avert my gaze, hug my knees, feel like a fool. I have violated an unspoken rule of this political setting. I have exposed my heart.

I gaze out the plate-glass windows, wondering if I'll ever be an effective advocate if I can't keep my emotions under wraps. Or if I'll ever want to. As I sag into the misery of my thoughts, a swallow-tailed kite arcs into view, alive, glinting white against the blue sky, just outside the window glass. It shouldn't be here now. The others of its kind are all at the Okeechobee roost, ready any day to set out across the Gulf for South America. I catch the eye of a friend. We smile, and I settle back into my body, into who I am. The others talk on.

I came to this story with what I thought was a simple intent: to be close to a bird I have loved for twenty years. But my story turns out to be much more than the natural history of the swallow-tailed kite: It's the natural history of us, in South Florida, us as North Americans in the late twentieth century. The story penetrates the way I live my life, the size of the house I live in, the food that I eat, the things I buy, the way I travel. I chose kites, or they have chosen me, but I could have selected the monarch butterfly or the parula warbler or a Florida black bear or a Haitian sugar cane worker to serve this story. Each creature is linked to every other in the intricate web of life. The lives of the migrant workers who harvest the cane are just as degraded as are those of the kites who breathe the canes' pesticide; as are the rivers and lakes that receive the cane's nitrogenous wastes; as are the teeth of our children and ourselves, who eat sixty-eight pounds of sugar every year; as are the souls of the rich few who get even richer off of the whole.

We each play a part. But we, the humans, get to choose our parts.

My part, at the moment, is to write what I see, to do as Allan Ginsberg says, "I write to shatter complacency, I write to shatter denial. I write to embrace paradox. I write to see the world whole."

And I, I write to follow the swallow-tailed kite—through the brokenness, and the beauty, of the world I share with God's bird.

Diane Boyd-Heger

For the past twenty years I've attempted to unravel the secrets of one of North America's most elusive carnivores, and in the process I have discovered many truths about wolves and myself. I grew up in a suburb of Minneapolis, in a neighborhood full of young baby boomers. Although city-raised, I was not city-souled.

Wild places became the fabric of my life, and wolves became the threads that wove place and heart together. I first encountered them in 1976 when I volunteered on a captive wolf research project directed by L. David Mech. Some of these captive animals were socialized to people, acting like a dog in wolf's clothing. But the shy, untamed ones restlessly pacing in the back of the wooded enclosures stirred fantasies of watching wild wolves pursuing a deer along a birch-lined lakeshore. My dream was realized the following year when I was offered the position of volunteer technician on Mech's wild wolf project in northeastern Minnesota. I packed my stuff for a summer of wolf research, whatever that might entail, and headed for the field station. About eight miles south of the station, a wolf darted out of the spruce, shot across the road in my headlights, and disappeared into the brush as I jammed on the brakes. The adrenaline flowing through my body assured me that I had, indeed, seen my first wild wolf.

That summer I learned about basic wolf ecology, trapping, radio-collaring, and radio-tracking wolf movements. Five days after we set out our traps for wolves, we discovered a trap missing. We trailed the drag marks of the trap anchor through the brush and came upon a wolf struggling to free itself of the foreign thing holding it fast. She stopped fighting and looked up at us from her vulnerable position. I gazed into her wild, wheat-colored eyes and felt astonishment and pity. "C'mon Diane, we got work to do," called Jim, the field biologist. His voice broke the spell, and I helped him radio-collar the lean wolf, wishing her well when we left the site. I wondered how this animal could cause so much controversy and knew I needed to learn more about wolf ecology and biopolitics.

I returned to northern Minnesota in the winter of 1978, which I spent holed up in a small cabin at an isolated ma-and-pa resort with my ninety-pound mongrel, Stony, for company. It was incredible country to explore on skis—endless miles of snowy frozen waterways stippled with tracks of moose, deer, fox, and wolves. The land lay sleeping, storing reserves needed for next year's growth, but the animals were hungry and seeking calories to ward off the cold. The only other occupant of the resort was a skinned bear carcass left in a shed by a hunter. The rancid fatty smells drew the attention of a starving wolf, whose tracks hauntingly circled the bear shed after a January cold snap. I propped open the door, and the wolf took advantage of this banquet many nights, careful to slip away before sunrise. The wolf didn't appear for several nights in a row when the temperature dropped to forty degrees below zero. When she returned, her tracks circled my cabin and headed into the shed, but had not exited. I cautiously peered in and was shocked to see the frozen wolf curled up tightly next to the bear carcass. Old age and many weeks of starvation had taken its toll: she lay dead next to one hundred pounds of frozen meat that she had been too weak to tear off and digest.

During the summer of 1979 I worked as a wolf trapper for Minnesota's livestock depredation control program. The job description sounded straightforward enough: The local game warden would call if a cow or sheep was reported killed by wolves, and together we would go to the farm to investigate the claim. When there were no depredations, I would capture the wolves and place radio-collars on them for an ongoing research project. When I arrived at my new post, in the midst of a tightly knit society of three hundred conservative farm folks in northern Minnesota, I was more than an anomaly. Word quickly spread through the community that the new depredation control agent was a "girl." Although wolves are very intelligent and difficult to catch, they were the least of my problems that summer.

Shortly after my arrival, I was mentioned in the local weekly paper in Bill's news column. Bill, an old-timer around whom the town revolved, wrote that he had heard that the new government wolf trapper was "an attractive blond lady and did anybody have a wolf he could borrow." The following week Bill ran a large photo of himself with a six-foot-tall cardboard cartoon wolf and stated he now had a wolf problem and would the lady wolf trapper come pay him a visit. I couldn't let this escalate, so I drove to Bill's house and introduced myself to him as we stood on his porch. He began to smirk as I acknowledged that I had heard about his wolf problem. I went back to the pickup and pulled out a perfect cardboard "wolf trap" I had constructed out of an old box and some electrical tape the night before. Bill's grin disappeared. I patiently explained to him how to set the trap and that the best bait for this sub-species of wolf would be some foul-smelling paper product. He stood there slack-jawed for a moment, then broke into a big smile, clapped me on the shoulder and invited me to come in for a piece of fresh blueberry pie that his wife had just pulled out of the oven. We had a very pleasant conversation over some of the best pie I've ever eaten. Much to his credit, the next week Bill ran a photo of my cardboard trap and declared that his problem had been resolved.

For the first time, I experienced the antiwolf sentiments of ranchers and farmers and realized that wolves cause both real and perceived hard-ships for some livestock growers. It was a very important discovery, and gave me a more balanced perspective about wolves. The polarization of the wolf huggers and wolf haters was detrimental to wolf conservation. There had to be some middle ground where wolves and people could mu-tually exist, relatively free of conflicts. I had lived in the rather sheltered world of the university and had little experience dealing with the contro-versial real world of wolves, politics, and women in the sciences. But I jumped in with both feet when I accepted a graduate fellowship with the University of Montana's Wolf Ecology Project in September of 1979 to study wolf recovery in the Rockies.

In an abandoned turn-of-the-century homestead bordering Glacier National Park I learned to live without electricity or running water, cut my own firewood, hunt deer, and love the winter isolation. I replaced the amenities of urban and social life with the rhythms of the biological world around me: the deep warmth radiating from the crackling wood-stove, the rush of the river, the bond with my dogs Stony and Max, and the howling of wolves. I wouldn't survive if I didn't learn to live with the elements. Mother Nature always wins, so you might as well team up with her instead of fight her.

The Wolf Ecology Project and I evolved together. Sometimes I spent long periods of time without seeing another human being. Other times I worked with dedicated volunteer technicians who gave us long hours for little or no pay. My graduate advisor later told me that I was "fiercely in-dependent" and often difficult to work with in those early years. I prefer to think of it as tenacity and the self-reliance necessary for survival, traits learned in northern Minnesota and just as valuable in the Rockies. But as time went on those hard edges softened, worn down by the natural world around me. The wolves were good teachers and I began to understand the benefits of pack life and cooperation.

My master's project revolved around coyote-wolf interactions near Glacier National Park. My study subjects were the only wolf in the western United States and as many coyotes as I could catch and radio-collar in the wolf's huge home range. The wolf, Kishinena, and I had several things in common: We had each traveled a great distance to discover the Glacier area, we were both pioneers in our niches, and we stayed. Kishinena eventually found a mate, produced pups in British Columbia (BC), a stone's throw north of Glacier in Canada, and catalyzed the successful natural recolonization of tens of thousands of square miles of formerly wolfless habitat in BC, Alberta, Montana, and Idaho.

Following Kishinena's trail was often difficult, despite the beeps emitted from her radio-collar. We were initially hoping to observe her directly, but abandoned that idea to avoid altering Kishinena's natural behaviors. This proved to be a wise decision because Kishinena was very shy of humans, avoiding ski tracks and human scent. Besides, she tirelessly trotted so many miles in one day that it would take me a week to catch up on skis. In winter a wolf's every step, pause, scent mark, and bed are recorded in an icy record waiting to be read like an adventure novel. After months and years of following the tracks of Kishinena and her descendants, I began to develop an intuitive sense for wolf routes, the favorite trails, good resting points, deer and elk wintering areas, easy river fords, and territory boundaries. I learned to trust my intuition, regardless of how "unscientific" that might be.

Kishinena's first litter of pups was born in 1982. As they grew, they were joined by wolves who survived the gauntlet run from Canada down the Rocky Mountains. Where I had once thrilled to the discovery of a single set of wolf tracks, we now had the exciting task of keeping tabs on four wolf packs along the western side of Glacier National Park and a growing number of satellite packs that had evolved from Glacier dispersers. I feel very privileged to have been witness to such a surprisingly successful story of wolf recovery. Since that tentative beginning, thirty litters have been born in my study area, containing approximately 170 wolf pups. We are now studying the sixth generation of Kishinena's bloodline. The U.S. Fish and Wildlife Service joined us in monitoring wolf activity outside Glacier in 1987, many new wolf education groups have sprung up, and several wolf-related graduate student projects have examined a piece of the wolf puzzle. Glacier became the springboard that launched western wolf recovery.

A white wolf named Phyllis, probably born to Kishinena in 1982, was one of the wolves instrumental in wolf recovery. She was accidentally captured in a research snare set for grizzly bears in 1985. The researcher put a Wolf Ecology Project radio-collar on her a few miles north of Glacier

National Park. Phyllis was a breeding female and had recently whelped seven black pups. The following year she denned in Glacier, the first wolf to den in the park in more than half a century. In just three years Phyllis contributed eighteen pups to the blossoming wolf recolonization of the northwestern United States. I captured and tagged many of her progeny but was never able to recapture her to replace her aging radio-collar with a new one. She was very elusive and even my best efforts could not outwit her. Sometimes she would carefully dig out my camouflaged traps, exposing them without triggering them. Other times she would leave a fresh, steaming scat within a few feet of the trap to let me know that she was not fooled by my efforts.

Because of her highly unusual white coat, she was easily identified even after the batteries in her radio-collar quit. One March morning while en route to the outhouse I saw a light-colored canid at the far end of my half-mile-long meadow. With the aid of binoculars I could see a black radio-collar nearly buried in the dense white fur and confirmed that this was Phyllis. This was particularly exciting because her radio-collar had ceased transmitting and we had been unable to locate her for several months. Phyllis trotted across the snowy expanse and stopped twenty-five yards from my cabin. She stood there for less than a minute, staring at my cabin, then turned and disappeared into the forest. She clearly went out of her way to approach my cabin, as if to say "Hi, I'm still here and more clever than you." And of course she was.

Phyllis left our study area and established a new home range in southwestern Alberta. She was occasionally seen by the local people, and sightings of the white wolf with the black collar were recalled with excitement. She began to frequent a bush camp, occasionally scrounging a meal or sleeping in an abandoned shed out of the wind. Just shy of her eleventh winter, eight years after I began tracking her, Phyllis was shot by a hunter.

During the early years of my research, I was told it was not OK to have feelings for your study animals. When wolves died it was part of the research to document as thoroughly as possible the date and cause of death. This involved long days of packing wolf carcasses out of the backcountry, and performing necropsies on stainless-steel tables in a university lab. It was legal to shoot wolves in the Canadian portion of the study area, and we often received wolf radio-collars returned by curious hunters. I phoned and visited many Canadian hunters to collect information or tissue samples for genetics work from our tagged wolves. None of the hunters I spoke with had any hatred of wolves, but had opportunistically killed them. This lack of malice made my task much easier. Also, the fact that I am a woman often opened up doors to these male hunters and ranchers that a male researcher may not have opened. I find that most "tough guys" are somewhat disarmed by a forthright woman seeking an honest discussion. They seemed to appreciate the fact that a woman biologist was out there getting dirty and sincerely liking the challenges of research, and listening to what they were saying.

I have often been asked if it is difficult to be a woman working in the male-dominated wolf research world. The first time I was asked this I was slightly puzzled by the question because I hadn't given it much thought. I was simply out to do the best job that I possibly could. But as I delved a bit deeper I realized my approach to science and wolves is innately shaped by the fact that I am a woman. Women and men postulate and resolve problems differently. Science has traditionally been dominated by men seeking quantitative answers to theoretical questions. Women can offer another perspective. Paul Paquet, who studies wolf behavior in Canada, gave me an example of this. Many years ago he was analyzing social behavior in captive wolves. He hired a young woman who was unfamiliar with traditional beliefs about wolf pack social structure. She observed the wolves, dutifully recorded their social interactions, and submitted a synopsis to Paul. He was surprised when she reported that the dominant female led the pack in behavioral interactions. It had been preconceived and previously reported by many researchers that the alpha male directs a pack's behavior. Paul again watched the pack and realized she was correct, confounding previous male-biased scientific observations.

The most pleasant days of my life have been spent following wolf tracks in winter, taking in the natural world around me from the pseudo-perspective of a wolf on skis. It's the best I can do, lacking the sensitive wolf olfactory system, the interaction of richly furred companions, the total awareness of the surrounding natural world inherent in wild predators. There are no human words to adequately express the inner energy I've felt when my howls are answered by wolf howls drifting through the lodgepole pines. The connection on such a primal level far surpasses the capabilities of human conversation.

For nearly two decades I have trapped and radio-collared wolves, monitored their movements with telemetry, skied along wolf travel routes, collected and analyzed data on kills, scats, habitat use, dispersal, survivorship, and dynamics of predators and prey. I attempted to sort through these data in my doctoral dissertation. But I've learned far more from wolves than what is recorded in the volumes of my field notes. The wolves have energized my passion for the wild spirit of the mountains and exposed me to myself. They have taught me the importance of working cooperatively and I've applied that to expanding conservation efforts. They have enriched my life, and I hope to repay their subtle guidance and enhance their survival. My hope is that if the ecological processes I've studied are explained to the public, wolf presence may be better tolerated by humans. Scientific research alone is not enough to conserve wild landscapes and their fragile inhabitants. Only through public education and cooperation will wolves be allowed to exist in an increasingly fragmented world.

My role of field biologist has evolved into that of a researcher/educator. More and more of my time is spent giving presentations, publishing scientific papers, writing nontechnical articles for popular magazines, and in discussions with opposing factions. Although lately I'm not in the field as much as I'd like to be, I feel I can better help wildlife through public education. True conservation involves understanding the interaction of people and other elements of an ecosystem, and the concern, yes even advocacy, of the researcher to touch people. Stephen Jay Gould stated so eloquently: "We cannot win this battle to save species and environments without forging an emotional bond between ourselves and nature as well—for we will not fight to save what we do not love." I have struggled with the perceived conflict of objective scientist vs. advocate for twenty years. I've concluded that it is OK to have feelings about the animals you study, without risking damage to your scientific credibility. We should not fear admitting these sentiments any more than we should allow them to interfere with our work. Objectivity and passion about study animals are not mutually exclusive; I wouldn't have devoted my life to studying wolves if I didn't love them.

GORILLAS IN THE MIST

Dian Fossey

Editor's Note: In 1966 Dr. Louis B. Leakey chose Dian Fossey to undertake a long-term field study of the mountain gorilla. Fossey established the Karisoke Research Centre within the Parc des Volcans in Zaire and Rwanda. For thirteen years, her groundbreaking research on mountain gorillas revealed to the world this "dignified great ape—a gentle yet maligned nonhuman primate." Known for her passionate involvement with and protection of mountain gorillas, Fossey was murdered, it is believed, by poachers. But her landmark research and close observations of these apes, so near extinction, lives on in her famous book Gorillas in the Mist. *Here is an excerpt from that book, from a chapter entitled "Decimation by Poachers."*

On the morning of January 1, 1980, someone knocked loudly on my cabin door. I opened it to find one of my food porters carrying a bulging potato basket on his head. I was about to tell him that I had not ordered any potatoes, when he excitedly exclaimed, *"Iko ngagi!"*—"It's a gorilla!" My heart sank. We put the basket into a large seldom-used room. I slowly opened it. Out crawled a pathetically weak female infant of about three years, Kweli's age.

She had been taken from Zairoise poachers attempting to sell her on New Year's Day to a French physician in Ruhengeri for the equivalent of $1000. Only because of the cleverness of Dr. Vimont was the captive acquired from the poachers, who were subsequently jailed. Again, active law enforcement is active conservation at work. I never learned how many group members had been killed for the infant's capture. All I could definitely discover was that she had been held for about six weeks in a damp, dark potato shed near the park boundaries below Mt. Karisimbi and fed bread and local fruits. Like all other gorilla capture victims, she was badly dehydrated and had developed severe lung congestion. Terrified of the presence of humans, the baby immediately hid under a bed when she saw me. For two days whenever anyone entered the room she retreated there. Fresh food vegetation and nesting materials were brought to her. I was pleased when she finally began eating and using the nests I built for her to sleep in at night.

Six weeks of care were required before Bonne Année was well enough to play in the meadows surrounding camp. An additional six weeks were needed for the infant to regain tree-climbing dexterity and food-preparation skills, such as peeling celery stalks, stripping thistles, and wadding *Galium*. The transformation of the sickly captive into a typically lively young gorilla was a joy to observe. Bonne Année's recovery was aided by Cindy, who cared for the infant exactly as she had watched over Coco and Pucker eleven years earlier. Although considerably aged, Cindy provided Bonne Année with cuddling or body warmth whenever the baby wanted to rest. The dog also participated in mild wrestling or chasing games during the gorilla's two-month convalescence.

The Rwandese park Director in Kigali had been informed of Bonne Année's arrival as well as of my intention to introduce her into a free-living group once she recovered from the trauma of capture and poacher confinement. I was pleased with his acceptance of my decision. The enforcement of legislation, both in Rwanda and abroad, had come a long way since 1969, when Coco and Pucker were exploited as pawns traded between Rwanda and Germany.

I felt that Bonne Année's best survival chances lay with the newly forming, heterogeneous Group 4, the only study group without strong blood ties or infants. The major drawback to the choice of Group 4 was Peanuts' inclination to lead his five followers into the saddle area west of Visoke, where poachers and traps were still being encountered. Would Bonne Année be freed only to fall victim to poachers once again?

By March Bonne Année's health was completely restored. The time for her release could no longer be put off. It was first necessary to "wean" her from Karisoke's commodities such as treat food, the cabin's warmth, and the numerous camp residents, including Cindy and visitors who provided the infant with constant attention and play opportunities. To accomplish this, a bivouac camp, consisting of only a small tent and sleeping bags, was set up in Group 4's range far from Karisoke. There, for four days and nights, Bonne Année learned to "rough it" along with a helpful student, John Fowler, and an African assistant.

The day of Bonne Année's attempted reintroduction to the wild was jinxed from the start. Not only was it pouring rain, but Group 4 had traveled far from the bivouac camp and were involved in an aggressive interaction with an unidentified fringe group. Because of their highly excitable state, it seemed unlikely that Group 4 would have accepted Bonne Année at that time. While returning to the bivouac camp, we reluctantly decided to attempt introducing the infant to Group 5 the next day. Group 5 could offer Bonne Année a relatively poacher-free range, although their strong blood ties could jeopardize acceptance of an infant from outside their own gene pool.

My greatest apprehensions about Bonne Année's introduction to Group 5 were centered on the dominant female Effie, who had the most to lose if alien bloodlines entered the group. Unknown to me, she was three months away from parturition (her sixth infant to be born into the group during the years of the study). I was also concerned about the provocative behavior of Effie's daughter Tuck, coming into regular cyclicity and being mounted frequently by Icarus. A third factor strengthening the kinship ties within Group 5 was the conception of Icarus' second offspring with Pantsy during the same month as the attempted release of Bonne Année. At this time, early spring 1980, I had yet to gain any evidence concerning the extreme lengths to which a silverback will go to protect the integrity of his familial bloodline, other than incidents that had occurred during interactions with extragroup silverbacks. For this reason, I did not consider Icarus a potential threat to Bonne Année.

As John and I took Bonne Année out to Group 5, my misgivings grew. I was surprised that my feelings were not conveyed to the youngster, happily riding piggyback on John during the long morning trek. On reaching Group 5, clustered together under drizzly skies during a day-resting period on Visoke's southern slopes, we were relieved to note that no other groups or lone silverbacks were around. Perhaps this second reintroduction attempt had a chance after all.

It was my intention to find a tree near the group. Being in a treed position would give Bonne Année the option to remain with us if afraid or to return to us if she was not accepted. The three of us climbed into a tall and gently sloped *Hypericum* about fifty feet away from the resting group. Five minutes passed before Beethoven, after a startled, "double-take" stare, gave a short alarmed scream. He looked at Bonne Année quizzically, as if trying to determine whether she was one of his group. The infant matter-of-factly returned his gaze as though she had known the old silverback all her life. It was hard to believe that Beethoven was the first gorilla Bonne Année had seen in three months.

Beethoven's vocalization alerted the other members of Group 5 to our presence. Immediately, Tuck left the group and strutted to the base of the tree wearing compressed lips and nervously whacking at vegetation during her approach. She was followed by her mother. Effie was also walking stiffly and wearing a none-too-pleasant facial expression.

Humans ceased to exist for Bonne Année. The baby slowly left John's arms and descended the tree to rejoin her own kind. As she passed me I reached for her almost as instinctively as a mother reaches out to protect her child from danger. Then, fully realizing that it was not for me to interfere with the infant's decision, I withdrew my arm. Bonne Année climbed down to Tuck. Both gorillas gently embraced. John and I beamed at each other, disregarding all our previous fears and doubts about the captive's acceptance into Group 5. It was the last time either of us smiled for the rest of the day.

All that I had feared came to pass. Effie strutted over to Tuck. The two females began fighting for possession of the baby, pulling at her extremities, dragging her away from one another and biting her. Bonne Année screamed with pain and fright. After ten minutes, I could not take any more. My intentions to remain a detached scientific observer dissolved. Yelling, "Get out of here! Get out of here!" I climbed down to rescue the baby. I passed her up to John, who then climbed higher above me. Effie and Tuck returned to the tree base after their momentary fright at my interference and glared up at us threateningly, as if intending to climb the *Hypericum* and retrieve Bonne Année.

Then, to the complete surprise of John and myself, the baby again left the protection of his arms and returned to Tuck and Effie. This time I made no move to stop her. Bonne Année was clearly determined to become a free-living gorilla.

Tuck and Effie instantly resumed their cat-and-mouse game of torture. Bonne Année's screams began anew. The brutality of Group 5's two females was agonizing to watch, the infant's cries unbearable to hear. The sounds prompted Beethoven to charge, roaring, to the base of the tree and caused Effie and Tuck to flee. Shaken, Bonne Année went directly to the old silverback, who smelled her with mild interest but did not open his arms to her pathetic attempts to be held or cuddled by him. As it started raining heavily, Beethoven turned his back on the infant to gain protection from the downpour in a dense clump of vegetation. Little Bonne Année huddled against his massive silvered back, drenched and shivering.

When the rain let up slightly, other Group 5 members came to investigate and smell the small stranger. The presence of young animals seemed to bolster Bonne Année's confidence. She moved in among them, sat down, and calmly began feeding. She was almost lost from our view as the gorillas crowded and displayed around her, strutting, and chestbeating as if trying to gain some kind of response from the infant. Suddenly Icarus entered into their midst, scattering the youngsters by strutting in a threatening manner, lips compressed. He made a direct run at Bonne Année and dragged her by one arm through the foliage. Effie and Tuck ran to join the young silverback in a combined attack on the baby, knocking her over whenever she tried to stand up. Their abuse became far rougher than before, because of Icarus' involvement. Ruthlessly, he grabbed Bonne Année away from the females and ran some sixteen feet, carrying her in his teeth. The infant screamed in terror. The noise brought Beethoven and other individuals charging toward Icarus, who hastily dropped the baby and fled.

My gratitude for Beethoven's intervention was short-lived. After about a minute the old silverback left and went downhill to feed by himself. It was as though physical limitations brought on by advanced age prevented him from active chastisement of Icarus. Also reproductive opportunities seemed at an end for Beethoven, whose remaining two females, Marchessa and Effie, were not likely to be sexually receptive again for at least three or four years. The future generations of Group 5, Beethoven's progeny, were now the responsibility of Icarus.

With Beethoven's departure, Icarus returned and, along with Tuck, resumed even more concentrated harassment of Bonne Année. It seemed to John and me as if they wanted to extend her suffering as long as possible for their own sport. Finally, the infant gave up her weak attempts at self-defense. She lay down, remained absolutely still, and gave no more vocalizations. This was a sign of total defeat.

For the last time Icarus chestbeat, grabbed her, and violently dragged her downhill, throwing her to the side before completing his display with a run and another chestbeat. Miraculously, Bonne Année managed to crawl back to the base of our tree, but she lacked the strength to climb up to us. Stunned at the extent of Group 5's xenophobic brutality, I was almost too slow to move to her rescue. However, I did manage to retrieve Bonne Année and hand her up to John just before Icarus and Tuck returned to the tree base to glare at us belligerently. John hid the baby under his rain jacket. We could only pray that she would not vocalize her usual dislike at being restrained. I had little doubt that the sound of her cries would provoke Icarus to climb the tree and forcibly retrieve her.

Four of Group 5's younger animals now surged around the tree before climbing up the trunk in an attempt to locate Bonne Année. As they tried to pass me, I had to pinch, lightly kick, or shove them away when Icarus was not looking. Puzzled by this unaccustomed treatment from me, they backed down, yet did not lose their interest in the newcomer. I was grateful that the shielded infant was neither moving nor vocalizing. Icarus scattered the youngsters, then he began climbing the tree. I'll never forget the feeling of the young silverback's hot breath penetrating my sodden boots, his head inches from my feet. It was only because John and I were positioned above him—and there were two of us—that Icarus did not continue his pursuit of Bonne Année.

During the next hour Icarus and Tuck maintained a hostile vigil at the tree base, barking or pig-grunting harshly at the slightest movement either John or I made. The male's head hair stood erect and he emitted a pungent silverback odor indicative of his tension. Both animals yawned repeatedly, exposing all of their teeth while shaking their heads rapidly from side to side. I received the impression that they wanted to attack, but neither had sufficient courage to risk climbing up the trunk with two human beings above them. I do not recall ever feeling so helpless.

Several times Icarus unleashed his stress by charging violently down the slope, chestbeating, and tearing at vegetation. To our dismay, he always returned to resume his guard position. After nearly an hour the rest of Group 5 moved away to feed. This prompted Icarus and Tuck to follow, but they soon strutted back to stare at us suspiciously. Only when the pair moved out of sight from us, some thirty feet below into dense foliage, was it safe for John to leap out of the tree and run uphill still carrying the silent baby gorilla under his jacket. Five minutes later I followed, expecting to be pounced on from behind at any minute. That evening John told me that he had had the same fear. Neither of us was at all relaxed until we were well over half an hour away from the group. The irrational behavior of Tuck, and especially of Icarus, had severed all ordinary bonds of rapport and communication. It was impossible to know if what certainly appeared to be xenophobia had rendered Icarus' behavior as unpredictable to himself as it was to us.

Once back at camp, Bonne Année was dried and put into her sleeping cage along with her treat box of fruit. Her wounds proved not to be serious and she seemed content to be back in familiar surroundings.

Twenty days later, when the injuries incurred from her encounter with Group 5 had healed, Bonne Année was successfully introduced to Group 4. Group 4's lack of strong kinship bonds permitted instant acceptance of the baby into the heterogeneous group of two young adult animals from a fringe group, the three males Beetsme, Tiger, and Titus of the old Group 4, and the group's young silverback leader, Peanuts, about eighteen years old at this time. Within an hour after meeting her foster family, Bonne Année was playing with five-and-a-half-year-old Titus. Bonne Année had become a gorilla of the mountains at last.

For a year Bonne Année was an integral part of Peanuts' Group 4, protected and cuddled by all the members. In May 1981 she succumbed to pneumonia after a prolonged period of heavy rains and hail.

Bonne Année's death raises the question as to whether she should have been released to the wild in the first place. My answer remains yes. A putative argument would claim that, if there are only some two hundred and forty mountain gorillas left in the wild, shouldn't Bonne Année have been preserved in a zoo? This line of reasoning would ask that the captive be exhibited simply for exhibition's sake because of the rarity of her kind. There are no mountain gorillas surviving in zoos, therefore even if Bonne Année had endured the adjustment she would never have had any opportunities to breed for the perpetuation of her species. She had that chance in the wild with others of her own kind. Bonne Année, at least, died free.

All too vividly I remember photographs taken of Coco and Pucker during the years of their confinement in the Cologne Zoo, photographs that revealed their depression even though they had one another for comfort and companionship. I would never have wanted Bonne Année to experience Coco and Pucker's trauma of captivity only to gain a few more years of sterile existence. By her successful reentry to a free-living group, where she thrived for a year, Bonne Année proved that it is possible to reintroduce captive gorillas to their natural habitat if a receptive free-living gorilla group is available. I believe that the benefits involved—especially the perpetuation of the species—outweigh the risks.

Eva Saulitis

It's been nearly three years, but I can't get Molly's question out of my mind. "Eva, what do you think it means that we have to do this? What does it mean for us to find this dead whale?" The orca whale is long-gone now, washed off the sloping beach where we found it. The shoreline has recovered itself from the imprint of its body by the roiling of stones re-settling themselves as the tide rises again and again. Its floating body has dissolved into the blue-green coldness of salt water. An everyday thing, a carcass is, in the life of a biologist. But this dead whale just won't leave me alone; this being of the deep, unconscious ocean, heaved up on land. One can ask it a question and it will lie there, or one may never see it at all, hidden in a crook of an island, visited only by gulls and eagles, ravens and bears.

The dead whale asks more of me. More than why it died, or how it arrived, or what had it been eating, more than was it poisoned by oil. Three years ago, Molly listened and heard the questions, and asked them of me. And then she left me to listen, to learn to ask. She left me to answer, in my own voice.

I dreamed that it was night, and I was at the ocean. I walked onto a long, wooden boardwalk that went straight out, miles out to sea. I walked along the wet planks, and there was no railing at the sides, just the blackened waves very close to me and the wind, and clouds torn open across the moonlit sky. Suddenly, I was surrounded by killer whales, their exhalations sounding on both sides of me. There were many whales and I could dimly see their blackness, blacker even than the waves, the sky. I sat down on the boardwalk, afraid I would lose control of myself, plunge recklessly into the dark water. I held my breath. My blood pounded in my ears. In that moment, someone could have put an ear to the shell of my ear and heard the sound of the sea.

Our gum-boots roll and slide off the algae-slicked stones of the beach as we approach the whale. Faltering steps mimic the tentative fear I feel inside. "Halloooo, bears, coming throooough, bears . . ." We send our calls with the southwest day-breeze blowing across the body of the whale, carrying our warning with the smell of decay over the island of bears.

Egged on by our resolve, we lay our buckets down and walk in opposite directions, circling the carcass. Molly stands near the withered dorsal fin. "God, it reeks!" Her face is contorted in a grimace of disgust, and I have to laugh. But underneath it all, I think, *Can I do this?*

Our instruction: to find this body, measure it, photograph it, cut it open and place pieces of its blubber in buckets, remove its stomach and take what is inside. The dead orca offers up no instruction of its own.

The whale's body roasts in the heat of the sun: skin cracked and dripping grease, its normally starkly contrasted black and white colors melted away to a streaked bronze. Its heaviness weights the beach. Its blood penetrates the stones.

I look past the rye grass above the rocks, into the moving green screen of the forest. I imagine invisible bears, whose eyes watch from the trees. "Halloooo, bears," I cry, remembering, suddenly, our invasion. I feel a cold cylinder of fear in my chest when I confront myself with our predicament. Montague Island represents for me fierceness, wildness, like the wind over the island grasses, it is uncompromising and irrevocable. The dead orca has, by chance or design, come to rest on the watery edge of the homeland of bears.

Three islands in Prince William Sound are inhabited by brown bears: Montague, Hinchinbrook, and Hawkins. Hinchinbrook and Montague are separated from each other by a notorious strait of water called Hinchinbrook Entrance. Ten miles across at the point where the islands are the closest, it opens like a wide whale's mouth to the Gulf of Alaska. The Entrance is streaked by currents and rip tides; winds rise unexpectedly. Through the mouth, storms enter, whirling off the Gulf.

Several years ago, a strong-willed bear made the crossing of the Entrance. It had been transplanted to Montague Island by the Fish and Wildlife Service, after raiding garbage cans in Cordova. Weeks later, the bear showed up again in town.

The Chugach Eskimo people tell of bears swimming in the opposite direction. One story involves a woman living at the now-abandoned village of Nuchek. She was betrayed by her husband, so transformed herself into a brown bear and killed him. Four fur seals disguised as men bore her by baidarka to Hinchinbrook Entrance. From there she swam into the Gulf, creating Middleton Island out of seaweed so she could rest. She finally arrived at Montague, her fury intact. That is why, say the Chugach, the brown bears on Montague are so fierce. I imagine these descendants of the betrayed woman: beings that shift from human to animal, volatile changelings.

The alders wave wildly, forming a visually impenetrable, moving curtain of green. Surely the smell of the carcass is passing through the cool forest air, bending around trees and into passages between boulders. I hope that the whale is too rancid for bears. Behind the green, are there eyes, watching?

Molly and I regroup. "Let's get this over with as fast as we can," I say, opening the top of a bucket. "Let's make a plan." Molly's thoughts are elsewhere. "Eva, why do you think we have to do this? What does it mean that we have to cut open this whale?" Her question inserts itself into my mind, trying to find purchase. I'm in science mode, nervous about bears, unsure of the task before us, wanting to do it right. I know what she is asking. As always, what she asks of me is to look deeper, beyond the surface, beyond science and task. I don't always know if I'll be able to live up to the challenges she poses. I load the question like film into my consciousness, hoping the picture will be taken, the moment preserved for later consideration.

We bend to the buckets, one of us rearing our head up every few minutes to shout our incomprehensions toward the edge of trees. Before we left the boat, we had changed into expendable clothing. In Valdez, eighty miles distant and a day's journey away, we had foraged through the local second-hand shop for clothing we knew we would burn after our encounter. Ill-fitting jeans, a dollar a pair. Pink sweatshirt with too-short arms, fifty cents, discarded T-shirts only a tourist would buy.

We prepared ourselves as best we could in Valdez. But looking at the sheer weight of the whale's carcass, the unimagined flesh, I realize that we could never be prepared for such a death. We could never be prepared for the eyes of bears we cannot see, for the impossibility of detachment in the face of the manifold implications of ourselves on this beach. Wildness accepts no predictions.

We pull on raingear and reach in for the fillet knives we bought in town. I glance at the enormity of the whale. The knives are absurd, but they will have to do. We move toward the carcass. "Maybe one of us should watch for bears, while the other cuts," suggests Molly. I agree, looking back down the beach to our inflatable raft, and then to the *Whale One*, floating blankly at anchor fifty yards offshore. I imagine scrambling down to the raft and paddling like mad for the boat. At least with the receding tide, it is floating closer to the beach. I turn away and, knife in hand, press its tip into the crisp skin of the whale's throat.

From a cartographer's perspective, this beach is part of a sickle-shaped peninsula separating Port Chalmers from Stockdale Harbor. These names hint at the commerce and the busy industry of the first half of this century in Prince William Sound. They do not apply to the current wildness of these two wide bays. They are shunned by most mariners. In 1964, the earthquake lifted the entire coastline of Montague Island; in some areas, the island rose thirty feet. Charts warn of hundreds of underwater dangers—reefs and ledges not marked on maps. At low tide, water curls whitely over shallow areas, and waves break themselves against the exposed rocks.

Montague Island is forty miles long, a jagged backbone of mountains. It bears along its length the force of the Gulf, protecting, and actually creating, the shelter of the Sound. Storms pile up along its south-facing coastline. We watch weather meet the mountains and spill down their sides like waterfalls of steam. Where clouds are held in the valleys, rain falls endlessly.

To me the tiny crook of island where we stand has always looked like a beckoning finger. I have placed my feet on Montague only a few times in eight years. The submerged rocks, unsuitable anchoring spots, and dangerous waters surrounding the island hold me away. The promises of the unknown—bears, huge trees, expansive green valleys, permanent snowfields—draw me closer.

Earlier in the summer, I ventured onto the island with three friends. In the late afternoon, I sat alone in a rye grass meadow, not facing the sea as I usually do, but facing the island, into an alder and salmonberry thicket. The meadow was a resting place for bleached and scattered logs, and I leaned my back against their sun-warmed solidity. Facing the thicket, I thought of the bears that inhabit the island, and wondered where the closest one was. I imagined its eyes among the alders, its tongue tasting the berries. I imagined the spirits of all the bears who had ever lived on the island watching me. Closing my eyes, fear left me. I thought of the ancient stories of women who coupled with bears, and with a strange, floating serenity, I asked to be filled with the spirit of the brown bear. For that brief drift of time, I wanted a bear to come to me. Before the thought could leave my mind and depart to wherever it was headed, I snapped to.

Are you crazy? I asked myself, quickly sitting up and looking around the meadow, with its graveyard of logs. I was suddenly terrified of the unknown power of my own thoughts. But that momentary letting go of the fear that I expected of myself asked me questions. What empty place inside myself could be filled by this fearful presence, what it represented: strength, a sense of territory, a fierce need for solitude, fidelity to place.

The heat of the sun sears my face and dampens my clothes with sweat as I push the knife blade through the leathery skin of the whale. I stand awkwardly, a few feet away, my arm extended, trying to keep my distance. As the knife penetrates the blubber layer, juice oozes out of the cut. I can feel its heat as it runs across my gloved hand. Inside this whale minute organisms are working, softening, consuming, dissolving the whale. They generate another kind of heat. I saw away a square of skin and hot, melting fat and drop it into the bucket that Molly holds toward me. A lab will whirl this flesh in test tubes and, by a process I can hardly imagine, gas chromatography, render it into data on hydrocarbon levels borne by the whale.

The open wound releases the thick, sweet rotten smell of decay. Molly's voice rings out as she paces the pale cobbles, calling to the bears. "How are you doing?" she asks. "It's so hot," I reply, wiping moisture from my forehead with the back of my gloved hand. "And this smell. . . . I'm trying not to judge it. If I describe it to myself, it's not so bad." I turn my face into the wind, gulping breaths of clean, salt-laden air.

She offers to start off cutting for the stomach. I hand her the gloves. We stand side by side, looking at the bulk of the whale. "Let's just cut it like we're gutting a fish," I suggest. I try to imagine where the stomach would be—above the chewed-open flesh near the belly button, and below the chest cavity. The giant, paddlelike pectoral flippers fold together like hands in prayer, blocking access to the upper belly. "Let's just lift the top one out of the way," says Molly, striding up and grasping the peeling slab with both hands. With both of us heaving, the flipper is unyielding, as improbable and unmoving as a grand piano. Molly bends down, crawls as far as she can under the flipper, and begins the cut.

Several moments have passed since we've shouted, so I send out calls to the trees as I walk around to the whale's head. The flesh is puckered where birds have picked out the skyward-facing eye. The mouth gapes, its rows of evenly spaced, conical teeth grinning. I bend down and stroke my fingers along their marble smoothness. They are cold to my touch.

I guess I should cut one out for aging, I think, and fetch our small hacksaw from the bucket. After several minutes of vigorous rasping I let my arm drop to check out my progress. The tooth is barely scratched. The hacksaw, like the knife, like ourselves, has been daunted by the reality of the whale. This tooth will resist my futile attempt at thieving. I leave it intact and move close to Molly.

She has emerged from under the flipper and is jerking the knife along, making a jagged cut through the blubber layer. She is on her knees, wallowing in the stiffness of the raingear, her face inches away from the whale. Her rubber-suited arms are smeared with juice and blobs of grease. The split-open rinds of flesh on the whale's belly pull away from the underlying layer of muscle.

We approach this task from a hundred different perspectives, Molly and I. I watch her working, her small form dwarfed by the whale. She is six years younger than I, but I often feel diminished by the power of her imagination and insights. Her small stature is belied by her physical strength and endurance. She grew up crewing on her father's fishing boat, the *Sweet Sage*. As a young child, she woke at 4:00 A.M. with her two sisters to set out for the fishing grounds in Cook Inlet.

Molly is my companion of three summers in the Sound. We share a wall-tent home looking out on the passage where we scan for whales. She is my companion of stretched-out days on the water in our small boat. She always asks the important questions, unwrapping me from anxiety over the quality of our work. She pulls me back from my worries and, my hand in hers, leads me toward the edges of things. She challenges me to peer over the side, to plumb the deeper waters. On this day, she calls me to the shadow side of what is before us: this body on the beach, on the island of bears, edged by waters of whales and fish and deepness and unknown. Sometimes, we speak the same language. Sometimes no words are necessary.

We take walks often, stretching our legs after long days on the boat. We explore stretches of beach, deer trails leading up to ridges, depressions in the forest that hint of hidden lakes where we might swim. On beaches, we search for Japanese glass fishing floats: round globes of colored glass that survive wave-driven landings. On the same fog-bound day last summer, we each found our first glass balls, on two separate beaches. In the afternoon, we lounged in the boat, holding them up to the light, peering through them. Molly's was small, fitting perfectly in the palm of her hand. The glass was a clear blue-green. My ball was larger, and the glass was opaque, with a scratched look. "See how these balls are different in the way we are, Mol," I pondered. "Yours is so clear-sighted and compact; mine is cloudy and uncertain, a little battered." We laughed. "I think yours is beautiful," Molly said.

This summer, I must face the certainty of Molly's decision that this will be her last season working with me in the Sound. She is a writer by vocation and avocation, and a scientist by neither. She moves on, toward her writing, and away from the eclipsing silences, the hourless days. She moves on from the precarious balancing act between science and pure experience.

Her absence asks of me why I stay. For I cannot imagine not staying. Our friendship has been the anchor point from which I have explored my place in the Sound. Within it, I have been able to move in this in-between place of conflict. In the world we have created together, questions of detachment and implication can live side by side.

The question of the whale, as she posed it, was to ask me how to be more authentic in this place. To let go of the easily resolvable. To climb into the body of the whale, to be not afraid of bears, of experience, of questions that have no answers. Of being alone. She left me with the challenge of seeing through my own eyes, and not relying on hers.

I take my turn at the whale. Molly lurches up, her face glistening with sweat. "I have to get away from this and breathe some fresh air," she says, stumbling down the beach to move the buckets closer to the edge of the water. "Heeeeyooo . . ." she yells over her shoulder.

I slice at the exposed muscle layer. The juice from the cut sizzles up. The meat is brown, softened, and fibrous. The huge body of a whale retains heat for days after death, cooking the flesh from the inside. The sun bakes it from without.

I think of the living whale that once moved this body through the secret realms of water. The streamlined form swam effortlessly, the once blood-red muscles conveying a life of constant, undulating motion; the ability to travel a hundred or more miles in a single day, to capture silver flashes of salmon, twirling porpoises. This is what happens to a body that has been supported by the sea when it is cast upon land, the realm of gravity. It falls, as the whale falls back to water mightily during a breach. It sags, collapses, breaks down. I am self-conscious for this whale's spirit. I am suddenly aware of our intrusion into the privacy of death. This slashed body reviles me.

So many times my own presence as a scientist in the Sound or amongst the animals feels repellent. It's an ever-present contradiction, the desire to learn about the whales, to "do science," and the conviction that the animals should be left alone. I hover above myself, watching this efficient persona, scanning with binoculars, wielding cameras and knives, scratching notes on wet paper with a mechanical pencil.

And sometimes I see myself from a different set of eyes. And I feel real. I watch the mountains of Montague in the distance, the streaked lenses of rock eddied by ice and snow. I want to imprint myself there on those slopes. And the image of the mountains pools inside of me, carves in me a certain solidity.

I pivot back and forth constantly, between my scientist self and the self that feels more true: the witness. There must be a balancing point there with the integrity of stone. I don't believe it's wholly the domain of a scientist to want to know why. It is a universal human quality, one that I can't separate myself from.

The mountain or the ocean itself cannot be asked with the hope of receiving an answer. And this is what holds me here. The sea is vast and yields its secrets randomly, slowly, if at all. It is willful, like a sleeping animal, wakening with heavy breathing, shaking itself. I peer down into the water, straining to see what is yielded up: the eye of a whale, or its shoulder, a flash of black and white in the greening world.

Two hours have passed. "We should go faster," I tell Molly. "Maybe we can both cut and yell at the same time." The sun has dipped to the west. "Sure," says Molly, grasping a knife. My blade glides along the taut, gray membrane that lines the cavity holding the organs. We carve away rinds of fat and muscle to expose a rectangle of lining. I push the tip of my knife through the shiny elastic surface. An instant whoosh of fetid air rushes out, and the membrane loses its tautness. We hold our breath and turn our heads away. "Jesus," says Molly releasing air in a gasp. "That was awful." I slice away a patch of lining. Cuts through the inner skin of membrane reveal the coils of glistening, veined intestines. My knife penetrates a loop and it oozes orange slime, the color of sulphur fungus.

The stomach is deep inside the whale. I stand back and pull the intestines onto the beach to make a space. We take turns grasping and feeling for the stomach, our arms reaching in to the pits. I feel for the end of the intestines; it seems impossible that there is an end. Finally, I feel the widening flask that welds into the stomach. My arms extended as far as they can into the body of the whale, bending under the ribs, lost in the mass of intestines. "How are we going to get this out?" I ask Molly. "We need a bigger opening," she says, knifing off more slabs of blubber and muscle, widening our rectangle. I wield the hacksaw, trying to carve away ribs to reach the stomach. As with the teeth, the saw makes nearly imperceptible scratches on the two-inch-thick bone.

Our only choice is to climb on top of the whale and heft the stomach up from under the lowest rib. Molly uses the pectoral fin as a step; she skids along the whale's side. I reach the knife into the body cavity, cutting away the transparent membranes holding the stomach pouches to the wall. When I have loosened a mound of stomach, I lean back and pull the slippery mass out from under the rib, and heave it to Molly. Bending her knees, she strains upward until the sack rests on the whale's side.

I climb onto the whale to help Molly pull the rest of the stomach out and up. My foot slips on the greasy skin, and I slide down into the body cavity. I am drenched in sweat, but am thankful for the protection of raingear now. I look up and see for the first time that we have an audience. A cadre of eagles and ravens looks down on us from the trees.

I try to imagine the sight: two ungainly humans, slipping, sliding, shimmying, cutting, probing, hefting, slicing. Do they wonder, what is the purpose, what is our place? We of the buckets and bags, notebooks, cameras. I often feel out of place in the eyes of the animals we encounter. Once, I stared over the bow of the boat at my reflection in the water. This is what the whale sees, looking up. An odd, flickering, white-faced shape flapping its orange wings, jabbering noisily in the bright, blinding air.

It takes both of us pulling, but soon we have hauled many sections of stomach up through the ribs and onto the side of the whale's belly. We reach for our knives, and draw them back and forth across pouches. The knives have dulled. Through the thick, outer skin of the muscled sack is a crenulated surface, like the underside of a mushroom. This pouch is empty, surprisingly white and clean.

"I think I've found something," Molly says quietly. Her two palms rest on a bulging section of stomach. It is hard and knobby, like the crop of a bird. The knife slices, and the contents spill out: a brown slimy soup of whiskers, claws, and shriveled strips of skin. We pull out handfuls of long, quill-like sea lion whiskers, and the white, pearly ones of seals.

Something curious catches my eye. I reach into the jumble of remains and pull out three square tabs. "What the heck . . ." I begin. They look disconcertingly like buckles from Helly Hansen raingear. It takes me a moment to recognize that they are numbered flipper tags. Somewhere, biologists snapped them to the flesh of living seals or sea lions, to trace their movements and fate.

We are excited at our success. We work quickly, slicing open more pouches, scraping the contents out with our fingers, and filling Zip-loc bags. We don't want to miss tiny fish scales that may cling to the stomach walls. When we finish, we slide off the side of the whale, our boots crunching down on the cobbles.

Stepping back from the carcass, its full view is shocking. Streaks of intestine have begun to dry, sticking to the rocks. The pull of gravity on the internal organs has caused them to sag toward the ground. The pit of the body cavity is filling with brownish fluid. I want to leave, to relish our accomplishment of what had at first seemed an insurmountable task. But my feelings are mixed with shame at seeing the gash in the whale's side, its innards spilling out of our jagged cuts. It seems a reckless, violent piece of work.

Later that summer we would get a radio call about an orca carcass floating in Montague Strait. The caller described a huge opening in its belly, so I knew it was the whale from the beach. But he also told us the carcass was headless. The picture flashed in my mind of a chain-saw-wielding someone, after the ivory teeth or perhaps the skull. How was this person different from me? Both of us, wanting something, and taking it, from the whale.

The gashed body of the whale offers up no reckoning. I remember a story. The Chugach Eskimos believed that when killer whales came into a bay with a village, death would come. The people were sad. The whales were after someone's spirit. There are spirits on this island, including those of the whale, the bears. My own spirit wants taking up. It is too full of contradictions.

Back on the boat, we prepare for our departure. Molly fills buckets with soap and salt water. Still in our raingear, we stand on the bow and pour water over each other, scrubbing away the offal of the whale with long-handled deck brushes. Several washes later, the smell remains, as it will for weeks to come. We peel down to our damp clothing, strip it off, and pile it in a plastic garbage bag for later burning. We take quick dives from the boat after soaping our bodies, but the scent of the whale has permeated our skin.

I pull up the anchor and Molly backs the boat away from the shore. The tide rises again, seeping up the beach. I look at the strange shape resting on the stones. "Remember that time we bowed to the forest, Molly?" I ask.

We had been on a hike in the high country. We stood on the beach afterward, looking back toward the stream-cut valley we had followed. "I feel the need to bow to that place, Eva," Molly had ventured. So we stood, side by side, our palms pressed together, like the hands of prayerful monks. We bent at our waists, with our faces turned up to the forest.

We kneeled on the beach and touched our foreheads to the wet gravel. And then we turned and walked away.

As we depart, we see the whale from the vantage from which we first saw it. The marks of our probing are not visible from this distance. The impression we had when we stood beside it, that the whale was cast from its element, dissolves. It is an illusion, in which our defilement of the whale disappears as the conflicts fade to the ordinary, day-by-day of our water life.

On one of the wooden supports inside our wall-tent is pinned a fragment of a poem by Rilke. It instructs us emphatically to live the questions. And doing so, he writes, *perhaps you will then gradually, without knowing it, live along some distant day into the answer.*

For this moment, the coppery form of the whale rests on the wild fringe of the island, with eagles perched in the high trees above it. The image imprints on my mind as the weight of the whale imprints its memory onto the beach. We leave the burnished form to the solitude of its resting place, to the company of waving grasses, patient birds, the spirits of ponderous bears. I imagine them biding time, waiting to reclaim what is theirs, their eyes in the alders, watching.

ELEPHANT MEMORIES

Cynthia Moss

There is a small national park called Amboseli at the base of Kilimanjaro in southern Kenya. In its 150 square miles live a variety of wild animals: lions, leopards, cheetahs, rhinos, giraffes, buffaloes, zebras, wildebeests, and elephants. The wildlife has lived there for several thousand years; I have lived there for most of the last 14 years, carrying out a study of the elephants.

Elephants are very special animals: intelligent, complicated, intense, tender, powerful, and funny. I consider myself immensely fortunate to have spent so much time with them. I have followed the lives of Amboseli's elephants through droughts to periods of superabundance, through times of heavy poaching and great losses to times of peace and relative security. I have watched them give birth and I have watched them die. I have observed young females reach sexual maturity and mate for the first time and young males leave the security of their families and strike out on their own. I have seen the grand old matriarchs leading and defending their families and I have also seen them lose all dignity and run around in play with their tails curled up over their backs and a wild glint in their eyes.

After so many years with elephants I wanted other people to know them, enjoy them, and care about them as I have. I wanted to share my knowledge and experiences, and therefore I have written this book. I think it is important to point out that this is not a tale of adventure about human hardship and bravery in the face of Africa's heat and dust and large, dangerous animals; in other words it is not about how I survived alone in the bush with 600 wild friends. It is about the elephants' lives, how they survived or succumbed to droughts, poachers, Maasai warriors, disease, injuries, tourists, and even researchers. It is about their families, their "friends," their mates, and their offspring; and their good times and bad times through the seasons and the years. I have merely gone along with them—a spectator at the *banquet or a witness to less happy events—in the role of voyeur, not as a participant. I am there, of course, but only as observer, interpreter, scientist, conservationist, philosopher, and sometimes just as a lover of elephants who puts aside the tools of the trade and simply enjoys being with them.*

In the early morning light, the large gray forms moved slowly, deliberately, and nearly silently along a well-worn path amongst lava boulders and small thorny *Balanites* trees. They walked in single file with a large female with long, upcurved tusks at the lead, many calves of varying sizes and ages along with more adult females in the center, and a straight-tusked, ancient, but immensely dignified female at the rear. Behind them rose the overwhelmingly dominant feature of the landscape—the 19,340-foot snow-capped peak of Kilimanjaro. The elephants headed north, away from the mountain; they walked without stopping to rest or feed, as if they had an appointment at a prearranged place.

Eventually they emerged into a habitat of open pan with no trees and little other vegetation. Here the quiet *sluff, sluff* of their feet kicked up the fine alkaline dust and their outlines became hazy. They did not linger here either, but continued on until abruptly the dry, bare ground gave way to lush, green vegetation interspersed with open water dotted with and surrounded by myriad water birds: ducks, geese, ibises, herons, cranes, plovers, jacanas, and many more. Other animals gathered along the edge of the swamp: zebras, wildebeests, reedbucks, waterbucks, and buffaloes. The elephants kept on their course, ignoring these smaller species, who stepped discreetly out of the way.

On reaching the swamp, the elephants spread out. Some began to feed immediately while still walking, snatching up large mouthfuls of the dark, green *Cynodon dactylon* grass, others continued on a straight course, and all arrived together at a channel of clear running water. Each of the adult females dipped the tip of her trunk into the stream, sucked the water up into her trunk, lifted her head up and back, placed the trunk in her mouth, and let the water flow back down her trunk and down her throat while swallowing at the same time. Most of the calves used the same technique, but one young calf was not yet adept with his trunk and he knelt down and drank with his mouth.

When they finished drinking some went on into the swamp and started feeding in earnest, while others walked over to a depression where a mud wallow had formed. The adults splashed themselves with the dark, glutinous mud by first picking it up in the curve of their trunks and then flinging it onto their chests, backs, sides, and heads. The mud hitting their bodies made a sharp, wet slapping sound. Soon they turned from a light gray to mostly glistening black. The calves, showing less restraint, waded right into the wallow and flopped down on their sides and then writhed and wriggled in the mud until one side, including head, ears, and eyes, was completely covered in mud. Then they sat up and flopped over to the other side. Young calves took the opportunity to climb on the older ones as soon as they were down, and in the process, got covered in mud themselves. Eventually there was a great heap of youngsters completely filling the mud wallow. Slowly they disentangled themselves and struggled out of the mud wallow, slipping and sliding up the small bank.

The calves joined the adults, who were now moving deeper and deeper into the swamp. There the elephants found grasses, sedges, including papyrus, and succulent creeping herbs. They ate steadily, building to a rhythm: first twisting the trunk around a bunch of vegetation, pulling to one side and ripping the bunch free, then placing it in the mouth, and immediately reaching for more as they chewed. Some kinds of plants came out by the roots and with these the elephants bit off the part that was palatable and let the other drop. The small calves found less that they could handle, only young shoots here and there and tender creepers. These younger calves also had some trouble trying to follow their mothers through the dense vegetation and deep water and at times they had to swim from one clump of vegetation to the next.

The elephants fed continuously until midday, when they moved to higher, dry ground, where they found a bare patch of dusty soil. They scooped the dust up in their trunk tips and blew it out over their heads and backs. Now they gathered together in a tight group, nearly a circle, standing close together, some touching. One female rubbed her head against the shoulder of the old, straight-tusked female. A calf leaned and rubbed against the leg of his mother. First one calf lay down, then three more subsided to the ground and lay flat on their sides. The females' heads hung down and their trunks became limp and stretched out until the tips touched the ground. Two of the females rested their trunks on their tusks. One simply draped her trunk over her left tusk. The upcurved female neatly curled her trunk like a snake and rested it on both her tusks. A half-grown calf placed his trunk on the back of a sleeping calf. All became quiet and breathing deepened.

The elephants slept for about 40 minutes, the calves soundly, but the adults much more lightly, occasionally opening their eyes, gently flapping their ears, or swishing a trunk or tail at an annoying fly. A young adult female was the first to show signs of stirring. She stepped forward a few feet and started dusting. Then the calves stood up and synchronously most of the members of the group defecated and urinated. Still they stood there as if waiting. Then the ancient female made a very long, soft rumbling sound, raised and flapped her ears against her neck and shoulders, letting her ears slide down with a rasping sound, and set off. This was the signal they had been waiting for and all the others followed after her.

They traveled north, forming a column two or three abreast. Once again they seemed to have a purpose in their movement and direction. Some of them raised their trunks in the air, sniffing the wind. They headed toward a channel of the swamp where the water continued to flow above ground. Feeding near the channel were two more groups of elephants. The original group moved steadily in their direction. When they arrived at the first of the two stationary groups there was a discreet reaching of trunks in each other's direction by some of the members, but the upcurved female and the old female ignored these elephants and walked on past toward the second group. When they were about 50 yards from this group, the upcurved female rumbled—a different, higher-pitched, and louder rumble than the signal the old female gave after they woke. This sound produced an instant reaction in the new group. The members raised their heads, lifted and spread their ears, and produced loud, throaty rumbles. At the same time the elephants in both groups began to secrete a clear liquid from the temporal glands on the sides of their faces. More answering rumbles came from the original group and then both started striding rapidly toward each other. When they were 20 yards apart they broke into a run and came together in a turmoil of earflapping, rumbling, screaming, trumpeting, clicking of tusks together, entwining of trunks, spinning and backing, and urinating and defecating. Their temporal gland secretions were streaming down their faces and they reached their trunks toward each other's glands. The upcurved female pushed through the milling calves and went straight to a large female with a big tear out of her right ear. They lifted their heads together and clicked tusks while entwining their trunks and rumbling deeply.

It was the wrong time to be leaving the protection of the swamp, but they had had no choice. They kept to the edge of the swamp, although on this side it was fairly open. They had almost reached the end of the Namalog drainage when suddenly, from behind a clump of young acacias, stepped three Maasai men, each with a long glinting spear. Slit Ear saw them first and gave an alarm, and they all turned and ran. The three Maasai sprinted toward the elephants at an angle, trying to cut Slit Ear off, but she swerved and got past with her family and Tolstoy, Tallulah, and Theo and their calves closely bunched behind. Out on her own, unable to run as fast as the others, was Teresia.

The men quickly raced toward her with spears poised in their right hands, raised parallel to the ground and above their shoulders. The first man threw his with a tremendous thrust combined with the momentum of his sprint. It hit Teresia in the left shoulder and drove deep into the muscle more than six inches. The next man flung his spear just as she turned to charge. It went through her ear and into her neck. The third man hesitated, aimed carefully, and with all his power threw his spear and hit Teresia behind the shoulder. He had aimed for the heart and had just missed. The blade went slightly to the right and between two ribs.

Teresia groaned in pain with each strike and staggered when the third spear hit, but she did not fall down. She charged, and with no more weapons the Maasai had to run. After chasing them only briefly she turned back toward Namalog and in agonizing pain made her way around to the northern side. Two of the spears had fallen out, but the first, the one that had gone into her shoulder, was still embedded. It scraped against the bone as she tried to run. She limped her way to the thickest part of the swamp edge and hid among the dense bush. There was no way she could catch up to the others, who were now halfway back to Olodo Are, running at full speed and very frightened.

When Teresia reached the thicket she stopped, her sides heaving with the effort. With her trunk she grasped the spear and pulled and twisted it until it came out. The original penetration had torn through her muscles and in wrenching it out she did more damage. She had made it to the thicket by sheer will. Now she could barely move. The three men had not tried to follow her. For the moment she was safe, but they or others could find her later and finish her off with more spears.

However, Teresia had had much experience in avoiding Maasai during her life and she managed to elude them by sticking to the thick bush and keeping just ahead of the herders when they came near. She was in considerable pain and was seriously crippled by her shoulder wound, but she was not near death because the spears had not severed any arteries, nor had they hit any vital organs. After two days of hiding while recovering her strength, she was able to move down to the swamp to drink and even feed for a while. She was not strong enough to try to make it back to the park and her family. She had to remain at Namalog on her own. A few Maasai saw her during this period and noticed that she was wounded but they were not interested in killing her. It was not very exciting or brave to kill an old wounded animal, so they left her alone. For her attackers it had been a spur-of-the-moment sport.

The danger to Teresia did not come from the Maasai, but in a more insidious form. Teresia's wounds were narrow and deep, which was very bad for an elephant. The thick, tough skin tends to nearly close up around the openings, making it difficult for puncture wounds to drain properly. Teresia's shoulder wound was draining well because it was kept open by her movement. The other two wounds were not draining and soon became infected. It was a slow process, but eventually the infection spread and turned to septicemia, a general poisoning of the blood. All three wounds oozed a greenish-yellow pus.

Ten days after she was speared, Teresia was still alive but losing the battle with the infection, which had spread throughout her body. She was in less pain now but feverish; she barely fed and just managed to get to the swamp edge to drink. She was thirsty most of the time because of the fever and so tried to stay as close to running water as possible without meeting Maasai.

After two more days Teresia could no longer move and stood in the shade of a tree, swaying slightly with unsteadiness and only semiconscious. She had reached a state of feeling little and she mostly dreamed, perhaps of vast swards of sweet new grass and clear, cool hill streams. Or the taste and feel of the sweet juices that squirted out when she crunched down on her favorite wild fruit. Or most likely the smell and touch and sounds of her family—those who were still alive and others who were long gone, her grandmother, mother, sisters and brothers, sons and daughters.

On her final day Teresia grew too weak to stand and slowly subsided onto the ground, first onto her chest and then over on her side. She was conscious of the sounds and smells around her for a while longer, but soon there was nothing. Her long life was over.

I am not going to try to pretend that I was not more affected by the death of Teresia than by that of any other elephant. I had grown very attached to that funny-looking old elephant and I knew I would feel sorrow and loss when she died. By the end of 1983, when I saw how slow she was and how old she looked I knew she was going to die in the next couple of years of natural causes if nothing else because of her age and her teeth. I had estimated her to be 60 and had put her year of birth at 1924. I now revised it to 1922.

It was intriguing to try to imagine what Teresia must have experienced in that long life. For half of her life she probably very rarely saw cars and encountered few man-made structures other than Maasai mud and dung huts. There were only elephants, other wild animals, the Maasai, their livestock, and sometimes people who came to hunt or poach. When she was well into her thirties, things began to change and more vehicles appeared and buildings went up in places where she used to feed. The cars probably frightened her for many years but eventually, when nothing bad seemed to occur around them, she got used to them. In the last ten years of her life she tolerated them completely and almost certainly knew by sight and smell the research vehicles with the particular people in them that followed her for hours at a time.

Changes in Teresia's habitat caused by conservation efforts and tourism may have been inconvenient and possibly irritating at times, but I suspect that they were basically extraneous and unimportant to her life in general. I think what mattered most to Teresia was her family—her calves and her other relatives; and her concern was how best to protect them and secure the resources that she and they needed to survive and flourish. I like to think that Teresia was able to pursue these goals without too much interference and that she had a relatively good life for an African elephant living in the twentieth century. Very few elephants are able to live out their full lifespan in the way that she did. Amboseli is probably one of the last places in Africa where she could have. Elephants have been pushed out of so many places where they used to be found and squeezed into small sanctuaries. To have to break with tradition, abandon well-known home ranges, give up old migration routes, and crowd into a restricted area must be stressful. Both inside and outside parks and reserves, most African elephants are pursued for their ivory and the older elephants are always the first to be killed because their tusks are bigger. In the few areas where poaching is under control, elephants are culled for a variety of reasons, usually "for their own good." Whole family units are killed from the matriarch down to the littlest calves, with only a few calves between one and three years old saved to be sold to zoos. As painful and agonizing as her death was, I would still prefer that Teresia died in the way that she did rather than be killed "cleanly, efficiently, and painlessly by a bullet" in a culling scheme in which she would have lost her whole family, all her female descendants, most of her genes, nearly everything she had lived 62 years for.

Looking back over Teresia's life provides an opportunity to review the full life cycle of a female elephant. When Teresia was born around 1922 she weighed about 260 pounds and stood approximately two feet nine inches at the shoulder. Her brain weighed 35 percent of what it would weigh as an adult. (The human brain is 26 percent of its adult weight at birth; most other mammal brains are 90 percent of the adult weight at birth.) She had a lot of mental and physical development ahead of her.

Teresia probably spent the first four years of her life in very close proximity to her mother and her siblings and other relatives in the family. She depended on her mother for both milk and care. When she was around four years old, a younger sister or brother was most likely born and Teresia was weaned. At four she would have taken great interest in her new sibling and lavished it with attention. At the same time she was developing her own social relationships within the family and learning elephant protocol. As a young calf she would have been tolerated in most situations, but as she got older she had to learn about dominance and aggression as well as affiliation. She would also have begun to know elephants from other families and her own family's position in relation to them.

The years from 4 to 12 or 13 were probably by elephant standards fairly carefree. Teresia was growing, learning, playing, and developing friendships and bonds. I am sure there were many bright-green, sun-filled days when Teresia and the other youngsters in her family and bond group were able to "be silly." I can imagine them racing about, beating through bushes and tall grass, heads up, ears out, eyes open wide glinting with mischief, or running across the open pans in the "floppy run," letting forth wild, pulsating play trumpets. On the best days everyone joined in, even the adults.

Starting sometime in her ninth or tenth year Teresia's body began to go through changes and in her eleventh or twelfth year, if conditions were adequate and there was not a drought, she probably came into estrus for the first time and experienced all the confusion, fear, and excitement of that event. She may or may not have conceived on that occasion. If she did not she probably came into estrus again a few months later and most likely conceived then. Her body went through further changes as the fetus grew and various hormones went into action. Her breasts filled out gradually over the months. By the time she was 18 months pregnant her sides were bulging and the weight of the fetus slowed her down. She probably had to feed more than before, because she, as well as the fetus, was continuing to grow. At her age she was only about two thirds the size of a full-grown adult female.

At 13 to 14 years old Teresia probably gave birth to her first calf. Most likely she would not be in synchrony with the other females in the family and she may also have given birth out of the main birth season. Given the odds for first calves, this one may not have survived, especially if it was a marginal year in terms of rainfall. But in a good year and in a close-knit family, it could very well have lived beyond its first year. Born around 1935, it would have been 49 the year Teresia died. She had no living daughter that old and there were only one or two big bulls of that age. I suspect that animal died somewhere along the way.

If her first calf lived out its early years, then Teresia would have come into estrus again when it was about two and given birth to a new calf when it was four and she herself was 17 to 18. For the next three decades of her life Teresia was either lactating or pregnant or both, as she would continue to suckle her youngest calf until the next one was born. If she gave birth to her first calf when she was 14 and had a calf every four years until she was 49, when Tolstoy was born, she could conceivably have had ten surviving calves. If she had her first calf at 12 and had a few very short calving intervals of only three years, then she might have had 11 calves in those years. After 50 Teresia's breeding slowed down considerably. We know that she did not produce a calf for nine years, and then gave birth to her final calf when she was 58. That one did not survive.

In those middle years, when she was reproductively most active, important social changes were also occurring. Whoever was matriarch when she was born, possibly her grandmother, would have died and the next-oldest female taken over. This may have happened two or three times before Teresia herself was the oldest female and therefore the matriarch. I know that she was the oldest female in 1964 because among the photographs that Norman Myers took there were several complete rolls of film on the Ts. They were standing in a group resting under some trees and he photographed them from all angles. Teresia was easily recognizable and she was definitely the biggest female there. Thus she must have been matriarch of her family and the senior member of the whole bond group for at least 20 years.

I think it could be said that in the last decade of her life Teresia was in her old age. I do not know if elephants become senile. Teresia always seemed to have all her faculties intact. She stayed with her family, continued to interact with them, and was as tolerant and sweet-natured as she was when I first knew her. Teresia must have been a particularly caring and in some way attractive grandmother because Theodora's calf spent far more time with her than with his own mother. In those last two years, whenever I saw the family, he was often following Teresia or standing next to her. He would go to Theo to suckle but then would return to Teresia. If I had not known the family I might have thought it was her calf. She also continued to maintain a close relationship with her strapping son Tolstoy, who was 13 years old and showed no signs of going independent up till the time she died. Thus, although slow and possibly not leading the family in the way she must have when she was younger, Teresia was still a vital part of the family in her old age.

I would estimate that 65 is probably about the oldest age an elephant can reach in the wild. By then the teeth would be completely worn down and malnutrition and its related diseases would follow. The famous Kenya elephant Ahmed of Marsabit mountain died in this way, although he was only 55; but he had an abscess under the molar on one side of his jaw and he could chew only on the other side. The molars on his chewing side were worn away to nearly nothing, while the other two were untouched. I saw pictures of him before he died; he was gaunt and emaciated. Postmortem examinations revealed no disease other than the abscess. He had probably died of starvation.

Very few elephants live out their full lifespan. The single greatest cause of death is killing by man, whether it be poaching, hunting, or culling. Natural mortality results from a variety of causes. As I have shown, mortality can be high among young calves in drought years. Again, this type of mortality is linked to nutrition. Once a calf becomes about five years old its chances of survival are much higher. There then seems to be a second small rise in mortality around the age of independence for males. We do not know how they die, but it seems to be a time of vulnerability for them. They may be more likely to be speared or poached, but in Amboseli we do not have direct evidence that this is occurring, only that young males are dying at a higher rate than would be expected. After this age natural mortality levels out to about 3 percent per year for adults.

Elephants may not have a graveyard but they seem to have some concept of death. It is probably the single strangest thing about them. Unlike other animals, elephants recognize one of their own carcasses or skeletons. Although they pay no attention to the remains of other species, they always react to the body of a dead elephant. I have been with elephant families many times when this has happened. When they come upon an elephant carcass they stop and become quiet and yet tense in a different way from anything I have seen in other situations. First they reach their trunks toward the body to smell it, and then they approach slowly and cautiously and begin to touch the bones, sometimes lifting them and turning them with their feet and trunks. They seem particularly interested in the head and tusks. They run their trunk tips along the tusks and lower jaw and feel in all the crevices and hollows in the skull. I would guess they are trying to recognize the individual.

On one occasion I came upon the carcass of a young female who had been ill for many weeks. Just as I found her, the EB family, led by Echo, came into the same clearing. They stopped, became tense and very quiet, and then nervously approached. They smelled and felt the carcass and began to kick at the ground around it, digging up the dirt and putting it on the body. A few others broke off branches and palm fronds and brought them back and placed them on the carcass. At that point the warden circled overhead and dived down in his plane to guide the rangers on the ground to the dead elephant so that they could recover the tusks. The EBs were frightened by the plane and ran off. I think if they had not been disturbed they would have nearly buried the body.

Even bare, bleached old elephant bones will stop a group if they have not seen them before. It is so predictable that filmmakers have been able to get shots of elephants inspecting skeletons by bringing the bones from one place and putting them in a new spot near an elephant pathway or a water hole. Inevitably the living elephants will feel and move the bones around, sometimes picking them up and carrying them away for quite some distance before dropping them. It is a haunting and touching sight and I have no idea why they do it.

When an elephant dies in Amboseli we let it rot for a while and then collect the lower jaw for aging. The jaws are often still smelly so we put them out in the sun on the periphery of the camp. Without fail these hold a fascination to all passing elephants. Recently one of the big adult females in the population died of natural causes and we collected her jaw after a few weeks and brought it to the camp. Three days later her family happened to be passing through camp and when they smelled the jaw they detoured from their path to inspect it. One individual stayed for a long time after the others had gone, repeatedly feeling and stroking the jaw and turning it with his foot and trunk. He was the dead elephant's seven-year-old son, her youngest calf. I felt sure that he recognized it as his mother's.

I have often wondered if elephants experience anything akin to grief when a close family member dies. Certainly the death of an important animal such as the matriarch has a profound effect on the family. There can be total disintegration of the group for a long period afterward, with some families never resuming their former cohesiveness. I have seen females whose young calves have died looking lethargic for many days afterward, sometimes trailing along way behind their family. They had shown no signs of illness before the calves died so it may be that they were "depressed" in some elephantine way.

Just the other day a university group to which Joyce [Poole] was lecturing told her that they had heard that Amboseli's elephants were going to be culled. I am sure this is not true, but a kind of momentum begins to build as people see the aesthetically unappealing scene of dead and dying trees and think that "something" should be done. Killing the elephants seems the simplest and most direct solution, but only to people who have not watched individuals over 14 years; have not seen elephants greet one another with trumpets of joy; seen elephants, adults and calves alike, running and playing across an open pan in the moonlight; seen elephants trying to lift and hold up a stricken companion; seen a female stand by her dead baby for four days; or seen a seven-year-old calf gently fondle and stroke and feel the jaw of his dead mother.

Elephants are not so many rodents to be exterminated; they deserve something better than that and I am not afraid to say that ethics and morality should be essential considerations in our decisions for their future. Preserving habitats and trees and maintaining species diversity are important goals in conservation, but nothing will convince me that killing Slit Ear, Tallulah, and Tuskless and their families would be worth the achievement of those goals. The world would not be a better place if they were dead.

In the last two years I have realized that more than anything else, more than scientific discoveries or acceptance, what I care about and what I will fight for is the conservation, for as long as possible, not of just a certain number of elephants, but of the whole way of life of elephants. My priority, my love, my life are the Amboseli elephants, but I also want to ensure that there are elephants in other places that are able to exist in all the complexity and joy that elephants are capable of. It may be a lot to ask as we are about to enter the twenty-first century, but I think it is a goal worth striving for.

ELEPHANT TALK

Katherine Payne

Spend a day among elephants, and you will come away mystified. Sudden, silent, synchronous activities—a herd taking flight for no apparent or audible reason, a mass of scattered animals simultaneously raising ears and freezing in their tracks—such events demand explanation, but none is forthcoming.

Some capacity beyond memory and the five senses seems to inform elephants, silently and from a distance, of the whereabouts and activities of other elephants.

I stumbled on a possible clue to these mysteries during a visit to the Metro Washington Park Zoo in Portland, Oregon, in May 1984. While observing three Asian elephant mothers and their new calves, I repeatedly noticed a palpable throbbing in the air like distant thunder, yet all around me was silent.

Only later did a thought occur to me: As a young choir girl in Ithaca, New York, I used to stand next to the largest, deepest organ pipe in the church. When the organ blasted out the bass line in a Bach chorale, the whole chapel would throb, just as the elephant room did at the zoo. Suppose the elephants, like the organ pipe, were the source of the throbbing? Suppose elephants communicate with one another by means of calls too low-pitched for human beings to hear?

Half a year later the World Wildlife Fund, the Cornell Laboratory of Ornithology, and friends in the Cornell biology department helped me, Bill Langbauer, and Liz Thomas return to the zoo to test this idea. We recorded near the elephants for a month. Then we made electronic printouts . . . and saw that we had recorded 400 calls—three times as many as we'd heard.

Elephant sounds include barks, snorts, trumpets, roars, growls, and rumbles.* The rumbles are the key to our story, for although elephants can hear them well, human beings cannot. Many are below our range of hearing, in what is known as infrasound.

The universe is full of infrasound: It is generated by earthquakes, wind, thunder, volcanoes, and ocean storms—massive movements of earth, air, fire, and water. But very low frequency sound has not been thought to play much of a role in animals' lives. Intense infrasonic calls have been recorded from finback whales, but whether the calls are used in communication is not known.

Why would elephants use infrasound? It turns out that sound at the lowest frequencies of elephant rumbles (14 to 35 hertz, or cycles per second) has remarkable properties—it is little affected by passage through forests and grasslands. Does infrasound, then, let elephants communicate over long distances?

Suddenly we realized that if wild elephants use infrasound, this could explain some extraordinary observations on record about the social lives of these much loved, much studied animals. Iain and Oria Douglas-Hamilton, Cynthia Moss, and Joyce Poole, in their long-term studies of elephants in Tanzania and Kenya, had reported many examples of behavior coordinated by some unknown means over distances of two miles or more.

For instance, how do male and female elephants find one another for reproduction? This was a question raised by Joyce's doctoral research on the lives of males. Adult males and females live independently from one another, moving unpredictably over a great territory, with no fixed breeding season. A male elephant spends part of each year in a condition called musth, when he crisscrosses large areas in an endless, irritable search for females in breeding condition. Well may he feel irritable, for receptive females are a truly scarce resource. With two years of gestation followed by two more of nursing, a female is receptive only a few days every four or five years.

But they do find one another. In fact, as Joyce observed, the amazing thing is that the female is no sooner in estrus than she is surrounded by males that gather from all directions, some from far away. The dominant musth male then guards the female and mates with her every few hours until her period of receptivity ends.

How has the estrous female informed males from far and wide of her condition? The answer may lie in a unique sequence of intense, low-frequency calls that a receptive female makes during her estrus. This sequence always has the same form and thus technically may be called a song.

*Zoologist Judith Kay Berg of the San Diego Wild Animal Park reported similar categories of elephant vocalizations, some at very low frequencies, in a 1983 scientific paper.

Slow, deep rumbles, rising gently, become stronger and higher in pitch, then sink down again to silence at the end. The performance may continue for half an hour, and before the day is out the singing elephant will be surrounded by male elephants.

I first saw and heard these things as a guest of Joyce Poole in Kenya's Amboseli National Park in 1985 and 1986. In two and a half months we recorded more than a thousand calls from the elephants that Joyce and Cynthia Moss know so well. The calls that seemed likely to interest distant elephants were rich in infrasound and powerful enough to travel a mile or more.

But how were we to prove that elephants responded across such distances? How could we study communication when we couldn't perceive most of the calls? Bill Langbauer figured out a way to solve these problems.

The answer, for elephants, seems to lie in lives of perpetual motion. Elephants coming to a water hole often arrive at a dead run, not because anything scary is behind them, but simply because water is, at last, in front.

Etosha elephants are leaner than the elephants in East Africa, there is more competition at water holes, and calf mortality is higher, probably because of the distances between water and food. We figured that if elephants had the ability to communicate over long distances, they would be particularly likely to use it in places like Etosha, where news about how distant elephants were faring might reduce the likelihood of bad decisions and death from exhaustion, predation, or dehydration.

From the platform of our observation tower 20 feet above ground we had a good view of an area of roughly half a square mile. An array of four widely spaced microphones enabled us to pinpoint elephant calls, whether or not we ourselves could hear them. Video recordings revealed which elephants were in the correct places to have made the sounds and documented the subtle interactions of elephants at a watering area.

Once again we marveled at elephants' "silent" mass coordination. Often it took the form of simultaneous arrival of several groups from different directions, after days in which we had seen no elephants at all. Sometimes it took the form of sudden group flights, when a moment before all had seemed peaceful and individuals had appeared relaxed. Sometimes we observed sudden synchronous freezing—two to a hundred individuals suddenly holding still in their tracks, as if a motion-picture frame had stuck in the projector. Other times there was sudden simultaneous calling by several adult females, which we would understand only later when a new group arrived and was greeted with excitement by others already present at the water.

Although males came to the water as often as females, the great majority of our recorded calls were made by females. A picture began to form in my mind of a communication system in which males and females played quite different roles.

Female behavior is richly illustrated by their calls—mothers, calves, and baby-sitting sisters settling questions of when to nurse or how far to wander, of family groups keeping track of one another, and so forth. Yet females also respond to distant happenings. How do they achieve the silence necessary for hearing faint, distant signals? "Freezing," which insures synchronous periods of listening, seems to solve this problem.

Adult males are less vocal than females, yet very responsive to female activities. Probably the noisiness of female groups enables males to learn much about the latter's location and sexual state simply by listening.

Are infrasonic calls, then, one of the means by which elephants normally coordinate their behavior over long distances?

The evidence that infrasound plays a crucial role in the lives of elephants is building up. Our experiments suggest that each elephant lives in a network of communication in which the animal-to-animal distance is potentially at least two and a half miles. It seems likely that this network has something to do with the ability of elephants to maintain an elaborate hierarchical society even in an environment as sparse as Etosha.

What would happen to a population too dispersed to use the long-distance communicative abilities that elephants appear to be endowed with? This question was in my mind two years ago when, as a guest of friends from the World Wildlife Fund, I was able to go into one of the sparsest environments in the world and see elephants living there.

A hundred miles west of Etosha along the South Atlantic is a strip of shifting sand dunes and gravel plains called the Skeleton Coast Park. My old friends, filmmakers Des and Jen Bartlett, have lived, filmed, and studied animal life there for the past five years. Amazingly, they told me, elephants inhabit the area, although rain almost never falls and there is little surface water except during the rare occasions when water from rain in the mountains far inland bursts through the dunes and creates a river flowing toward the sea.

However, succulent bushes in dry riverbeds reveal that water is not far beneath the surface. The desert elephants eat leaves and branches from these bushes. To get from browsing areas to drinkable water, they may walk as far as 30 miles in a stretch. They sometimes go four days between drinks.

Pioneer conservationist Garth Owen-Smith took us to see some of the elephants' sources of drinking water. Words fail to describe those barren, empty distances, the intense heat, the unquenchable thirst, or the longing I felt for signs of life. Each time we reached water, I wondered how any animal that had found it could ever leave. But there was not enough vegetation near water to feed a herd of elephants for more than a few hours.

In a dry riverbed just outside the park we came to a dozen or so wells dug by the elephants, each just wider than an elephant's trunk. Reflections showed water about a foot down. All around were animal tracks.

Years ago, we learned, the largest population of elephants in the coastal desert had lived nearby in the Hoarusib Valley. There, too, in the bed of a tributary, were wells that supplied not only the elephants but also many other wild animals with water. When water in the wells was too low for little elephants to reach, adults would fill their trunks and pour the contents into the calves' mouths.

But by 1982 the elephants had all but vanished. Many left when a drought harsh even for the Skeleton Coast struck the region, but piles of bones revealed that poachers also took a toll. With the elephants disappeared all traces of their wells.

So it had been a wonderful surprise for Garth when, one day four years later, he happened upon a family of ten elephants in the Hoarusib area. They walked up the valley where the old wells had been, dug new holes in the same place, drank, and left. After this, footprints of other animals leading from all directions to the wells revealed that it had again become a place of life.

These were the sort of tales we heard about the desert elephants. We heard no tales of magically synchronized movements among separated groups. I believe, in fact, that the distances between groups are usually too great for their calls to reach.

The remarkable—almost unbelievable—thing about the desert elephants is their endurance through the dry months. They must be guided not by the voices of distant relatives but by their own heritage, which we may think of as the voices of their ancestors. The experience of many generations is what leads these elephants over gravel plains and rocky mountains, across dunes and down dry riverbeds to the few sources of life-giving water in a vast and hostile desert.

If the Skeleton Coast lineage dies out, it seems unlikely that other elephants lacking this heritage could ever repopulate the area. I suspect, rather, that the present elephants' tracks and their wells would be filled in with windblown sand, and that would be that.

Thus it is terrible to learn that in the past two decades the desert elephant population has declined from several hundred to a few dozen, badly reduced by ivory poachers. The elephants' tusks were torn out, sold to middlemen, and illegally shipped to Japan, China, Europe, and America.

By the time the tusks reached their final destinations, all the experience of the living elephants had gone out of them—the dust and the musth, the smells and sounds of fighting and mating, the long, urgent songs of fertile females, and the stillness of the night as elephants froze in their tracks to listen.

Gone, too, the long dry treks over dunes and gravel plains, guided by matriarchs with generations of memory in their heads. Gone the finding, the digging, the drinking from their own fresh wells. Gone the memories of heat and the vastness of the barren land—the patience. And the river breaking through.

All of this vanished with several hundred desert elephants. Nothing is left of them but little white carvings in ladies' jewel boxes, smelling faintly of French perfume.

THE CASE FOR THE PERSONHOOD OF GORILLAS

Francine Patterson and Wendy Gordon

We present this individual for your consideration:
She communicates in sign language, using a vocabulary of over 1,000 words. She also understands spoken English, and often carries on 'bilingual' conversations, responding in sign to questions asked in English. She is learning the letters of the alphabet, and can read some printed words, including her own name. She has achieved scores between 85 and 95 on the Stanford-Binet Intelligence Test.

She demonstrates a clear self-awareness by engaging in self-directed behaviours in front of a mirror, such as making faces or examining her teeth, and by her appropriate use of self-descriptive language. She lies to avoid the consequences of her own misbehaviour, and anticipates others' responses to her actions. She engages in imaginary play, both alone and with others. She has produced paintings and drawings which are representational. She remembers and can talk about past events in her life. She understands and has used appropriately time-related words like 'before', 'after', 'later', and 'yesterday'.

She laughs at her own jokes and those of others. She cries when hurt or left alone, screams when frightened or angered. She talks about her feelings, using words like 'happy', 'sad', 'afraid', 'enjoy', 'eager', 'frustrate', 'mad', and, quite frequently, 'love'. She grieves for those she has lost—a favourite cat who has died, a friend who has gone away. She can talk about what happens when one dies, but she becomes fidgety and uncomfortable when asked to discuss her own death or the death of her companions. She displays a wonderful gentleness with kittens and other small animals. She has even expressed empathy for others seen only in pictures.

Does this individual have a claim to basic moral rights? It is hard to imagine any reasonable argument that would deny her these rights based on the description above. She is self-aware, intelligent, emotional, communicative, has memories and purposes of her own, and is certainly able to suffer deeply. There is no reason to change our assessment of her moral status if I add one more piece of information: namely that she is not a member of the human species. The person I have described—and she is nothing less than a person to those who are acquainted with her—is Koko, a twenty-year-old lowland gorilla.

For almost twenty years, Koko has been living and learning in a language environment that includes American Sign Language (ASL) and spoken English. Koko combines her working vocabulary of over 500 signs into statements averaging three to six signs in length. Her emitted vocabulary—those signs she has used correctly on one or more occasions—is about 1,000. Her receptive vocabulary in English is several times that number of words.

Koko is not alone in her linguistic accomplishments. Her multispecies 'family' includes Michael, a twenty-three-year-old male gorilla. Although he was not introduced to sign language until the age of three and a half, he has used over 400 different signs. Both gorillas initiate the majority of their conversations with humans and combine their vocabularies in creative and original sign utterances to describe their environment, feelings, desires, and even what may be their past histories. They also sign to themselves and to each other, using human language to supplement their own natural communicative gestures and vocalisations. Tests have shown that the gorillas understand spoken English as well as they understand sign.

Sign language has become such an integral part of their daily lives that Koko and Michael are more familiar with the language than are some of their human companions. Both gorillas have been known to sign slowly and repeat signs when conversing with a human who has limited signing skills. They also attempt to teach as they have been taught. For example, one day Michael had been repeatedly signing 'CHASE' (hitting two fisted hands together) but was getting no response from his companion, who did not know this sign. He finally took her hands and hit them together and then gave her a push to get her moving. Similarly, Koko has often been observed moulding the hands of her dolls into signs.

Many of those who would defend the traditional barrier between *Homo sapiens* and all other species cling to language as the primary difference between humans and other animals. As apes have threatened this last claim to human uniqueness, it has become more apparent that there is no clear agreement as to the definition of language. Many human beings—including all infants, severely mentally impaired people, and some educationally deprived deaf adults of normal intelligence—fail to meet the criteria for 'having language' according to any definition. The ability to use language may not be a valid test for determining whether an individual has rights. But the existence of even basic language skills does provide further evidence of a consciousness which deserves consideration.

Conversations with gorillas resemble those with young children and in many cases need interpretation based on context and past use of the signs in question. Alternative interpretations of gorilla utterances are often possible. And even if the gorillas' use of signs does not meet a particular definition of language, studying that use can give us a unique perspective from which to understand more directly their physical and psychological requirements. By agreeing on a common vocabulary of signs we establish two-way communication between humans and gorillas. We can learn as much from what they say as we can by evaluating how they say it.

Our approach has been to give Koko and Michael vocabulary instruction but no direct teaching of any other language skill. Most of the signs were learned either through the moulding of the gorillas' hands into signs or through imitation. But Koko and Michael have both created signs and used the language in diverse ways not explicitly taught. In a very real sense, the study has involved the mapping of skills, rather then the teaching of skills.

The gorillas have taken the basic building block of conversation (signs) and, on their own, added new meaning through modulation, a grammatical process similar to inflection in spoken language. A change in pitch or loudness of the voice, or the addition (or substitution) of sounds, can alter the meaning of a spoken word. In sign language this is accomplished through changes in motion, hand location, hand configuration, facial expression, and body posture. The sign BAD, for instance, can be made to mean 'very bad' by enlarging the signing space, increasing the speed and tension of the hand, and exaggerating facial expression. Koko, like human signers, has exploited this feature of sign language to exaggerate a point, as when she signed THIRSTY from the top of her head to her stomach, instead of down her throat.

A conversation with Koko that involved this kind of creativity with the sign ROTTEN has been documented on film. Koko demonstrated the standard form of the sign in an exchange of insults after her companion called her a STINKER. Koko then inflected the sign by using two hands (perhaps meaning 'really rotten') and in the same sequence, brought the sign off her nose toward her companion, conveying the idea 'you're really rotten'. Koko's use of ROTTEN in this conversation also demonstrates her grasp of the connotation of a word rather than its denotation or concrete or specific meaning.

Another way Koko and Michael have created novel meanings for basic vocabulary signs is through an unusual coining process in which they employ signs whose spoken equivalents match or approximate the sounds of English words for which no signs have been modelled. For example, Koko uses a modulated *knock* sign to mean 'obnoxious'. This indicates that she knows:

1. That the sign KNOCK is associated with the spoken word 'knock'.
2. That 'knock' sounds like the spoken word 'obnoxious'.
3. That the sign KNOCK can therefore be applied semantically to mean something or someone obnoxious.

When signs have been repeatedly demonstrated that are difficult or impossible for Koko to form, her solution has often been to make substitutions based on the sound of the corresponding English word: KNEE for 'need', RED for 'thread', LEMON for 'eleven', and BIRD for 'word'.

The gorillas also communicate new meanings by making up their own entirely new signs.

An analysis of the 876 signs emitted by Koko during the first ten years of the project revealed that fifty-four signs, 6 per cent of her total emitted vocabulary, were her own inventions. Another 2 per cent (fifteen signs) were compounded by Koko from signs she was taught.

These invented signs indicate that the gorillas, like human children, take initiative with language by making up new words and by giving new meanings to old words. On the next level, there is evidence that Koko and Michael can generate novel names by combining two or more familiar words. For instance, Koko signed 'BOTTLE MATCH' to refer to a cigarette lighter, 'WHITE TIGER' for a zebra, and 'EYE HAT' for a mask. Michael has generated similar combinations, such as 'ORANGE FLOWER SAUCE' for nectarine yogurt and 'BEAN BALL' for peas. Other examples in the samples of the gorillas' signing are 'ELEPHANT BABY' for a Pinocchio doll and 'BOTTLE NECKLACE' for a six-pack soda can holder. Critics have commented that such phrases are merely the pairing of two separate aspects of what is present. Many of the above examples, however, cannot be explained in this way—when Koko signed 'BOTTLE MATCH', neither a bottle nor a match was present.

The gorillas have applied such new descriptive terms to themselves as well as to novel objects. When angered, Koko has labelled herself a 'RED MAD GORILLA'. Once, when she had been drinking water through a thick rubber straw from a pan on the floor after repeatedly asking her companion for drinks of juice which were not forthcoming, she referred to herself as a 'SAD ELEPHANT'.

Another creative aspect of the gorillas' language behaviour is humour. Humour, like metaphor, requires a capacity to depart from what is strictly correct, normal, or expected. For example, when asked to demonstrate her invented sign for STETHOSCOPE for the camera, Koko did it on her eyes instead of on her ears.

We have often noticed Koko giving an audible chuckling sound at the result of her own and her companions' discrepant statements or actions. She discovered that when she blew bugs on her companions, a predictable shrieking and jumping response could be elicited. Originally, she laughed at this outcome, but now she chuckles in anticipation of the prank as well. Accidents and unexpected actions by others can also cause Koko to laugh. Chuckles were evoked, for instance, by a research assistant accidentally sitting down on a sandwich and by another playfully pretending to feed sweets to a toy alligator.

In stark contrast to the gorillas' ability to express humour is their ability to communicate their thoughts and feelings about death. When Koko was seven, one of her teachers asked, 'When do gorillas die?' and she signed, 'TROUBLE, OLD.' The teacher also asked, 'Where do gorillas go when they die?' and Koko replied, 'COMFORTABLE HOLE BYE.' When asked, 'How do gorillas feel when they die—happy, sad, afraid?' she signed, 'SLEEP'. Koko's reference to holes in the context of death has been consistent and is puzzling since no one has ever talked to her about burial, nor demonstrated the activity. That there may be an instinctive basis for this is indicated by an observation at the Woodland Park Zoo in Seattle, Washington. The gorillas there came upon a dead crow in their new outdoor enclosure, and one dug a hole, flicked the crow in, and covered it with dirt.

In December of 1984 a tragic accident indicated the extent to which gorillas may grieve over the death of their loved ones. Koko's favourite kitten, All Ball, slipped out of the door and was killed by a speeding car. Koko cried shortly after she was told of his death. Three days later, when asked, 'Do you want to talk about your kitty?' Koko signed, 'CRY'. 'What happened to your kitty?' Koko answered, 'SLEEP CAT'. When she saw a picture of a cat who looked very much like All Ball, Koko pointed to the picture and signed, 'CRY, SAD, FROWN'. Her grief was not soon forgotten.

17 March 1985, with Francine Patterson
F: How did you feel when you lost Ball?
K: WANT.
F: How did you feel when you lost him?
K: OPEN TROUBLE VISIT SORRY.
F: When he died, remember when Ball died, how did you feel?
K: RED RED RED BAD SORRY KOKO-LOVE GOOD.

Arthur Caplan argues that animal interests and human interests should not be counted equally, claiming that nonhuman animals lack certain traits that make a moral difference. He uses the following example to illustrate his point:

> If you kill the baby of a baboon the mother may spend many weeks looking for her baby. This behaviour soon passes and the baboon will go on to resume her normal life. But if you kill the baby of a human being the mother will spend the rest of her life grieving over the loss of her baby. Hardly a day will go by when the mother does not think about and grieve over the loss of her baby.

But in this example the comparison is between outward behaviour in the case of the baboon mother, and a private mental state in the case of the human mother. In most such cases, the human mother also resumes her normal life: returning to her workplace, caring for her other children, going about her daily activities as before. Her grief is not necessarily apparent to the casual observer. Because the baboon mother cannot (or chooses not to) communicate *to us* her internal feelings about the death of her baby, it is assumed that it does not matter to her. While we cannot make any claims here about the emotional life of baboons, we have considerable evidence that Koko continues to mourn the loss of her adopted 'baby', All Ball, even years after his death.

19 March 1990
Koko comes across a picture of herself and All Ball in a photo album.
K: THAT BAD FROWN SORRY [emphatic] UNATTENTION.

Koko has also displayed a capacity for empathy in her comments about the emotional states of others:

24 September 1977
Koko is shown a picture of the albino gorilla Snowflake struggling against being bathed. Koko signs 'ME CRY THERE', indicating the picture.
3 November 1977, with companion Cindy Duggan
Koko looks at a picture of a horse with a bit in his mouth.
K: HORSE SAD.
CD: Why?
K: TEETH.

27 December 1977
Michael has been crying because he wants to be let out of his
room. Koko, in the next room, is asked how Michael feels.
K: FEEL SORRY OUT.

7 April 1986
Mitzi Phillips tells Koko about a problem that is making her
feel sad.
MP: What could I do to feel better?
K: CLOSE DRAPES . . . TUG-OF-WAR.
As Mitzi writes in the diary, Koko quietly comes up to her.
K: SAD? [Making the sign a question by raising her eyebrows
and leaning forward, a standard ASL question form.]
MP: I feel better now.
Koko smiles.

Michael frequently expresses himself creatively through sound play.
He uses various objects and parts of his body to produce a wide variety
of sounds and intricate rhythms. In creating his 'sound tools' he experiments with different materials in his environment. In addition to rhythmic drumming and tapping, for example, he sometimes strums a rope or
fabric strip held taut between his feet and his mouth. He made a rattle by
filling a PVC pipe end with hard nutshells and shaking it vigorously with
his hand covering the open end. Then he filled his mouth with the nutshells and shook them around, making a contrasting 'wet' rattling sound.

Koko regularly expresses her creativity through fantasy play, alone
or with her companions. Often this play involves her plastic reptile toys
and centres on their tendency to 'bite'.

13 October 1988, with Mitzi Phillips
Koko is lying down with one of her toy alligators. She looks at
it and signs 'TEETH'. She examines its mouth. She kisses it, puts
two alligators together as if to make them kiss each other, then
gives them a three-way kiss. She puts her hand into the toy's
mouth, then pulls it out and shakes her hand.
MP: Oh, did it bite you?
K: BITE.
MP: Oh, no! Does it hurt?
Koko kisses her finger.
MP: May I see that bad alligator?
Koko gives it to Mitzi. Mitzi 'asks' the alligator why it bit
Koko and pretends to listen to its answer, then hands it back
to Koko. Koko kisses the toy again and again.

K: ALLIGATOR. GORILLA. BITE. GORILLA NUT NUT NUT. STOM-
ACH TOILET.

They are intelligent and emotional, they express themselves creatively through language, art, music, and fantasy play; but are gorillas self-aware? Once considered unique to human beings, self-awareness is an elusive concept. Its many definitions are both varied and vague, although almost everyone has some notion of what it means. Through their signing, Koko and Michael have shown a number of generally accepted cognitive correlates of self-awareness, including the use of personal pronouns, references to their own internal and emotional states, humour, deception, and embarrassment.

Human children begin by using personal pronouns and self-referents in their speech at about the same time that they begin to recognise themselves in mirrors. Similarly, at the same age that she began to exhibit self-directed behaviours in front of a mirror, Koko acquired the signs for 'me', 'mine', 'myself', 'you', and proper nouns, including 'Koko'. The gorillas have also demonstrated self-awareness in their ability to describe themselves as the same as or different from others. For example, research assistant Maureen Sheehan questioned Koko about the differences between gorillas and humans:

MS: What's the difference between you and me?
K: HEAD.
MS: And how are our heads different?
Koko beats on her head with her open hands quite hard, harder than a human would ever do.
MS: What else is different between us?
Koko moves her hand up to her stomach, a gesture resembling BLANKET.
MS: Do you mean something about your stomach?
K: STOMACH GOOD THAT.
MS: Oh, but what were you saying about blanket, different?
Koko moves her hands up and down her torso, then pulls the hair on her belly. Maureen interprets these new gestures as meaning 'body hair'.
MS: Now can you name something the same?
K: EYE.
MS: Yes, that's right, we both have eyes.
K: LOVE.

Michael was once asked a related question: 'What makes you different from your cat?' He responded, 'GORILLA ME MIKE'.

Self-awareness is also shown by the gorillas when they talk about themselves in situations removed in space or time from the current one. This capacity for displacement is clearly and repeatedly demonstrated in conversations such as the following:

10 July 1984, with Francine Patterson, six days after Koko's birthday
F: What happened on your birthday?
K: SLEEP EAT.
F: Didn't something special happen on your birthday?
K: OLD GORILLA.
F: Yes, you're thirteen years old and big.

Michael began at an early age to tell stories about past events. In 1979, when the project was still located on the Stanford University campus, the gorillas witnessed a violent, screaming argument between a red-haired woman and a research assistant at a nearby laboratory building. The woman apparently hit the assistant and had to be subdued at gunpoint by the police. When Michael's companion Barbara Weller arrived, knowing nothing of the incident, she found him at the window . . .

M: GIRL.
Michael stares out of the window for a few more minutes.
M: KNOW HIT-IN-MOUTH.
B: Know hit-in-mouth?
M: HIT-IN-MOUTH RED BITE.
B: Why are you signing hit-in-mouth?
M: KNOW.
B: Who do you want to hit-in-mouth?
M: HAIR GIRL RED.
B: What? Red hair girl?
M: LIP [The gorillas use LIP to mean 'woman'.]
B: Lip?
M: LIP LIP LIP BIG-TROUBLE.

Michael Lewis suggests that there are certain emotional states that only the self-aware can have. One such state is embarrassment. In order to be embarrassed animals must be capable of reflecting on their own behaviour and comparing it to standards set by society or themselves. Koko seems embarrassed when her companions notice that she is signing to herself, especially when the signing involves her dolls. One incident recorded when Koko was five years old provides an example. Her companion observed her creating what appeared to be an imaginary social situation between two gorilla dolls. She signed, 'BAD, BAD' while looking at one doll, and 'KISS' while looking at the other. Next, she signed, 'CHASE, TICKLE', hit the two dolls together, and then wrestled with them and signed, 'GOOD GORILLA, GOOD GOOD'. At this point she noticed that she was being watched and abruptly put the dolls down.

There is no reason to think that Koko and Michael are significantly different from other gorillas in their inherent linguistic capacities, self-awareness, or other mental abilities. They are two individuals selected more or less at random from the total population of gorillas, and the circumstances of their first few years were very different. So it is fair to assume that they are representative of their species. Nor is there reason to consider them essentially different from other gorillas because of their experience with human language. Indeed, a few zoo gorillas who have been exposed informally to sign language have shown that they, too, can learn signs, even later in life and without intensive teaching. By teaching sign language to Koko and Michael we have not imposed an artificial system on them, but rather have built upon their existing system to provide a jointly understood vocabulary for mutual exchange.

In December 1991 a third gorilla joined Koko and Michael. Ndume, a male born at the Cincinnati Zoo in 1981, arrived on loan as a potential mate for Koko. Ndume has not been instructed in sign language, but he uses natural gorilla gestures, postures, and facial expressions to communicate with both gorillas and humans. For example, Ndume regularly uses an arm-shaking gesture similar to the sign 'PLAY' to invite his caregivers to play. Ndume and Koko have been observed simultaneously using the gesture 'AWAY' toward each other. And Ndume has on several occasions spontaneously made the sign 'DRINK' in the context of being given a drink, a sign he apparently learned by observation without any direct instruction.

Perhaps our most interesting findings relate to how astonishingly like us gorillas are—or how like them we are.

Through what they have taught us about gorillas, Koko and Michael are helping to change the way we view the world. They force us to re-examine the ways we think about other animals. With an emotional and expressive range far greater than previously believed, they have revealed a lively and sure awareness of themselves as individuals. Asked to categorise herself, Koko declared 'FINE ANIMAL GORILLA'. Indeed. Fine animal-persons, gorillas.

LIFE AMONG THE WHALES

Alexandra Morton

I sat next to the aquarium tank in the warm California night in 1978 and watched the two killer whales below me. The loudspeaker on the wall reverberated with a plaintive call that I had heard again and again from the female. Two days before, following the death of her third calf, Corky had begun to call every few seconds. Her cry was starting to sound hoarse and raspy. When her dead calf was winched from the tank, Corky had thrashed against the concrete-and-glass walls, but now she lay motionless on the bottom, rising only to breathe. Occasionally her mate called out in response, but she ignored him, and her pitiful cries continued.

Corky had lost her calf to starvation. Although she was extremely attentive to her baby, she didn't know how to nurse it. The calf had chirped endlessly for nine days as its mother's milk flowed uselessly into the water. Corky had been taken from the wild, removed from her mother and the rest of her family pod when she was very young, and had never learned how to nurse.

I heard the male, Orky, vocalize again, and this time Corky answered him. She rose to the surface and exhaled beside him, and then the pair dove together. Soon, I heard them calling back and forth. As they undulated gracefully, Corky's pectoral fin rested lightly against Orky's side. I was deeply touched by the comfort Corky had finally found in her mate.

Exhausted from my 72-hour vigil, I decided that I could no longer study killer whales in captivity. I had already spent several years researching cetacean communication, first with bottle-nosed dolphins, then with Corky and Orky at Marineland in Los Angeles. I longed to understand the complex repertoire of orca vocalizations, and now I felt it was time for me to join killer whales in their natural environment. There was nothing more than tragedy to observe in captive whales.

Killer whales, or orcas, are found in all oceans and major seas at any time of year. Next to humans, they are the most widely distributed species of mammals on Earth. They are formidable predators of both fish and marine mammals. The larger males can weigh 11 tons, attain lengths of up to 32 feet and swim at speeds as great as 20 knots (23 miles per hour). They use echolocation to find and track their prey, emitting a constant stream of "clicks" that bounce back from surrounding objects and give the whales a mental sense of what lies in the murky waters ahead. They communicate with other orcas by using whistles and various calls.

Canadian researcher John Ford discovered that each killer whale pod has a slightly different language or dialect. I had learned the sounds and cadences of Corky's pod dialect, and I felt that if I could find her family in the wild I could seek relationships between what the whales were doing and saying.

I quit my job, packed my belongings into my pickup and headed north. Rolling off the tiny ferry at Alert Bay, a Vancouver Island fishing village on the Johnstone Strait, the first thing I saw, staring at me with unblinking eyes, was a totem pole crowned by a killer whale motif.

I unfurled my Zodiac inflatable boat on the beach, mounted the engine, stowed my assorted gear and paddled to the closest wharf. I had arranged for Paul Spong, a killer whale researcher, to guide me to his small research facility on a nearby island. In the northern twilight the sky turned dark red, and my stomach knotted in apprehension as I waited for him. Where would I go if he didn't come, and how would I ever find Corky's family pod?

Across the water I spotted silver plumes erupting from the brilliantly colored surface; proud, straight black fins emerged. There they were, wild orcas. Adrenaline rushed through my body, but I clung to the dock. I knew nothing of these waters or this northern wilderness. But the sight of the whales so close to me was magnetic. With my eyes riveted to their rippling flukeprints, I timidly pushed off from the wharf.

In Johnstone Strait I was no longer peering down at whales in a tank, I was among them. They swirled the water beneath me and rose beside me. I was the visitor; they were at home. I lowered my hydrophone, an underwater microphone, placed the headset over my ears and pressed the "record" button. Echoing in the vastness of the deep, numbing water were the familiar calls of Corky's dialect. As I watched calves nuzzle their mothers and splash in the red-gold waters, I knew then that I belonged there. I only wished Corky could be with her family, too.

Shortly, Spong appeared and led the way to his research station, where I set up camp. The summer flashed by in a blur—whales passing under my boat, their breath fogging my camera lens and their calls filling my head. I also learned about engine breakdown, drying wet bedding in a northern rain forest and the incompatibility of electronic equipment and salt water. But I was able to record hours of tape of Corky's pod.

I spent my first two summers in Canada living in a big canvas tent. I arrived with a stack of blank tapes, hoping to fill them with whale sounds. I would get up very early and head out in the 12-foot Zodiac to find whales. Days would go by without my seeing orcas, and I would drift, listening and watching for them. On the days that I found whales I would record their calls as well as verbal notes about their behavior. Stormy days were welcome; I could catch up on sleep.

My initial research suggested that the primary function of killer whale communication is to keep all pod members in touch and traveling in the same direction in the murky green waters off British Columbia. The calls also appeared to inform the group about what was going on; whales made different sounds when foraging or at play. Most dramatic was the call used during a change of direction: the same sound Orky had made to rouse his grieving mate. I roughly interpreted this special call as "swim with me, in this direction." But I had no explanation for why the whales produced so many different sounds or why some calls seemed random and unconnected to any specific behavior. Obviously there was a great deal going on that I knew nothing about.

GREETING DAWN WITH A FLICK OF THE TONGUE

Before going to Canada I made some observations that suggested complex social behaviors no one else had described. Every morning that I'd spent with captives Corky and Orky I saw them select a spot along the tank wall in the predawn light and gently squirt water at it. Then they opened their mouths and flicked their tongues at the chosen spot. When the sun appeared, the first beams of light invariably hit the exact spot the whales had marked. As the seasons changed, the spot moved, but the whales always knew where it was. In the early morning sunlight the whales played boisterously, chasing each other, spiraling nose-to-tail in tight circles and creating huge swells that sloshed out of the pool. If a cloud passed, the activity stopped until the sunlight reappeared. Because of the position of their tank they didn't respond to sunsets, but once during a thunderstorm, I saw Orky flick his tongue at lightning and make a low groaning sound.

Corky and Orky also engaged in precisely synchronized forms of play. The most intricate took weeks to perfect. Just after dawn, when no trainers were around, they would lie side-by-side, their tails resting on the trainer's platform while each held a pectoral fin aloft. At first they had timing problems and sometimes held the wrong fin up or collided when trying to flip their tails out. When the performance went smoothly they stopped doing it. The fun was apparently in learning.

In Canada I watched Corky's pod perform similar highly synchro-nized behaviors and energetic play at day's end. I saw two bulls float head-to-tail, oriented toward the pink blaze of the setting sun, and hold their pectorals aloft in a kind of cetacean salute. Another evening I saw four whales "spyhop"—poking their heads vertically above the water to take a look around—side by side, in perfect unison, facing the sinking sun.

These ritual-like behaviors hint at a rich, vibrant social core. The need to respond to the sunrise was so strong in Corky and Orky that 12 years in a tank had not thwarted the behavior. It is clear that orcas re-spond to what is going on above, as well as below, the water.

During the early years I spent bobbing among killer whale fins, Corky's pod became tolerant of my presence, and slowly I became famil-iar with each of the individual personalities.

Killer whales are a matriarchal society, and the grande dame of Corky's extended family was named A9. (Alpha-numeric code names make it easier to track the whales by computer.) Killer whales mature at a rate comparable to our own, sexual maturity beginning in the early teens, full maturity in the early 20s. Females have a life expectancy of up to 80 years in the wild, bulls to about 60 years.

The identity of Corky's mother, A23, was known because at the time of Corky's capture the calf was swimming tightly against her mother's side. All calves exhibit this behavior, or swim just behind their mother's dorsal fin, except when playing with other youngsters. Several photo-graphs from the 1969 capture show mother and daughter in their last hours together. When I found the pod, she was with two more-recent off-spring. She swam with another female, probably a sibling, whose female calf was about the same age as Corky when she had been taken. The calf was dubbed "Sharky" because of her unusually sharklike dorsal fin.

Sharky was an exceptionally outgoing calf, and she often approached my boat with her year-old brother in tow. She seemed curious about my actions. As I lowered the hydrophone she would come as close as she dared and then wriggle off in excitement. If I put my bare hands into the bone-chilling water I could feel her echolocation clicks against my skin as she tried to make sense of this strange creature.

Years later, when Sharky suddenly lost interest in me, her shift in be-havior was so dramatic that I was worried. The explanation came 18 months later when, at the age of 14, Sharky gave birth to a daughter, who was named Charlotte. Sharky no longer swam at her mother's side but re-mained in the pod, with Charlotte tucked behind her dorsal fin.

Newborn orcas are very well developed at birth. Within the womb the little whale is curled sideways, its nose against its tail. The calf emerges with deep creases running vertically from the base of the dorsal fin to its belly, due to the way it was curled. At birth the tail lies folded together like resting butterfly wings, and the tiny dorsal fin is flopped to one side. Within the first 20 minutes of life the fins stiffen, giving the whale its proper shape and the ability to swim. However, a newborn is weak and requires help swimming. The mother tows her baby, which rides in her current, between her dorsal fin and tail, behind the widest point of her body.

Orca pods stay together for life and are composed of up to four generations of related females and their offspring. The young calves grow up in the company of their brothers and uncles, but not their fathers. Whenever I encountered A9, she was usually flanked by two magnificent sons who remained at her side until her death in 1991. After she died, the two no longer traveled with their pod but lingered all winter within a few miles of the spot where they had last seen their mother alive. Then they vanished. As each family returned the following spring, I searched for the brothers' distinctive dorsal fins without success. I thought that they, too, had died, a common occurrence with orphaned bulls.

A WELCOME SUMMER REUNION

During July and August huge numbers of spawning salmon funnel through Johnstone Strait en route to their birth streams. This annual concentration of fish draws orca pods from throughout the region for a community gathering. Early arrivals often swim north and greet newcomers. Late in August 1992, while I traveled with one of these groups, A9's two sons suddenly appeared. As the escort whales surrounded the pair, goosebumps rose on my arms. I had truly missed them.

The oldest son, A5—also called Top Notch—carries one of the most massive fins on the coast. Despite his immense size I have always felt at ease near him. He was the first whale to approach me on the day I discovered Corky's pod.

I took pictures whenever I found new calves or teen males—who change in appearance rapidly as they grow—or any adults with which I was unfamiliar. These photographs helped Mike Bigg of Canada's Pacific Biological Station fill out his orca genealogies. Taking ID photographs of whales isn't easy; I had to photograph them from the left side for consistency (markings differ from side to side), up close and in perfect focus. Proximity is the key. I learned to follow a pod slowly and quietly.

Whenever the whales did focus their attention on me it was incredibly powerful. Once, when I was charged by a teenage male, I knew there was nothing to be gained by fleeing, so I maintained my speed and paralleled his course. He dove and, I was relieved to see, reappeared at his mother's side.

Another time he appeared out of nowhere, inches from the stern of my boat. I'd been floating for an hour and had seen no indication of whales nearby. Suddenly he exhaled in a mighty *WHOOSH* right beside me. I jumped and my heart slammed into my ribs. Though I was startled, his manner was nonthreatening. I took it to be a form of whale joke and laughed as he skimmed alongside, his eye swiveling up to get a look at me. I noticed that he was nearly the same length as the 22-foot boat I was using.

On a drizzly afternoon in the summer of 1980 a young Canadian filmmaker pulled alongside my boat. He invited me to a field studio he and his partner had built on Vancouver Island, complete with an underwater camera that was aimed at a submerged pebble beach. This beach is a playground for the whales, who seem to enjoy rubbing their sensitive skin on the rocks. The two cinematographers wanted to film my reaction to watching the objects of my study frolicking in their world.

THE MAN WITH AN ORCA ON HIS SHOULDER

I was skeptical and unimpressed: I was sure their camera would never work. When I arrived, the other partner was underwater attending to the equipment, so I waited on the beach. The lean figure in a wet suit that emerged smiling from the green water held my attention as he waded ashore and peeled off his insulating suit. He had a killer whale tattooed on his shoulder. "Who is this man?" I thought to myself.

The camera did work. I watched in amazement as Top Notch loomed into view, somersaulted and rubbed the entire length of his back on the pebbles. I had always longed to see what wild whales did beneath the surface. I was ecstatic.

Seven months later I married the cameraman, Robin Morton. His films on killer whales have been shown internationally and were used to protect the submerged beach as a provincial ecological reserve. We bought an old boat, the *Blue Fjord*, and dedicated ourselves to whales. At the end of the year our son, Jarret, was born. To make money we chartered out our boat for a variety of non-whale-watching uses and explored the coast looking for a site for basing a year-round study.

On a cool, wet October day in 1984 we took our Zodiac and followed Corky's pod as it entered a steep-sided, mainland inlet surrounded by snowcapped peaks. As we traveled farther into this mist-enshrouded place we felt as though we were entering another world. So it was quite unexpected when we spotted a small house floating on a raft of logs. It looked warm and inviting with smoke curling out of the chimney. Other houses lay beyond. Soaked and cold, we left the whales and turned to meet the people who lived there.

We were welcomed by an eclectic group of residents and realized this was the place we'd been looking for. We knew there were whales because they had led us there. There was a post office where mail arrived by seaplane, a place for us to moor the *Blue Fjord* and, incredibly, a cheerful one-room school. Jarret, who had spent more time among whales than children, was definitely ready for playmates of his own species. And so we began to moor the boat there and adopted Echo Bay as our home. Our community had no power, roads or waterworks. There were no telephone lines for staying in touch with our families. But for the three of us it was perfect. Jarret had playmates and the warm, cozy homes of new friends, while Robin and I had endless miles of coastline to explore.

Whale sightings were infrequent, but so little was known about the winter activities of killer whales that we saw something new with every encounter. When we came upon other boats we pulled alongside, inquired if they'd seen whales and asked them to call us on the marine radio if they spotted any. A few of them called in, and slowly we built a network of spotters. Today more than half of my sightings come from these people.

That winter we learned that because of the depleted food supply, the big pods of summer fragment into smaller "subpods" made up of one or two mothers—probably sisters—their offspring and their brothers. These groups are quieter and less boisterous as they forage in kelp beds and along the base of steep inlet cliffs.

The killer whales off British Columbia are split into three different social groups: residents, transients and offshores. The differences between residents and transients are remarkable. Residents eat fish, travel in larger associations, vocalize often, remain with their mothers for life and travel predictable routes. Transients eat mammals—seals, sea lions and other cetaceans. They are quiet and their pods are small—five or fewer. Their fins are more sharply pointed. They are difficult to locate because they travel unpredictable routes. Transients are difficult to study because they suddenly disappear, with years passing between sightings. The offshores have only recently been discovered, and we know little about them. They live in open waters and only occasionally come inshore.

As we followed Corky's pod—residents—during the winter months, we began to encounter more transients. They were wary of us when we tried to approach and reacted as though we were stalking them. Residents had become familiar with our photographing behavior, and basically ignored us. Transients, however, did not. Their uncanny ability to simply disappear, even in open water, I think was used in efforts to lose us. Sometimes they surfaced three or four times, heading one way, only to reappear minutes later, swimming far behind us and in the same direction. At other times they resurfaced and spouted behind islands or rock piles. We always presented ourselves as entirely predictable, and the pods we encountered most often soon relaxed enough for quick photography sessions.

Several months later I spotted a large group of transients from several pods. Robin had left on a film job, and Jarret was at a friend's, so I departed alone and followed the orcas. They were spread out, so I moved slowly from group to group, trying to identify them. We came to a large bay, and the lead whales stopped at the entrance and floated while the others caught up. All breathed rapidly for several minutes, saturating their blood with precious oxygen. Then they rolled into steep dives, showing their entire backs to their tails.

I started my stopwatch to time their dive. There was a sea lion haulout in the bay, so I positioned my boat, turned off the engine and dropped the hydrophone. I waited in a torrential downpour, counting the minutes. Resident pods dive for 2 to 3 minutes, so after 15 minutes I thought I had been given the slip.

Suddenly the still, dark water exploded ahead of me in a wall of white foam. The cliffs reverberated with gunshotlike sounds from the whales as they heaved air from their lungs. Over the hydrophone their eerie, haunting calls began. I quickly pressed the record button to catch these rarely heard vocalizations and raised my binoculars. I thought I knew the power of killer whales; I'd been traveling with them for five years. But as I witnessed bodies of bull sea lions weighing up to 2,000 pounds sailing through the air, the show of power was so great that it seemed unreal.

RECORDING THE SOUNDS OF UNDERWATER BATTLE

The whales tore through the water, spray flying off their dorsals as they tried to land blows with their heads or tails while managing to avoid the huge canines of their agile sea lion prey at the same time.

I was content to observe from a distance and record the sounds of underwater battle. I was pretty sure that if I moved within range one or more of the sea lions might try to escape the attack by jumping into my boat. Neither the craft nor I could have survived the landing.

Shortly, as the whales were consuming a hard-won meal, I sped home in the rain-soaked twilight, my mind replaying the sight of whales and sea lions suspended in midair, each fighting for the right to survive. I had valuable data and a new awareness of my physical fragility.

On September 16, 1986, my life unraveled. Robin was filming A9 underwater at the pebble beach. One way orcas threaten one another is to release a cloud of bubbles. Robin believed that they might be more accepting of his underwater presence if he weren't releasing air with each exhalation. That day he was using a rebreather system, scuba gear designed to emit no bubbles. He had used it before. But this time a tiny valve became clogged, reducing the flow of oxygen. Although everything seemed to be running normally, I sensed something was wrong when A9 approached him and then immediately departed. I jumped overboard but was unable to do anything more than retrieve his body. He had died among the whales he loved, a hundred yards from where I'd first watched him walk out of the sea.

My research faltered as I learned to deal with the rigors of wilderness living on my own. Every detail seemed to require monumental effort. I sold the Blue Fjord. The Zodiac was lost in a storm. Jarret and I moved into a small floathouse, and the first thing I had needed to learn was how to use a chain saw. If I couldn't get my own firewood I would be dependent on my neighbors. I thought of the chain saw as a monster machine, and at first I operated it only when the weather was calm enough to fly to a hospital for emergency care. Eventually I got the hang of it and found a certain pleasure in cutting and squirreling away my own wood. A visit from a bear that tried to force its way into my home convinced me to learn how to handle a rifle. The most difficult challenge was living as a single woman with a young child in a community of 30 people. My remedy was to embrace my research and remain firmly focused on my purpose for being there—the whales. Finally, I was accepted by my neighbors.

I spent the next seven years researching killer whales on my own from my new 22-foot vessel, the Blackfish Sound. The boat allowed me to follow whales for days at a time; Jarret and I could anchor wherever the evening found us or tie up to the floating homes of friends. My son developed into a capable deckhand. He often steers, and his steady hands make him a natural at videotaping whale encounters. On one occasion he caught the surfacing of a newborn calf.

The advantage of a long-term field study is the learning that unfolds over time. As the seasons run by I have a growing sense of how complex these creatures are. With each encounter I acquire more pieces of the puzzle. Most of the time I don't know where they fit until I have a day when I observe how several variables are related, and suddenly I gain one more insight into their behavior. Undoubtedly part of what attracts me to orcas is the certainty that beneath their impassive and regal exterior, deep pools of character and experience swirl. Their lack of facial movement imparts a certain "unknowability" to us humans, whose first language is the change of facial expression. A whale never frowns, grimaces or laughs. There is only the ever-present Mona Lisa smile. Whales don't offer their secrets freely.

On a crisp fall day in 1980, I was tagging along behind Corky's pod, watching through binoculars as they socialized with other members of their community. We were in a large body of open water. Ahead, a bank of fog rolled thick and dark along the horizon. It looked much farther away than it was, and soon it rolled over me, dampening the paper I was writing on. When I looked up I was completely disoriented. Very foolishly I had left without a compass and now had absolutely no idea of which way to go.

My predicament was compounded when I realized I was in an active and narrow shipping lane. Over the hydrophone the dull roar of a luxury liner became louder as it approached swiftly. To a small boat, cruise ships are massive monoliths with knife-edged bows. Panic started to take over; I didn't know which way to turn. Then the pod—A9, Top Notch and the others—surfaced serenely beside my boat.

I didn't care where they were headed; I knew they would avoid the ship and I'd be safe. But my relief was tempered by the worry that tracking them would be impossible in the thick gray fog. The whales had been on such an erratic travel pattern all day, it was amazing I had stumbled onto them at all. Nonetheless, I started the engine and puttered along parallel to them. The next time they surfaced the group was even closer, tightly bunched alongside me. As they dove, Sharky and her mother veered beneath me; several times I shifted into neutral, concerned they might graze the propeller with their flukes.

I assumed we were heading deeper into the fog, but after 20 minutes I saw the vague outline of a tiny island crowned with twisted cedars. The pod vanished, and I sped for the islet, bursting into the glorious evening sunlight. As I got my bearings, I realized the whales had turned 180 degrees and taken me back home.

My mind was reeling. Had they rescued me? Was that even remotely possible? Whatever their motivations, they had turned around, stayed close to me until I was safe, then apparently returned to their original course.

I think that during the 15 years I've spent with them, these whales have gotten to know me. They probably know where I live, the extent of my range and that I scurry home when darkness falls. I don't mean that they have ever demonstrated any recognition—for the most part they ignore me. I have tried to present myself as predictable and reliable, and I let them know that I will pull back and let them enter narrow channels first, as well as maintain a steady speed and straight course if young calves come near me to investigate. I shut off my engine and float at a distance when they rest.

As the first southeaster of fall bends the tops of the trees around my house and scatters the summer tourists, I look forward to what I might learn this winter. My list of questions still runs longer than my answers. The most wonderful aspect of studying such fascinating creatures is that my job will never be finished. All of my adult life has been spent in their company, and I can see no reason that should change.

LISTENING TO THE SEA BREATHING:
AN INTERVIEW WITH HELENA SYMONDS

Brenda Peterson

For the past seventeen years Helena Symonds has lived on isolated Hanson Island, off the northwest coast of British Columbia. This island is largely uninhabited, except for Helena; her husband, Dr. Paul Spong; and daughter, Anna, though summer brings many research assistants to their OrcaLab. The surrounding area is also home to resident orca pods that gather to feed, engage in complicated socializing, and to create what Helena Symonds calls "sound sculptures" so stunning and sophisticated they require both a well-trained ear and computers to begin to fathom.

We may never be able to actually translate orca vocalizations into human speech or vice versa. Helena and Paul's approach is to listen, record, and learn to recognize the orcas by their voices. This means memorizing and acoustically identifying each orca family's unique sound. Anytime orcas are passing near Hanson Island, or gathering around Parson, Flower, or Cracroft Islands, Helena is listening through a system of underwater hydrophones. Speakers broadcast from the rafters of her wooden home, her bedroom, the Lab, and even from the moss-hung trees in the surrounding rain forest. In the middle of the night, throughout the day, whether she's baking bread or working in the Lab, when Helena hears orca vocalizations, she stops everything and rushes to record them.

Coeditor Brenda Peterson paid a visit to Hanson Island in October 1996 and spent two days listening to Helena share the wonders of her orca world.

Helena: What we do here is a lot of listening. I never particularly thought I was an auditory person. I was more visually oriented toward drawing and painting. I have a background in theater, of all things. Suddenly, in coming here, I was placed in a world where listening is an important skill. Our ability to understand what we are listening to is our main research tool. Each day, with the help of our hydrophone network, we try to track the whales within a forty-square-kilometer area. A lot of our work is at night when there are no possible complementary visual reports of the whales' whereabouts. We can discern from their vocalizations where the whales are, who they are gathering with, what they're doing, whether they're resting, fishing, or socializing. It's really exciting. Remember, this is all *live*. Do you hear those calls coming through the speakers? That's the A36s.

Brenda: How can you tell them apart?

Helena: It's largely a process of elimination. We have been following this group for many years now and they have become very familiar, so the task is not as difficult as it once was. When we started we learned to make gross distinctions. Within the main community of whales we study there are three main groups, called clans. Within each clan are a number of pods that share an acoustic tradition passed on from generation to generation through the orca mothers. So you say, okay, I'm hearing "A" clan calls and you know that in "A" clan there are nine pods. Even though these pods have several calls in common, each pod has a unique sound, and may even have particular calls that set them apart from the other pods. Once you have been able to identify the pod, the work becomes more complicated. Members of a pod are very closely related, rather like an extended family, and they all make the same calls.

Hear that call? That's distinctive of the A36s. The A36s, one of three subpods that belong to the A1 pod, are Sophia, the orca mother, and her three sons, Cracroft, Plumper, and Kaikash. As Sophia's family does not always travel with the other two A1 subpods, we had to be able to distinguish her family's calls to keep track of their movements. Luckily, Sophia's family has visited this area quite often and we are able to tune our ears into their sounds. It's just a matter of becoming familiar with their voices.

Brenda: Just how important is family in the world of orcas?

Helena: Very. An orca mother and her offspring, even adult sons, spend every day of their lives together. These groups are incredibly bonded; only death or capture will separate them. In 1990, we experienced a very clear illustration of the strength of those bonds. One night, late in November, we began to hear calls. As the night wore on we began to notice that many of the calls sounded very strange, agitated. We didn't realize until the morning that we were probably hearing the death of Eve, one of the older orca mothers. She and her two sons, Top Notch and Foster, had been seen the evening before. The next day her sons charged around Hanson Island very fast, first one direction, then the other. The mother was nowhere to be seen. We knew something was terribly wrong, because the three whales had never been apart. Eve's body was discovered ten days later.

When summer and the whales returned, Top Notch and Foster were missing. Some believed the sons had died without their mother. All of us were concerned. Finally, one day, the two brothers suddenly came swimming close to our shore. They joined the A36s, who are relatives but not their closest kin. The brothers at first seemed to keep a distance from the A36s. If the A36s swam on one shore the brothers swam on the opposite side. After a while, the younger brother, Foster, began to befriend Sophia's oldest son, Cracroft. And soon after, the youthful antics of Kaikash, A36's youngest, seemed to enliven Top Notch, who soon began to play too. It occurred to us that the brothers' alienation and grief was finally over. Not long afterward, the brothers rejoined their own family. After this experience I think we began to understand that the whole orca community is very significant, providing an extensive support system for each whale.

Brenda: Why are the females in orca society so important for the pod's survival?

Helena: Once past infancy, female orcas may live a long life. The average life span is about fifty years, but many live longer. The oldest females in this community are about seventy-three years old; many are in their sixties and fifties. This longevity provides a great deal of stability in orca society. Young females grow up and establish their own families while still having the influence and wisdom of an older female at hand. The sons, who live much shorter lives on average, are able to remain with their mothers all or most of their lives. Each orca knows his or her place in the family, the pod, the community. They are very secure.

Orca societies are highly social, cooperative, and peaceful. Even after spending many years following and mapping the daily movements of the whales I am still impressed with how the whales coordinate their activities and how excited they seem to be with each other. We believe specific sub-pods may act as "hosts" to other visiting groups. Almost every season, Tsitika's group is the first to arrive here. As the summer progresses, Tsitika's family often wait on the outskirts of the area for new arriving groups which they then escort into the area proper.

Early one evening in mid-August, many years ago, about thirty whales passed the Lab. The orange glow of the setting sun shone on their bodies as they spyhopped and rushed northward. As the long summer twilight finally gave way to the night, a spectacular show of Northern Lights held us spellbound for what seemed like a long time. Just when we could hardly absorb any more wonders we started to hear the whales returning in the distance. Soon the ocean in front of the Lab was filled with the sounds of whales breathing and calls upon calls, a virtual mirror, as

Paul put it, of the Northern Lights above us in the sky. As the eighty whales moved together toward Johnstone Strait the August full moon rose and spilled its light into the remaining sky. Not hard to guess why I stay, is it?

Brenda: How is your work different from other whale research?

Helena: Hanson Island has always been special. There has been a field research station here ever since Paul set up camp back in 1970, so we have been gathering data for nearly thirty years. I've been here for almost eighteen years. Interestingly, our method today is very similar to what it was in 1970. We decided back in the early 1980s we would only work from land. Several events contributed to that decision.

In September 1981, A24 gave birth to a calf right in Johnstone Strait. It is the only birth that has ever been witnessed in the wild. It was very exciting. A group of reporters, in the area to cover the efforts to save the Tsitika Valley from logging, just happened to be returning from a visit to Robson Bight when the birth occurred. They, of course, photographed the new mum and the calf and the news was out! The next day the Strait was jammed with sightseers, ourselves included. Eventually, the boats made a complete circle around the new mum and her little one leaving the rest of the pod restlessly waiting outside.

It was a circus. There I was, sitting trapped in our boat with my young baby daughter in my arms, and there was A24, trapped out there with *her* baby, surrounded by so many people. I thought *there must be a better, a less invasive way, to study the whales.* That's when we decided to stop going out in boats and began to explore other ways to get information. We were fortunate to meet a local electronic wizard who expressed an interest in building remote transmitting systems. We began to experiment with these systems, trying to find the best locations that would allow us to listen to as wide an area as possible, including adjacent waterways. We always had at least one hydrophone in front of the Lab before, but now suddenly we could hear where we couldn't see. We could follow the whales for hours.

Our hydrophone network is quite unique. Each year we record about a thousand hours of tape. We record every time we hear whales and this means we have to monitor twenty-four hours each day. Fortunately, we now have a lot of help from volunteers.

Each morning we listen to the tapes and try to retrace the whales' path from the day before. The summer months are very busy and I am seriously sleep-deprived most of the time. I get very wrapped up in the whales and would rather be in the Lab than anywhere else. If I can't be there then I listen and keep track through the speakers in the house.

Brenda: You and your husband are very active in the movement to release and rehabilitate wild orcas captured and held in captive parks like Sea World. What is that research and work about?

Helena: In the sixties and seventies almost seventy whales were captured from the Pacific Northwest. Most of the whales were taken from the Puget area. Terrible damage was done. Many whales were killed outright during capture attempts. The pods involved in the captures are only now recovering, three decades later. Of those seventy whales, only three have survived—Corky, Yaka, and Lolita. Corky and Yaka were caught here in BC in 1969. They are Northern Resident orcas, the same whales who visit our area each summer. Lolita is a Southern Resident and was caught a year later in Penn Cove, Washington. We feel that they need to be returned to their families as soon as possible. No one can say how much longer they will continue to live. Usually, orcas survive less than ten years in captivity. These three are nearing thirty years! They are old in captive terms but in the wild they would be young mums with probably a couple of kids each and many more years to live.

We are fighting to convince Sea World to free Corky. Anheuser Busch, the beer company, owns Sea World and they have huge resources, power, and influence. But we have managed to draw a lot of attention to Corky's plight and thousands of people have added their voices to the protest. We all believe Corky deserves a chance to come back home.

Brenda: If it were possible to get Sea World to release Corky after so much protest, it would set a precedent for the release of other captive orcas. Do you think it can be done successfully?

Helena: Absolutely. We are not proposing that Corky be just dumped back into the ocean. She would be trained to catch live fish in her present tank and given extensive medical check-ups before she was brought to a halfway house near here, where she would have time to get adjusted before the whales arrived back for the summer. We would watch to make sure she and the other whales were ready before she was released.

Corky has lots going for her. Her mother, Stripe, is still alive, as are several others who were in her pod when she was taken. She still makes the same calls as her family. She has survived losing seven babies, being attacked by another captive, and twenty-seven years of sterile concrete walls. Imagine that moment when she again feels her home waters surround her and hears her mother's voice.

Brenda: Do you think Corky's mother will remember her?

Helena: Of course. Orcas have the second-largest brain of all animals, almost four times the size of a human brain and at least as complex. A good memory is certain. Corky was about four years old when she was caught. She has memories. When *Prime Time Live* played her family's calls to her, she lay on the surface and shuddered. It was a powerful moment. Orcas have to learn many skills and memorize huge, complex, geographical areas. Their range is hundreds of kilometers long, a maze of islands and waterways. All this knowledge is stored and retrieved with ease. When a calf is born, the pod takes the calf on a tour of their range to imprint knowledge of all the special areas. Perhaps that is why older individuals, especially long-living females, are important to the pod. Last summer, the oldest female—she is over seventy years old—toured this area with her son. As she swam along, every other whale came up to her, spent a few moments with her, and then moved away to allow her to pass. We have also seen other older females spend long hours with young whales, usually male, and often from a completely different pod.

Brenda: Do you think orcas are as aware of you and your family as you are of them?

Helena: [laughing] I don't know that the orcas pay much attention to us. We're fairly secondary to them. I suspect it doesn't take a lot of energy on their part to take us in. They can easily do it and keep going. I think the most important thing for orcas is themselves, their families, their society.

There are times when I do wonder. One beautiful day in late fall we were heading back to the island and this young mum, Simoon, and her calf, Misty, were traveling toward us. We stopped and turned off the engine. Misty veered away from her mum and came close to the boat. As she swam past, in the clear water, she crooked her neck and looked straight at us for a long moment before straightening up and swimming back to her mum. We all felt intuitively connected.

What always amazes me about orcas is how intensely focused they are despite disturbances. It is quite hard to gauge how boats are affecting the whales. Researchers keep getting confusing results when they observe boats and whales together. However, when we listen on the hydrophones, we get another impression about what is happening. We often hear the whales go quiet when a boat is approaching. They seem to be listening. After a while, they will echolocate, figure out where the boat is going and then carry on.

Brenda: How do you think your intuitive feelings affect your understanding of the whales?

Helena: I think they fill in the gaps. There is so much we don't understand. Hydrophones, time, and experience all help, but so much remains hidden. After all, the ocean is not our natural home. We can only imagine. I think the total immersion, the constant presence of the whales in our lives has made us develop new awareness. I'm always thinking about what the whales are doing. Sometimes, when it's late at night, when the sea is smooth and velvety under the moon and the whales are passing by, I just listen to the sea breathing. I believe staying here in one place, listening, not chasing, has changed me. We humans have so few models in our history of successful, peaceful coexistence within families and societies. Orcas have all of this. They can teach us—if we can only learn to listen.

Editor's Note: There was a capture of ten orcas off Taiji, Japan, in February 1997. Under the guise of an "academic" permit given by the IWC, the Japanese captured these orcas for entertainment and business purposes. Five of those originally captured were released, but the other five orcas were forcibly separated from their families and shipped to three different Japanese aquariums. One of the captured female orcas was believed to be pregnant. Helena Symonds and Paul Spong have been helping with the widespread international protest against this capture. For more information look up the Free The Taiji Five! site on the Internet: http://paws.org./activists/taiji

I ACKNOWLEDGE MINE

Jane Goodall

It was on December 27, 1986, that I watched the videotape that would change the pattern of my life. I had spent a traditional Christmas with my family in Bournemouth, England. We all sat watching the tape, and we were all shattered. Afterward, we couldn't speak for a while. The tape showed scenes from inside a biomedical research laboratory, in which monkeys paced round and round, back and forth, within incredibly small cages stacked one on top of the other, and young chimpanzees, in similar tiny prisons, rocked back and forth or from side to side, far gone in misery and despair. I had, of course, known about the chimpanzees who were locked away in medical research laboratories. But I had deliberately kept away, knowing that to see them would be utterly depressing, thinking that there would be nothing I could do to help them. After seeing the video I knew I had to try.

In March of 1987, I was given permission to visit the laboratory, LEMSIP, of Sema, Inc., funded entirely through federal taxes in the United States. Even repeated viewing of the videotape had not prepared me for the stark reality of that laboratory. I was ushered, by white-coated men who smiled nervously or glowered, into a nightmare world. The door closed behind us. Outside, everyday life went on as usual, with the sun and the trees and the birds. Inside, where no daylight had ever penetrated, it was dim and colorless. I was led along one corridor after another, and I looked into room after room lined with small, bare cages, stacked one above the other. I watched as monkeys paced around their tiny prisons, making bizarre, abnormal movements.

Then came a room where very young chimpanzees, one or two years old, were crammed, two together, into tiny cages that measured (as I found out later) some twenty-two inches by twenty-two inches at the

159

base. They were two feet high. These chimp babies peered out from the semidarkness of their tiny cells as the doors were opened. Not yet part of any experiment, they had been waiting in their cramped quarters for four months. They were simply objects, stored in the most economical way, in the smallest space that would permit the continuation of life. At least they had each other, but not for long. Once their quarantine was over they would be separated, I was told, and placed singly in other small cages, to be infected with hepatitis or AIDS or some other viral disease. And all the cages would then be placed in isolettes.

What could they see, these infants, when they peered out through the tiny panel of glass in the door of the isolette? The blank wall opposite their prison. What was in the cage to provide occupation, stimulation, comfort? For those who had been separated from their companions—nothing. I watched one isolated prisoner, a juvenile female, as she rocked from side to side, sealed off from the outside world in her metal box. A flashlight was necessary if one wanted to see properly inside the cage. All she could hear was the constant loud sound of the machinery that regulated the flow of air through vents in her isolette.

A "technician" (for so the animal-care staff are named, after training) was told to lift her out. She sat in his arms like a rag doll, listless, apathetic. He did not speak to her. She did not look at him or try to interact with him in any way. Then he returned her to her cage, latched the inner door, and closed her isolette, shutting her away again from the rest of the world.

I am still haunted by the memory of her eyes, and the eyes of the other chimpanzees I saw that day. They were dull and blank, like the eyes of people who have lost all hope, like the eyes of children you see in Africa, refugees, who have lost their parents and their homes. Chimpanzee children are so like human children, in so many ways. They use similar movements to express their feelings. And their emotional needs are the same—both need friendly contact and reassurance and fun and opportunity to engage in wild bouts of play. And they need love.

Dr. James Mahoney, veterinarian at LEMSIP, recognized this need when he began working for Jan Moor-Jankowski. Several years ago he started a "nursery" in that lab for the infant chimpanzees when they are first taken from their mothers. It was not long after my visit to Sema that I went for the first of a number of visits to LEMSIP.

Once I was suitably gowned and masked and capped, with paper booties over my shoes, Jim took me to see his nursery. Five young chimps were there at the time, ranging in age from about nine months to two years. Each one was dressed in children's clothes—"to keep their diapers on, really," said the staff member who was with them. (Someone is always with them throughout the day.) The infants played vigorously around me as I sat there on the soft red carpet, surrounded by toys. I was for the moment more interesting than any toy, and almost immediately they had whisked off my cap and mask. Through a window these infants could look into a kitchen and work area where, most of the time, some human activity was going on. They had been taken from their mothers when they were between nine and eighteen months old, Jim said. He brings them into the nursery in groups, so that they can go through the initial trauma together, which is why some were older than others. And, he explained, he tries to do this during summer vacation so that there will be no shortage of volunteer students to help them over their nightmares. Certainly these boisterous youngsters were not depressed.

I stayed for about forty minutes, then Jim came to fetch me. He took me to a room just across the corridor where there were eight young chimpanzees who had recently graduated from the nursery. This new room was known as "Junior Africa," I learned. Confined in small, bare cages, some alone, some paired, the youngsters could see into the nursery through the window. They could look back into their lost childhood. For the second time in their short lives, security and joy had been abruptly brought to an end through no fault of their own. Junior Africa: the name seems utterly appropriate until one remembers all the infants in Africa who are seized from their mothers by hunters, rescued and cared for in human families, and then, as they get older, banished into small cages or tied to the ends of chains. Only the reasons, of course, are different. Even these very young chimpanzees at LEMSIP may have to go through grueling experimental procedures, such as repeated liver biopsies and the drawing of blood. Jim is always pleading for a four-year childhood before research procedures commence, but the bodies of these youngsters, like those of other experimental chimps, are rented out to researchers and pharmaceutical companies. The chimpanzees, it seems, must earn their keep from as early an age as possible.

During a subsequent visit to LEMSIP, I asked after one of the youngsters I had met in the nursery, little Josh. A real character he had been then, a born group leader. I was led to one of the cages in Junior Africa, where that once-assertive infant, who had been so full of energy and zest for life, now sat huddled in the corner of his barred prison. There was no longer any fun in his eyes. "How can you bear it?" I asked the young woman who was caring for him. Her eyes, above the mask, filled with tears. "I can't," she said. "But if I leave, he'll have even less."

This same fear of depriving the chimpanzees of what little they have is what keeps Jim at LEMSIP. After I had passed through Junior Africa that first day, Jim took me to the windowless rooms to meet ten adult chimps. No carpets or toys for them, no entertainment. This was the hard, cold world of the adult research chimps at LEMSIP. Five on each side of the central corridor, each in his own small prison, surrounded by bars—bars on all sides, bars above, bars below. Each cage measured five feet by five feet and was seven feet high, which was the legal minimum cage size at that time for storing adult chimpanzees. Each cage was suspended above the ground, so that feces and food remains would fall to the floor below. Each cage contained an old car tire and a chimpanzee. That was all.

JoJo's cage was the first on the right as we went in. I knelt down, new cap and mask in place, along with overalls and plastic shoe covers and rubber gloves. I looked into his eyes and talked to him. He had been in his cage at least ten years. He had been born in the African forest—shipped to America, probably, by Franz Sitter himself. Could he remember, I wondered? Did he sometimes dream of the great trees with the breeze rustling through the canopy, the birds singing, the comfort of his mother's arms? Very gently JoJo reached one great finger through the steel bars and touched one of the tears that slipped out above my mask, then went on grooming the back of my wrist. So gently. Ignoring the rattling of cages, the clank of steel on steel, the violent swaying of imprisoned bodies beating against the bars, as the other male chimps greeted the veterinarian.

His round over, Jim returned to where I still crouched before JoJo. The tears were falling faster now. "Jane, please don't," Jim said, squatting beside me and putting his arm around me. "Please don't. I have to face this every morning of my life."

I also visited Immuno's two labs in Austria. The first of these, where hepatitis research is conducted and where chimpanzees are used to test batches of vaccine, was built some time ago. There I got no farther than the administration building. I was not allowed into the chimpanzee rooms because I had not had a hepatitis shot. And—how unfortunate!—the closed-circuit TV monitors could not, for some reason, be made to work that day. In the lobby, though, were two demonstration cages, set there so the public could see for itself the magnificent and spacious housing that Immuno was planning for its chimpanzee colony. (This they felt was necessary because of all the criticisms that were being made about the small size of the existing cages, dangerous criticisms leading to expensive lawsuits.) The present cages, I knew, were not very large. The new ones looked identical to those at LEMSIP. To my mind, it should be required that all scientists working with laboratory animals, whatever the species, not only know something about the animals and their natural behavior, but see for themselves how their protocols affects individual animals. Researchers should observe firsthand any suffering they cause, so that they can better balance the benefit (or hoped-for benefit) to humanity against the cost in suffering to the animal. Laboratory chimpanzees are prisoners, but they are guilty of no crimes. Rather, they are helping—perhaps—to alleviate human suffering. Yet in some of the labs I have described, and in others around the world, they are subjected to far harsher treatment than we give to hardened criminals. Surely we owe them more than that.

Even if all research labs could be redesigned to provide the best possible environment for the chimpanzee subjects, there would still be one nagging question—should chimpanzees be used at all? Are we really justified in putting our closest relatives in the animal kingdom into cages and subjecting them to lives of slavery for the sake of human health? Just because we have decided that it is not ethical to use human "guinea pigs"? We have far more in common with chimpanzees than the physiological characteristics that make them, in the eyes of some scientists, so suitable for certain kinds of research. We should not forget that there are equally striking similarities in the social behavior, intellect, and emotions of human beings and chimpanzee beings. And I personally believe that if we have souls, then probably chimpanzees have them too.

I have been described, by the director of one large chimpanzee colony, as a "rabid antivivisectionist." That kind of language is used regularly by individuals, extremists on both sides of the animal-rights issue, who wish to imply that those holding views in opposition to theirs are irrational, even dangerous. Often such talk is a way of avoiding debate. It certainly is not useful.

Of course I wish I could wave a wand and see the lab cages standing empty. Of course I hate the suffering that goes on behind the closed doors of animal labs. I hate even more the callous attitude that lab personnel so often show toward the animals in their power—deliberately cultivated, no doubt, to try to protect themselves from any twinge of guilt. But it would not be constructive to go around denouncing these individuals as "sadistic vivisectionists"—or whatever may be the counterpart of "rabid antivivisectionist." The animal-rights movement is here to stay, and because scientific investigations have now shown conclusively that the higher animals have minds and feelings and are capable of making complex decisions, the movement will continue to grow in strength. For too long we have used and abused the nonhuman animals with whom we share this planet, without even pause for thought—not just in the lab, but in the slaughterhouse, the hunting field, the circus, and so on. Our children are gradually desensitized to animal suffering. ("It's all right, darling; it's only an animal.") The process goes on throughout school, culminating in the frightful things that zoology, psychology, veterinary, and medical students are forced to do to animals in the process of acquiring knowledge. They have to quell empathy if they are to survive in their chosen fields, for scientists do things to animals that, from the animals' point of view, are torture and would be regarded as such by almost everyone if done by nonscientists.

Animals in labs are used in different ways. In the quest for knowledge, things are done to them to see what happens. To test the safety of various products, animals are injected with or forced to swallow different amounts to see how sick they get, or if they survive. The effectiveness of medical procedures and drugs are tried out on animals. Surgical skills are practiced on animals. Theories of all sorts, ranging from the effects of various substances to psychological trauma, are tested on animals. What is so shocking is the lack of respect for the victims, the almost total disregard for their living, feeling, sometimes agonizing bodies. And often the tortures are inflicted for nothing. There is an angry debate, ongoing and abrasive, about the role of animals in medicine. Even though I am not qualified to judge a dispute of this magnitude, which has become so polarized, it seems obvious that extremists on both sides are wrong. The scientists who claim that medical research could never have progressed at all without the use of animals are as incorrect as the animal-rights activists who declare stridently that no advances in medicine have been due to animal research.

Let me return to chimpanzees and to the question of whether we are justified in using them in our search for medical knowledge. Approximately three thousand of them languish in medical research laboratories around the world, somewhat more than half of this number (about one thousand eight hundred) in the United States. Today, as we have seen, they are primarily used in infectious-disease research and vaccine testing; even though they have seldom shown even minor symptoms of either AIDS or hepatitis, the experimental procedures are often stressful, the conditions in which they are maintained typically bleak. Yet they are so like us that some people believe that they and the other great apes should be reclassified and placed, along with humans, in the genus *Homo*. Chimpanzees, instead of being *Pan troglodytes*, would become *Homo troglodytes*. Proponents of this plan believe that such a taxonomic change would result in greater appreciation for the sentient, sapient nature of apes—but I doubt it. It seems more likely that it would backfire, incensing thousands of people, particularly those in certain religious groups.

I think it is more important to educate people to a better understanding of the true nature of chimpanzees (and other nonhuman animals), particularly an appreciation of the extent to which they can feel—feel pain, feel emotions. Humans are a species capable of compassion, and we should develop a heightened moral responsibility for beings who are so like ourselves. Chimpanzees form close, affectionate bonds that may persist throughout life. Like us, they feel joy and sorrow and despair. They show many of the intellectual skills that until recently we believed were unique to ourselves. They may look into mirrors and see themselves as individuals—beings who have consciousness of "self." Do they not, then, deserve to be treated with the same kind of consideration that we accord to other highly sensitive, conscious beings—ourselves? Granted, we do not always show much consideration to one another. That is why there is so much anguish over human rights. That is why it makes little sense to talk about the "rights" of chimpanzees. But at least where we desist from doing certain things to human beings for ethical reasons, we should desist also from doing them to chimpanzee beings. We no longer perform certain experiments on humans, for ethical reasons. I suggest that it would be logical to refrain also from doing these experiments on chimpanzees.

Why do I care so much? Why, in order to try to change attitudes and actions in the labs, do I subject myself repeatedly to the personal nightmare of visiting these places, knowing that I shall be haunted endlessly by memories of my encounters with the prisoners there? Especially their eyes, those bewildered or sad or angry eyes. The answer is simple. I have spent so many years in the forests of Gombe, being with and learning from the chimpanzees. I consider myself one of the luckiest people on earth. It is time to repay something of the debt I owe the chimpanzees, for what they have taught me about themselves, about myself, about the place of humans and chimpanzees in the natural world.

When I visit JoJo in his tiny steel prison I often think of David Greybeard, that very special chimpanzee who, by his calm acceptance of my presence, first helped me to open the door into the magic world of the chimpanzees of Gombe. I learned so much from him. It was he who introduced me to his companions, Goliath and Mike and the Flo family and all the other unique, fascinating personalities who made up his community at that time. David even allowed me to groom him. A fully adult male chimpanzee who had lived all his life in the wild actually tolerated the touch of a human hand.

There was one especially memorable event. I had been following David one day, struggling through dense undergrowth near a stream. I was thankful when he stopped to rest, and I sat near him. Close by I noticed the fallen red fruit of an oil nut palm, a favorite food of chimpanzees. I picked it up and held it out to David on the palm of my hand. For a moment I thought he would ignore my gesture. But then he took the nut, let it fall to the ground and, with the same movement, very gently closed his fingers around my hand. He glanced at my face, let go of my hand, and turned away. I understood his message: "I don't want the nut, but it was nice of you to offer it." We had communicated most truly, relying on shared primate signals that are deeper and more ancient than words. It was a moment of revelation. I did not follow David when he wandered off into the forest. I wanted to be alone, to ponder the significance of what had happened, to enshrine those moments permanently in my mind.

And so, when I am with JoJo, I remember David Greybeard and the lessons he taught me. I feel deep shame—shame that we, with our more sophisticated intellect, with our greater capacity for understanding and compassion, have deprived JoJo of almost everything. Not for him the soft colors of the forest, the dim greens and browns entwined, or the peace of the afternoon when the sun flecks the canopy and small creatures rustle and flit and creep among the leaves. Not for him the freedom to choose, each day, how he will spend his time and where and with whom. Nature's sounds are gone, the sounds of running water, of wind in the branches, of chimpanzee calls that ring out so clear and rise up through the treetops to drift away in the hills. The comforts are gone, the soft leafy floor of the forest, the springy branches from which sleeping nests can be made. All are gone. Here, in the lab, the world is concrete and steel; it is loud, horrible sounds, clanging bars, banging doors, and the deafening volume of chimpanzee calls confined in underground rooms. It is a world where there are no windows, nothing to look at, nothing to play with. A world where family and friends are torn apart and where sociable beings are locked away, innocent of crime, into solitary confinement.

It is we who are guilty. I look again into JoJo's clear eyes. I acknowledge my own complicity in this world we have made, and I feel the need for forgiveness. He reaches out a large, gentle finger and once again touches the tear trickling down into my mask.

III: BORDERLINES

The Domesticated Wild

*T*he edge between the known and the unknown is the place where the human and animal meet. This borderline does not necessarily open to the wilderness. These pieces are about our familiar companions, in all senses of the word, dogs, cats, horses, llamas. They are about the animals we think we know best, who live among us, whose lives are threaded through our own. But being accustomed to their presences, relying upon them for food, security, or companionship, does not mean we know or honor them. It is a brave and difficult task to attempt to know those who dwell beside us. It requires us to set aside assumptions, to offer ourselves in hope that the other will trust and reveal itself as well.

In these times, to change the relationship between ourselves and the others among whom we live is a recognized need. And what is gained besides some real glimpse of the other? A flash of self. As Gretel Ehrlich tells it: "Animals hold us to what is present, to who we are at the time. What is obvious to an animal is not the embellishment that fattens our emotional résumés but what's bedrock and current in us: aggression, fear, insecurity, happiness, or equanimity. Because they have the ability to read our involuntary tics and scents, we're transparent to them and thus exposed—we are finally ourselves."

HOW I TITHE

Susan Chernak McElroy

I was surprised to find myself so smitten with Phaedra. I've never been especially enchanted with llamas, probably because I worked with a zoo's llama herd that spit on me five days a week for almost a year. I first saw Phaedra out in a field of grass and daisies, her fluffy white coat frosted with dried leaves. When her owner invited me into the pasture for a look at his herd of magnificent, extra-woolly llamas, it was Phaedra alone who approached me, sniffed my face and breath, and hummed a tone that sounded like summer wind in my ear. She was a good few heads shorter than the other llamas, her face round and babyish. In fact, I mistook her for a youngster until her owner, Andy, told me that she was mature, just dwarfed. Something wasn't growing right with Phaedra, and most likely never would. I left Andy's farm that day thinking that I maybe wanted a llama. I ignored the quiet inner voice that said it wasn't a llama I wanted, but Phaedra, who just happened to be packaged as a llama.

Phaedra didn't come to live with me, but within three months, my husband and I were given two llamas. Unlike tiny Phaedra, Mandy and Fernando were impressive beasts that towered over our small herd of miniature donkeys. Fernando was disinterested in us at best, leery at worst. Mandy, a huge white bus of a llama, suffered from a gone-haywire burping mechanism that made her drool bucketloads of smelly foam all over herself. When winter set in, the cold got to her and she shivered and trembled even when I covered her in old blankets.

Late that winter, settled into a new home at our neighbor's farm that came complete with a heated barn, Mandy died in my arms as Fernando looked on. The cruel east wind that had hammered us for months had proven too much for her old body to endure. I sobbed for days, stricken with remorse that I hadn't been able to offer her a longer life, better care. As the rendering man hauled her away, my husband, Lee, said, "No more llamas." Then, he went one better. He said, "No more nonproductive animals." We had animals of every sort, but the larger ones, the stock animals, were our "business," the creatures we prayed would help us with tax write-offs to feed the rest. They "produced" babies, which we sold.

So that spring, we sold off our nonproducing stock. It was agony. Our girls, the small group of show-winning breeding jennies, were— aside from the dog, cats, and a few free-ranging chickens—the only animals who remained. The workload shrank. So did the very heart and soul of the barn.

I went to visit Andy and Phaedra that summer. As our farm had shrunk, his had exploded. His pastures danced with curly-haired baby llamas and infant miniature donkeys as adorable and cuddly as stuffed toys. As Phaedra walked across the pasture to greet me, I could hardly believe I was looking at the same animal I'd seen the year before. Her white coat was caked with dirt and burrs. Black flies feasted in the crusty discharge around her eyes and drew blood around her ears. When I put my hands on her, I felt ribs beneath my fingers. She was a skeleton.

As the other llamas had grown tall and powerful, the pasture became unsafe for tiny, deformed Phaedra. Too small to compete for food, she waited and starved. She had become the object of the herd's abuse, and the special target of the herd sire. In his formal courtship, he struck Phaedra down endlessly, coming at her like a battering ram, eventually breaking apart her small face and jaw. After a while, she learned to stay on the ground. Then another complication had set in. Phaedra's eyesight had gone bad, perhaps from her injuries. She had no night vision, and spotty vision during the day. Andy had to put out a night-light for her in the barn, and she would sleep beneath it, unsteady on her feet if she left the small circle of glowing yellow.

From the first, I knew Phaedra was mine. Yet even in the midst of her suffering, I didn't ask to bring her home. I hinted at it, but I didn't use my voice, loud and direct, to ask as I wanted to ask.

So I returned home and Phaedra stayed out in her pasture. My own voice seemed small before that of my husband, who had clearly asked for no more nonproductive animals. Lee had made room in his life for the farm and its creatures, a life he would never have chosen for himself. He had offered to keep us financially afloat while I stayed home and worked on my book and flower gardens. I loved my life at home as much as I felt guilty for loving it. For the first time in twenty-two years, I wasn't earning money, yet I was spending Lee's as fast as he brought it home. Fences, pasture seed, feed, tack, and animals all came our way through Lee's wallet.

I felt it was more than fair of him to ask that no more of our limited financial resources go to vets and feed stores.

Still, drawn to Phaedra like a magnet, I went to visit Andy again. He told me that earlier in the week, Phaedra had fallen in the field and couldn't get to her feet without help. Andy, swamped with the demands of a large llama and donkey herd, a new business, a new marriage, and a new baby, had sparse energy left for Phaedra. I said, "Let me take her home, please." And he said, "yes." I imagined that convincing Lee would be a hard task, yet when I spoke to him of bringing Phaedra to our farm, he agreed surprisingly easily. And so, later that week, Phaedra came home.

She stumbled out of our old brown van and into our green pastures, a timid, frail creature with an uncertain future. As she took her first tentative steps toward our red barn with its overflowing mangers and cool, clay flooring, my heart fairly melted in my chest. I saw a dainty white fairy blessing the pastures with beauty and tranquillity where anyone else would have seen a ragged dirt ball with four legs.

She became my summer project. Each day, I sang songs to her as I washed the fly crusts off of her ears and eyes and brushed the dirt away from her cotton-soft fur. I treated her swollen eyes with drops and wiped bug repellent on her face and ears. My hope was that good food and good care would be enough to bring Phaedra back to health. But fate fought me at every turn. First it was a bad abscess on her cheek, near her broken jaw. Then it was diarrhea brought on by the antibiotics to fight the abscess. Next, she quit eating. Finally, she developed a stress ulcer. I poured Maalox down her throat three times a day, marveling that she didn't spit it back at me. The vet became a regular visitor, and I joked with him about setting up a permanent cot in our barn. Eventually we realized that Phaedra's old jaw injury had made it impossible for her to swallow any grass at all. She would come to me at the pasture fence with grass packed in her mouth. And I would wrap my arms around her, slip my fingers into her mouth, and pull out fist-sized wads of sticky green stuff. If I didn't, there would be no room in her mouth to accommodate the grain and pellets she *could* eat.

As the weeks passed, I asked myself—as Lee often asked—what in the world I was doing? There were other projects, other tasks, that demanded my time and attention. Yet I let them fall by the wayside, focusing my energy on Phaedra, my precious, gentle, trusting little fairy. For reasons I could never hope to explain to anyone, including myself, Phaedra simply enchanted me. I would find myself just watching her move about in the pasture or sprawl luxuriously in the sun. Sometimes I'd see her gaze upward at a flock of birds or sniff at a cluster of bees on a patch of clover. Once, I saw her leap around the pasture like a gazelle, all four legs stiff beneath her, bouncing straight into the air as she tossed her head left and right in what looked like rapturous llama abandon. Her presence at BrightStar somehow filled the desolate empty spaces in the barn and in my heart that came on the heels of our decision to be "practical" about the animals. Phaedra *sustained* me in a very special way.

Despite all my loving care, Phaedra's condition failed to improve. She lived in a standstill state of frail health, not gaining a pound, not eating well, not responding to any of my efforts to strengthen her. Her vet and food bills were hitting the catastrophic mark when I told Lee, out of deep guilt and frustration, that I wouldn't spend any more money on her, that I would put her down before she ran up more bills. Lee looked me in the eye and said, "No more charity cases."

For the next few days, Lee's words rang like a siren in my mind. No more charity cases. I've learned to listen closely when my inner alarm goes off. It usually means that I'm about to be graced with something of importance, provided I do the work of keeping my heart and my mind wide, wide open.

So one evening I sat in the barn with Phaedra while she ate, and asked her, out loud, the questions I had only asked myself. I asked her what she was doing at our farm, why she had called so strongly to me, and what she needed to teach me. Sitting on a bucket beside her, I stretched my arms out to her and closed my eyes and waited for whatever thoughts might come to me to help me reconcile my needs, her needs, Lee's needs. Sitting and asking—out loud—is a technique I'd used before, sometimes with no results, sometimes with stunning effect. Its success seemed to be a matter of how well I listened, and of pure and simple grace.

No more charity cases. Visions of a lifetime of hurt and lost animals drifted before me. I had taken them all home—dogs, kittens, orphaned birds, half-squashed toads—spent my last dime on them, found them new homes, healed them, loved them, too often buried them. Familiar faces bubbled up in my mind: Beau, a gangly starved Doberman-mutt I found in the parking lot of a movie theater who vomited and leaked bloody diarrhea in the back of my girlfriend's fancy new car as we drove him home to my place. I don't remember where the money came from to get him to the vet, get him on mange medicine, get him wormed, vaccinated. Probably, it was my parents who footed the bill. The day I found him a new home at a local auto-body repair shop, we all rejoiced at money and effort well spent: The dog who went eagerly to the young man's truck was sleek, well-fed, with eyes that danced.

I remembered the pigeon I'd found on a winter day, decades after Beau, and dozens of strays and orphans later. It was Christmas Eve and I was busy, as busy as a body could get without self-destructing. On a dirty street near one of my then-boyfriend's grimy rental houses, the bird sat—the last of its infant down still trailing around its ungainly neck. When I approached, the pigeon never moved, never opened its eyes. It had just enough life left to scream piteously when I picked it up, its wings flapping in unfathomable terror. I held the bird close and quickly searched through its greasy feathers to see if I could find any immediate problem. Revulsion washed over me when I found the army of skittering, ugly lice of a sort, racing through the pigeon's feathers and across its skin like small, scuttling roaches. The bugs crawled off the bird and onto my hands, then leapt off onto the sidewalk. Only a very sick animal would house that massive an army of parasites. I stood on the sidewalk and thought of my boyfriend waiting at home in our expensive, executive-style home, filled with his visiting relatives. It was getting dark and I was already late. The house was so clean, the bird filthy. My boyfriend would be livid. I took a deep breath, and, in a quiet way, I killed myself. Carrying the pigeon to the open backyard of the rental house, I placed it in a bush. Out of the warmth of my hands, the bird shivered and grasped at the winter-bare branches of a shrub that offered no warmth, no protection from the night wind, no hope. And I turned away to hurry off and celebrate Christmas.

A year later, at a dock in Santa Barbara, I saw a young brown pelican with a splotch of oil circling its breast. The oil was destroying the bird's natural waterproofing and already the pelican was floating deeper in the water than it should. Soon, it would become fully water-saturated and drown. Once again, I was late for a Christmas party. The same boyfriend waited for me—this time on our yacht—tied just down the dock. Over the year, our relationship had degenerated to a perverse master-slave alliance. He would be furious with me if I showed up with a sick bird. I thought of our spotless deck. I thought of my lover's ice-blue eyes glaring down at me. I thought of the pigeon I had left sick and shivering in a leafless bush a scant year before.

There was still one piece of old bait fish in the sack I'd fed to the gulls and the pelican on the wharf. I used it to lure the pelican within reach, then grabbed the startled bird by the neck and hauled its thrashing body onto the pier. I raced to our boat, grabbed a large deck towel and wrapped the pelican up into a huge, argumentative bundle. The commotion drew my lover up on deck, surprised and angry. After unleashing a few expletives, he demanded I release the bird and get ready to go. My knees went to Jell-O before him, and the voice piping out of me that said "No!" sounded too high and thin. The pelican added an exclamation point to my wavering denial by ejecting a forceful blast of poop that splattered up my lover's pant's leg. I swallowed a hysterical giggle, then turned my back and marched off to demand that the harbormaster find good care for the bird. When I returned to the boat, I was met with a silence that continued through the evening. To the silence, I said out loud, "It would have died. I'd do it again. It would have died." Beneath the agony of fear that I had learned to expect in every confrontation with my lover, I felt the first small churning of power. The power was my voice, brought to life by a huge, needy bird. I vowed that Christmas that I would never again turn my back on an animal because of someone else's agenda.

I remembered telling Lee before we married that sometimes my affinity for animals wouldn't look very cute. It would look like stopping in the middle of the road to carry a snake to the curb when we were already late for some party. Or it might look like a bathtub full of some sick creature that honks or cries all night. It would be money spent, and emotion and tears. "You will get frustrated with it and sick of me," I told him. He had not—or if so, only fleetingly. In the past years, I suddenly realized that it was me who had finally gotten sick of it, sorry for it, ashamed of it. *Ashamed of it. "It's only an animal." "Are all your llamas that ugly?" "Why don't you adopt children instead?"* I had spent decades explaining, justifying, apologizing.

Could I have chosen my passion, I would not have chosen animals. In my weakness and almost pathological need to be liked, to be approved of, I would have chosen a more acceptable, more noble cause on which to spend my life's energy: child welfare, world peace, hunger, poverty. But I did not choose. Instead, I was chosen. Chosen long before I could even talk. My first words were about animals, my first joys, my first deaths, first births, my first sense of the mystery of God. When I was stricken with cancer in my late thirties, it was a lifetime of experience with animals living and dying in my home and in my arms that offered me a vision of deep healing and a way back to health. In a very real and fully spiritual sense, they had given me my life and given me my voice.

Phaedra finished off her grain and turned to me. In the outstretched circle of my arms, she settled down on her knees and began working on her cud. I stayed very still and continued to listen. The small lives I had nurtured had given life and vigor back to me tenfold. *Tenfold. This is how I tithe.* My eyes flew open and met the deep brown of Phaedra's luminous eyes peering back at me. Her face was soft, her gaze clear, kind, and bottomless. The banana ears that swiveled my way were white and clean. She leaned forward and gently sniffed my face, and I scratched her thin neck. There had been improvements, albeit small ones. She would be fine. We would be fine. Shame melted. The world returned. This is how I tithe. Not with money and checks but with time and love and nurture to a decades-long chain of creatures who found their way to me, who chose me. And in the choosing, healed me, taught me, empowered me: the charity cases. God grant me a never ending stream of charity cases: "Bring it over to Susan. She'll take care of it. She knows how."

When I left the barn that night and returned to the house, it was to tell Lee that I would be cutting off my very arms and legs if there were no place in our home for the nonproductive ones, the charity cases. And of course, he understood. Understood quickly. It was I who needed to understand, and it was Phaedra who had chosen to teach me: This is how I tithe.

THINKING LIKE ANIMALS

Temple Grandin

Language-based thought is foreign to me. All my thoughts are full-color motion pictures, running like a videotape in my imagination. It was always obvious to me that cattle and other animals also think in pictures. I have learned that there are some people who mainly think in words and I have observed that these verbal thinkers are more likely to deny animals' thought; they are unable to imagine thought without words. Using my visual thinking skills, it is easy for me to imagine myself in an animal's body and see things from their perspective. It is the ultimate virtual reality system. I can imagine looking through their eyes or walking with four legs.

My life as a person with autism is like being another species: part human and part animal. Autistic emotion may be more like an animal's. Fear is the dominant emotion in both autistic people and animals such as deer, cattle, and horses. My emotions are simple and straightforward; like an animal's, my emotions are not deep-seated. They may be intense while I am experiencing them but they will subside like an afternoon thunderstorm.

For the last fifteen years I have designed chute systems for handling cattle in slaughter plants. The conveyorized restraint system I designed is used in slaughtering one third of all the cattle in the United States.

Cattle are not afraid of the same things that people fear. The problem is that many people cannot observe this because they allow their own emotions to get in the way. To design a humane system I had to imagine what it would be like if I were the animal. I had to become that animal and not just be a person in a cow costume.

Cattle and people are upset by different things. People are repulsed by the sight of blood, but blood does not bother cattle. They are wary of the things that spell danger in the wild, such as high-pitched noise, disturbances of the dirt, and sudden jerky movements. A high-pitched noise may be a distress cry, and dirt or grass that is displaced may mean that there has been a struggle to avoid being eaten. Abrupt motion may be associated with a predator leaping onto its prey. These are all danger signals.

Many times I have observed cattle balking and refusing to move through a chute at a slaughter plant. They may balk at a jiggling gate, a shadow, a shiny reflection, or anything that appears to be out of place. A coffee cup dropped on the floor can make the cattle stop and turn back. But cattle will walk quietly into a slaughterhouse if the things they are afraid of are eliminated. Solid sides on chutes prevent them from seeing people up ahead and muffling devices lessen the shrill sounds that alarm them.

Cattle are sensitive to the same things that disturb people with autism. Immature development in the lower brain systems causes some people with autism to have a heightened sense of hearing, and an intense fear is triggered when anything in their environment is out of place. A curled-up rug, or a book that is crooked on the shelf, causes the same fear as being stalked by a predator. The autistic brain is acutely aware of details that most other people ignore. Sudden high-pitched sounds in the middle of the night cause my heart to race as if a lion was going to pounce.

Like a wild animal, I recoil when people touch me. A light touch sets off a flight reaction and my oversensitive nerve endings do not tolerate hugging. I want the soothing feeling of being held, but the sensations can be too overwhelming, so I pull away. My need for touch started my interest in cattle.

Puberty began the onslaught of hormones that sensitized my nervous system and started the constant fear and anxiety. I was desperate for relief. At my aunt's ranch I observed that when cattle were placed in a squeeze chute for their vaccinations, the pressure from the side panels squeezing against their bodies relaxed them. Pressure over wide areas of the body has a calming effect on many animals. Pressure applied to the sides of a piglet will cause it to fall asleep. Firm touch has a calming effect, while a light tickle touch is likely to set off a flight reaction.

Many parents of autistic children have observed that their child will seek pressure by getting under sofa cushions or a mattress. Therapists often use deep pressure to calm autistic children. I decided to try the squeeze chute and discovered that the intense pressure temporarily made my anxiety go away. When I returned home from the ranch I built a squeezing machine. Early versions pressed against my body with hard wood. When I first started using the machine I flinched and pulled away from it like a wild animal. As I adjusted to being held I used less intense pressure and I remodeled the side panels with foam rubber padding to make the machine more comfortable.

As I became able to tolerate being held I became more interested in figuring out how the cattle felt when they were handled and held in squeeze chutes at the feed yards. Many of the animals were scared because people were rough with them. They chased them, yelled at them, and prodded them. I found that I could coax most cattle to walk through a chute to be vaccinated by moving them quietly, at a slow walk. When an animal was calm I could observe the things that would catch his eye, like shadows or people leaning over the top of the chute. The leader would look at the things that concerned him. He would stop and stare at a coffee cup on the floor or move his head back and forth in time with a small chain that was swinging in the chute. Before moving forward he had to carefully scrutinize the things that attracted his attention. If the handlers tried to force him to move before he had determined that the chain was harmless, he and all the other cattle would panic. Cattle moved quietly and quickly through the chutes as soon as the swinging chain was removed.

I found that the animals were less likely to resist being held by the squeeze chute if pressure was applied slowly. An animal would panic if suddenly bumped. I also discovered the concept of optimum pressure. The chute must apply sufficient pressure to provide the feeling of being held but not cause pain. Many people make the mistake of mashing an animal too tight when it struggles. And the chute always needs solid sides, so that the cattle do not see people deep inside their flight zone. The flight zone is the animal's safety zone. They become anxious and want to get away when people get too close.

Years later, when I designed a restraint chute for holding cattle for slaughter, I was amazed that the animals would stand still and seldom resist the chute. I found that I could just ease their head and body into position by adjusting the chute. When I got really skilled at operating the hydraulic controls, the apparatus became an extension of my arms and hands. It was as if I could reach through the machine and hold each animal very gently. It was my job to hold the animal gently while the rabbi performed the final deed.

During the last ten years, more and more women have been hired to handle cattle and operate chutes in both feed yards and slaughter plants. At first the men were skeptical that women could do the work, but today progressive managers have found that women are gentler and work well with the animals. Some feed yards now hire only women to doctor sick cattle and vaccinate the new arrivals. In slaughter plants, two of the best operators of kosher restraining chutes are women. They were attracted to the job because they couldn't stand to see the guys abusing cattle.

When I first started designing equipment I thought that all the problems of the rough treatment of animals in slaughter plants could be solved with engineering. But engineering is only part of the equation. The most important thing is the attitude of management. A strong manager acts as the conscience of the employees in the trenches. To be most effective in maintaining high standards of animal treatment the manager has to be involved enough to care, but not so much that he or she overdoses on the constant death. The managers who are most likely to care and enforce humane handling are most likely to have close associations with animals, or are close to the land.

I am often asked how I can care about animals and be involved in their slaughter. People forget that nature can be harsh. Death at the slaughter plant is quicker and less painful than death in the wild. Lions dining on the guts of a live animal is much worse in my opinion. The animals we raise for food would have never lived at all if we had not raised them. I feel that our relationship with animals must be symbiotic. In nature there are many examples of symbiosis. For example, ants raise aphids and use them as "dairy cows." The ants feed the aphids and in return they provide a sugar substance. It is important that our relationship with farm animals is reciprocal. We owe animals a decent life and a painless death.

I have observed that the people who are completely out of touch with nature are the most afraid of death, and places such as slaughter houses. I was moved by Birute Galdikas's book on her research on orangutans. The people in the Borneo rain forests live as a part of nature and have a totally different view of life and death. To the native people, "death is not separate from life." In the jungle they see death every day. Birute states, "For me, as for most middle-class North Americans death was just a tremor far down, far away at the end of a very long road, not something to be lived with every hour of every single day."

Many people attempt to deny the reality of their own mortality. When I designed my first system I had to look my own mortality straight in the eye. I live each day as if I could die tomorrow. I want to make the most of each day and do things to make the world a better place.

Stacy Young

Having rescued and cared for animals all my life, I had always thought of myself as having an enlightened relationship with them. Horses, ducks, rabbits, flying squirrels, baby robins, field mice, dogs, and cats had all been part of the family at one time or another. But it was a small, black feral kitten who would force me to confront a level of prejudice toward animals that I had never realized I had.

I volunteered one summer at the adoption desk of our local animal shelter. To my horror, people dumped their companion animals at the shelter for the most trivial reasons: Their dog was shedding; their cat was clawing the furniture. One woman dropped off her fifteen-year-old cat because he didn't match her new couch.

But at least they brought them into the shelter. Many people, I discovered, simply dump their unwanted cats in the woods, or at the side of the road. If they survive at all, they do so by becoming wild, or feral. Trapped on the edges of civilization, these outlaw cats are feared and despised. People either are afraid of them for the diseases they may carry or hate them for preying on the local bird population. Almost without exception local laws allow for feral cats to be trapped and destroyed.

Of course, any cat who did make it into the shelter ran the risk of being killed. There had to be several empty enclosures every day to accommodate new arrivals, so every afternoon the shelter manager went through the cat room to decide which ones to euthanize that night. She chose the least adoptable: older cats, cats that hissed at people, cats with scars. People only wanted the young, cute cats.

The longer I worked there, the more certain I became that killing these perfectly healthy animals was wrong. I rescued as many as I could by adopting them myself. But I couldn't save the ferals.

The first time I saw Animal Control bring in a feral cat I didn't even know what the word meant. This one had obviously once been a magnificent longhaired beauty. Now his fur was filthy and matted, one eye was cloudy, and the other stared malevolently at me.

"His owner should be arrested for animal abuse," I remarked heatedly.

"Oh, he's got no owner," the officer replied. "This here's a feral. He's a useless son of a bitch." He put the paperwork on top of the carrier and left.

Stunned, I followed the shelter manager as she took the carrier to the back. "What's happened to this cat?"

She shrugged. "Maybe his owners left him behind when they moved. Maybe he got sick and they didn't want to pay the vet bill. Who knows?"

"Let me foster him," I said. "I'll bring him round so he's adoptable."

The shelter manager frowned at me in surprise and shook her head. "He's *feral*. You can't bring him round. He'll never be adoptable."

"Then what will happen to him?" But I knew as I asked the question. I felt the hackles rise on the back of my neck.

"We can't even find homes for all the domestic cats that come in here," she said quietly. "Nobody wants to adopt the ferals. We euthanize them." With that, she carried the doomed animal into the euthanasia room. I was horrified.

I started searching for people sympathetic to feral cats and discovered a national network, linked by newsletters, e-mail, and word of mouth, dedicated to rescuing them. They vaccinate the cats, alter them to prevent more litters, and return them to their feral colonies in the suburban wild. Via the network I found a group of people who had already launched a project to stabilize the cat population in our neighborhood park, and I began helping them.

One day I got a call from Eileen, another woman on the project. "We trapped three kittens this morning," she said. "They don't look any older than three months. I think there's a chance they're young enough to be socialized. Would you foster them?"

I knew what she was saying, of course. Word among veterans of this work was that three months was the limit; any older than that and they would be irrevocably feral. But if these kittens could learn to adapt to humans, they had a chance to be adopted. The alternative was to release them back to the colony, where we both knew that, despite our best efforts, they would be in constant danger. She had them vaccinated and altered and drove right over.

As soon as I saw them I knew they were older than three months— at least four, maybe five. They were terrified, huddled together in the back of their carrier, a black male and two white females, one with black spots, one with gray.

The gray spotted female already seemed tame enough to hold, so I picked her up and held her carefully against my chest. "Annie," I whispered. Her fur was as soft as a rabbit's and luxuriously thick. She was otherworldly, almost ethereal, and I was thrilled to hold her. But then I saw the fear in her eyes and realized she wasn't tame at all; she was being submissive because she was terrified. I wanted these kittens to grow to trust me, not fear me. It was going to take time. Gently I put her down.

I named the black male Simon. He was the most magnificent cat I had ever seen. His coat was long and hauntingly black, and he was just beginning to have a thick lion's mane around his head. His long nose and piercing emerald green eyes reminded me more of a wolf than a cat. I felt I was face-to-face with a creature as wild as any on Earth.

My husband, Vaughn, whose heart went out to these hapless kittens, helped me set them up in the large bathroom off our living room. We left the door to the carrier open so they could come and go as they pleased. Every morning their plates of food were empty and the kitty litter had been used, but I never saw them out of that carrier. Day after day when I went in to check on them, they huddled together in the back of it, Simon protectively shielding his sisters, pure hatred in his eyes.

I had never tamed a wild animal before. I became obsessed with taming Simon. I imagined that he would become my lap cat, that he would love to have me pet him. It didn't occur to me that there was anything wrong with my attitude. Patiently I set out to bring him around as if he were a recalcitrant child.

I sat on the floor next to the carrier for hours every day so Simon could learn to trust me. Sometimes I read a magazine or book; often I spoke in low, soothing tones, telling him what it would be like to live in our house, assuring him he would be happy with us. I wanted to be his friend, I told him.

But Simon refused to respond. Sometimes I sat watching him, willing him to give in. But his implacable stare never wavered, and it was during those long, tense silences between us that I began to realize what I was doing. I was taking it for granted that I had the right to ignore Simon's will. What I was doing was *for his own good*. But what gave me the authority to decide what was good for him? With mounting uncertainty I tried to explain myself to Simon.

For three weeks he and his sisters huddled in the open carrier and refused to come out as long as I was in the room. I was becoming increasingly discouraged when Joyce, another woman from the rescue project, arrived one afternoon with a huge cage, four feet tall by three feet deep by two feet wide. A cat playpen, she called it, perfect for socializing these feral kittens. Set it up where they would have a chance to see Vaughn and me interacting with our other cats, she advised. Let them get used to being part of the household.

I frowned doubtfully. Simon would hate being in a cage.

"They'll come around, you'll see," Joyce said.

I thought if it had worked with other feral cats, maybe I should try it. Reluctantly, I helped Joyce set it up with a litter box, food, and a towel draped over one corner to give the kittens some privacy. Then we put the open end of the carrier against the door of the cage and, with some prodding, got the three ferals to jump in.

Vaughn and I made it a point to spend time near the cage, but it was no use. The two females stayed in their hiding place behind the towel, and Simon crouched, motionless, on the carpeted ledge above them. He refused all offers from our other cats to sniff noses through the bars. No matter how much I talked to him, cajoled, begged, cried, his look of profound contempt didn't change.

Doubts assailed me. Maybe this was just a game of power, after all. Did I really want to help him, or was I offering my protection only if he was willing to become my pet? Perhaps I really did enjoy my superiority over this creature. I wanted to own this animal, to possess him like a beautiful toy. These thoughts tortured me until I was too ashamed to look Simon in the eye.

One day, when he had been in the cage for two weeks, I put my face close to the bars and whispered hello to him, as I always did. He backed up and stared at me with the same hatred I had grown to expect, but this time his loathing struck me like a physical blow.

A crushing shame overtook me. *My God*, I thought, *I have no right to cage this animal.* I put my hands on the bars and pressed my face against them and imagined that I was in the cage and not Simon. I could feel the anger he felt. I could feel his primal fear.

Soon the paralyzing moment of empathy passed and I was the superior again, but now the role was repugnant to me, and I renounced it in one swift action. I opened the cage, knowing that it would only be a matter of time before he found the cat door, his window to the outside.

"You're free to go, Simon," I whispered. He sat up and pricked his ears as if he had understood what I said. "Your sisters, too. You're welcome to live here if you want to. I'll always have food for you, and a warm, safe place to sleep. But I won't impose my will on you anymore."

Slowly I got up and went out of sight of the cage, leaving Simon and his sisters alone with the open door. Already I missed him unbearably. But for the first time, I had truly done something for *him*. I collapsed on the couch, exhausted.

Nearly an hour later, I reached for a magazine and saw a movement out of the corner of my eye. I looked around just in time to see Simon trot over to the chair where one of our cats was sleeping. He stood up on his hind legs like a bear and sniffed her paw, then turned and surveyed the room. When he saw me he froze, and I held my breath. Simon lowered his front paws to the floor, still watching me. Then slowly he crawled under the chair, curled up, and, with one last look my way, put his head on his paws and closed his eyes.

Simon's simple gesture made my heart stop. I lay there motionless, my hand still outstretched for the magazine, unwilling to move and risk having him change his mind. Then slowly, cautiously, I relaxed. Still Simon didn't move, and finally I let myself believe what had just happened: I had given him back his dignity; in return, he had honored me with his trust. In that moment I knew the nature of my relationship with all animals had undergone a profound change. I was still the human, the most powerful animal on Earth. I couldn't change that. But never again would I take it for granted that my power gave me license to dominate.

That evening after dinner, when all the rest of the cats left the house through the cat door, Simon and his sisters went with them. I watched them go and wondered sadly if I would ever see them again. A few hours later, they returned. After that, they lived in our house but kept a cautious distance.

Simon in particular remained aloof.

One rainy afternoon about a month later, I answered the doorbell and found our neighbor, drenched, holding a tiny, bedraggled bundle of light green and blue and yellow feathers. It was a parakeet, nearly dead, she had found on the beach near our house.

I knew why she was bringing the little creature to our house: People thought of us as the unofficial neighborhood animal shelter. But this was a *bird*. Even if we saved her, how could she stay with us? What chance would she have in our houseful of cats?

"We'll try to save her," I promised.

We hauled an old hamster cage out of the basement, made a little nest out of soft rags and strips of newspaper, gave her a bowl of water and a two-inch bar of seeds, fruit and nuts all held together with honey. Then we put the cage in the bathroom and shut the door to give her some peace and quiet. We both knew there was a good chance she would not make it through the night. At least we could give her a safe haven in death.

But when I tiptoed into the bathroom early the next morning there she was, hopping back and forth on the floor of the cage. When she saw me she began to sing with wild, raucous abandon. The two-inch bar of seeds and fruit had completely disappeared and she had made an astonishing recovery.

I named her Sidney, bought her a large cage, and gave her my writing table in the dining room, right by a window overlooking Puget Sound. For two weeks we had to guard her from our electrified cats during the day and lock her in the bathroom at night to keep her safe. It became clear that for this little bird, the cage was something very different from what it had been for the feral cats. They were predators; for them it had been a prison. But Sidney was prey. Yes, the cage was a prison, but it was also a sanctuary, and she seemed content to call it her home.

The cats finally got used to having a bird in the house and even seemed to enjoy her company. Soon people walking by could see three or four cats napping in front of the window, curled up around Sidney's cage and on top of it. Simon was the only one who never jumped up on the table to see Sidney. He watched her curiously but kept his distance.

Then one afternoon, I walked into the dining room and found Simon at the cage. He sat spellbound as the little bird ran back and forth on her perch, wings flapping furiously, head poked way out at Simon, singing loudly. It seemed clear that she wanted him to play. Simon was so flabbergasted he stood up on his hind legs like a bear and stared at her with his mouth open.

Finally Sidney fell silent, one claw poised in the air outside the bars, as if reaching for Simon. Clearly the ball was in his court. Simon seemed frozen on his hind legs, front paws folded on his chest, eyes wide. Sidney cocked her head and raised her foot a bit higher.

Then Simon reached out and slowly, gently, pressed his paw against Sidney's outstretched claw. The room was silent. I held my breath and watched as predator and prey set aside their most basic instincts to forge a relationship born of unusual circumstance, two creatures in an artificial habitat created by humans.

It was Sidney who finally broke the spell. Suddenly she let out a screech and flapped her wings at Simon, chirping wildly. Simon settled down then with his back against the cage, eyes half-closed, more relaxed than I had ever seen him. Our brave parakeet seemed to have gotten through to this proud, wild creature in a way I hadn't been able to in nearly three months.

From then on Simon was almost always at Sidney's cage. They played together endlessly, Sidney pecking delightedly at Simon, Simon swiping at her feet with his paw. Often he curled up against her cage for his nap. Sometimes he just sat next to her gazing out the window, bird and cat watching the world go by.

And after Simon made friends with Sidney, he began to interact with Vaughn and me as well. If we moved very slowly, he let us touch his paws. After a while, he let us stroke the soft fur on his back, very briefly.

Then one night we discovered Sidney lying on the floor of her cage. We raced her to an emergency clinic, but she died before the doctor could help her. Did we know why there was blood on her leg? the doctor asked. Perhaps it would explain how she died. But we had no idea.

I wrapped Sidney in a soft blue cloth and put her back in her cage that night so Simon could say goodbye, but he didn't understand. The next morning I found him nuzzling the cage, waiting for the little bird to come out and play. Seeing Simon with his paw up on the bars of the cage, I thought about what the doctor had said, that there was blood on Sidney's leg. Suddenly I knew that it had been a cat's claw that killed her. Even a human could get sick from a cat scratch. The bacteria in that claw would have been way too much for Sidney's tiny system. Simon had played with her the most; it had probably been his claw. The thought tore at my heart. Theirs had been the most fragile of alliances, between predator and prey, and I wondered if I had done the right thing, letting them play.

Simon slept next to her all day. He woke up when I took her out of the cage, and he watched as I stroked her dear little green and blue body. He lifted his paw and I held her out so he could touch her for the first time without bars between them. He listened as Vaughn and I bade her a final farewell, and he followed us outside and sat quietly as we buried her. Later on, Vaughn took Sidney's cage down to the basement, and I put my laptop back on the dining room table.

A few days later as I was working, Simon jumped up onto the table and curled up next to my keyboard. I reached out and gently rubbed his paw. He closed his eyes and, for the first time, began to purr.

JUSTICE IN VENICE BEACH

Vicki Hearne

I was with my dog Annie on the boardwalk in Venice Beach when I dis-covered that there is something to the notion that it is a complex fate to be an American. Annie is a registered American Staffordshire Terrier (AmStaff, for short) and at the moment this was interesting, because that year, 1986 as I recall, the *American Kennel Club Purebred Dog Gazette* conducted a poll to find out which breed would be voted the all-American dog. The AmStaff won. AmStaffs, like pit bulls, English Bull Terriers, and some others, are among the breeds and lines of dog various groups in this country are proposing to muzzle, outlaw, generally abolish, or at least require special licenses for, on the grounds that they are vicious and un-American. The enthusiasm in question has spread, so that there are now breeds that are un-Irish, un-English, un-Norwegian, un-German, and un-Australian.

The day Annie and I were at the beach—it was June, and everything sparkled—I wasn't thinking about all that, Venice Beach not being a place where I worried too much about running into members of the House Un-American Activities Committee. Annie was walking formally at heel, the kites were flying, the peddlers were peddling various things legal and illegal, the skaters were skating, the lovers were loving. I must say that Annie was a bit nervous about the whole situation, since she does worry about the moral lives of those around her.

Suddenly, from behind a kiosk selling entrancingly unwearable gar-ments, appeared two excited American males, respectable, each with a dog, a Collie and a German Shepherd. They asked me what sort of dog Annie was. I said she was a pit bull, which is the answer I give when I am alarmed, and it is in any case true from certain points of view. Respectable-looking American males who are excited always alarm me.

One of these gentlemen—he had a distinctly Santa Monica lawyer-ish look about him—started howling about people like me with vicious dogs like Annie being responsible for the ruination of the country. His friend, a Stanford alumnus as it seemed, added that if it weren't for people like me the Stanford football team wouldn't have had to change its name from the Indians to the Cardinals, thus betraying everything Stanford stands for. (There may be something to this.)

Now, you have to understand that Annie is definitely a matriarchal sort of dog. She thinks people and dogs should behave themselves, and she also thinks that she is in charge of seeing to this, so she was look-ing very much like an alert and ready-to-move version of Mount Ever-est. This caused the Stanford man to move threateningly toward me. Annie growled at him. He retreated, while his Collie, Lad, responded to the excitement by attacking Cracker, the German Shepherd. (Both dogs were males.)

This was too much for Annie. Coming as she does from a long line of noble fighters, she disapproves of street brawls the way a great boxer might. So she leaped in between the snarling pair and performed the acro-batic feat of simultaneously grabbing in her mouth one of the ears of each. The snarling became screeching, and a policeman of sorts appeared to break up the fight. But there was by now no fight, of course, because both dogs had instantly apologized profoundly, promising Mama never to do it again.

Annie said, "See that you don't!"

Cracker and Lad recognized genuine authority. They sat down obe-diently, symmetrically and formally, putting all they had into announcing their intention to go forth and sin no more. They were dogs, of course, and dogs know what people rarely do—the female is in charge. Always. The respectable male *Homo sapiens*, however, were confused and mut-tered something uncivilized about feminists. Annie looked at them with a Look of Meaning, and they quieted down.

So the breed that is to be outlawed, muzzled, etc., because of its fighting history, was the one that broke up the fight and restored order. And this is the breed voted the all-American dog. Which tells me that to be authentically American is exactly to be misunderstood. There is justice in America, just as Thomas Jefferson hoped there would be, but her true name and nature is a secret.

GOAT'S MILK

Charlotte Zoë Walker

This woman has come from afar. She can be seen walking in the meadow near her cabin, followed by two goats, three tiny kids, and a big, bearlike white dog. Wildflowers grow in the meadow, and birds make beautiful sounds, bits of song, which she strings together on the silver lines of her flute. It seems to be the most peaceful life imaginable, this life in the meadow, and that is why she sought it and worked so hard to bring it into being.

But even she, with her vision of harmony, does not know how beautiful she is, this tiny, dark woman, strolling in the meadow grass, making music as her small menagerie straggles and scampers around her and behind. As she lies down in the soft-and-pricking grasses and looks up at the small clouds in a suddenly blue sky, one of the kids puts its nose against her cheek, its long-lashed brown eyes gaze into the long-lashed brown eyes of a woman who's come from afar.

This peaceful life is not easily maintained, for it means rushing home from work each night, traveling an hour from the city where she translates letters from Spanish to English, and then her employers' replies, from English back to Spanish. And then, after the long drive through gradually thinning traffic, the animals greet her needily, and must be fed and petted, and her dog, her big, beloved friend, must have a walk, while the goats come along for company. And the lamps must be lit with care, because there is no electricity yet on this road, and wood must be split and restacked inside the cabin. But all this effort to maintain her refuge helps keep her mind clear and free, helps her to forget where she came from—afar—which was what is called a police state, though the only police were not protectors, maintainers of order, but victimizers, virtuosos of chaos.

When Cecilia lies in the meadow looking up at small clouds in azure, she sometimes finds the sky going suddenly black, sometimes hears an iron door clanging shut—or worse, open—or the lovely afternoon sun, when it is turned on again, becomes a glaring interrogation lamp. And she is forced to remember that somewhere in the world, at this very moment, a woman, maybe a hundred women and men, maybe more (no longer, for now, in her own country, but elsewhere, many elsewheres)—are caught in that tearing, searing reality. It lacerates her spirit, tears her open again, to know that she cannot change such an impossible truth.

And she wills to them, to those who are still caught, or newly caught in the same old web, a soft, tender nose-nudge from one of these kids. She sends them good goat's milk, or her own soft, pure goat cheese in small rounds, like those clouds above—floats them there by azure delivery. Here, she says, partake of this and be nourished, be strong for reclaiming your freedom.

But her anger and terror rise up just the same. Almost suffocating, she sits up suddenly in the meadow and looks about her, counting all her gentle creatures, calling the big, fluffy dog, who comes bounding toward her with a smile on his friendly bear face. She looks at the row of trees at the edge of the meadow, hoping to see the blue heron. But the heron is not there today. So she lifts her flute from the grass and rises to her feet to walk some more. As she walks, her fingers and her breath find a market song from her childhood, a song about fruits and gourds and many-colored birds.

One day, in mid-autumn when the trees around the meadow are burgundy and orange and gold, Cecilia receives a letter from a woman she met on the day they were all released from the prison. For months they had suffered in neighboring rooms, but had never seen each other. When the doors were opened, they all became sisters in a moment, in a few waiting hours, an afternoon of blindingly pure new light. This woman, Rosa, who was tall and must have been blond once, when her hair knew the sun, was heavily pregnant on that day of release.

When Cecilia, sitting on a wooden bench beside her, asked how long she had been in prison, Rosa said, "Almost a year, I think." Looked down at her belly then, and after a moment whispered, "Yes."

Now Rosa is writing to ask that her friend of a day, of the day of liberation, her friend of a few brief letters, sponsor her entry to the new country. "It is the only chance I have," she writes. And though Cecilia knows the torturers are gone, or merely, mildly, walking the streets of their country now like innocent citizens, she can imagine the family's pain over the coming of that child, now three years old. The husband, who had been out of the country when Rosa was arrested, had not been able to bear the knowledge of that child's beginnings and left very soon.

Rosa's parents did better, and the little one's grandmother will even weep with anguish when they drive Rosa and little Jesús to the airport. She will be losing her only happiness, her only joy, after all the pain. But Rosa must begin in a new place, begin from afar.

It is late winter when Cecilia drives along the snow-flanked highway to the airport to meet her friend. She knows it is insane to do this, she may not even have the strength to manage it. Her cabin is small. There is a man at work that she was just beginning to trust a bit, and now there will be no time for him, no easy place to get to know him in her life. And worst—the past will be with her every day now, it will be much more difficult to keep it afar.

And yet she could not refuse. To give goat's milk in a small cup, directly into two small hands and a rosy, drinking mouth. That is God's reply to her shipments of goat's cheese sent effortlessly away on small clouds. Now you may truly nourish! But not until spring, for the goats are dry now, waiting for their new babies to come and their milk to flow again.

"*Hola!* Rosa! There you are!" she laughs, as the tall, weary-looking blond woman with a child on her hip walks from the customs gate.

"Cecilia! Oh, I was afraid you wouldn't be here!" Rosa lets her fingers slip from the handle of the heavy bags as Cecilia lifts it away from her. The freed hand goes first around her child to steady him on her hip, then back to greet Cecilia, warmly gliding past her shoulder as they hug one another.

"Of course I am here," says Cecilia. She pauses, a bit shyly, then looks from Rosa's hazel-colored eyes to the dark brown ones of her child, who studies Cecilia solemnly.

"So you are Jesús," she says. A chill comes over her, at the back of her neck especially, as she looks at him.

"Jesús, this is Tía Cecilia," his mother says. She kisses his cheek and sets him down on the dirty marble floor. Cecilia squats down to be at his level.

"*Buenos dias*, Jesús," she tells him. "Do you want to see the goats at my house?"

He nods slowly.

Rosa laughs. "Mamita too! I want to see them as much as Jesús does!"

Cecilia smiles and says something kind. She leads them quickly to her car, limping with the weight of the heavy bag that is too big for her. But she is doing it all automatically, with a heart that is frozen in shock at one fact—her instant recognition of the child's face.

She is taking into her refuge a miniature, a tiny replica of the one who tormented her most.

What a relief, when they get home, to remember that she decided not to give them her beloved tiny sleeping loft. It is such a perfect place for a child, she almost felt required to offer it. Thank heaven, she made up the downstairs bed for them instead, in the open living space that's most of her little cabin. She will need to retreat to the loft, she will need to hide from her memories of that face. How can Rosa bear it? Why didn't she run away when her husband did, leave the baby with his grandmother, give him to an orphanage, do *something* to escape being haunted this way? It could have happened to me, he could have been born to me!

They are in the house now, away from the winter cold. She has done everything automatically, she has not really heard Rosa's answers to all her questions, she has not heard her own answers to Rosa's questions, her exclamations of amazement over winter and snow. All the time this haunting has taken over her mind—even as she stirs up the coals in her wood stove and adds a new log and offers Rosa and Jesús something warm to drink.

"*Qué lindo!*" says Rosa as they wander about the snug, one-room space of her cabin with its sleeping loft above. "How beautiful you make it here!"

"It's just a small log cabin," says Cecilia. "But I love it." She shows Rosa the small kitchen alcove and the bathroom—the only room with a door that the cabin has.

Rosa touches a richly colored handwoven rug from the mountain country near their home—red and burgundy, goldenrod, deep blue and brown. It hangs on the wall near the back door. She looks at Cecilia with tears in her eyes. "Home," she says, and smiles a wonderfully sad, loving, and ironic smile. Only the most courageous spirits can make such gentle, complicated smiles!

"*Sí,*" says Cecilia, responding with a smile almost the same. "I tried to find some sweet memories of home to look at here." She leads them across the room to the mattress on the floor, with its bright woolen blanket from home. "Here is your bed," she says. "And this cupboard is empty for you to put your things." She swings the doors open to show them the welcoming space. A little blue truck sits on the top shelf. "Who is this for?" she says to Jesús. He eyes her seriously. "Who do you think it is for?" she says again, and she is able to smile.

"*Para mí?*"

"*Sí!* For you," she says. "Take it." And his little hand reaches shyly up to the shelf, just within his reach it is, and his fingers close over the blue truck. For a moment he is just a child. That face that he has, in his innocence, genetically borrowed disappears for a moment in his baby smile.

Late that evening she looks down at them from the railing of her loft. Rosa has fallen asleep with her arm around Jesús, who sleeps curled toward her, with the little blue truck held tightly in one fist. Cecilia told them she would leave one lamp burning low for them.

Really she is the one who is afraid of darkness this night. She is afraid of waking up in darkness. But even with the light on, the dreams come to her. That face comes back, a face so handsome in its way that one could learn to hate beauty forever. Face so ugly that one could never see beauty again. She sits up abruptly, shaking. The dim light is a torture too. Darkness would be better.

Shaking, she descends the ladder from her loft, goes to the kitchen alcove for a glass of water.

"NO! NO!" Rosa shouts. So she has dreams too! The child begins to whimper.

"It's all right, Rosa," she says softly, walking across the room to her.

She kneels down to the mattress on the floor and puts her hand on Rosa's shoulder. "You are in my house, Rosa, you're safe."

Rosa looks up at her with lovely eyes. "Ahh, Cecilia! Oh, I'm so sorry I woke you!"

"No, it's I who woke you. I had a dream too."

"But we're safe?" Rosa says. "We're safe in your house?"

"Yes," says Cecilia. "Safe in my house. I'm going to turn off the lamp now. We won't dream anymore. Or if we do—we'll dream with the angels."

She leans forward to kiss Rosa's forehead, to adjust the blankets round Jesús' shoulders. *"Que sueñes con los angelitos."*

"Con los angelitos," says Rosa, smiling up at her ... with haunted eyes.

In the first few days they set up a routine that makes the loss of privacy, the harshness of memory, easier for Cecilia to bear. There is the pleasure of sharing her food, her shelter. There is the comradeship of Rosa's presence, and the child's delight in the animals. And very quickly Rosa begins to keep house for her while she is at work.

When she comes home, dinner has already been cooked, the kerosene lamps have been lit. One night the animals have been watered and fed also, but Cecilia quickly explains that this is her special pleasure—not so much a chore as the joy of her day. And Rosa gladly leaves that to her, just taking care of the house, the wood stove, and the cooking. Even that Cecilia misses somehow, but she relinquishes it for her friend's sake. Rosa needs to feel she is doing something to pay her own way. Before the time in prison she had been a teacher of young children.

"When you have had time to improve your English, you can get a teaching job here," Cecilia says, as they take coffee outdoors together, one mild afternoon in early spring. "They need teachers who know Spanish."

"Not yet," says Rosa. "I'd be so afraid." She laughs nervously, giving Cecilia a brief imploring glance. And Cecilia realizes that as far as

Rosa is concerned, this arrangement could be very comfortable for a long, long time.

They sit, without chairs, on the deck of her cabin, their coffee mugs beside their knees, as they watch the rushing spring waters of the nearby stream. Jesús is lying astride Leo, her big white dog, burying his face in the soft fur.

"No, not yet, of course," says Cecilia. Unspoken between them both—the fears each has of the other. For Rosa—the fear of being sent into the cold world; for Cecilia—the fear of never being alone again.

Only a few nights later, she comes home to find the smell of smoke heavy inside the cabin, and black soot up the side of one wall. The tapestry from home is singed partway up, and the bottom edges burnt. Her mind knows immediately what happened—but her emotions are frantic with shock, with possibilities of chaos.

"Cecilia—I'm so sorry!" Rosa says. Her beautiful long face is taut with worry and fear. "Jesús was playing with the cat on top of the table somehow—and the lamp fell over! I was cooking dinner, I didn't watch him close enough." She pauses, looks desperately for some sign from Cecilia. "I'm so ashamed!" she says.

Fire is licking at Cecilia's eyes, it is singeing her feet, her heart. Nothing is safe. There is no refuge. "I'm—glad you weren't hurt," she manages to say. "It's—a shock, is all. Let me sit down a minute."

"I know," says Rosa quietly. She follows Cecilia to the couch.

Cecilia leans forward, places her head in her hands a few moments. Then looks up again. "For you too—it must have been worse, with the flames here, the danger!"

"Maybe not," says Rosa. "I had to move so fast—I had to put it out! If Jesús was hurt—or if we destroyed your house—I would have killed myself."

"You don't mean that." Cecilia is annoyed by such a declaration. How would that help?

"I do. Even now—I am sick with shame that we did this to your home!"

"I have to do something about getting electricity," Cecilia says. "In a few months—the lines may come through."

"Until then—we will be very careful," says Rosa.

"But how can a child be trusted to be careful? How can you—be sure he didn't do it on purpose?" Cecilia feels horrible as she says it—but she is afraid it might be true. Fate is very strange. How can they be sure he is not somehow an enemy? She looks at the child for the first time since she came in. He is sitting on the bed, his own safe territory, his eyelids lowered and his straight little mouth firm with fear and solemnity. She cannot bear to have him here, the danger, the dreams. There are so many things she can't speak of.

It is almost a normal evening. They eat dinner quietly. Talk gently of spring, of lamps, of electricity. Jesús is first instructed and then reassured by his mother, though Cecilia can barely speak to him, and is relieved when Rosa puts him to sleep.

When the dishes are washed and things put away, they sit down together on the sofa, a pot of peppermint tea on the old trunk Cecilia uses for a coffee table. Cecilia pours a mugful for each of them, hands Rosa hers. They have become close, like sisters—but always with these unspoken things between them.

"There is something I need to ask you," says Rosa. "Even before today—I have feared sometimes that you don't really like Jesús. You are kind to him, of course, but—"

"He brings back memories for me," says Cecilia.

"Oh." Rosa sips her tea, though it is too hot and she puts it down, hastily.

"He is a wonderful child," Cecilia says. "Forgive me if I don't seem to understand that. I do. But tonight has shaken me up—terribly."

"I know," Rosa says. "It has shaken me also."

"And I wonder sometimes . . ." Cecilia plunges ahead. "I wonder sometimes—how were you able to keep him, after all that happened?"

"How was I able to love him, you mean?" Rosa turns to face her friend more directly from her end of the sofa, gives Cecilia an almost-challenging look from her hazel eyes. Her delicate mouth with the deep lines beside it is half open, ready to respond.

"Both. First—just to keep him. Even before that—to give birth at all—how hard it must have been!"

"Yes. It seemed like their ultimate triumph over me, making me carry their seed in my body." She looks out the darkened window opposite them.

"Yes," Cecilia breathes out. "That's how I thought it would feel. It could have been me too, you know. I could have left prison in the same condition you did."

"Then you know completely," says Rosa softly. Her gaze swings to Cecilia's eyes, offers a look of sympathy.

"That part of it—I know completely. But the rest of what you went through—I don't think I could do it."

"The way I got through," says Rosa, "was that I promised myself I would kill the child when it was outside of me."

"Ah!" There is a long silence between them. Then Cecilia confesses. "It's what I think I would have done. What I would really have done."

"But then you can't," says Rosa. "Then your breast is full of milk and the child is itself. It came from heaven, not from prison. That's what you say, that's what you hope, when you hold it for the first time."

"And now—" Cecilia hesitates—"Do you love him now as if he were born out of love?"

"I love him even more fiercely, perhaps. I can't say why. Maybe it's an angry love, maybe it's a tender love, I don't know. But he is himself, you know, he exists free of that time." She looks again directly into Cecilia's eyes. "He is just a little boy, Cecilia."

"And the resemblance never—haunts you?"

"Resemblance?" Rosa looks at her in surprise. "What do you mean?"

"I . . . I don't know. I . . . get confused sometimes." Cecilia looks at Rosa, begging for silence or understanding, or innocence, perhaps. She is not sure which of these Rosa gives her—but something is given.

"I do . . ." says Rosa slowly, "I do . . . almost always . . . love him as if he came from me alone."

"Yes, I'm glad, I'm so glad it's that way," says Cecilia. But she has to repeat that phrase, ". . . almost always."

"And also—to protect us from any memories that might come—"

"You named him Jesús."

"*Sí.*" Now they are both looking at each other's tears. It is a moment when they might embrace, comfort one another. But they cannot. Cecilia reaches forward, lifts the lid from the teapot. A frail wisp of steam comes forth.

Rosa twists her hands in her lap. Nods, as Cecilia lifts the teapot and gestures with it toward Rosa's empty mug.

How can it matter how he was fathered? But it does. It still does.

Maybe Rosa, with her mother's bond, is able to forget—but not really, no not really. Jesús may be named to remind them constantly of the power of forgiveness, and maybe it is a real power—but Cecilia refuses that betrayal, refuses to forgive. And now every evening when she comes home she imagines the scorched smell is still in the cabin. She brings home flowers, she burns incense to mask it. She waits for the lilacs to bloom. On the news, she hears that her countrymen have voted to let the torturers continue to walk freely among them—out of fear that otherwise they will suddenly take power again, begin the horror all over again. Commentators say that perhaps it was a wise decision, perhaps this is true democracy, a haunted people's compromise. Cecilia only knows that the torturers mildly, smugly, menacingly walk among her people, as their genes walk along pathways inside this little boy's body. And she longs for her solitude.

In May, the lilacs do bloom, and five kids are born—Sarita has twins, and Blanca triplets. Cecilia takes the day off from work when Rosa calls her:

"I think Sarita's in labor!" By the time she gets home, both kids are born, and Sarita has cleaned everything up, looks quite pleased with herself and these two lovely black creatures with the same dun-colored spots as their mother. Blanca watches enviously. When will her time come?

That very midnight, before she goes to sleep, Cecilia goes out to the shed to find Blanca with one kid born, the second dangling in mid-dive from the birth canal, one wet little head and one hoof reaching out.

"*Dios!*" Rosa cries out, and Cecilia looks up to see that her friend, wrapped in a cotton bathrobe, has followed her. "Should I drive to the neighbors, call the animal doctor?"

"No. This doesn't look so bad," Cecilia says. She kneels on the straw beside the laboring animal and puts her slender arms inside to push back a bit and fish in the wetness and warmth for the tiny hoof that's lost its way. Then how easily the little creature completes its dive into life on this planet, lands gently in the straw. Then, as she watches for the placenta to come, Cecilia gives a laugh of surprise. "Blanca! You competitive thing!" Another kid is pushing fast against the second one, and soon the three wet, amazing little creatures are all struggling to stand up.

"How can she feed all three?" Rosa asks. She reaches into the pen to touch one tiny, glorious baby.

"She rotates them pretty well," Cecilia says, as she watches Blanca cleaning up the afterbirth, caring for everything with a fine skill. Cecilia strokes the newest kid and helps it to stand up. "And we'll help out with the bottle."

"Oh, I'd love that!" says Rosa.

"Then you can take the three A.M. feeding," Cecilia teases. Rosa's laughter is part of the warm, safe feeling as she works with the new kids, helping Blanca's work of cleaning them—she wipes with a cloth as Blanca licks the wobbly creatures with her tongue. Then dipping the umbilical cords in iodine so that they can dry cleanly and fall off in their own time.

Finally she is ready to leave the pen, comes out to stand beside Rosa and admire the little ones.

Rosa's eyes are shining like a child's. There is a wonderful energy weaving among them, women and goats alike. "But I *will* help you with the three A.M. feeding," Rosa says eagerly. "I'm used to it!"

"Me too," says Cecilia. "It will be nice to have some help this year. And at last—" she looks gravely at Rosa with a sudden, surprising, and generous flow from within her spirit—"at last, I can give Jesús some goat's milk to help him grow stronger!"

Rosa takes her hand away from the kid she has been touching. Its mother has nudged forward and is licking it tenderly. She looks from the goat to Cecilia.

"I was thinking you needed us to go soon," she says. "I was thinking— you still haven't got used to Jesús somehow."

This strikes Cecilia sharply, between two ribs on the left side, like a sharp instrument, or the ping of a strange tuning fork. "I wasn't used to having the memories come back," she says. "And then the fire—but it's spring now. Things are changing, Rosa. Look at these babies! I'm feeling stronger now."

"And you don't need us to go soon?"

"I do, Rosa—you and Jesús have been good for me. I've learned from you more than I can say. But—I do need to go on, I do need my solitude again." She looks at the tears rising once again in Rosa's eyes, feels them once again in her own. "But not," she says, pauses almost breathlessly—"not until Jesús has drunk enough of this good goat's milk! Not until the goats are dry—in November. Maybe you can be ready by then?"

"I can try," says Rosa.

"*We* will drink goat's milk too," Cecilia says firmly—"to make us strong. And glad. And ready!"

Rosa laughs. She gets up from the straw-colored floor and gives Cecilia a quick hug, before they walk out of the shed together, into the starlight.

The next day they introduce the tiny kids to Jesús. He looks at the winsome, dainty creatures in amazement. He watches them drinking from the two pleased mother goats. He follows their every move with adoring eyes.

"Come, Jesús," Cecilia says to him toward evening. "The mother goats have enough milk for you too. Shall I show you?"

He follows her into the goat shed, where Sarita and Blanca have come in from the yard by their own door. The kids are nestled in the sweet-smelling straw of the sleeping pen. Her girls bleat passionately as they follow their old pattern, remembered from a year ago, and enter the milking area.

"*Sí, sí,*" she comforts them. "I'm here, I'm here. Jesús is here too," she says importantly, and looks down at the tiny boy whose hand she is holding.

"*Sí,*" he whispers with gleaming almond eyes at their widest. Those other eyes have disappeared. She doesn't have to let the thought in. (But it waits at the edge, it is already in, no she banishes it.) These eyes of innocence are Jesús' alone.

"*Mira,* Jesús! Look," she says. "Blanca and Sarita are going to give us milk. Blanca always comes first." She sits down at the milking bench, and puts her arm around Jesús, guiding him down to the bench beside her. He gasps as Blanca, with her teasing face and her three black spots, jumps quickly up to her higher level of the bench, and pokes her head into the stanchion to munch at the feed Cecilia has placed there.

"There, lovely Blanca, you're first again, you fine girl," says Cecilia. She strokes Blanca's side and, as if she were a goat herself, nudges Blanca affectionately with her forehead. She positions the pail and puts her hands around the two soft teats so full of milk.

"*Mira!* Jesús, here comes the milk!" she says. A strong, sweet-smelling stream of it zings into the pail.

"*La le-che,*" he agrees, saying it slowly and affectionately in his sweet child's voice.

The intimacy in the small shed overwhelms her. Her dear girls, the playful, loving, motherly goats patiently, and yet exuberantly, letting down such abundance of milk. The tiny child needing it, that his bones and spirit may grow.

CALVING HEIFERS IN A
MARCH BLIZZARD

Ann Daum

I grow numb. Not from the cold so much as from the sight of the dead baby calves that litter the barnyard. Each night I step over a tiny red white-faced heifer on the way to the gate. She was born dead, froze to the ground where we threw her. Two black calves stiff as fence posts in the bed of the yellow Dodge; a chocolate bull calf, too broad through shoulder and hip for his mother to deliver, laid out by the shop like a frozen steak for the dogs to gnaw.

I keep meaning to throw them all in the back of the Dodge, dump their hard little bodies onto the growing heap of calves down by the southern curve of the river. I'll do it tomorrow. Or maybe the next day, when I have a few more to add.

It's not usually so bad, I'm told. This spring blizzards have hit one after another, snow thawing into mucky puddles that freeze and thaw again, spread to brown lakes with the next storm. Usually my dad has two hired men who alternate night duty during calving season. This year our foreman, Jim, quit in February, leaving Mike, who is new to South Dakota and the ranching life; his wife, Diana; and myself, the rancher's daughter just out of college, to calve out the heifers. In a blizzard. I have learned about the signs of impending birth in heifers, the way a vulva slackens and gapes just before labor begins. I have learned to cut one black heifer from sixty and drive her into a barn she has no intention of entering. I have learned to slam the head gate shut on a wild heifer, grease my cupped hand and naked arm with Beta-dyne solution and lubricant before reaching in to check her cervix. But mostly I have learned about walking through endless pen slop and calves dying in the ice-skimmed snow between my hourly nighttime checks. This has nothing to do with the herd health classes I aced in college. This has everything to do with death and the hundreds of different ways a heart can freeze.

Nights run into days and again into nights, every hour the same, interrupted only by the wet of scorched coffee and birth water. I was supposed to be good at this. My father brags about my way with animals, my dedication to caring for sick foals, my soft heart toward any creature in pain. He hasn't seen me kick the poor dumb calves for dying. Throw their lifeless bodies into the truck a little harder than I have to. It's not that I don't care, but that I can't. It overwhelms.

And it never seems to end. Tonight is my turn to check the heifers, spare Mike the few hours he'll sleep until feeding begins just after dawn. The white-faced heifer staring at me from the labor pen of the tilting, red barn won't wait till dawn to calve. She's been laboring since ten o'clock, and it's two now. Time to give her a hand.

Outside I hear the wind pick up, dash pellets of ice against the ancient wall boards. I pray no other heifers will choose tonight to calve.

I chase the black white-face into the head gate as gently as I can, but I am not really gentle. She wouldn't move if I were. She struggles briefly, breath rushing through her open mouth, brown eyes rolled to white. She doesn't understand. I am washing down, scrubbing Betadyne in an orange smear nearly to my shoulder, when she moans with the next contraction. Her breath comes quickly, hanging in clouds above her nostrils. She moans again, back humping up this time to push.

I cup my hand, slide my fingers past her vulva, into the heat of her vagina. She clenches down on me in a hot fist, and I move no farther until she relaxes. I thrust farther inside, up past my elbow before the next contraction, then wait. Grope, wait, grope, wait. Everything feels the same in there: wet, tense, slick. I shift positions, tilt downward, toward the cervix, wonder if I'm helping things at all.

Then I feel the calf, catch the slick rod of a foreleg for an instant before it slips away. Wait, grope. Feel a hoof brush my wrist—a soft, porous hoof, pointing down, as it should.

The calf should be pointing out toward the vulva with his nose resting on his outstretched forelegs. This time something feels wrong. Both forelegs are there, pointing down, but no nose. The heifer shivers, mouth-open groan with the next push. I will my arm to relax, wait through the contraction, then slide my cupped hand up the slick little leg. No nose. Farther, and I find the nose pushed down, caught on the rim of the heifer's pelvis.

The calf moves a little with the next push, wet-moth flutterings under my hand. This is one I can save, and I will. I push the stiff front legs back toward the cervix, back against nature, hoping to realign the calf's head between his front legs. The cow doesn't help, resists in the way that is known to her. She pushes harder. Pushes her calf's skull deep into her pelvis's bony pocket. There is no way out for the calf in this position.

I push harder too, waiting for another break between contractions to wrestle the heavy calf farther back into his mother's womb. Finally feel the snot-slick ball of forehead tucked deep between his knees. I slide my palm down the curve of his nose, insert two fingers into his spongy mouth. He holds my fingers with his unborn tongue, tasting blood and air and life. The next contraction nearly breaks my arm and I groan with the cow. Nothing is so lonely and yet so entwined with another life as assisting a birth. I am up to my armpits in the creation of life. I feel three heartbeats pulse as one.

"Hold on, mother," I say to the heifer. "We're almost there." She seems to hear me, breaths out in short little gasps, prepares to push again.

The calf still clamps my fingers in his mouth, tight between his hungry pad of gums. I push backwards again on his front legs, hard this time, then pull his head up by the gums and lay it between his knees. Yes! He is outside his mother in under a minute, bleeding gently from the torn umbilical, sneezing straw tickles from his wide, wet nostrils. The heifer rests, uncaring, as I string the black bull calf upside down from one hind foot to weigh him. He protests, bawling through his birth-wet mouth. His mother hears this finally and stumbles up to take a look. Wonder, snuffling mother love.

I watch for a while, marvel with his mother at curious brown eyes fringed with thick black lashes, at tottering legs unfolded and propped up, one in each corner. The heifer noses her baby, then jumps when he falls back into the straw. I laugh, rinse my puckered arms in rust-flecked well water, then shrug back into my coat. The calf is on his feet again, and this time open mouth and curling baby tongue connect with teat and all is well. I'll check them again at three-thirty, but right now I want to go back to sleep. Dream for an hour of life, rather than death.

Outside, wind dries the sweat from my face, presses sleet through my woolen scarf. I pull open the barnyard gate, whump it closed, and begin a boot-clumping run for the house. The cold whistles through and around me, scorching my cheeks and the back of my throat. I laugh into the wind, and I am not numb.

AN INTERVIEW WITH
LINDA TELLINGTON-JONES

Mary Anne Fleetwood

Early in life, Linda Tellington-Jones became a professional equestrian. She studied dressage, a type of horsemanship in which the rider uses slight movements to control the horse, and competed in western pleasure, steeplechasing, jumping, and endurance racing events. Later, she combined a natural ability to relate to animals, keen intuition, and training in the Feldenkrais Method to develop a unique system of bodywork, called Tellington-Touch. These touches can alleviate physical and behavioral problems in animals and are often effective in similar ways when used with humans.

Today, Ms Tellington-Jones is as committed to working with humans as she is to working with their animal companions. In February 1995, for example, she travelled to Israel as an animal ambassador to present Tellington-Touch to 40 Arab and Jewish children through a program sponsored by the Tel Aviv SPCA. During the finale, the tension broke between these two rival groups when the youngsters spontaneously formed a circle, started making the touches on the child ahead, and began a snake dance around the room, screaming, yelling, and laughing as if they were old friends.

Ms Tellington-Jones is also an astute observer of the relationships between people and animals—and what these relationships have to teach us. In fact, this is a major focus of her work, as the following interview confirms. Acknowledging a bond with all species, she connects with them as spiritual, not as lower beings existing merely to be manipulated and controlled. In every sense, her work is holistic, encompassing physical, emotional, and spiritual aspects of being.

Increasingly, she is in demand as a trainer and presenter of Tellington-Touch in the US and abroad. She attributes her popularity to the growing numbers of people who prefer nonthreatening techniques for changing negative behavior and initiating healing in animals.

An anonymous poet once wrote of animals: "They are not brethren, they are not underlings, they are other nations, caught with ourselves in the net of life and time, fellow prisoners of the splendor and travail of the earth." From just such a mystical consciousness, the Tellington-Jones touches began.

WHAT THREE QUESTIONS WOULD YOU LIKE TO DISCUSS ABOUT YOUR WORK?

The first would be: how can we understand the role that animals have in our life as teachers? Second, how can we, through working with animals in a gentle, nonthreatening type of bodywork, come to a deeper level of connection with animals using nonverbal communication? Third, through that deeper understanding and connection with the animals, how can we understand and communicate with our own species in a more successful and effective way?

WHAT ROLE DO ANIMALS HAVE IN OUR LIVES AS TEACHERS?

In working with difficult animals, I look at problems as opportunities for learning. For instance, I work a great deal with animals who have all kinds of behavioral issues that people would prefer to change. We also work with physical dysfunctions or problems in the body. Let's take an aggressive dog, for example. I see aggression as coming from lack of confidence or fear. By finding the areas of the body where a fearful or aggressive dog does not like being touched, and gently working on that area with the TTouches, fear can be released, resulting in a new level of self-confidence and an end to aggression, except in the rare cases of tumors or rage syndrome in dogs.

I worked with a dog in Switzerland in May 1994 who was raised by a woman who has been breeding and training for over 15 years. Simona Mueller brought the dog to one of my trainings because she just didn't know what to do with him. He was fine in the show ring. But as soon as Simona came out of the ring, if anybody got within about seven feet of her, the dog would lunge for that individual's throat. This was not a comfortable situation!

I sensed the dog was picking up the fear of his owner. She would encourage the dog to cling to her. Whenever the dog got a foot away from her, he lost his confidence because he wasn't complete without her. So I worked on him with what we call the "journey of the homing pigeon." We led the dog from two sides with a dog halter so he could not attach to either person. I had Simona on one side, and I was on the other side, each one of us being about three feet away. We stroked him with what we call a "wand." In the horse world, it's called a dressage whip. It's four feet long, stiff and white. By the fourth session, the dog could run free in the arena, and 20 people could be standing around talking without fear of being attacked. He could sit or stand quietly, six to eight feet away from Simona, and not be aggressive or nervous without her physical support.

In the third session, I said to her, "I find it interesting that your dog is so aggressive. How do you feel about strangers?" She said, "I'm afraid of people." She realized some of the dog's problem had been caused by her fear. Simona learned a lot about herself by seeing her own fear reflected in the fear of her dog, and as he released his fear, she had the opportunity to work on the release of her own fears.

We, as a species, are so afraid of other people. I find that when people can begin to recognize fear in animals, they can often see these fears in themselves. I also find that with animals, there is a level of unconditional love that occurs that we just don't get between people, or very rarely.

I think there are times when an aggressive animal is reflecting suppressed aggression in the human companion. When their animal friend changes as a result of new awareness in the body, the person frequently realizes they can change also. I get many people who come to my trainings with companion animals who have never had bodywork. By learning to work with their animals, they begin to realize what they are missing. I get a lot of people who wind up getting a massage and many different types of bodywork because they are so amazed at the changes they see in their animals.

Another example of how animals teach us involves a three-year-old quarter horse mare. A number of years ago in Texas, I had this mare in the training who was very difficult. And she did not want to be touched anywhere with any type of touch. The horse had very little handling and had never been abused. She had been that way since birth. Nobody could understand why she was so touchy. At first, the mare was very resistant and uncomfortable when I worked with her, moving constantly and tossing her head, but after thirty minutes, she relaxed and began to enjoy the work. As this horse was able to release her fear of contact and relate to us, she actually appeared to be enjoying herself. During the break, a woman came up to me and said she had just learned one of the most important lessons of her life. Since she was a child, she had been terrified of being touched. She had been to several doctors, and they all told her it was in her head. She realized, while watching me work on the mare, that her sensitivity wasn't just in her head; it was really in her body. It gave her permission to trust her own feelings, and a hope that she could overcome her fear.

I think it's important to recognize the role of animals as teachers. I find, for example, in working on animals who are stiff or arthritic, that

206 • MARY ANNE FLEETWOOD

they are often irritable and moody, as are many people who have such pain. By seeing this behavior in an animal, people can understand their irritability more and are able to accept their own behavior. Seeing their condition mirrored in an animal gives them new tools for understanding themselves.

I get many calls each year from people whose animals are close to death and they themselves need help in letting go. What I've been doing for some years now is suggesting that instead of sending an animal to the vet to be euthanized, or denying their sadness and grief, that they have a ceremony at the end of the animal's life. In the case of any animal who is starting to go downhill and appears to be suffering or weakening significantly, I suggest they ask the animal whether it is ready to go or not. I've said this to so many people who have never communicated with an animal and didn't know it was possible, but many have success with this question.

You'd be amazed at how many people come to me and say, "At the end, I asked my cat or my dog or my horse, and they did tell me it was time to go, and it was very clear to me." I've frequently known devoted animals who would hang on long after they were ready to depart because their human companion could not release them. Just giving permission to die often allows the animal to go on their own without the assistance of the vet.

I suggest having a ceremony when the time has come. Call in a few friends who know the dog, cat, horse, or other beloved animal companion. Sit quietly and do some TTouches, groom the animal, and give a bath when appropriate. Give them a little massage, talk about how important that four-legged (or feathered, scaled, or finned) friend has been. Talk about and acknowledge the sadness and the joy and see the weaving between sadness and joy. Hold the animal when they make the passage.

We're taught not to grieve in this culture. We're taught that it's not okay to be sad. The British attitude of "keep a stiff upper lip" still pervades in the lives of many folks.

HOW, THROUGH USING A NONTHREATENING TYPE OF BODYWORK, DO YOU COME TO A DEEPER LEVEL OF NONVERBAL COMMUNICATION WITH ANIMALS?

When I say "nonthreatening," I mean the type of bodywork that develops a trust with the animal. There are many types of bodywork that are being done on animals that I feel are really inappropriate. You see, I don't think it's appropriate to hurt an animal. Lots of people get bodywork done on animals where the animals go through a lot of pain and have a release at the end. I heard of a llama who was put in a squeeze chute for eight hours and had deep bodywork done on it, and the whole time was resisting. I don't understand that.

What I find happening is there is a level of trust established through

TTouching the body that goes beyond the normal mental or emotional connection. That kind of physical connection is really worthwhile. Anybody who does the circular touches will find after a couple of sessions, sometimes after one session, that the animal wants to follow them everywhere. I just love it. I love the look the animals get on their faces. A two-way connection begins to happen.

I've had a good relationship with animals since I was two or three years old. I've always had deep connections with animals, but since I've been doing the TTouch, I can work on an animal for maybe 10 minutes, and it will relate to me much more closely than it had before and much differently than if I simply pet or stroke or talk to it.

DO YOU KNOW WHY THE TOUCHES WORK?

No, I don't know why they work. I know that my intent is to awaken the intelligence of the cells and to activate their effectiveness. The intent is not to use energy to do the work. It's not about doing something to an animal or fixing or curing it. It's about giving the animal new information in order to help it function more effectively. So it doesn't put us in the position of doer and fixer. For me, when I look at an animal, I see it in a state of perfection. I don't care if it's afraid, or if it's aggressive or physically disabled. What I look for is that perfection at a cellular level.

HOW CAN WE COME TO A BETTER LEVEL OF UNDERSTANDING WITH HUMANS AS A RESULT OF OUR CONNECTION WITH ANIMALS?

In my latest book, there's a story about dolphins that I was with on the west coast of Australia at Monkey Mia a couple of times. I thought of one dolphin named Holy Fin every day for two years. I would send my thoughts to her and imagine me being there, imagine doing the touches on her. Two years later, I went back and that very same dolphin, identifiable because she happened to have a hole in her fin (she was shot at some point) swam up to me and touched her beak to my cheek and swam away. I never saw her do it to anybody else the whole time I was there, nor did she do it to me again. It's like she greeted me, and it was an acknowledgement. It's such a gift, you know, there's something special when an animal connects in a special way.

On the third question of how we can come to a better understanding of our own species through animals. I find so many people who like animals better than people. It's very, very common among animal lovers. As a matter of fact, I have many incredibly talented, successful friends who are in their forties or fifties today who feel that they wouldn't have made it through their teenage years if they had not had an animal in their life at that time.

Again, I get back to the TTouch, often called "the TTouch that teaches." By reaching out and nurturing an animal, and by opening our hearts to the animals and seeing all these other aspects of fear, aggression, fight, flight, or freeze—we begin to see these responses mirrored in ourselves. Humans have all those same fight, flight, or freeze aspects, and we begin to have more empathy and understanding.

It took me a long time to find the courage to actually open my heart. I've been a professional in the horse world since I was 16 years old. Things are changing, but generally the feeling is "don't touch that animal . . . you'll spoil him". Most training is based on domination. Short, sharp, harsh commands are common because there is some strange thinking that animals are stupid and learn slowly. That is such denial of what really happens with animals.

I found that all I have to do is dare to have the courage to open my heart, and once people "got that" about me, I lost my fear of people. I began to see people like the animals. As I did that, I realized we all have those same fears, and that the unconditional love which animals give us is rarely found among humans. Although I love working with animals, my real work is with people who come to work with the animals. And it's such a gift to myself to be able to open my heart and acknowledge the importance of this attitude.

IS THERE A SECRET TO YOUR KIND OF RAPPORT?

Many people ask me how I can be so successful with so many species of animals. How do I know so much? When I approach an animal, I acknowledge my Oneness with that animal and my Oneness with the Spirit of all animals. Whenever I get in a situation where I'm not quite sure what to do, I "see". I have to put the word "see" in quotation marks because it's not a physical seeing. Many people have observed what I do and experience the love that flows from me. I don't experience that connection as love. I experience it as deep appreciation. Maybe that is unconditional love, love that an animal is capable of giving and receiving.

Ken Kerry in his book, *The Starseed Connection,* made a statement which I think is really significant in terms of the world of animals and our lives. He said that since the Fall of Man in the Garden of Eden, man lost his ability to speak with the animals. Nature and animals represent the "Negual", or Great Spirit. I believe that's why so many people are attracted to animals. Because the way that most people live today is not at one with nature. We've cut ourselves off from nature. The animals are here as representatives to remind us that we need to be at One with Nature and with All That Is.

Susan Griffin

THE HUNT

Is it by its indefiniteness it shadows forth the heartless voids and immensities of the universe, and thus stabs us from behind with the thought of annihilation when beholding the milky way?
—HERMAN MELVILLE, *MOBY-DICK*

And at last she could bear the burden of herself no more. She was to be had for the taking. To be had for the taking.
—D. H. LAWRENCE, *LADY CHATTERLEY'S LOVER*

She has captured his heart. She has overcome him. He cannot tear his eyes away. He is burning with passion. He cannot live without her. He pursues her. She makes him pursue her. The faster she runs, the stronger his desire. He will overtake her. He will make her his own. He will have her. (The boy chases the doe and her yearling for nearly two hours. She keeps running despite her wounds. He pursues her through pastures, over fences, groves of trees, crossing the road, up hills, volleys of rifle shots sounding, until perhaps twenty bullets are embedded in her body.) She has no mercy. She has dressed to excite his desire. She has no scruples. She has painted herself for him. She makes supple movements to entice him. She is without a soul. Beneath her painted face is flesh, are bones. She reveals only part of herself to him. She is wild. She flees whenever he approaches. She is teasing him. (Finally, she is defeated and falls and he sees that half of her head has been blown off, that one leg is gone, her abdomen split from her tail to her head, and her organs hang outside her body. Then four men encircle the fawn and harvest her too.) He is an easy target, he says. He says he is pierced. Love has shot him through, he says. He is a familiar mark. Riddled. Stripped to the bone. He is conquered, he says. (The boys, fond of hunting hare, search in particular for pregnant females.) He is fighting for his life. He faces annihilation in her, he says. He is losing himself to her, he says. Now, he must conquer her wildness, he says, he must tame her before she drives him wild, he says. (Once catching their prey, they step on her back, breaking it, and they call this "dancing on the hare.") Thus he goes on his knees to her. Thus he wins her over, he tells her he wants her. He makes her his own. He encloses her. He encircles her. He puts her under lock and key. He protects her.

(Approaching the great mammals, the hunters make little sounds which they know will make the elephants form a defensive circle.) And once she is his, he prizes his delight. He feasts his eyes on her. He adorns her luxuriantly. He gives her ivory. He gives her perfume. (The older matriarchs stand to the outside of the circle to protect the calves and younger mothers.) He covers her with the skins of mink, beaver, muskrat, seal, raccoon, otter, ermine, fox, the feathers of ostriches, osprey, egret, ibis. (The hunters then encircle that circle and fire first into the bodies of the matriarchs. When these older elephants fall, the younger panic, yet unwilling to leave the bodies of their dead mothers, they make easy targets.) And thus he makes her soft. He makes her calm. He makes her grateful to him. He has tamed her, he says. She is content to be his, he says. (In the winter, if a single wolf has leaped over the walls of the city and terrorized the streets, the hunters go out in a band to rid the forest of the whole pack.) Her voice is now soothing to him. Her eyes no longer blaze, but look on him serenely. When he calls to her, she gives herself to him. Her ferocity lies under him. (The body of the great whale is strapped with explosives.) Now nothing of the old beast remains in her. (Eastern Bison, extinct 1825; Spectacled Cormorant, extinct 1852; Cape Lion, extinct 1865; Bonin Night Heron, extinct 1889; Barbary Lion, extinct 1922; Great Auk, extinct 1944.) And he can trust her wholly with himself. So he is blazing when he enters her, and she is consumed. (Florida Key Deer, vanishing; Wild Indian Buffalo, vanishing; Great Sable Antelope, vanishing.) Because she is his, she offers no resistance. She is a place of rest for him. A place of his making. And when his flesh begins to yield and his skin melts into her, he becomes soft, and he is without fear; he does not lose himself; though something in him gives way, he is not lost in her, because she is his now: he has captured her.

THE ZOOLOGICAL GARDEN

Wild, wild things will turn on you
You have got to set them free.
—CRIS WILLIAMSON, "WILD THINGS"

In the cage is the lion. She paces with her memories. Her body is a record of her past. As she moves back and forth, one may see it all: the lean frame, the muscular legs, the paw enclosing long sharp claws, the astonishing speed of her response. She was born in this garden. She has never in her life stretched those legs. Never darted farther than twenty yards at a time. Only once did she use her claws. Only once did she feel them sink into flesh. And it was her keeper's flesh. Her keeper whom she loves, who feeds her, who would never dream of harming her, who protects her. Who in his mercy forgave her mad attack, saying this was in her nature, to be cruel at a whim, to try to kill what she loves. He had come into her cage as he usually did early in the morning to change her water, always at the same time of day, in the same manner, speaking softly to her, careful to make no sudden movement, keeping his distance, when suddenly she sank down, deep down into herself, the way wild animals do before they spring, and then she had risen on all her strong legs, and swiped him in one long, powerful, graceful movement across the arm. How lucky for her he survived the blow. The keeper and his friends shot her with a gun to make her sleep. Through her half-open lids she knew they made movements around her. They fed her with tubes. They observed her. They wrote comments in notebooks. And finally they rendered a judgment. She was normal. She was a normal wild beast, whose power is dangerous, whose anger can kill, they had said. Be more careful of her, they advised. Allow her less excitement. Perhaps let her exercise more. She understood none of this. She understood only the look of fear in her keeper's eyes. And now she paces. Paces as if she were angry, as if she were on the edge of frenzy. The spectators imagine she is going through the movements of the hunt, or that she is readying her body for survival. But she knows no life outside the garden. She has no notion of anger over what she could have been, or might be. No idea of rebellion.

It is only her body that knows of these things, moving her, daily, hourly, back and forth, back and forth, before the bars of her cage.

THE GARDEN

And the man said, The woman whom thou gavest to be with me, she gave me of the tree, and I did eat. . . . Therefore the Lord God sent him forth from the garden of Eden, to till the ground from whence he was taken. So he drove out the man; and he placed at the east of the garden of Eden Cherubims, and a flaming sword which turned every way, to keep the way of the tree of life.

—GENESIS 3:12, 23, 24

She was in the garden, sequestered behind bushes, as night came, just as the other children were called in, and so she stayed quiet, she said, as a mouse, so that she could be out there alone. And when the cries of the others had gone indoors, in this new silence she began to hear the movements of birds. So she stayed still and watched them. Then she felt, she said, the earth beneath her feet coming closer to her. And she began to play with the berries and the plants and finally to whisper to the birds.

And the birds, she said afterward, whispered to her. And thus when, hearing her mother's frightened voice, she appeared finally from the dark tangle of trees and shrubs, her face was so radiant that her mother, amazed to see this new joy in her daughter, did not tell her then what she knew she would soon have to say. That those bushes her daughter hid behind can also hide strangers, that for her shadows speak danger, that in such places little girls must be afraid.

PETRA

Flor Fernandez Barrios

By the time I came into grandmother Petra's life, she was an old woman tired of birthing and raising so many children. Nevertheless, time and a hard life could not erase the beauty and kindness of her soul. Grandmother in her seventies was still as strong as the large and wide trunk of the *ceiba* tree that grew by the riverbed. She had solid legs with veins that popped from the skin, just like roots wrapped around the earth. She could easily wrestle a man down with her wiry arms, which were also gentle, like branches holding her babies and protecting them from the wind. Grandmother had long white hair, braided and rolled into a bun on the back of her head. Such a hairdo gave her profile the appearance of a flamenco dancer and the wise look of an old gypsy. When she looked at me I could see her Portuguese bloodline in her clear blue eyes.

Grandmother worked as hard as a man. She didn't believe in having servants, and even when Grandfather hired two assistants for cooking and housework, she did most of the work by herself. Every morning she was out of bed before five, filling the huge *cantinas* that stored the milk the men brought in from the barn in aluminum buckets. I would wake to the metallic click clack made by the accidental clashing of all these containers thrown around in the kitchen. As soon as I heard the sounds, I knew it was time to get up and get a taste of the foamy, sweet, warm milk fresh from the cows.

Occasionally, Grandmother sat with me, and we both enjoyed sipping our *cafe con leche* while the rest of the household was still asleep. Once, she told me this was her favorite time of the day—when everything is quiet and one can still smell the moist, minty, refreshing scent of morning dew.

I was eager to learn from her. There was a certain kind of pride I experienced in being able to do the things Grandmother did. Even though I was young, maybe seven or eight years old, I enjoyed the attention she gave me. I followed her to the cornfields to pick fresh corn for lunch, or when she went looking for the eggs of wild hens carefully hidden in the tall grass. When we were out there, Grandmother was softer and she seemed to smile more than when she was around people. She loved the land and the animals.

One afternoon coming home from getting some *malangas*, a root similar to potatoes, we were walking across the *potrero*, where golden grass intermingles with dark green patches of *Dormidera* weeds, when Grandmother suddenly stopped. She put her bag of *malangas* on the ground, and listened.

"It's the pregnant mare Alazana! Something is wrong with her!" Grandmother took off toward some tall bushes, where I could distinguish the figure of an animal resting on the grass under an old *tamarindo* tree with large thick branches that extended in a circle, like a gigantic umbrella providing protection from the hot sun. I followed her. The mare was on the ground, lying on the right side of her belly, making frantic attempts to get up. But every time she tried, her left leg bent and failed to support her. Alazana was a beautiful horse. Her smooth dark amber fur shone under the sunlight. Right above her dark round eyes, in the center of the forehead, was a spot of white hair that was inviting to the touch.

"Her left leg is broken!" Grandmother said as she moved closer to the animal. "Stay where you are, Teresa!"

"Grandmother, can we help her get up?"

"No . . . no, don't move any closer! We don't want to scare her."

I watched as my grandmother walked closer and closer to the mare. Her movements were slow and gentle. She looked like a tai chi dancer, totally focused in her dance. Her eyes were like those of a hawk fixed on the eyes of the animal. I felt as if there was a hypnotic exchange between them. I was amazed to see the mare become more relaxed as Grandmother approached her side. Taking her time, and making no sudden moves, Grandmother knelt next to the wounded creature. She placed her hand on Alazana's head. Then she moved to examine the broken leg. As she touched the area right above the hoof, the animal arched back, kicking the air with her front legs, just barely missing Grandmother. After a few minutes the mare settled down.

"Teresa, go back to the house and get your grandfather or one of the workers, or whoever is there. Tell them what happened, so they come prepared. And bring a wood box that is right inside the utility room," Grandmother instructed me. "Yes, Grandma, I'll be back soon." I didn't want to leave the scene, but I knew it was best not to contradict her.

I ran to the house as fast as I could. On my way there, I met Manuel, an old cowboy who spent most of his time in the barn, making sure the animals had plenty of water and food. I told him what had happened. Manuel was probably seventy-two years old, but he looked much older. His unshaven face and missing teeth gave him a sick and fragile appearance.

"Manuel, go, she needs help with the mare," I said.

"*A carajo,* I'll go, but that mare is not worth the hassle!" he said, spitting a wet ball of tobacco into a pile of hay.

I couldn't find Grandfather, but Matias, a handsome young farmworker who was coming back from town, volunteered to help. I found the box and Matias offered me a ride on his horse. When we arrived, Grandmother and Manuel were trying to restrain the broken leg by tying a stick to it. Matias joined them, while I stood a couple of feet away, watching the animal.

"Hand me the box," Grandmother said.

Grandmother opened the wood box, and took out a roll of ordinary black electrical tape. She proceeded to wrap the tape around the mare's leg and the stick. It was then that I noticed a red bubble coming out of what looked like the mare's rear end. The bubble looked just like a balloon, and was gradually getting bigger. "Grandmother . . . Grandmother . . . look!"

"I can't look now. What is it?" she said without taking her eyes from the tape she was wrapping around the leg.

"Grandmother, there is a funny-looking balloon growing from Alazana's *pipi.*"

"Oh no! Not now! Here Manuel, go ahead and finish this. Let me take a look back there. If it is what I think it is . . ." she said with a frown on her face.

"What is it, Grandmother?" I asked.

"She is giving birth, *esta pariendo,*" she said to me calmly.

"Is she going to be okay?"

"*Sí mija,* but because of her broken leg, it's going to be very difficult for her," Grandmother said, kneeling down and taking a closer look at the growing bubble. "Look, Teresita . . . the head is beginning to show!" I had never seen Grandmother so excited. She looked like a little kid. And I was thrilled. I'd never seen a horse giving birth before.

"Matias, go and bring some water for the mare," Grandmother ordered, gently petting Alazana on her head.

"*Ven,* Teresa, let's leave her alone for now." Grandmother gently pulled me into the shade of the *tamarindo* tree.

"These things take a little while, so we better get comfortable," she said, sitting on the ground and signaling me to join her.

"Is Alazana in a lot of pain?" I asked Grandmother, thinking about the times I heard my aunts talk about their labor pains.

"If *yeguas* are like women, I'm sure she's in lots of pain." Grandmother pulled from her dress pocket a white cotton handkerchief and wiped the sweat from her face.

"Is there anything we can do to help her?"

"Not really. This is the mare's job." Then she looked at me and smiled. "Maybe there is one thing we both can do—pray. Pray to the Virgin to help her."

"Which one?"

"Your favorite Virgin. Do you have a favorite virgin?" she asked.

"Yes! La Caridad Del Cobre."

"Well then, this is your chance to ask her for a favor." She became quiet, absorbed in her own thoughts. I didn't know how serious the situation was, but I was afraid for the animal. I tried to imagine the kind of pain Alazana was in. I thought about the time when I got very ill and my stomach hurt and hurt all night. Maybe Alazana was having the same sharp pain in her big swollen belly.

Time went by slowly. The afternoon sun began to soften, but the temperature was still in the upper eighties at four o'clock. Manuel decided to go back to the barn. Matias brought us cold lemonade and coffee. Grandfather Jose joined us, and tried to lighten the tense mood with jokes. I kept my eyes on Alazana. I didn't want to miss the birth.

Around four-thirty, the mare became restless. She moved her front legs in an attempt to get up, but her broken leg crippled her. A few minutes later, the transparent and bloody sac hanging from her behind started to grow again. I could see the foal, cushioned by the fluids inside the bag. "What a miracle!" I said to myself.

"That's it, Jose, *el potro* is coming!" Grandmother shouted.

Alazana pushed out the entire sac, and without wasting any time, she proceeded to lick the foal with long gentle strokes. She cleaned away the thick envelope covering the body of her baby till everything was gone, and dark walnut fur shone. The long thin legs of the little foal wobbled in his effort to stand up. The mother mare encouraged his efforts, prodding him on with the steady touch of her tongue and nose. She was struggling to stand, too.

"What a shame!" I heard Grandfather say.

"Yeah," Matias replied. I wondered what they meant.

"Grandmother, what are they talking about?" Grandma looked at me with a somber face.

"Nothing that you need to worry about now." She got up from her place, shaking pieces of grass and dirt from her dress. She walked toward Grandpa and Matias, leaving me puzzled.

"Do you think Alazana is going to be able to stand up?" she asked the two men.

"The injury is bad, but I think with a little help . . ." said Matias.

"Let's see if we can take her to the stable," said Grandfather, grabbing a bundle of rope from beside his saddle. Grandfather walked up to the mare and tried to place the rope around her neck. Alazana kicked and moved her head away from him.

"Come on Alazana! I'm not going to hurt you." Grandfather tried to edge closer and again he was greeted with resistance.

"Jose, give me that piece of rope," Grandmother said, looking into the eyes of the mare with the same intense gaze I had seen earlier. Alazana didn't move. Grandmother patted the animal on her long neck and rubbed her narrow forehead. Grandmother started to talk to the mare in a soft low voice. I couldn't hear what she was saying, but it was working. The new mother appeared relaxed and open to Grandmother's words and gestures. It was then that the young foal, perhaps inspired by the moment, pushed and pulled his body up, his hind legs shaking and his weight resting on his front legs. The little creature tried once more and managed to straighten all four legs at once. As the foal stood next to his proud mother, Grandmother tied the rope around Alazana's neck and started to pull, coaxing the mare to stand up.

"Come on . . . come on, come with me. You can do it, my brave Alazana. You can do it."

Alazana tried. The first effort failed when she put weight on her broken leg.

"Come on, you guys, come and help. Don't move too fast, just come from the other side and help her lift her body, while I pull the rope."

"Can I help, Grandma?" I asked, walking toward the group.

"Stay away, Teresa." I was upset. I wanted to be part of the whole thing, and I wanted to be close to the baby horse. I wanted to touch him.

Finally, Alazana was up and we all cheered and laughed. The young foal stayed close to his mother, taking small steps with his trembling legs.

"Now, let's take this slowly. I don't want her to fall down again," Grandmother said, walking beside Alazana.

"Yes, Capitan," replied Grandfather with a smile on his face.

Alazana made it to the stable, where she was kept in the shade with plenty of water and food. I watched the little colt suck milk from his mother's breast. He didn't seem to get satisfied. After making sure everything was fine, Grandmother and Grandfather joined me. I had been sitting on top of a pile of hay by the entrance.

"What do you say the name of this colt should be?" asked Grandfather, putting his arm around my shoulders.

"I don't know . . . maybe . . . uhm . . . what about Almendro, since his skin is like a dark walnut?" I said, looking at the colt, who now was resting next to his mother.

"Petra, do you think we should let Almendro be Teresa's horse?" Grandfather looked at Grandmother with a smile, knowing the answer was going to be yes.

"I don't know, Jose, maybe we should wait and see if she stops arguing with her teachers in school." Grandmother winked.

"Grandmother, please . . . I promise I will be good in school. Please let me have Almendro," I begged, putting my arms around her waist.

"*Esta bien*. Almendro is your horse. But you must take good care of him. I'll ask Matias to teach you, in time, how to groom and keep him healthy."

I was so excited. I couldn't believe the little horse was my own. I could ride anytime. I felt so lucky to have Almendro. "Thank you Grandmother! Thank you Grandfather!" I gave hugs to each one, and then ran to the house so I could tell Mother and my brother Victor the news.

Later that evening I overheard a conversation between Grandfather and Matias. They were sitting out on the porch. The fresh smell of gardenias and wild jasmine filled the air. Rain had fallen earlier and cooled the ground, leaving puddles all around the garden, which attracted happy frogs. I was busy chasing a tiny green frog. The smart creature kept jumping on top of the flat stones of the entrance walk. I held my flashlight firmly, moving fast, trying to keep the trickster under the spotlight.

But my green friend disappeared in the bushes. Disappointed with myself, I turned off the flashlight and began to walk away. It was then I heard Grandfather say to Matias, "We'll have to see how Alazana does with her broken leg."

"She is such a good horse. It is a shame to have to get rid of an animal like her," Matias lamented.

"I know, I wish we could do something."

I went inside the house and found Grandmother in her sewing room, mending some socks. She lifted her eyes, looking at me over the thick lenses of her glasses. She could tell something was disturbing me.

"Come in, Teresa, what kind of trouble have you gotten yourself in? You look like the dog who kicked the can."

"I haven't done anything, Grandmother, but I heard Grandfather and Matias talk about killing Alazana."

"Come and sit here." Grandmother pointed at a chair next to the window, by her side. "*Mira hijita*, there are things which are painful to talk about, and this situation with the mare is one of those hard balls to swallow." Grandmother got up from her place and put the sewing kit away on top of a small oak table. "There is no way around this." Grandmother took my face into her hands. "We don't want to do it, either, but we have to do it."

"Why . . . why . . . why do you have to kill her?" I cried.

"Because her leg is not going to heal. Alazana is going to be in a lot of pain."

"Why don't you call a vet? Ask him to come and fix her broken leg."

"It will be useless. Believe me, there is nothing anyone can do."

"Not even God?" I asked defiantly.

"That . . . I can't answer. That's for you and God to discuss privately," she said, looking me straight in the eye.

I was angry at her. I wanted a different answer. I wanted Alazana to stay alive. I couldn't imagine how anyone could kill such an animal—so kind and beautiful. I looked at the old woman, not recognizing her.

"Teresita *hija*. Listen to me," Grandmother continued in a soft tone of voice. "It is not that we haven't tried to save the animal. Your grandfather and I have talked all day long about what to do." She became pensive. "That mare will suffer if we let her live."

I ran out of the room. I didn't want to hear any more. I slammed the door on my way out, went to my room, and threw myself on my bed, hiding my face in the soft pillow. I expected Grandmother to follow me, but she never came. That night I fell asleep crying about Alazana and feeling sorry for Almendro, who was soon to be an orphan.

The next morning I met Grandfather Jose in the kitchen. I asked him, "Grandfather, if Grandmother is so good with animals, why can't she talk Alazana into getting her leg healed?"

"Ay *carino*, that's a different story." He got up from the wood box where he had been sitting, trying to end the conversation.

"Grandfather, why is that a different story?" I insisted. He sat back on the box.

"When a horse breaks a leg . . ."

"Yes, I know it never heals!" I interrupted him, upset with the same story. He was surprised by my reaction.

"It is true, Teresa, it is true! We don't want to kill Alazana, but we have to, for her own good. You know sometimes when these things happen and a horse breaks a leg, we are able to fix it, but in this case . . ." He paused and looked in the distance. "The fracture is quite big and right in the joint that connects the leg with the thigh. Something like that never heals."

"I don't want you to kill Alazana. What's going to happen to Almendro?" I cried.

"Almendro will be fine. We'll make sure he is fine."

"I don't believe it. He is going to be sad, very sad without his mother."

Grandfather put his arm around my shoulders and pulled me toward him. He didn't say any more. He let me cry while he ran his finger through my long dark hair, combing back the rebellious curls falling on my forehead. I could feel the rough skin of his hand brushing my forehead. Grandfather's hands were big and calloused from working the land for so many years.

"How did it happen? How was she hurt?"

"Well, we think that Alazana got scared by something. She ran and maybe stepped in some hole in the ground. Maybe she was scared by the train, the wheels on the track, or the high whistle from the engine."

I saw Grandmother coming toward us with a bucket full of milk. Grandfather was quick to get up and take the load from her hands, as any perfect *caballero* should do, and Grandfather has always insisted on being one.

"You always get your way," I heard Grandfather say to her in a teasing way.

"Not always," she replied in a meaningful, grave tone, speeding past and leaving Grandfather behind with the bucket.

Years later, I realized the truth in Grandmother's words. She did not get her way. Life had been tough. She lost her homeland. She lost some of her children. Then, Fidel Castro took away the land she had claimed as her second home.

"Come on, Teresa, let's see how Alazana is doing," Grandmother invited me.

We found both Alazana and Almendro resting, laying in the hay, next to each other. I saw Grandmother frown and shake her head.

"It doesn't look good. Her leg is quite swollen."

I took a look at the swollen leg. It was hard to tell whether the animal was in pain, but the leg was swollen to almost double its normal size. Grandmother examined the broken limb carefully, trying hard not to cause any more damage.

"There is infection," she said almost to herself. She patted the mare on the back. Alazana lifted her beautiful head and looked into my eyes. A chill of energy ran up and down my spine. Alazana's eyes were like two black marbles, with tiny sparks of light shining through. There was something she was trying to communicate to me and I saw images in my head of Alazana galloping above the hills, like a Pegasus, opening her wings wider and wider, getting higher and higher . . .

"Grandmother. Grandmother, I saw . . ."

"Yes, Alazana needs to go," Grandmother said, before I had a chance to say anything.

"She had wings and she was flying!" I said, joyful and sad at the same time.

"You saw her spirit. Alazana is wanting to go. She is going to be okay." Grandmother continued patting the mare with gentle strokes along her neck. Alazana appeared to be soothed by this because she allowed her head to rest on Grandmother's lap. Almendro came closer to me, and sniffed my right arm with his little nose. The colt needed attention as well, so I rubbed his face with my hand. I felt an immediate connection with Almendro. A feeling of warmth and laughter inside my heart.

That was the last time I saw Alazana. The next morning I woke up early, before six, and ran to the stable looking for her and Almendro. I found only Almendro and Grandmother feeding him milk from a baby bottle. Alazana was gone.

"Where is Alazana?"

"She is gone," Grandmother said without looking at me.

"Gone where?"

"Grandfather Jose took care of her earlier this morning." This time she looked me in the eyes. "She was in too much pain." She motioned for me to come closer. "Here, feed Almendro. Life goes on, *mi hijita*. This little one is going to need care now that his mama is gone. I'm too old to do all this work by myself. Do you want to help with Almendro?"

Of course, I was thrilled. For a moment I forgot about Alazana.

"Oh *sí*, Grandmother. I'll help you!" My eyes met the eyes of Almendro, and I saw Alazana flying away, with her golden wings spread wide as an eagle's. She was smiling at me. At that moment I knew, in the way that only children know, that even though Alazana was dead, some part of her was there with us watching over young Almendro.

"You can stay here if you want to play with Almendro. But don't let him out of the barn," Grandmother said and began to walk toward the house. I watched her for a few seconds, noticing for the first time that she was limping a bit with her right leg. Of course, she would never say a thing about her pain. Grandmother was tough as cowhide.

In 1968, Grandmother suffered a massive stroke that left her paralyzed and unable to utter any words. For days and nights her daughters and sons took turns sitting by her bed. They said prayers, talked and read to their fragile and pale mother. Her son Tomas, a doctor, told everyone that Grandmother was going to be bedridden for the rest of her life.

When I heard the diagnosis from Uncle Tomas, I knew that Grandmother would rather die. She was not the kind of woman to settle for a vegetative existence. For Grandmother, like the mare Alazana, living with broken legs would have been a pain too difficult to endure.

For two weeks, Grandmother wrestled with death. When I visited her, I sat by the bedside, looking at her wrinkled and tired face. I could see her internal struggle, as she occasionally attempted to utter words through her closed mouth. Only her dried lips moved, in a contorted, twisted gesture. With her eyes shut she appeared to be far away. I disliked seeing my grandmother in such a defeated posture, a ghost figure against the white sheets.

Miraculously, Grandmother recovered from the stroke. First, she began to mumble words. She became restless in bed, and gradually her legs and arms began to respond to her commands. One night, my mother caught Grandmother out of bed. She was standing on her feet, leaning against the wall, trying to keep her balance with her weak legs, shaking but determined to walk. From then on, she did not go back to bed.

When Grandmother Petra died many years later in 1982, I was not there for her funeral and burial. I was in exile. I remember my mother called me and said, "We just finished talking to Cuba." Silence. "Mami died."

I looked out the window of my bedroom. It was a clear California night with a sky full of shining stars and a silver half moon. For a moment, I thought I saw Grandmother riding on Alazana's back, smiling at me while galloping across the galaxy. A sudden soft breeze blew inside the room and gently caressed me. The smell of fresh-cut grass impregnated the air and took me back across time and space to the golden green landscapes of the farm. There, standing like a royal palm tree, firmly rooted in the earth, was Grandmother Petra, waving at me, saying good-bye.

FRIENDS, FOES, AND WORKING ANIMALS

Gretel Ehrlich

I used to walk in my sleep. On clear nights when the seals barked and played in phosphorescent waves, I climbed out the window and slept in a horse stall. Those "wild-child" stories never seemed odd to me; I had the idea that I was one of them, refusing to talk, sleeping only on the floor. Having become a city dweller, the back-to-the-land fad left me cold and I had never thought of moving to Wyoming. But here I am, and unexpectedly, my noctambulist's world has returned. Not in the sense that I still walk in my sleep—such restlessness has left me—but rather, the intimacy with what is animal in me has returned. To live and work on a ranch implicates me in new ways: I have blood on my hands and noises in my throat that aren't human.

Animals give us their constant, unjaded faces and we burden them with our bodies and civilized ordeals. We're both humbled by and imperious with them. We're comrades who save each other's lives. The horse we pulled from a boghole this morning bucked someone off later in the day; one stock dog refuses to work sheep, while another brings back a calf we had overlooked while trailing cattle to another pasture; the heifer we doctored for pneumonia backed up to a wash and dropped her newborn calf over the edge; the horse that brings us home safely in the dark kicks us the next day. On and on it goes. What's stubborn, secretive, dumb, and keen in us bumps up against those same qualities in them. Their births and deaths are as jolting and random as ours, and because ranchers are food producers, we give ourselves as wholly to the sacrament of nurturing as to the communion of eating their flesh. What develops in this odd partnership is a stripped-down compassion, one that is made of frankness and respect and rigorously excludes sentimentality.

What makes westerners leery of "outsiders"—townspeople and city-slickers—is their patronizing attitude toward animals. "I don't know what in the hell makes those guys think they're smarter than my horse. Nothing I see them do would make me believe it," a cowboy told me. "They may like their steaks, but they sure don't want to help out when it comes to butchering. And their damned backyard horses are spoiled. They make it hard for a horse to do something right and easy for him to do everything wrong. They're scared to get hot and tired and dirty out here like us; then they don't understand why a horse won't work for them."

On a ranch, a mother cow must produce calves, a bull has to perform, a stock dog and working horse should display ambition, savvy, and heart. If they don't, they're sold or shot. But these relationships of mutual dependency can't be dismissed so briskly. An animal's wordlessness takes on the cleansing qualities of space: we freefall through the beguiling operations of our own minds with which we calculate our miseries to responses that are immediate. Animals hold us to what is present: to who we are at the time, not who we've been or how our bank accounts describe us. What is obvious to an animal is not the embellishment that fattens our emotional résumés but what's bedrock and current in us: aggression, fear, insecurity, happiness, or equanimity. Because they have the ability to read our involuntary tics and scents, we're transparent to them and thus exposed—we're finally ourselves.

Living with animals makes us redefine our ideas about intelligence. Horses are as mischievous as they are dependable. Stupid enough to let us use them, they are cunning enough to catch us off guard. We pay for their loyalty: they can be willful, hard to catch, dangerous to shoe, and buck on frosty mornings. In turn, they'll work themselves into a lather cutting cows, not for the praise they'll get but for the simple glory of outdodging a calf or catching up with an errant steer. The outlaws in a horse herd earn their ominous names—the red roan called Bonecrusher, the sorrel gelding referred to as Widowmaker. Others are talented but insist on having things their own way. One horse used only for roping doesn't like to be tied up by the reins. As soon as you jump off he'll rub the headstall over his ears and let the bit drop from his mouth, then just stand there as if he were tied to the post. The horses that sheepherders use become chummy. They'll stick their heads into a wagon when you get the cookies out, and eat the dogfood. One sheepherder I knew, decked out in bedroom slippers and baggy pants, rode his gelding all summer with nothing but bailing string tied around the horse's neck. They picnicked together every day on the lunch the herder had fixed: two sandwiches and a can of beer for each of them.

A dog's reception of the jolts and currents of life comes in more clearly than a horse's. Ranchers use special breeds of dogs to work live-stock—blue and red heelers, border collies, Australian shepherds, and kelpies. Heelers, favored by cattlemen, are small, muscular dogs with wide heads and short, blue-gray hair. Their wide and deep chests enable them—like the quarter horse—to run fast for a short distance and endow them with extra lung capacity to work at high altitudes. By instinct they move cows, not by barking at them but by nipping their heels. What's uncanny about all these breeds is their responsiveness to human beings: we don't shout commands, we whisper directions, and because of their unshakable desire to please us, they can be called back from chasing a cow instantaneously. Language is not an obstacle to these dogs; they learn words very quickly. I know several dogs who are bilingual: they understand Spanish and English. Others are whizzes with names. On a pack trip my dog learned the names of ten horses and remembered the horse and the sound of his name for years. One friend taught his cowdog to jump onto the saddle so he could see the herd ahead, wait for a command with his front feet riding the neck of the horse, then leap to the ground and bring a calf back or turn the whole herd.

My dog was born under a sheep wagon. He's a blue heeler–kelpie cross with a natural bobbed tail. Kelpies, developed in Australia in the nineteenth century, are also called dingoes, though they're part Scottish sheepdog too. While the instinct to work livestock is apparent from the time they are puppies, they benefit from further instruction, the way anyone with natural talent does. They're not sent to obedience school; these dogs learn from each other. A pup, like mine was, lives at sheep camp and is sent out with an older dog to learn his way around a band of sheep. They learn to turn the herd, to bring back strays, and to stay behind the horse when they're not needed.

Dogs who work sheep have to be gentler than cowdogs. Sheep are skittish and have a natural fear of dogs, whereas a mother cow will turn and fight a dog who gets near her calf. If kelpies, border collies, and Australian shepherds cower, they do so from timidity and because they've learned to stay low and out of sight of the sheep. With their pointed ears and handsome, wolfish faces, their resemblance to coyotes is eerie. But their instinct to work sheep is only a refinement of the desire to kill; they lick their chops as they approach the herd.

After a two-year apprenticeship at sheep camp, Rusty came home with me. He was carsick all the way, never having ridden in a vehicle, and, once home, there were more firsts: when I flushed the toilet, he ran out the door; he tried to lick the image on the screen of the television; when the phone rang he jumped on my lap, shoving his head under my arm. In April the ewes and lambs were trailed to spring range and Rusty rejoined them. By his second birthday he had walked two hundred miles behind a horse, returning to the mountaintop where he had been born.

Dogs read minds and also maps. Henry III's greyhound tracked the king's coach from Switzerland to Paris, while another dog found his owner in the trenches during World War I. They anticipate comings and goings and seem to possess a prescient knowledge of danger. The night before a sheep foreman died, his usually well-behaved blue heeler acted strangely. All afternoon he scratched at the windows in an agony of panic, yet refused to go outside. The next day Keith was found dead on the kitchen floor, the dog standing over the man's chest as if shielding the defective heart that had killed his master.

While we cherish these personable working animals, we unfairly malign those that live in herds. Konrad Lorenz thinks of the anonymous flock as the first society, not unlike early medieval cities: the flock works as a wall of defense protecting the individual against aggressors. Herds are democratic, nonhierarchical. Wyoming's landscapes are so wide they can accommodate the generality of a herd. A band of fifteen hundred sheep moves across the range like a single body of water. To work them in a corral means opposing them: if you walk back through the middle of the herd, they will flow forward around you as if you were a rock in a stream. Sheep graze up a slope, not down the way cows do, as if they were curds of cream rising.

Cows are less herd-smart, less adhesive, less self-governing. On long treks, they travel single file, or in small, ambiguous crowds from which individuals veer off in a variety of directions. That's why cowboying is more arduous than herding sheep. On a long circle, cowboys are assigned positions and work like traffic cops directing the cattle. Those that "ride point" are the front men. They take charge of the herd's course, turning the lead down a draw, up a ridge line, down a creek, galloping ahead to chase off steers or bulls from someone else's herd, then quickly returning to check the speed of the long column. The cowboys at the back "ride drag." They push the cows along and pick up stragglers and defectors, inhaling the sweet and pungent perfume of the animals—a mixture of sage, sweet grass, milk, and hide, along with gulps of dust.

What we may miss in human interaction here we make up for by rubbing elbows with wild animals. Their florid, temperamental lives parallel ours, as do their imperfect societies. They fight and bicker, show off, and make love. I watched a Big Horn ram in rut chase a ewe around a tree for an hour. When he caught and mounted her, his horns hit a low branch and he fell off. She ran away with a younger ram in pursuit. The last I saw of them, she was headed for a dense thicket of willows and the old ram was peering through the maze looking for her.

When winter comes there is a sudden population drop. Frogs, prairie dogs, rattlesnakes, and rabbits go underground, while the mallards and cinnamon teal, as well as scores of songbirds, fly south because they are smarter than we are. One winter day I saw a coyote take a fawn down on our frozen lake where in summer I row through fragrant flowers. He jumped her, grabbed her hind leg, and hung on as she ran. Halfway across the lake the fawn fell and the coyote went for her jugular. In a minute she was dead. Delighted with his catch, he dragged her here and there on the ice, then lay down next to her in a loving way and rubbed his silvery ruff in her hair before he ate her.

In late spring, which here, at six thousand feet, is June, the cow elk become proud mothers. They bring their day-old calves to a hill just above the ranch so we can see them. They're spotted like fawns but larger, and because they are so young, they wobble and fall when they try to play.

Hot summer weather brings the snakes and bugs. It's said that 80 percent of all animal species are insects, including six thousand kinds of ants and ten thousand bugs that sing. Like the wild ducks that use our lake as a flyaway, insects come and go seasonally. Mosquitoes come early and stay late, followed by black flies, gnats, Stendhalian red-and-black ants, then yellow jackets and wasps.

I know it does no good to ask historical questions—why so many insects exist—so I content myself with the cold ingenuity of their lives. In winter ants excavate below their hills and live snugly in subterranean chambers. Their heating system is unique. Worker ants go above ground and act as solar collectors, descending frequently to radiate heat below. They know when spring has come because the workers signal the change of seasons with the sudden increase of body heat: it's time to reinhabit the hill.

In a drought year rattlesnakes are epidemic. I sharpen my shovel before I irrigate the alfalfa fields and harvest vegetables carrying a shotgun. Rattlesnakes have heat sensors and move toward warm things. I tried nude sunbathing once: I fell asleep and woke just in time to see the grim, flat head of a snake angling toward me. Our new stock dog wasn't as lucky. A pup, he was bitten three times in one summer. After the first bite he staggered across the hayfield toward me, then keeled over, his eyes rolling back and his body shaking. The cure for snakebite is the same for animals as it is for humans: a costly antiserum must be injected as quickly as possible. I had to carry the dog half a mile to my pickup. By the time I had driven the thirty miles to town, his head and neck had swollen to a ghoulish size, but two days later he was heeling cows again.

Fall brings the wildlife down from the mountains. Elk and deer migrate through our front yard while in the steep draws above us mountain lions and black bears settle in for the winter. Last night, while I was sleeping on the veranda, the sound of clattering dishes turned out to be two buck deer sparring in front of my bed. Later, a porcupine and her baby waddled past: "Meeee ... meeee ... meeee," the mother squeaked to keep the young one trundling along. From midnight until dawn I heard the bull elk bugle—a whistling, looping squeal that sounds porpoiselike at first, and then like a charging elephant. The screaming catlike sound that wakes us every few nights is a bobcat crouched in the apple tree.

Bobcats are small, weighing only twenty pounds or so, with short tails and long, rabbity back feet. They can nurse two small litters of kittens a year. "She's meaner than a cotton sack full of wildcats," I heard a cowboy say about a woman he'd met in the bar the night before. A famous riverman's boast from the paddlewheel days on the Mississippi goes this way: "I'm all man, save what's wildcat and extra lightning." *Les chats sauvages,* the French call them, but their savagery impresses me much less then their acrobatic skills. Bobcats will kill a doe by falling on her from a tree and riding her shoulders as she runs, reaching around and scratching her face until she falls. But just as I was falling asleep again, I thought I heard the bobcat purring.

PARTNERING PEGASUS

Susan F. Boucher

The goddess Demeter was depicted with the head of a beautiful black mare; her priestesses were referred to as foals. Why? And what about the mythical race of centaurs—part horse, part man? What is it about humans that makes some wish they were part horse?

Only a virgin can approach a unicorn. Only National Velvet can reason with a rogue. The mythology of the American West is filled with tales of mustangs who can be tamed only by honorable, virtuous men. All the stories about the wild, free thing that surrenders to the touch of a human hand—what are they about?

It's not that there aren't answers. I'm skeptical of today's Freudian answers, but it's true that many girls lose interest in horses once they acquire an overt interest in sex. It's also true that being able to claim ownership, at least by proxy, of an impressive penis has its compensations. It was useful when a man came out of the bushes while a friend and I were riding, and directed our attention to a limp little dangle emerging from his pants. My friend giggled. "You know," she told him, "I don't think you want to be doing that around a barn—we see bigger and better every day."

While that's an answer, it's not *the* answer; it simply reflects contemporary myth. The stories of the affinity between wildness and purity aren't *the* answer either; they reflect older, sweeter myths.

Perhaps the answer lies in the nature of the horse, so extraordinarily other than our own. We can say that about all our companion animals, but only the horse, among our companions, is not a predator. Horses are the eaten, not the eaters.

Because teeth and claws can come from any direction, it's useful that, unlike humans, horses don't have stereoscopic vision. Their vision encompasses about 360 degrees, but they see a different landscape out of each eye, and changes in either landscape could mean danger. My horse is a good horse, so he spooks when something in the landscape changes. Not only does he spook the first time he sees it, he often spooks again when we encounter it coming 'round the other way—his right eye doesn't know what his left eye knows. But because he's a good horse, he knows better than to expend energy fretting about things he's learned won't harm him, so once the thing that spooked him takes its rightful shape in his landscape, he won't spook at it again.

For a lot of people, spookiness is not a characteristic of good horses. A human who startles and runs from a rustle in the bushes is thought cowardly by many; we expect our heroes to stand and hold their ground. Spookiness is not a human virtue.

There are far too many people who think that simply *being* human is a virtue, and if they treat other animals as though they too were human, that is likewise virtuous. However, humans, like any other animal, range in temperament from peaceful to aggressive. Because a particular inclination is *their* nature, they tend to assume it's natural to all others. Therefore, at one extreme, there are those who think that human love alone will persuade an animal from its nonhuman nature. Their horses tend to walk all over them, and their dogs steal food off dinner plates. At the other extreme are those who, because they think aggression is natural, see that characteristic predominant in all living things—the villains in stories who beat their animals into submission tend to beat their children too.

It's not human love alone, nor power, that writes the real stories about horses and humans. The horses have a lot to say.

The wild, free creature of *our* stories is generally a stallion. Head erect, nostrils flaring, mane and tail whipping in the wind, he stands overlooking his herd, protective and wise. Fair enough—one of our contemporary myths says guys get to be wild and free. This very same wild, free guy, the story goes, can be reined in by a gentle, loving woman. Her gentleness invites his protection and his protection her respect. This is how, in our time and place, some say things ought to be.

The horses have a different story. In the wild, each herd is, indeed, accompanied by a stallion. Wild and free. And he does protect his mares—from other stallions. The leadership of the herd, however, falls to a mare, and the stallion respects the leader. She may not be the biggest or the strongest, but she's the wisest, with a self-assurance that inspires confidence. If the lead mare is relaxed and grazing, the others eat, and if she startles and bolts, the others follow. In the landscape of horses, spookiness is in fact a virtue.

The mares, among themselves, determine hierarchy—not only their own, but that of their offspring. According to their own status, and by example, they teach their foals when it's appropriate to insist and when it's smarter to defer. People who want to raise a foal are wise to watch it in the field. Is it confident around the others? Is it healthy and playful? Is it polite to other horses? What, and how, does its mother teach it?

Orphaned foals often grow up to be bullies when there are no mares to teach them manners. Humans who think love will gentle a horse are only half right. Mares love their foals, but, because survival depends on it, they're firm disciplinarians. Mares don't say to an unruly offspring, "Mummy doesn't want you to do that, honey." Mares say, *"Whack."* A mare's feelings aren't hurt if a child misbehaves; she doesn't worry what the neighbors will think. She doesn't lie awake nights wondering if she's done the right thing; she just does it. If she's a good horse and a wise mare, her children will grow up to be like her—alert survivors, and confident of what's owed them as well as what's owed to others.

Charles de Kunffy, an artist among horse trainers, once said that the reason royal children were required to study the equestrian arts was to learn humility. A good horse will give when it is asked properly and politely and becomes a monster in the hands of a despot. A good horse teaches the consequences of disrespect and the arbitrary exercise of power.

As I said, my horse is a good horse. His job on this earth, his story goes, is to reward humility. When I met him, he was standing in a pen, covered with flies and mud. His new owner, who'd bought him to compete on, had stopped riding him, having grown discouraged by his disinclination to make her look good. In many respects, he'd have been perfect for the job. He's a Trakehner, a particular breed of European sport horse, and he's a lovely example of his kind. So valued are Trakehners for their character and athleticism that humans risked their lives to bring the mares out of East Prussia at the end of World War II to save them from the invading—and hungry—Soviet troops.

He'd been a commodity for all his twelve years—he was sold from the breeding farm for thirty-five thousand dollars because of his potential. Things had never seemed quite to work out with him, however, and he'd gone from owner to owner, his price declining, until the young woman had picked him up for forty-five hundred. When she found him, he'd been off work for a year because the previous owner was afraid to ride him. The young woman wanted a horse who would make her a star, and instead she got a horse who was heavy and sullen in her hand, and ran away with her on cross-country courses.

As it happened, I already *had* a perfectly nice horse whose inclination was to be a pet and, while I wasn't learning much about riding from him, I wasn't looking for a second horse. I bought Anders because someone pointed him out to me, exclaiming, "Isn't it a shame? Such a lovely horse.

He needs someone to rescue him." When I approached him, however, it seemed the other way 'round. He somehow let me know I needed him.

I think all creatures know who they are, and what they're meant to do. How they came to be that way is, in some respects, irrelevant. There are people who claim that the domesticated animal is a degraded form of life, and others who believe that animals were created to serve humans. The moral and ethical questions implicit in those two positions are profound, but the fact is that mutually useful alliances have always existed between various species of living things. And the fact is that by 3,000 B.C., long after the artists of Lascaux so reverently depicted horses as prey, humans as far apart as Siberia and Egypt had been breeding and training horses.

The domestic horse is so profoundly different from its ancestors that it's not only temperamentally and physically different, it's genetically different. Przewalski's horse, the only remaining wild horse, has 66 rather than 64 chromosomes. The fact is that humans *have* shaped their horses, and the writer Vicki Hearne takes her place in a long tradition of trainers when she talks about the consequent responsibility of humans to honor what they breed their animals to do—to allow and even challenge them to do it.

And even though a breeder breeds for specific characteristics, it's only fair that trainers ask the individual what it's best fit to do. My Willie wants to be a pet. Anders likes to be a teacher. In Europe, the breeding of horses is a serious, honorable way of life, and a great deal of attention is paid to breeding horses who can be happy in their work. Character, in Europe, is as important as conformation and athleticism. In Holland, I met a stunning four-year-old gelding who'd recently been castrated. "Why?" I asked. "His balls bothered him too much," the trainer said. He went on to explain that the horse couldn't keep his mind on his work. It wasn't fair to ask him to work when he was so easily distracted, nor was it fair to let him father children who might be as distractible as he. And even though some bloodlines typically produce better dressage horses, or better jumpers, the foal is nevertheless asked, even before it's a weanling, what it particularly wants to do.

I watched this same trainer working with mares and their foals in an indoor arena. "Look how it moves," he said about one leggy child. "I think this one likes to jump." He sent the mare over a low jump, and the foal followed, bucking exuberantly on landing. The trainer raised the jump and sent the mare over again. Again, her child followed, tucking his knees under his chin and rounding his back into a fluid curve. "If they don't like to jump, they will not follow the mother over," the trainer told me.

He watched weanlings in the fields, too. "You learn if you see them play," he said. I remembered my own four-year-old thoroughbred in the field. Hughie loved feed sacks. He'd pick them up in his teeth, shake them until their crackling spooked him, and then tear 'round the field, trailing the sack over his shoulder so it chased him. Eventually he'd shift into a stately passage, watching to see if I saw how beautiful he was. What better way to tell me that he was the dressage prospect of my dreams? Not every horse makes a game of the energy and control required to go forward in such a slow and elevated trot.

As a two-year-old, Hughie'd been taken from the field and given a brief trial as a racehorse. He was big and ungainly, and timid—clearly not a racehorse—so he was put back out with the mares for another two years. Eventually his owner remembered there was a useless gelding out there somewhere and undertook to sell him. When I met him, his primary experience with humans had been the harsh three weeks in race training, when he was "broke."

He was seventeen hands and still growing. When he stepped off the trailer the first time I saw him, he seemed calm, but there was ring of anxious white around his eye. He hadn't a mean fiber in his whole big body, so he didn't do what many frightened horses do. He didn't try to strike, he didn't try to mash me against a wall, he didn't try to get away. That didn't mean these things weren't possible, however. In order that Hughie could come to feel safe with me, I'd have to treat him as though I were a mare.

Of course I'd have to love him, but I'd also have to be clear and dispassionate about what I expected. I'd have to correct him, fast as a rattlesnake, when he broke my rules, and—above all—I'd have to be fair. I'd have to learn his body language in order that I not violate the rules he came with. One of his rules was that I not mess with his ears, and another was that I not wave blankets at him. The humans who had handled him before were of the "might makes right" school of horse breaking, and one of their tactics was to subdue a horse by twisting its ear. Another was to "sack" it. Sacking isn't such a bad idea, as it happens. To touch, and then flick, a horse all over with a piece of cloth so it comes to understand the cloth won't hurt it, and that the human's intentions aren't evil, can be a step along the road of building partnership between horse and human. Intention is everything, however, and sacking is often done with the goal of reducing the horse to a sense of helplessness, and finally to passivity.

The horse has an acute memory. Along with bilateral vision, it is crucial to the survival of a prey animal. Poor Hughie. His future as a dressage horse required him to tolerate hands on his ears and cloth on his back. It was a long, slow process to renegotiate the rules. In the end, because ear rubs feel good, Hughie let me mess with his ears, but I always had to show him the saddle pad and let him smell it before I put it on. Because I was a mare, I had the right to require him to learn to deal with what I told him was safe; because I was also a human, he had the right to require me to respect his experience.

Building a relationship with a horse—riding it, in fact—is a delicate dance. The one who leads isn't necessarily the strongest one, or the one who knows most about the dance, it's simply the one the partners have, for the time, agreed is in charge of the pattern.

It is this delicacy, perhaps, that gives rise to our stories about girls and horses. In them, girls are understood to be fragile and so, for all their massive strength, are horses. Men are predators, some of our stories tell us, and in stories about dogs, it's often men who tame them. Our stories reflect what some of us believe to be true about male and female, strength and fragility, and stories are a means of teaching us to see. In the case of humans and dogs, both eyes tell a version of the same story. While it's both absurd and presumptuous to suppose we could see like other animals, the fact that horses see so differently can help us to imagine there are other ways the world might look.

Men who listen to mares' stories learn that it isn't only strength that teaches horses, and women who listen learn that gentleness is not enough. When horses were our helpers, crucial in some cases to our survival, humans did as much training as was necessary to get the job done. And even in those times, while many humans were devising ever harsher bits and spurs, others were listening to the horses.

In 400 B.C., Xenophon wrote a book on the art of training horses that influences, even now, the work of serious riders. Based on his own observations as well as the aesthetic tradition that shaped him, he said, "Anything forced or misunderstood can never be beautiful."

Indeed. Half a century later, like some contemporary fathers, the father of Alexander the Great gave his young son the best-bred horse money could buy. The horse was as unmanageable as he was beautiful, and was given up as vicious by those who saw the world solely in terms of dominion. While that was true of Alexander in relationship with other humans, he didn't make the mistake of assuming that horses see the same world humans do. He recognized Bucephalos's unruliness as terror and won his confidence by helping him understand he had nothing to fear.

Individual horses are as different from each other as we or roses are, or snowflakes. It could be entirely possible for someone to gain control of horses like my timid Hughie through domination alone. When material survival is at issue, for many people control is enough. It isn't mere survival, however, that creates the need in some of us to work with horses. There are some of us who would be centaurs; neither human nor horse, but something else. We are the ones who *must* listen to the horses in order that they may listen to us.

"Watch mares," a cowboy told me. A friend of mine had taken her young mare to him in desperation. The mare, Wasabi, had consented to training as long as it was fun, or interesting. Working on the longe line was fun—she was beautifully balanced and rhythmic and drew a crowd whenever she worked. It was interesting when a person sat on her back and another person led her around and told her, "Good *girl*, Wasabi." However, the presence of a rider on her back disrupted her balance, and once the novelty wore off, she got rid of the rider, and *that* was fun. Wasabi was, from her perspective, an excellent mare. She was by no means afraid, but balance and rhythm pleased her and things on her back disrupted them, and there wasn't, in purely human terms, a way of explaining to her that she could adapt.

The cowboy put Wasabi in the cross-ties, and every time she pawed, he smacked her. "I wouldn't do her like this if she was scared," he said, "but look at her expression. She's just being ornery. Her mama wouldn't put up with that kind of foolishness." Once Wasabi had agreed to stand quietly for a few minutes, he tacked her up and took her into a small pen where he mounted her. She walked a bit, trotted a bit, cantered a bit; then got fed up and exploded. Since the cowboy was an extraordinary rider, he stayed with her and simply whacked her every time she went up. Suddenly she stopped bucking and just stood there, her ears back. "She's thinking," he said. If her ears had been pinned, he would have been in big trouble, but they were just back, focused on her rider. He asked her to go forward, and she didn't, so he asked again, and then whacked her. She went up instead. He corrected her, and she stopped and thought. He asked her to go forward, and after a brief hesitation, she did so in an energetic, marching walk. "That's right, darlin'," he said, and got off. Thus ended the first lesson.

I went home and thought about what I'd seen. From the perspective of a human who believes love conquers all, the whole encounter might seem pretty brutal, but one of the reasons people with horses sometimes won't turn them out together is because they whack each other. They play king of the hill games, and tag, and can come in with superficial cuts and bruises. They come in with even more serious injuries when there have been disputes about hierarchy. An experienced horse owner knows that when a new horse joins a set of established pasture mates, the status of everyone in the group is called into question. Peace reigns in the long run, but in the short run even old friends can turn on each other. Once things have settled down, the boss mare doesn't have to pick fights—she knows who she is, and so does everyone else.

What Wasabi was learning in her first lesson is that you don't pick fights with the boss mare. The cowboy never picked a fight with her, he just responded, as mares do, to inappropriate behavior. In all the weeks he worked with her, he never asked her for more than she was physically or mentally equipped to do. While it mightn't have made sense to some humans, Wasabi's relationship with the cowboy made perfect sense to her. Once the boss mare's status is a given, she doesn't need to kick and bite; she can warn transgressors with a lifted hoof or squeal, and she can direct operations by example or with a gesture. In the same way, the cowboy's whacks became slight pressures of the calf, a delicate shift of balance or a lifting of the rein. And every time he went to take her from her stall, Wasabi would greet him with alert enthusiasm. Because, from her perspective, he told a credible story about the relationship between horse and human, she enjoyed their work together.

Sometimes the horse knows the story better than the human, and the human does better to believe the horse. When Anders was new to me, a trainer with a fancy reputation watched me ride him. "The horse isn't round enough through his body," he told me. I knew that much, I just hadn't figured out what to do about it. "You must hold him with the outside rein until he gives. *Hold him!*" I spent several lessons struggling, and failing, to do so. Nevertheless, the trainer assured me, it must be done, and I would just have to get stronger. "You have to *make* him give." Finally the trainer himself got on Anders to demonstrate. Anders, shaped by the years when people insisted on *making* him, fought back. Eventually, the trainer wrestled him into a shape approximating the proud carriage of a dressage horse and handed him back to me saying, "If I had more than five minutes, I would get him soft, too, but that takes time." Since, until that moment, I'd thought giving and softness were supposed to go hand in hand, I wondered if, perhaps, I'd been listening to the wrong person. I should have listened to my horse. In every way but English, he'd been saying, "I can't do it like this!" He felt so strongly about it that he'd wrenched his back and it was eight weeks before we could go back to work.

It's so delicate, I've learned, to work with Anders. In the instant before I want him to give, I have to give, and then he'll give back. On good days, when I'm listening carefully, there are moments when we are neither horse nor woman, but centaur—each given access to the other's vision.

It's taken him months to teach me that, and months to teach me that what I do with my seat and legs *really matters* to him. Because I've been willing to listen, he's been patient. Others who insisted they knew better than he made him resent all humans for a while. People who knew him in some of his former lives talk of how dangerous he was—how he used to strike at people in the field, how it had been necessary to walk wide around his stall for fear of being bitten. "What have you done?" they ask me. "How did you make him so peaceful?" I have to say I haven't *made* Anders anything. If anything, he's made me.

While I had to learn to defer to him when it came to riding, he had to learn to defer to me when it came to manners. It wasn't acceptable that he pin his ears at me when I came into his stall. It wasn't acceptable that he bolt on the leadline, or that he crowd me. He couldn't threaten me with a hind leg when I attended to his grooming. In these circumstances I knew better than he did, because I knew he could hurt me badly—what bruises a horse can concuss a human. In the agreement between horse and human, no harm should be done by either party.

One of the writers quoted by Xenophon said, "If a dancer was forced to dance by whips and spikes, he would be no more beautiful than a horse trained under similar conditions." Anything unnatural to a horse cannot be taught, it can only be forced. There is no movement in dressage that is not natural to the horse. What *is* unnatural, from a purely horse perspective, is that the movements occur at the behest of the human—the horse is ridden. And even if it *is* natural, what is forced cannot be beautiful.

There are whole categories of riding competition that rely on force. The horse is made to go forward through fear—trainers and friends surround the arena and shout, whistle, and crack whips to energize the horse as it passes them. Its natural carriage is enhanced unnaturally by the building up of hooves to heights just short of crippling, and chains are fastened above the hooves during schooling that elevate the action of the legs. Tails, naturally flagged aloft by excited horses, are cut, then set in a perpetually high, unnatural carriage. For those who find beauty in the partnership of horse and human, these tense and artificial horses are hideous to the eye. Alois Podhajsky, a former director of the Spanish Riding School in Vienna, writes about what he calls "false success," the "personal vanity and the desire to show off [which results in] a caricature of the various movements and to premature wearing out of the horse. Nature," he adds, "cannot be violated." In dressage, as in other disciplines that respect the character and not just the appearance of the horse, the quality of the movements depends on the extent to which a horse can respect and trust the rider.

In *The Oxford English Dictionary*, the first definition of "submission" is the "agreement to abide by a decision or obey an authority." Dressage judges define it similarly: "Attention and confidence, harmony, lightness, and ease of movement, acceptance of the bit." This also defines the relationship between good horses and good riders: the agreement between the dancers about who is in charge of the pattern. The British horseman, Henry

Wynmalen, says, "No one can avoid occasional upsets in a highly strung, high-couraged horse. But the talented rider shall ensure that no upsets or excitement are caused by his own conduct." He goes on to say that "the merit of the horse's calmness is in the confident and willing acceptance of his rider's requirements; there is no merit in the extinction of the horse's liveliness and brilliance."

Not only should a horse's liveliness and brilliance not be extinguished, they must be cherished, and good riders must pay attention to their horses about the difference between liveliness and pain or fear.

To an insufficiently attentive rider, fear can seem like liveliness. Early in our partnership, I took Anders to another barn for a riding clinic. He was a bit tense when I warmed him up away from the arena, but I thought it was because of me, since I'm often nervous in new places. That certainly was responsible for part of his excitement, but I wasn't paying enough attention. When I took him into the arena, located close to a cow pasture, and suggested that he settle down and get to work, he blew up. Afraid that if he threw me once, he'd throw me always, I wrestled him to a standstill. "You *idiot*," I yelled. "*You* idiot," the clinician said. "Can't you tell your horse is terrified?" I took a deep breath and willed myself to peacefulness. Only then could I hear what Anders was telling me—he was quivering, and his heart was beating so hard I could feel it through my boots. It was thus I learned that Anders was afraid of cows. In the miles and months since then, Anders has come to believe I won't willingly take him in harm's way, that I'll keep him from it if I can. So now, when we meet them, he's willing to take my word for it that cows won't hurt him, but, in return, I respect a brief, initial skepticism on his part before he refocuses his attention on me.

Submission is an agreement that can't be coerced, it can only grow from mutual respect. Gary Rockwell was reported to say of his good mare, Suna, who's been his partner in World Class dressage competition, "She has her own idea of what's reasonable and what infringes on her rights." Early in their relationship, though she was willing in her work, there were certain things Rockwell simply avoided asking of Suna because, as she hadn't yet gained confidence in him, he wasn't entitled to ask. She was also distracted by her cycles, which, as much in mares as women, can be uncomfortable and moody. Rockwell took his time, and brought her along slowly until her trust in him and confidence in her own ability enabled her to disregard such distractions. Suna and Rockwell, between them, are centaur, while separately they retain their individuality. Suna insists on her lively version of submission wherein, as her rider says, "She does things to remind me that she's in this project with me but that I don't dominate her."

There are people who say another animal couldn't possibly be a willing participant in the work they do with humans. Why on earth not? Perhaps it depends on circumstance. Two prisoners in a work party, digging at gunpoint, probably aren't working any harder than two people who, because they want one, are engaged in the creation of a garden. The only difference at the end of the day is that one pair feel oppressed, and the other fulfilled.

So why can't horses enjoy their work with us?

There are many things essential to survival—food, shelter, and procreation, to be sure, but almost as essential are alliances with others, and communication. Even if those of us who believe we were given dominion over all the earth may not prefer to see it, communication goes on all the time among and between all living things. The sounds we make, our body language, the pheromones we emit, the way we display our feathers, or feather our nests—all these say something not only to others of our species but to *all* the others.

Why is that so scary? Why do some of us so resist allowing our vision to expand?

I was reciting to my husband all the ways people in our culture have, over time, had to eat their words regarding the perceived inferiority of animals. First, the fact that humans had souls, and animals were declared not to have them, was sufficient proof that animals were inferior. As time went on, however, and science made inroads on articles of faith, the question of ensoulment became more and more murky. Later still, some argued that, whether or not *any* creatures had souls, animals didn't have language, but primates came along who learned to communicate in sign. Well, but animals weren't capable of abstract thought—and then the gorilla, Koko, told a joke. Finally coming to grips with the fact that animals *do* use tools, humans, still insisting on separatism, said, "Yes, but they can't make them"—only recently to learn that crows have been observed doing just that. "Aha!" said my husband, who very much enjoys a devil's advocate position, "but they can't program in 'C.'" "Why would *anyone* want to?" I snapped. Only a computer nerd would even know what he was talking about. "Because it's fun," he said.

Fun?

The Judeo-Christian myth that has partly shaped my vision tells me that not only is fun irrelevant, it's probably bad for me. This is the same tradition that holds among other things that we better not wear any mixed fibers, that we shall make no graven images, and that dancing leads to perdition. Because the human drive to create is so compelling that tradition has been modified somewhat to permit such doings if they can be defined as art. Art as defined, most particularly, by that tradition. Yet there are artists who are willing to suffer, and even to die, when they defy tradition for the sake of communicating to others what *really matters*.

Granted, as in all things, the compulsion to communicate varies in kind and strength from one individual to another. Some of us are satisfied if we can only tell one other that we're hungry. Others want to tell the world, and change it if we can. With our voices, with color, with music, with stones and steel and the way we touch, with everything at our disposal we reach out to communicate pleasure, anger, fear, wonder—all the things that make us what we are. And if all the things that make us what we are matter more to us than material survival, we seek to make art of the telling.

How subtle words are—one of our primary means of communication. The single word *fun* is both noun and verb in the dictionary, and its meanings range from cheat, to cajole, to amuse. In other words, to persuade. And yet we speak far subtler languages as well—touch, look, sound, smell—and, in all its implications, we have fun with them. To communicate is *fun* and it can range from high art to low comedy.

Watch horses. With pinned ears, they tell each other, and us if we're listening, that they're angry. Flagged tails say they're excited, and if one chooses to look further, very subtle differences in the shape of mouth, nostrils, and eyelids tell one whether the excitement is the result of curiosity, anxiety, exuberance, or something else. Just because we aren't listening, or don't know how to listen, doesn't mean they aren't talking.

Feel horses. To a rider, a tense back may mean fear, discomfort, anxiety, or something else. Even if the amount of weight in the hand through the rein is the same, its character can communicate whether the horse is resistant, or engaged—or something else. If the rider responds with a shift of weight, a relaxing of the back muscles, or a thump, the horse responds with a shift, or relaxation, or a thump of its own. It's a constant conversation: "Is this okay?" "Kinda." "Well, how about this?" "*No.*" "What do you mean, *no*?" "I mean you better try something else." "Oh . . . This?" "Yup." Whether it's the horse or the human asking questions depends on who wants to know, and who wants to know depends on the circumstances.

Just as humans vary wildly in their generosity, so do horses, but on the whole I suspect more horses are inclined to be generous than humans. (They're teaching me to see that.) A remarkable number of horses will accept ignorant riders on their backs. Small children get up on big, normally high-strung horses who simply ignore the whooping, thumping cowboy imitation on their backs and go quietly forward. These are horses who wouldn't put up with that behavior for a minute if it was someone who should know better.

I've seen more than a few riders at shows whose horses will do almost anything to stay under them. I watched a particular grey gelding in a dressage test whose rider not only hadn't mastered how to sit the trot, he hadn't begun to imagine how. In his comments, the judge wrote, "Generous, *patient* horse. Rider can reward him by learning how to sit." He added, "I admire adult beginners, but you're not quite ready for this level. You've got plenty of time, just be as patient with yourself as your horse is."

I've learned enough about horses to know that this one was not just a passive, defeated creature, but a teacher who, rather than being didactic, was actively engaged in supporting what it was his rider wanted to learn. I mentioned him to a friend, and she said, "Hey, I know that horse! He belongs to the guy's daughter, but she's off at school, so she asked her dad to keep him fit." The father had barely ever sat on a horse, but he agreed to try and found himself, rather to his astonishment, really wanting to learn to ride. Although the horse had been rather fractious with the daughter, he'd grown devoted to the father. The truth is that the more experienced daughter caused him less physical distress, but the horse was nevertheless willing to put up with significant discomfort for the sake of telling someone—who wanted to know it—what he knew about the art of centaur. He was having fun.

And maybe that's part of the answer. Between the two of us, my horse and I can agree to have fun together. Each of us can share with the other our perceptions of what matters in the particular world we inhabit, and for each of us the world becomes a little bigger, a little richer. I know it has value to me, and I find it hard to doubt it has value to him as well. As it happens, I'm not the one who feeds him, I'm the one who works with him. I'm the one who opens the gate and asks him, "Want to play Centaur?" And, in spite of the argument that other animals are capable only of cupboard love, Anders, knowing as well as I do we're both going to be sweaty when it's over, watches me walk across the pasture with a halter in my hand, nickers, and ambles amiably to meet me.

IV: RELATIONSHIPS

Learning from Animals

These pieces chronicle unique meetings between women and animals as members of different cultures fully entering into exchange, struggling to find points of commonality, to understand each other. These meetings between women and animals are not casual relationships. Much depends upon them, not only the life of the animals in many cases, but the emotional and spiritual life of the women.

Sometimes the animals determine the parameters of the relationship. It was not within Anna Merz's imaginings that she would raise a rhinoceros by hand in the wild. In order for the rhinoceros, Samia, to thrive among her own species, Merz had to be exquisitely sensitive to her needs and particularities, to meet the animal as a distinct and intelligent being, to come forth with respect and with love.

The interactions between humans and animals are not always benevolent. The unknown territory between human and animal is fraught with danger, particularly for the animals. Many of the women in this section learn about death from living alongside animals. They also enter the animal's worlds often guided by a sister creature, as Diane Ackerman was when she swam with a humpback mother and calf. Surrendering to their underwater element, she tried to communicate to these great-hearted mammal kin what so many of us want to say to the animals with whom we share a learning relationship: "I wish you well."

LEFT SINK

Ellery Akers

The first time I saw Left Sink I was brushing my teeth and almost spit on him. I wasn't expecting to find a frog in a Park Service bathroom, but there he was, hopping out of the drain and squatting on the porcelain as casually as if he were sitting beside a pond.

He was a small green tree frog, no bigger than a penny, and his round, salmon-colored toes stuck out like tiny soupspoons. For a few minutes I stared into his gold eyes, each pupil floating in the middle like a dark seed.

I was so close I could see his throat pulse, but I was probably too close, for he looked at me fearfully and leaped onto the silver "C" of the cold-water faucet.

Then he must have thought better of it, for he jumped down again, and sat, hunched over, by the soap. He kept making nervous little hops toward the safety of the drain, but my looming face was obviously in the way, so I ducked below the basin for a moment, and when I looked again he was descending into the hole, head first.

Feeling I'd disturbed his evening hunt, I decided to make amends. I grubbed around the floor for a dead moth, found one (though it was a little dried up), and offered it to the hole. The wing slanted into the drain, but nothing happened. I thought perhaps he'd hopped back down into the pipe. Trying to find something a little more appealing, I picked around the windowsills until I discovered a really decent-looking moth, pushed it up to the drain, and waited. After a few minutes, I got discouraged and walked away. When I turned back to sneak one last look, both moths had vanished.

The next day was so hot I forgot Left Sink completely. It is always hot in the California chaparral in September, especially in the Gabilan

245

Mountains. I spent the afternoon in the shade, lying on the cool pebbles of a dry wash and looking over my field notes. I had been camping for weeks, studying birds, and by now I had gotten used to the feeling of expectation in the landscape.

Everything seemed to be waiting for rain. The streambeds were dry, the fields were dry, and when the buckeye leaves hissed in the wind they sounded like rattlesnakes. Ravens flew overhead, croaking, their wings flapping loudly in the air. The rocks baked. Once in a while a few thirsty finches fluttered up to a seep in a cliff and sipped from a damp clump of algae.

I leaned against the cool flank of a boulder and fanned myself with my hat. From far away I could hear the staccato drill of a Nuttall's woodpecker. All the animals had some way of coping with the heat. The wrentits could last for several weeks without drinking. The deer found beds of shade and waited patiently until evening. Even the trees adapted. I knew that somewhere beneath my boots, one hundred feet down, the root of a digger pine was twisting along a crevice in the bedrock, reaching far below the surface to tap into the water table.

And the Pacific tree frogs—the normal ones—were sleeping away the summer and fall, huddled in some moist spot in the ground in a kind of hot-weather hibernation.

That night, when I went back to the bathroom, I discovered Left Sink had neighbors. Just before I turned on the water in the right-hand basin I noticed a second frog, and when I stepped back to look at both of them in their respective sinks, I started to laugh: They reminded me of a couple of sober, philosophical old monks peering out of their cells.

Overhead was a third frog, puffy and well-fed, squatting on top of the fluorescent lights, surrounded by tattered moths. I decided to call him the Light Buddha.

In the world of the bathroom, the light shelf was a delicatessen of the highest order, and the Light Buddha sat there night after glorious night, lazily snapping up moths as they fluttered past. The other two frogs seemed content to stake out the sinks, which weren't quite as dependable a food source, though they weren't bad. Almost every night I found a damp moth thrashing around in one of the basins, one little flopping death after another.

Right Sink was extremely shy, and spent most of his time crouched far back in the pipe. Usually I saw his gold eyes shining in the darkness, but that was all. Left Sink was more of an adventurer and explored the whole bathroom, darting behind the mirror, splatting onto the porcelain, hopping onto the windowsills, leaping onto the toilet, and climbing the slippery painted walls toe pad by toe pad.

From time to time I was tempted to pick him up as he was climbing. But I didn't think it would be fair; I knew this geometrical universe, and he didn't. Besides, there was no place for him to hide on those smooth, painted bricks. Even though tree frogs can change color in ten minutes, there was nothing in Left Sink's repertoire that could possibly match white paint; the best he could do was a sickly pink.

I could always tell if he had just emerged from the drain because he would still be a murky gray-green. As the evening wore on he got paler and paler. Once I couldn't find him for half an hour. Finally I caught sight of him over my head. Plopped on a narrow ledge, he looked like a pale pebble in all that metal and paint. I climbed onto the toilet for a better look. To my horror he began hopping along the ledge, which was no wider than half an inch. It was a ten-foot fall to the floor—for a frog that small, an abyss. He bounded past me, his grainy throat quivering. He headed toward a swarm of moths and flies that circled the fluorescent lights. A fly drifted down from the glare; Left Sink, his pink mouth flashing, snapped it up.

I was never quite sure just how skittish he really was. Sometimes he tolerated my watching him, sometimes he didn't. I got in the habit of sidling up to the plumbing, bent over so as not to be seen, and I must have looked pretty peculiar. One night a woman came into the bathroom and caught me hunched over like Quasimodo, staring intently at the drains, my hands full of dead moths.

"Left Sink! Right Sink!" I was saying. "Got a little treat for you guys!"

The woman bolted out the door.

I checked on the frogs every morning and evening. Sometimes when I saw Left Sink skidding down a length of plastic, unable to hold on in spite of his adhesive toe pads, I worried. I couldn't help thinking there was something unnatural about a frog in a bathroom.

Of course, I knew there were a few oddballs that *had* managed to live with us in our artificial world, but they were mostly insects. One year in school I had learned about the larvae of petroleum flies: They live in the gunk of oil fields, so numerous at times that, according to my textbook, they imparted "a shimmering effect to the surface of the oil." Their world was oil; if you deprived them of it, took them out and cleaned them off, they'd curl up and die in less than a day.

In that same class I'd learned that furniture beetles live in our table legs, and occasionally in wooden spoons; drugstore beetles float happily in bottles of belladonna, mating, pupating, dying. We have cheese mites in our cheese, and flour mites in our flour.

But no one mentioned anything about frogs.

Actually, considering the drought, Left Sink had a pretty good setup. It was already October and still no rain. Once in a while a few drops would plop into the dirt and gravel, and I would catch a whiff of wet dust, soaked cheat grass, and buckwheat. But that was all.

All the other frogs were holed up in the dirt, huddled in a moist crack or an abandoned gopher hole, waiting for the first rains of winter to wake them up. There were probably a few hiding in the field next to Left Sink's bathroom, their eyelids closed, their toes pulled under them to conserve moisture, unmoving, barely breathing, their heartbeats almost completely stilled. If I dug them up they would look like small stones.

One night just before I was about to leave the campground, I had a nightmare. It was a dream I had had many times, a dream of a city so polluted the air rose in black plumes above the granite and cement. I was at the entrance of a tunnel. Inside I could hear a whoosh of air: Millions of butterflies were flashing in the dark, thousands of ducks, eagles, sparrows, their wings making a vast rustling as they flew off and vanished.

I heard a low shuffling. After a while I realized it was the sound of feet: the slow trudge of bears, the pad of badgers, the pattering of foxes, the rasp of a hundred million beetles, rabbits, ants, mice. I looked around, panicked, to see if any animals were left. There were still cockroaches scuttling over the windowsills. There were pigeons, flies, starlings. I named them over and over in a kind of chant: the adaptable, the drab, the ones who could live with us, who had always lived with us.

A fox coughed close to my camp and woke me up. I unzipped the tent and looked out at the stars: Rigel, Algol, clear, cold, and changeless. A golden-crowned sparrow chirped from a nearby branch, then sputtered off into silence. For a while I tried to stay awake, but soon drifted off.

The next morning huge bluish clouds rolled across the sky. A couple of ravens sailed past the cliff in front of me. One of them jackknifed its wings, plummeted straight down, and then, at the last minute, unfolded them and flapped away. It was still early, but when I reached the bathroom it had already been cleaned. It reeked of ammonia, and a mop and bucket leaned against the door.

I rinsed off my face, brushed my hair, and looked sleepily into the drains. As usual, Right Sink was huddled far back into the dark pipe; he retreated still further when I bent over.

Left Sink, however, was gone. I wondered if he had slipped behind the mirror, or had come up in the world and was squatting with the Light Buddha. The shelf was empty. I looked on the windowsill—not there either.

It was not until I opened the door to the toilet that I found him. There, in the center of the ammonia-filled bowl, his green bloated body turning gray, was Left Sink, splayed out in the milky liquid, dead. Floating in front of him was a dead damselfly. I suppose he must have jumped in after his prey, convinced he was at the edge of a strange-looking pond, his toe pads gripping the cold, perfectly smooth surface of the porcelain.

His skin looked curdled, and it occurred to me he might have been there all morning, waiting to die. Then I remembered that frogs breathe through their skin; it must have been a hard, stinging death, but a quick one.

I flushed him down, wishing I could think of something to say as he made his way through the pipes and rolled out to the septic tank, some acknowledgment of the link between my kind and his, but I couldn't think of anything except that I would miss him, which was true.

When I opened the door a couple of nervous towhees blundered into the bushes. It was beginning to rain.

MAKING PEACE

Barbara Kingsolver

When I left downtown Tucson to make my home in the desert, I went, like Thoreau, "to live deliberately." I think by this he meant he was tired of his neighbors. For me the problem wasn't specifically my neighbors, whom I loved (and it's a good thing, since our houses were so close together we could lean out our bedroom windows and shake hands), but the kids who spilled over from—and as far as I could see, never actually attended—the high school across the street. They liked rearranging the flowers in my front yard, upside down. They had art contests on my front walk, the point being to see whether a realistic rendition of the male sex organ could be made to span the full sweep from sidewalk to front door. They held very loud celebrations, daily, on my front porch. When my brain was jangled to the limits of reason, I would creep from my writing desk to the front door, poke my head out, and ask if they could turn the music down. They glared, with So What eyes. Informed me this was a party, and I wasn't invited.

The school's principal claimed that kids outside the school grounds were beyond his jurisdiction; I was loath to call the city police, but did (only after the porch party ratified a new sport involving urination), and they told me what I knew they'd say: the principal ought to get those kids in school. My territory was up for grabs, by anyone but me.

After some years had passed and nobody seemed to be graduating, I struck out for Walden. My husband and I sold our house, collected our nerve, and bought four acres of rolling desert—a brambly lap robe thrown over the knees of the Tucson Mountains, a stone's throw beyond the city limits. There was a tiny cabin, which we could expand to suit our needs. I anticipated peace.

Like a pioneer claiming her little plot of prairie, I immediately planted a kitchen garden and hollyhocks outside the door. I inhaled silence, ecstatic with the prospect of owning a place that was really my own: rugged terrain, green with mesquite woods and rich in wildlife. No giant penises waiting to impale me when I threw open my front door. Only giant saguaros. Only bird song and faint hoofprints in the soil, evidence of wild creatures who might pass this way under cover of darkness.

Sure enough they came, the very first night: the javelinas. Woolly pigs. They are peccaries, technically, cloven-hoofed rooters of the New World, native to this soil for much longer than humans have known it—but for all the world they are pigs. I pressed my face to the window when I heard their thumping and rustling. Their black fur bristled as they bumped against one another and snuffled the ground with long, tusked snouts. I watched them eat my hollyhocks one by one.

Pioneering takes patience. I thought maybe that first visit was some kind of animal welcome-wagon tradition in reverse, and that over time we could reach an accord. Night after night, they returned. The accord seemed to be: You plant, we eat. The jackrabbits were hungry too, but I discovered that they shun the nightshade family—which conveniently includes tomatoes and eggplants—and that I could dissuade them from my flowers with chicken wire (although a flowerbed that looks like Fort Knox is a doubtful ornament). Not so picky, the pigs. With mouths of steel and cast-iron stomachs, they relished the nightshades, and in their eagerness I swear they even ate chicken wire. Over the weeks I tried the most pungent flowers I could think of: geraniums, marigolds. They ate everything. Rare is the epicurean pig who has feasted at such a varied table as the one I provided.

I tried to drive them off. Banged on the windows, shrieked, and after a goodly amount of accomplishing nothing whatsoever through those means, cautiously opened the door a crack, stuck my head out, and hollered.

"Shoo, pigs!" said I.

"Not by the hair of my chinny chin chin," thought they, apparently, in what passes for thought within those bony skulls. They ignored me profoundly, inciting me to extremes. I stooped to throwing rocks, and once by the wildest of chances, so help me God, I hit one, broadside. With a rock the size of a softball, and a respectable thud. The victim paused for half an instant midgobble and sniffed the air as if to ask, Was that a change in the weather? Then returned to the hollyhocks at hand. On the He-Man Scale of Strength, my direct hit scored "Weenie." I seethed between the four walls of my house like Rochester's mad wife in the attic.

In a fit of spite I went to a nursery that specializes in exotics, and brought home an *Adenium obesum*. This is the beautiful plant whose singularly lethal sap is used by African hunters to poison their darts.

Javelinas understand spite: they uprooted my *Adenium obesum*, gored it, and left it for dead.

Over the months our house slowly grew, with javelinas watching. We framed up an extra room, which we would eventually connect to the old house by tearing out a window, once it was sealed, to the outside. We laid out sheet-metal ductwork, which would go into the ceiling, for heating the new addition. In the middle of the night we woke to the sound of the devil's own celebration: hellacious hoofs on tin drums. The pigs had found their way into the new room and were trampling the ductwork, sending their tinny war cry to the stars above.

Ownership is an entirely human construct. At some point people got along without it. Many theorists have addressed the question of how private property came about, and some have gone so far as to suggest this artificial notion has led us into a mess of trouble. They aren't talking about *personal property*, like a toothbrush or a digging stick to call one's own, which has probably always been a human tradition. Even a bird, after all, has its nest, and chimpanzees in a part of central Africa where there's a scarcity of nut-smashing tools are known to get possessive about their favorite rocks. But to own land, plants, other animals, more stuff than we need—that is the peculiar product of a modern imagination.

In the beginning, humans were communal and social creatures; this is agreed upon by all scientists who've given our species retroactive study. The habit and necessity of cooperation is what led us, like other social species, toward the development of an elaborate communication system. Other social primates that live in large groups, like Japanese macaques and baboons, communicate with a much richer repertoire of sounds than the solitary primates like orangutans. Many social mammals use not only verbal but olfactory signals—a language of the nose. An example of complex communication among birds, familiar to any rural child, is that of the socially cooperative chickens, who use different calls (in the wild, as well as the barnyard) to refer to important events in their lives: krk krk krk (food over here); kark kark KARK (*really good* food over here); RRRR-rrrr (hawk overhead). Parrots, another famous category of garrulous birds, are presumed by scientists to have developed their gift of gab because of social habits and longevity in the wild.

It's safe to presume that the most talkative of all primates, *Homo sapiens,* evolved in the context of cooperative social groups also, hunting and gathering on the African savannahs. The theory that has percolated best into popular imagination is the one that claims men clobbered the animals, providing intermittent jubilations of protein for the home crowd, while women dug roots, picked fruits and seeds, and harvested edible plant parts. The latter activities presumably would provide the bulk of the steady calories, but for many decades the burgeoning science of human origins was captivated by the hunting scenario: the need to peer out over the savannah grass as incentive for walking upright; the necessities of spear making and cooperative hunting giving rise to language, dexterity, and a large, complex brain.

This neat boy-girl theory smacks of sexist backward projection, I've always thought, while I do concede (having carried a toddler on my own hip for a few years) that it's more feasible to go berry picking than lion hunting with a nursing child in tow. But many early anthropologists, unable to resist drama, apparently overestimated the importance of "the hunt" as a shaper of our body, character, and destiny. It's now understood that the earliest evidence of meat eating in the human archaeological record comes from East African sites that are less than two million years old. Considering that we have been walking upright and approximately human for more than twice that long, carnivory may have been an afterthought. Anthropologist Adrienne Zihlman argues that the challenge that shaped us was most likely the savannah environment itself, which is not a monoculture of tall grass but a complex mosaic of grassland, hills, and forested areas along watercourses. Potential food sources were abundant but seasonal and widely scattered: the early human's home range would have been much larger than that of living savannah baboons and chimpanzees. The best survivors would be those with a good locomotor system and the capacity to carry water and food, as well as offspring. Based on the fossil record, and on close study of living hunter-gatherers and our primate relatives in similar habitats, Zihlman has estimated that plant foods, insects, and small vertebrates made up more than 90 percent of the early hominid diet, and that "scavenging and consumption of large dead animals found by chance" was probably infrequent. This scenario, which has our ancestors shooing off hyenas and vultures from the *carcass du jour*, isn't going to sell any movie rights, but it has the advantage of evidence behind it.

In any case, the best perspective on the notion of a natural division of labor was given me long ago by one of my most influential college professors, Preston Adams, a botanist who studied human evolution. He pointed out that all "man the hunter" theories implicitly establish women as the first botanists. He also liked to tell restless zoology majors that it takes a superlative mind to appreciate a plant. He kindly allowed me to put two and two together.

When it began to dawn on our insightful ancestors that they could save some edible seeds, put them in the ground, and have a whole new edible crop right on the front stoop, we had agriculture on our hands. It's a giant step, the historical materialists maintain, to go from appropriating the products of nature to increasing their supply through human labor. The first evidence of cultivated grains comes from archaeological sites that are in the neighborhood of eleven thousand years old. Joseph Campbell, in his *Atlas of World Mythology*, identifies at least three independent points of origin for "The Way of the Seeded Earth": the Middle East, Southeast Asia, and Central America. Domestication of animals followed right along. A handful of seeds, like Jack's magic beans, turned our fortunes head over heels.

Friedrich Engels, the nineteenth-century economist and close associate of Karl Marx, examined our history under the bright lamp of a new paradigm set forth by his contemporary Charles Darwin. Engels also had access to the prodigious work of anthropologist Lewis Henry Morgan. Countless modern scholars have addressed the history of private property, but it's hard to beat the elegance of Engels's simple outline of human social evolution, laid out in his wonderful classic, *The Origin of the Family, Private Property, and the State*. In the natural progression to a more controlled form of hunting and gathering, he theorized, the community efforts of planting and harvesting remained the female domain, while animals that could "belong" to someone belonged to men. Goats and sheep, being mobile and tradable, became currency. Rather suddenly men got the purse strings. Rather suddenly "purse strings" was a concept. So was "inheritance." The family tightened its boundaries, the better to serve as conduit for property passed from father to son.

If we can divine religion from relics, it seems pretty clear that up to this point human societies stood most in awe of female power: the pregnant Venus of Willendorf; the Woman with the Horn carved on a cliff in Dordogne, France; the fecund clay figurines that preclassical Mexicans buried with their dead; pregnant torsos carved from the tusks of woolly mammoths in Asia; the pale stone fertility figures strewed along the Mediterranean coast like so many dragons' teeth. The one that gets my vote for blunt reverence is a mammoth-ivory disk from a gravesite in Moravia, cut with a single, unambiguous vulval slit. So many goddesses, so little time—for they fell, and fell *far*, from grace. It's pretty difficult now even to imagine female body parts as sacrament: when the kids spray-painted vulvas on my front steps, their thoughts were oh so far from God.

How fiercely doth the sacred turn profane. Our ancestors in the Fertile Crescent appear to have dropped Goddess Mother like a hot rock, and shifted their allegiance to God the Father, coincident with the rise of Man the Owner of the Flock.

Since then, most of us have come to see human ownership of places and things, even other living creatures, as a natural condition, right as rain. While rights and authority and questions of distribution are fiercely debated, the basic concept is rarely in doubt. I remember arguing tearfully, as a child, that a person couldn't own a tree, and still in my heart I believe that, but inevitably to come of age is to own. When we stand upon the ground, we first think to ask, Whose ground is this? And NO TRESPASSING doesn't just mean, "Don't build your house here." It means: "All you see before you, the trees, the songbirds, the poison ivy, the water beneath the ground, the air you would breathe if you passed through here, the grass you would tread upon, the *very idea of existing in this place*—all these are mine." Nought but a human mind could think of such a thing. And nought but a human believes it. Javelinas, and teenagers, still hark to the earth's primordial state and the music of the open range.

Now, territoriality is a different matter. Birds do that. Dogs do it. Pupfish in their little corner of a mud puddle do it. They (meaning, usually, the males of territorial species) mark out a little plot and defend it from others of their own kind, for the duration of their breeding season. This is about reproduction: he is making jolly well sure that any eggs that get fertilized, or babies that get raised, within that hallowed territory are, in fact, his own. Often, it's also a matter of securing an area that contains enough resources—nuts, berries, caterpillars, flower nectar, whatever—to raise a brood of young. Just enough, usually, and hardly a caterpillar more. The minute the young have flown away, the ephemeral territory vanishes back into the thin air, or the bird brain, whence it came. The male might return to establish a breeding territory in the same place again next year, or he might not. The landscape lives on, fairly untouched by the process.

When a male bird—a vireo, for example—sings his belligerent song at another male vireo that approaches his neck of the woods, he is singing about family. It's a little bit like grumbling over the handsome delivery person who's getting too friendly with your spouse; a *lot* like coming with a crowbar after an intruder at your child's bedroom window in the night; and nothing at all like a NO TRESPASSING sign. The vireo doesn't waste his breath on the groundhogs gathering chestnuts under his nose, or the walnut trees using the sunlight to make their food, the grubs churning leaves into soil, the browsing deer, or even other birds that come to glean seeds that are useless to a vireo's children. Worm-eating birds have no truck with seedeaters; small-seed eaters ignore big-seed eaters. This is the marvelous construct of "niche," the very particular way an organism uses its habitat, and it allows for an almost incomprehensible degree of peaceful coexistence. Choose a cubic foot of earth, about anywhere that isn't paved; look closely enough, and you'll find that thousands of different kinds of living things are sharing that place, each one merrily surviving on something its neighbors couldn't use for all the tea in China. I'm told that nine-tenths of human law is about possession. But it seems to me we don't know the first thing about it.

It did not take me long in the desert to realize I was thinking like a person, and on that score was deeply outnumbered. My neighbors weren't into the idea of private property, and weren't interested in learning about it, either. As Kafka frankly put it, when it's you against the world, bet on the world.

So I dispensed with lordship, and went for territoriality. I turned a realistic eye on my needs. I don't really have to have hollyhocks outside my door. But I'd like some tomatoes and eggplants. Oak-leaf lettuce on crisp fall days, and in the spring green beans and snowpeas. Maybe a *little* bed of snapdragons. It wouldn't take much. Since I had no plans to raise a huge brood, sixty square feet or so of garden space would serve me very well.

I revised my blueprints and looked hard at Pueblo architecture, which shuns the monumental for the more enduring value of blending in. The Pueblo, as I understand their way of life, seem to be more territorial than proprietary, and they've lived in the desert for eight centuries. Between the javelinas and me it had come down to poison darts in about eight days. Enough with that.

I settled on a fairly ancient design. The wings of my house enfold a smallish courtyard. My territorial vireo song is a block wall, eight feet high. Inside the courtyard I grow a vegetable garden, a few fruit trees, and a bright flag of flowerbed that changes its colors every season. The acres that lie beyond the wall I have left to cactus and mesquite bramble, and the appetites that rise to its sharp occasion.

Life is easier since I abdicated the throne. What a relief, to relinquish ownership of unownable things. Engels remarked at the end of his treatise that the outgrowth of property has become so unmanageable that "the human mind stands bewildered in the presence of its own creation." But he continues on a hopeful note: "The time which has passed since civilization began is but a fragment of the past duration of man's existence; and but a fragment of the ages yet to come. . . . A mere property career is not the final destiny of mankind."

Indeed. We're striving hard to get beyond mere property career around here. I've quit with the *Adenium obesum*, and taken to leaving out table scraps for the pigs. I toss, they eat. I find, now that I'm not engaged in the project of despising them, they are rather a hoot to watch. On tiny hooves as preposterous as high-heeled pumps on a pirate, they come mincing up the path. They feel their way through the world with flattened, prehensile snoots that flare like a suction-cup dart, and swivel about for input like radar dishes. When mildly aroused (which is as far as it goes, in the emotional color scheme of the javelina), their spiky fur levitates into a bristly, spherical crown—Tina Turner laced with porcupine. I don't even mind that they come and eat up our jack-o'-lanterns at Halloween; it's worth it. They slay me every time with their hilarious habit of going down on their foreknees and walking along, pious supplicants in awe of life's bounty, pushing whole pumpkins before them.

Meanwhile, in the cloistered territory of the courtyard, so many things come and go it would feel absurd to call it mine: I've seen an elf owl picking through the compost pile; Gila woodpeckers fighting over the tree trunks; hummingbirds at the flowers; doves who nested in the grape arbor; a roadrunner who chased off the doves and gulped down their eggs; a pair of cardinals and a Pyrrhuloxia couple who nested in adjacent trees and became so confused, when the young fledged and flew to the ground, that they hopped around frantically for a week feeding each other's kids. A pair of Swainson's thrushes stopped in for a day on their migratory flight from Canada to Peru; to them, this small lush square in a desert state must have appeared as Moses' freshet from the rock.

The cardinals, of course, eat the grapes. In some years the finches peck a hole in every single apricot before I get around to throwing a net over the tree. A fat, clairvoyant rock squirrel scales the wall and grabs just about every third tomato, on the morning I decide that tomorrow it will be ripe enough to pick.

So what, they all declare with glittering eyes. This is their party, and I wasn't exactly invited.

Trish Maharam

I came to horses knowing only that my child loved them, and that because of her age much of the responsibility would fall to me. What I didn't know was that as a woman I would develop a love of horses that I'd never fostered as a young girl.

My six-year-old daughter had been passionate about horses since the age of two. In the park we'd come upon them and Hanae would call out from her stroller, her bike, her lanky growing body. Finally we sought out horses and ponies a year ago at the urban Overlake Farm just twenty minutes from home.

I left a note inquiring about riding lessons. Hanae and I knew this as the right spot to begin our horse adventure.

Just a week later the phone rang. "Trish, it's Gloria from Overlake Farm. I found the perfect pony. I was up in the Colville Flats rounding up cattle and we went into the slaughter pens."

I was listening but did not understand. I wanted to lease a pony, or just use one for infrequent lessons, but there was no room in Gloria's rhythm for questions and I didn't want to sound ignorant.

"This old mare, swayback and bony, came trotting toward me with her ears up high. I got as good a look as I could and she's just perfect for Hanae. It's better when they're old, they're gentler around children. But we have to move fast. She's bound for auction, then slaughter, in a week. I'm sure she'll cost next to nothing."

"I have to think about it," I heard myself say.

"Don't wait too long."

Gloria gave me the number of someone at the auction yards, someone who might know the mare's history, make it more palatable. I called, eager to hear anything that would persuade me to say "No."

"Well, John's not here and I can't be sure I know the mare. But you know, there's usually a good reason why they're here. If they were any good to anybody they'd have kept 'em."

I thought about the plants I'd rescued from friend's compost heaps. They were thriving in the garden.

I called Gloria. "I can do this. It'll be the perfect birthday surprise." But I wasn't really sure. This was my way, to leap into experiences, often with a surge of fear.

But by the time I drove with Hanae and my husband, David, to the farm the idea of a horse had already taken root. When we arrived I smiled at David, gave Hanae a firm hug and said, "We've gotten you your very own pony, a mare. We're all going to meet her for the first time."

Gloria was waving from a lower pasture. "Oh she's just the sweetest Appaloosa. You should have seen her trotting before. She's got a lot of spunk; must be twenty-five from the look of her teeth, maybe thirty. I heard this is your six-year birthday present." Hanae pulled back shyly. "Maybe we can get you on her back for a little ride today."

We approached the pony. She had a thick, gray-spotted, shaggy coat, a rug really, and she was big, more a horse than a pony. I rubbed her coat and mane shyly, feeling a layer of slippery grime cover my palm.

"She's loaded with lice powder. They're bound to get it in those slaughter pens. She and this mare over here." Gloria pointed to a thin brown horse with a quivering underlip. Her expression was deerlike. I thought hard about lice. I cringed but smiled.

The pasture was full of thistles and muddy earth. It felt cold and dank. My toes were already wet. This was unfamiliar territory. I suddenly realized this was not just the rescue of a pony—it was taking on responsibility for another living creature. She was ours and I knew absolutely nothing about horses. I looked toward David for consolation. He averted his gaze and looked somewhere far off. This was my project. He had clearly communicated that he did not want a large animal at this point in our lives.

We drove over every other day. An hour's visit would turn into three. Large bags of carrots were consumed over the winter by Diamond Feather, Hanae's chosen name for her pony. Minnie, another rescued horse, shared the shed. She was bony and meek, like a victim. Diamond stood beside her, an experienced matron, concentrating deeply on the chewing of her oats. They bonded with each other and whenever Hanae would ride bareback to the arena, Diamond and Minnie would neigh their good-byes loudly. It was always a woeful moment, that parting.

Often when we went to the farm I'd be sure that we could only remain for a certain stretch of time. But the sound of Minnie and Diamond's unified chewing was comforting, and errands or work paled beside the simple smell of horses and hay and the sound of rain on the shed roof.

By the time spring came along we'd been taught grooming. Jenny, Hanae's riding instructor, met with us once a week. I sat in on the lessons, observing my daughter as she became tall and confident. I learned the methodical rubbing and lubricating of bridles, the brushing and currying, but there was a stiffness in my gestures. I moved around Diamond and the other horses with caution. My touch was distant, wary. I assumed they had a language I could not learn.

Diamond's left eye began to cloud over in the early spring and a series of vets dispensed ointments that I put into her eye once a day. Sometimes I'd let a day or two pass and often the ointment would coat more of the eyelash than inner eye. She was losing her patience with me. Her ears went back, which in horse language means "Clear out," but my ignorance kept me standing there. I'd rub her soft nose and kiss it until she lowered her head. This was the beginning of my knowing her.

No one properly diagnosed the eye, and it clouded over completely. We had to speak to Diamond when approaching from her blind side, touch her, so she knew our presense.

Gloria would come to us often, introduce us lovingly to the many other women who rode at the farm. Fifteen- and seventeen-year-olds, women in their forties, in their seventies. Comrades now. They would stop and chat about how well Diamond was looking. What I hadn't counted on was the deep sense of community. These women loved animals and it bonded us.

On a warm spring day Hanae ran ahead of me to the pasture. Diamond was down flat in the dirt. I sprinted toward her.

"Sharon," I called. She was grooming her horse. "Diamond Feather's down."

"Trish, it's all right, she's just sunning herself. I checked her already."

I still ran. It was the first time I'd ever seen a reclining horse. Minnie was quietly preening beside her. I sat cross-legged beside Diamond while Hanae collected bouquets of fresh grown grass for every horse within view. Diamond lifted her head and put it in my lap. It was a remarkable sight, the huge head settled on me and I rubbed her, stroked her, and wondered what her life had been before this. Had people loved her as I was loving her now? I brushed and curried her in spots that made her lips stretch far out and her teeth made silent nibbles; I felt then like we were becoming familiar with one another.

Gloria called one steamy summer day. "Trish, this is the perfect bath day. Come on over. Jenny's here and we've got Diamond grazing in wait."

I hung up. I'd been in the garden digging. There were ten plants waiting to get out of their cramped pots; Hanae was in her treehouse. But Gloria was on a mission. I laughed. Oh well. We grabbed some carrots and were off.

Diamond was already hooked up to Gloria's beauty parlor. She had a wild look in her eyes. Gloria had turned on her electric shears and the hair from Diamond's chin was dropping. I stroked her forehead and massaged around her temples, telling her it was all right. We were all with her, her congregation of women friends. We swept the hair away and hooked up the hose to warm water.

Her body stiffened at first and her head craned toward the sky. Gloria continued scrubbing and Diamond reluctantly relaxed.

"Oh, doesn't this feel good?" Gloria said, dragging the hose over Diamond's body. "I'll bet this is the first bath she's ever had." Words and water mingled. Dirt poured off her and Gloria chirped along. "There was an article in *Practical Horse* about a college girl with no money and a young man who was her trainer. They scoured the slaughter pens. The trainer was set on a big brown thoroughbred, but she was determined to have a little chestnut she'd spotted. She loved the face and the eyes on him. As of July he was the top First Year Green Working Hunter, which made him worth about six figures. There was a cover photo of them and the caption read something like, 'She had an "eye for an eye." ' Of the fifty slaughter horses the trainer got at the pens he's only brought two back."

Summer melded into fall. We were visiting the farm every other day with lessons twice a week. I barely noticed the leaves changing because the air was still warm. Hanae had begun first grade and our visits to the farm were infrequent.

It was early November when we noticed that Diamond's right eye, her only good eye, was draining. Gloria thought it might be a plugged duct. I didn't think to call the vet. The next Saturday, Diamond's energy seemed low. Her eye was very cloudy. I knocked hard and fast on Gloria's door. Before I spoke, her words came. "I saw her eye, Trish. The vet's doing a group call this afternoon. She's great. I think you'll like her."

I had to wait for the vet. She was checking other horses. Horses were running in the pastures, basking in the warmth of the day. I wondered what would happen if Diamond went blind. I'd keep her and nurture her. They say you can still ride a blind horse. All their senses heighten. Diamond's winter coat was coming. I stroked it, remembering the hair she'd shed the previous spring. I massaged her forehead; my hands now knew her body, face, neck. She'd begun to rest her big head in the crook of my arm and close her eyes. I loved the smell of her: the combination of hay and mulching leaves and wind. All the elements clung to her.

"Sorry it's taken so long." My eyes opened, came back to Diamond grazing. The vet had a firm spirited gait and her hair was silky red. She felt familiar.

"So this is Diamond Feather." Emily gently took Diamond's head in her hands and looked carefully at her eyes. "This looks like uveitis for sure. If you want to stop it where it is you have to be aggressive. I'd say six times a day with ointment for starters."

She gathered an ample bag of supplies, educating me about their purpose, while I stood dazed at the idea of six hours each day, the back and forth of it.

I looked at Diamond Feather. My posture was straightening, a sure sign of determination. Medicating a horse's eye can be a two-person job but I was sure I could do it alone. I roped off a part of Diamond's pasture for her and Minnie. I told her I needed her cooperation to make this eye better. She must have understood those first few days because she was very patient with my attempts. Gloria's daughter Linda showed me how to use a human twitch, a kind of nose pincher that focuses the pain on the nose so you can tend the eye, but I couldn't use it. I barely ever raised my voice with Diamond. It never occurred to me to be strict or severe with her.

I'd begin at 6:00 A.M., go home, get Hanae off to school, then again at 9:00, 1:00, 4:00, 7:00, and finally ten at night. Those first drives were arduous. I counted them off like a relay. Then I noticed that the weather was beautiful, the fall its most colorful in years. I urged myself to see the shapes as I drove along the lake. In the morning there was a mist like a snowfield, the schoolbus was picking up children. Hanae came infrequently. She was consumed with school and friends. This nurturing was tedious for her.

Often I turned the drive into a contemplation of the present, thinking about random significant questions: What is friendship? I'd ponder the mostly female relationships I maintained, those that gave and those that took away. It dawned on me how different it was to love an animal. There are no expectations in the giving. Not so with love of humans. There's a thread of need coiling through, a desire for something to be returned. I wondered if I could change this dynamic.

When I arrived at the pasture, Minnie and Diamond looked toward me. No false smiles, just a blasé acknowledgment. I felt a surge of love and friendship. They wanted carrots. Diamond put her head near mine. I breathed on her, found the bonyness of her face with my fingers. "I'm tired, Diamond, I want you to get better." She farted loud and long, pulled her head away, then gave it back. I had an immense love for this horse, this once mother. I wished she could tell me her story.

When I came home from the farm the phone was ringing. "Trish, it's

Emily, the vet. I did some bloodwork yesterday on Diamond. It's not good news. It showed a high calcium count, which means a tumor or cancer. I'm sorry. You've given her such a good home. Maybe she's got a year. Sometimes these things snowball so you should watch her closely, her appetite, her bowel movements. We don't want her to be in pain. Go to three times a day with the ointment and keep in touch."

David and Hanae and I sat down that night. I explained that there was something growing inside Diamond Feather and we didn't know how long she'd be with us. We'd dealt with death—birds on our property, raccoons, fish. We'd created ceremonies for them, made little graves. But we'd never lost anyone we loved.

Hanae cried. It seemed effortful, like she thought she was supposed to. I held her and we conjured memories until bedtime.

Three days later I was headed for Diamond's last creaming at four o'clock. It was near dark on that gloomy day and I shone my headlights on the stable. Diamond was down and obviously in pain. She was rocking her body on the ground, her breath was heavy and fast. Minnie was sniffing her. It was obvious that she'd been down for hours. I drove quickly to Gloria's. The door was open but no one was home. I called the vet and left a note, hoping Gloria would arrive soon.

In the pasture I got down on the ground and stroked Diamond. I wondered if this was colic. There was a strong smell of ammonia. I threw my weight into her body, imagining I had the strength to lift her like I would my child. I cajoled her with words and kisses, and finally she rolled herself up and stood. We tromped around the little space to get some movement going inside her. I prayed for long loud farts but she just fell onto her front knees and lay panting. I made her a bed of fresh yellow straw like a wreath around her.

A woman I'd never met appeared, set up a lantern, and stood by me silently. Then Gloria drove up, bringing life and possibility to the solemn air.

Emily finally arrived. She was all action. Listening to the heartbeat. Me holding Diamond's head while Minnie looked over my shoulder; the steam rising in the ray of a flashlight.

"There's bad blockage and huge gas pockets. We've got to put her on a longe line and get her running." Emily tugged from the front, I pushed from the back, Robin opened the gate and we finally got her out of the muddy pasture onto the drive. Gloria ran after her with a rake. It seemed so inhumane, but the result would be her health. I took her halter and ran beside her, with her, all the time telling her she could do it. But she fell in a heap on the ground.

Emily faced me. "It's bad, Trish. This gas colic needs surgery and with her history I couldn't say if she could even make it through. She's in a lot of pain and there isn't another way to make this better."

I began to cry. "What are you saying?"

"We could keep her alive but she'd be in pain. In the past I've let illness go too long. It just doesn't seem right. My advice is to euthanize her."

I'd never had any experience making a decision like this. Diamond stood before me, big in the night, the steam from her body so alive. It wasn't until she fell again that I understood it might be her time. They all left me alone with her. I wanted Diamond to tell me, to give me some sign, but there was only the heavy sound of breath and a steady rain. What equipped me to make this decision? Only that I owned her. The concept of owning seemed ludicrous to me just then.

Gloria came to my side. "She's had a good year, Trish. Look how flared her nostrils are. She's trying too hard. There's a grave already dug up by Crystal. You can have it for Diamond. This way she'll be near us."

I thought of Hanae planting a bed of yellow and purple crocus and poeticus like slender fairies, and of Diamond Feather lying peaceful beneath them. She looked broken, her legs kicking on the gravel surface, and for one moment I felt sure, long enough to say, "It's time." The women gathered and we waited for Diamond to stand again.

It was a procession, a betrayal. It was the path we had taken so many times as Hanae rode bareback along the wooded path that led to the arena. As we turned and faced the hill heading away from her pasture Minnie neighed, and Diamond, weakened, stood in her familiar stance and neighed in return. I could not promise Minnie that I would reunite them and their ritual tore at me. My whole body was sobbing. I remembered my mother saying that when we grieve it is for everything we have held or are holding. My sobs were open and unbarred like cats fighting in the night, or coyote cries and wolves howling.

At the top of the hill Diamond Feather fell, panting, and we urged her up, urged her to walk to her grave. There was an eerie light there, a kind of iridescence cast from the orange and yellow leaves. Gloria had to leave. In all the years of being a horsewoman she had never witnessed a horse being euthanized. I had to stay. I had to hold Diamond Feather so she would feel love.

Emily said it would only take about two minutes. Time felt hollow. I wanted to grip this moment, as though I weren't present enough. I didn't just want to observe her dying. I needed to be with her. A shot of blue liquid pierced through her neck and within moments her front knees thudded to the ground. I wished then that we'd waited until she'd come down by herself. I realized how controlled her other falls had been as her weight pounded the earth beneath us.

There are aftershocks in the muscles and the jaw and I rubbed the places I had massaged in the past until a silence settled over her body and all we could hear were the leaves falling upon one another. I kissed her temples for the last time.

Gloria was in the stable. She was crying as she told Minnie that Diamond was gone. I held Gloria close. It was the kind of hug that penetrates like a deep rain. Then I went home.

At dusk the next day we came as a family to say good-bye before Diamond was settled into her grave. Hanae had been very emotional and was angry with me because Diamond was her horse and she had not been present at her death. When we arrived, Diamond Feather lay undisturbed. Large colorful leaves had fallen on her body and neck. Her face was so tranquil, eyes closed, skin relaxed. She seemed already far away; only her body was left. We caressed her, my big hands beside Hanae's smaller ones. We let our hands rest finally on her eyes. Such a big gift she was.

FEAR IN THE SHAPE OF A FISH

Pamela Frierson

Until a few years ago, I had done my best not to think about sharks. Then one morning I picked up the *Honolulu Star Bulletin*, and read the headlines about the attack on Martha Morrell.

On November 26, 1991, Martha Morrell and a friend, visiting from Canada, went snorkeling in the calm waters in front of her home at Olowalu, on the leeward coast of Maui. The swells from a recent storm had stirred up the shallow, sandy bottom between stretches of coral, so the two women swam out a hundred yards to where the reef dropped off steeply and the water was clearer. Morrell and her friend spotted a flash of fin and a large, dark shadow passing nearby; thinking it was one of the spinner dolphins that often range near shore, they swam toward it. Their first clear glimpse of the shark came as it hurtled toward them, seizing Martha Morrell. At first her friend tried to fend off the shark, hitting and kicking, its rough skin raking her flesh. Then she fled to shore to get help.

By the time rescuers were able to launch a boat to reach Martha Morrell, it was too late. Teeth marks on the woman's body identified the killer as a tiger shark. It was the same species of shark that had fatally attacked Billy Weaver, a boy who lived just down the beach from me when I was a twelve-year-old growing up on the coast of O'ahu.

Because of my acute childhood memory of the news of Billy Weaver's death—I had known Billy, and the waters in which he died were visible from my house—the official response to Morrell's death seemed eerily familiar, as though it followed a pattern that earlier tragedy had set. When Billy had been killed in December of 1958, his father, a prominent Honolulu businessman, helped the state fund a year-long shark hunt. A total of 697 sharks was caught. If anybody objected to this killing, they did not air their feelings publicly.

Since the "Billy Weaver Shark Control Program," there had been five other state-funded shark hunts, but the last had been in 1976. Since Billy was killed there had been no deaths at sea that were indisputably the result of shark attacks. But the attack on Martha Morrell had happened close to a major resort area, and the tourist industry was particularly anxious that the state do something to allay fears. A state representative from Maui lobbied the legislature to appropriate money for "shark research and control."

Having returned to Hawai'i a few years before after several years in the West, where I had lived in backwoods bear country much of the time, I found the idea of a shark hunt astounding; I could not imagine, for example, the state of Idaho funding a year of bear slaughter after one of the rare incidents in which a bear had killed a human being. The shark hunt seemed like a primitive ritual of retaliation, particularly since one *chose* to go into shark territory—it was not as though these animals came ashore to raid our garbage cans.

But I was even more surprised to find that my intellectual sympathy for the shark seemed to grow in tandem with a fear that shortly made me, an avid snorkeler and ocean swimmer, afraid to go into deep water, and uneasy even in the shallow, coral-ringed bay where I often swim. I began to develop an obsessive interest in the details surrounding Morrell's death, and I followed the debate about shark hunting with a fascination that came only partly from my interest in issues of wildlife "management."

Aside from my own obsession with the topic, the immediate protest against state plans to hunt sharks was intriguing. Where in the past there had been little debate about the shark hunts, this time there was a strong outcry. I was not surprised that members of the marine science community, with a much-strengthened understanding of ocean ecology, spoke out against another shark hunt. But I had not expected the issue to be raised as one of ethics and cultural values by the Native Hawaiian community.

The day after the attack on Martha Morrell, a Honolulu paper announced: "State Sending Hired Gun to Get Killer Maui Shark." Veteran fisherman Jim Stegmuller, a former Maui policeman, had offered his services to the Department of Land and Natural Resources (DLNR).

The night after Morrell died, Stegmuller and his fishing partner set baited hooks in eighty-five feet of water off Olowalu. When they returned to dock, they were met by several Hawaiian men. The word had gotten out about the shark hunt, and a local Hawaiian radio announcer, Charlie Maxwell, had been flooded with calls from Hawaiians objecting to the shark hunt on the grounds that it violated cultural beliefs in the shark as 'aumakua—family guardian or, in some cases, ancestor. Every Hawaiian family had an 'aumakua, which was usually an animal but could be a plant as well, and many Hawaiians still paid respects to their guardians. The Hawaiians who accosted Stegmuller had a simple message to deliver: "If you hunt the shark, we feed *you* to the shark."

When Stegmuller and his partner returned to their lines the next morning, they found two large (they estimated twelve feet) tiger sharks on the hooks and a larger one swimming nearby. Stegmuller cut the lines and let the sharks swim away, and returned to let the state authorities know he was quitting the shark hunt.

Hawaii's economy is dependent on tourism, and tourists come here expecting to enjoy the beaches and the ocean. The shark hunt plan was not abandoned: The state legislature moved to set aside $150,000 for "shark control." Meanwhile Bill Paty, head of the DLNR and an avid swimmer and spearfisherman, quietly met with Hawaiian leaders on Maui and received their agreement for the state to pursue a very limited shark hunt in the Olowalu area, arguing that it was imperative the public know *something* was being done. Paty promised that the state would set up a task force that included Hawaiian leaders to address the larger question of whether a shark control program was needed.

The new fishing crew, made up partly of Hawaiians, put out their baited lines each night and checked them in the morning. A week later, the crew caught a thirteen-foot tiger shark. Only the remains of a lobster were found in the shark's stomach. Two weeks had gone by, and the likelihood of identifying the shark by surveying its stomach contents were slim. Nevertheless, the local press made it sound as though the shark had made a full confession. The shark's skin was donated to Hawaiian groups for making traditional drums, and the carcass was dumped out at sea. The head, to be taken to O'ahu for research, was displayed in large photographs in the daily newspapers, upright in a galvanized tub, jaws agape, surrounded by bloody water—an object of ritual revenge, like the head of John the Baptist.

In the weeks after Morrell's death, local media interest in sharks had reached a crescendo. Various experts discussed tips on avoiding encounters with sharks, and tips on surviving attacks. I read the information, and it seemed that no one really knew much about shark behavior. Some people argued that sharks were territorial; others thought not. It was generally agreed that it was safest to swim in broad daylight, preferably midday, although some shark attacks had happened at that time. Avoid murky waters, some argued, avoid places with steep drop-offs. Bright-colored bathing suits might be a bad idea. Anyone with open cuts should perhaps stay out of all but very shallow water. Rings and bright objects should not be worn. Swimming erratically might be dangerous, since sharks were attracted to sound pulses in the water and could mistake you for a wounded fish.

I had already limited my swims to a small cove at the southern end of Hilo Bay, but the next time I went swimming there I was muddled and nervous. What did I know about sharks? I had never seen one in the water, even though I grew up on the beach, some days spending nearly as much time in the water as I did on land. I knew from an early age that the ocean was not all benign. I had shed tears while trying to pick off the stinging tentacles of Portuguese men-of-war; I had learned to avoid the sharp-spined sea urchins. My parents loved the sea as a backdrop, as a bathing place; they had come from elsewhere because they loved the beauty of the islands but they never felt the need for any practical knowledge of the ocean. The fish we occasionally ate came in fillets from the market; the only name I remember is *mahimahi*.

I needed information about sharks, but there was something else I would have to come to grips with. I knew it as I watched the TV coverage on the Morrell attack, the interviews with the survivor and with those who brought the body to shore, but particularly those shots that showed where it happened—a long camera pan over empty blue sea.

A month after Martha Morrell's death, I stood at the kitchen window of my parents' home on the coast of O'ahu and looked out to where waves breaking on the reef formed a horizon. I was thinking back over thirty years, remembering a photograph published in the newspaper the day after Billy Weaver died. It must have been taken directly in front of our house. It showed the two islets called the Mokulua Islands, the southern one shaped like a gumdrop, and the northern one vaguely like a sphinx. The islets straddle a reef that parallels this stretch of windward coast about a half-mile from shore. In the photograph an enormous black arrow had been superimposed over the image, descending from the sky to the left of the sphinx islet. Its point marked the spot known locally as "the passage"—a break in the reef caused by the 1946 tidal wave that had wreaked considerable damage on this side of the island. I knew they brought a body back from the reef that day, but in my mind Billy never came back. He vanished into that black arrow.

Remembering that newspaper photograph so many years later, I felt drawn to go out there, to be near the place where, in my imagination, the tip of a black arrow still broke the line of the horizon. I hauled my brother's kayak down to the beach and paddled out. It was late afternoon. I let myself be possessed by an old dread that only now had declared its name. When a green sea turtle broke the surface of the water, it sent a jolt through my body. Every shadow on the water had the same effect. It didn't matter that I knew I was more likely to die of a bee sting, or be brained by a coconut, that I was fifty times more likely to die on the highway in the next year than I was to be eaten by a shark in my lifetime. The fear seeped in.

I could barely remember what Billy looked like (he was three years older than I, fifteen at the time of his death). I recalled the facts that I had been told later: He and a group of friends had taken air mattresses and a couple of surfboards and a small rowboat for some surfing on the break that came through the passage in the reef. Billy had one of the air mattresses, and was having to thrash hard to get on top of the waves. After one of the boys, Garrett, had caught a wave, he looked back and noticed Billy fifty yards behind him clinging to his air mattress and hunched over in the water. As he swam toward him he heard Billy give a feeble cry for help. When Garrett reached Billy, he saw the blood in the water; then he saw that Billy's leg was gone from the knee down. He shouted for the other boys to bring the boat over and, supporting Billy on the air mattress, started to swim toward the boat. The boys in the boat struggled with the anchor and the oars, then screamed at the boys in the water when they saw a large shark surface thirty feet away. Garrett pushed Billy toward a shallow ledge of reef and swam for the boat. Billy disappeared from sight. The boys, jammed into the small boat, fled toward shore.

Thinking about those boys, and the memory that must have haunted them ever since, I paddled toward the line of white water just beyond the reef. The noise of the waves increased to a steady low boom, and I could see unbroken waves roll into the passage. The water was a deep, serene blue inland from the reef. I had paddled to within a hundred yards of the passage, but now I couldn't make myself go further. I knew one of the boys who was with Billy that day—he sat next to me in the seventh-grade classroom. When he returned to school a week after Billy's death, he kept his head down and didn't talk. The black arrow that had sucked up Billy had sucked up part of him, too.

The shark and the black arrow were one, inseparably inside me, no matter how much time I spent reading about sharks. I realized how little the fear had to do with the animal itself, and how much harder it was going to be to make peace with it. I turned the kayak around and paddled jerkily toward shore. By the time I reached the beach, the bellies of the hills were in deep shade, and the coconut trees threw long spiky shadows across the sand.

Billy's death frightened me, but not away from the ocean, any more than having a friend die in a car wreck a year later made me afraid of cars. It did not make me think that since a shark had killed Billy, a shark might kill me. I surfed and swam without a thought about sharks through my teen years. I never saw one.

But I knew now the fear had stayed with me, an amorphous shape joined to the nightmares of childhood, to the darkness that drives our oldest, most powerful fairytales. There are no sharks in Grimm, but there are the wolves who inhabited the thick, dark forests that covered the land in the childhood of Europe. The fear we invest in them can be easily transferred elsewhere, for they are form made visible of something else: an evil intent lurking out there in the universe. Sharks can then play characters in a cosmic battle with the dark, as they do in that most extended monster-of-the-deep fable, *Moby Dick,* swimming up out of that beautiful, fecund, murdering sea.

Fear can turn to fury, a blind flailing at a universe we suspect cares not the least about human fate. In *A Sailor's Life,* Dutch seafarer and novelist Jan Hartog writes of that frenzy of hatred that can grip the human soul and be visited upon the shark:

> The shark embodies all that is evil. . . . When a shark is caught and hoisted on board ship, as occasionally happens on long voyages, the aft-deck turns into a slaughterhouse. The men go berserk in a prehistoric orgy of fury and blood. When the orgy is over, there is a bewildered sense of shame and they will pretend that the slaughter had a purpose. I have seen a grim, fat bosun struggle for weeks with a bit of corrugated iron skin, trying to make a handbag.

Berserk is a word we borrow from another culture, as is *amok.* But the "fury and blood" is still in us, even if our own culture shuns words to describe it. I once saw a man at a Zen meditation retreat beat a snake to death with a stick of firewood. That was in sheep ranch country, and later while out walking I came across a dead coyote crucified upon a barbed wire fence, his head lolling at a grotesque angle.

Clearly sharks—some kinds at least—are fearsome predators, and their fine-tuned adaptation to their environment compared to our clumsy vulnerability in the water makes them more so. They belong to the part of nature beyond our control. Yet I wondered what the Western view of the sharks as primitive monster, as, to quote Melville, "pale ravener of horrible meat," had to do with the animal itself.

Brad Wetherbee, a graduate student in marine biology at the University of Hawai'i, told me there are about 250 species of shark. They are incredibly various in shape and behavior. Some are herbivores, like the enormous whale shark—a gentle polka-dotted giant, who filter-feeds through a mass of spongy tissue in its mouth. There is the angel shark, so-named because its pectoral fins have lengthened into wing-like projections and its body flattened out with the eyes migrated to the top of the head, so that it can lie on the bottom and wait for prey to blunder into it. And of course there is the great white shark, the JAWS prototype.

Brad showed me the first shark I ever touched. It was called a cookie-cutter shark, and it was no longer than a dachshund.

The cookie cutter is a deep-sea dweller who survives by darting in to take perfect little circular bites out of larger fish. Brad pulled the shark out of a plastic bag by its tail and handed it to me. The fish was cold and limp as a much-used handbag. Its lower jaw looked like an ice-cream scoop, and the teeth appeared loosely set in the jaw, like ill-fitting dentures. The skin was nearly smooth when I ran my finger head to tail, and felt like fine sandpaper when I rubbed the other way, against the scales.

Brad also showed me two other small deep-sea sharks: a pygmy shark and a kitefin shark. At the top of the pygmy shark's head, an area dipped in like a human baby's fontanel. The pineal gland, Brad explained, is directly underneath, and scientists speculate that this area is photo-sensitive and acts like a "third eye," perhaps to help the shark orient to light from the surface.

On the kitefin shark we examined the tiny black pores that dot the underside of the head—peculiar organs called the ampullae of Lorenzini, common to all sharks, skates, and rays. These mucous-filled pores lead to electroreceptor nerves, and probably allow these fish to zero in at close range to their prey (all living organisms are surrounded by a weak electric field).

Brad told me that sharks possess a sophisticated sensory system—possibly unmatched by any other vertebrate. He pointed to what looked like a long vein down the side of the pygmy shark: "This is called the *lateral line*—it's lined with sensory cells that connect up to the brain. The cells in here may detect chemicals or vibration, or water currents and pressure; they may even help with hearing. The olfactory organs are here, they're called nasal sacs, and they are incredibly acute: They can detect blood in as small a quantity as one part per million from a mile away. This system is what's made some sharks apex predators."

I visited the University's Hawai'i Institute of Marine Biology at Coconut Island to talk further with Brad Wetherbee, and to meet Chris Lowe, another graduate student working on electroreception in hammerhead sharks, and their mentor, Kim Holland, head of the research station. The island is a small, flat piece of land in the middle of Kane'ohe Bay, and the bay is the world's largest pupping ground for hammerhead sharks.

The two graduate students and Holland are adamantly opposed to the state shark-hunting program. Chris and Brad have been putting together a critique of conclusions drawn from previous shark-hunt programs. "If you eliminate sharks, you may be eliminating a key part of the ecology, and that's our concern as biologists," said Brad. "Reducing numbers of an apex predator in any system can set off a chain of effects. But the main point for us, in regard to the shark hunts, is that there is no solid evidence that there is more danger from sharks nowadays, not if you look at the record correctly."

According to Chris Lowe, the record shows fifteen attacks during the fifteen years prior to the first shark-control program in 1959. In the time between the first shark hunt and last one (1976), the record shows sixteen attacks, an average of 0.9 attacks per year over that eighteen-year period. From 1976 through 1991, the record shows thirty-three attacks, which averages to 2.2 per year.

"So if you take only these factors into consideration," said Lowe, "it looks as though shark attacks have increased since 1976. But if you *exclude* the incidents that aren't provable attacks, such as where someone may have drowned first and then been bitten by sharks, the rate of attacks since the last hunt (1976) drops to 1.3 a year, and there were no *fatal* shark attacks between Billy Weaver's death [1958] and Martha Morrell's death in 1991.

"Add to that the enormous increase in people using the coastal waters ... you could expect a considerable rise in shark attacks, but in fact that hasn't happened. That alone should be proof that sharks don't normally prey on humans—that they must actively work to avoid us."

"Otherwise," said Brad, "Waikiki would be one big buffet for sharks."

Kim Holland and his two students had all sat in on Task Force meetings. Their agenda was to persuade the state to fund research—particularly a tiger shark–tracking program. Holland had done some fish-tracking studies, and he assured the Task Force that equipment was available to make a study cost-effective: telemetric devices that could send a signal considerable distances for up to a year would be attached to a number of tiger sharks; boats could be sent out periodically to pick up the signal and follow the animals' movements.

In April of 1992 the Task Force set aside funds for Holland's tiger shark–tracking project. There had been only one documented attack since the beginning of the year. In March a woman was surfing off Kaua'i when a large shark grabbed the end of the board and knocked her into the water. When the shark released the board she paddled into shore unharmed.

For the Shark Task Force members it was a blessedly quiet summer. Then came the fall. On October 23, a surfer named Rick Gruzinsky, lying prone on his board off O'ahu's North Shore, was lifted out of the water. He clung to his board as it flipped and found himself face-to-face with a large tiger shark, its teeth closed around the midsection of his board. The shark broke loose a chunk of surfboard, rolled away, and was gone. Gruzinsky paddled frantically to shore. The missing crescent-shaped "bite" of board was found the next day.

The state launched a hunt in the area. A large tiger was caught. The chunk of board was tried in the shark's mouth. "A perfect fit," the shark hunters proclaimed.

There had been several shark sightings on the north and northeast shores of O'ahu, the most popular surfing areas. At a November 2 Task Force meeting the sightings were discussed, and a vote was taken as to whether to hunt in that area. The state offices had been deluged with letters, mostly against shark hunts. The one Hawaiian on the Task Force, Charlie Maxwell, was adamantly against more hunts. The decision was not to hunt.

The day after that decision a young bodyboarder was attacked at the northeast shore. Blood loss from the leg wound proved fatal. A state hunt hooked two large tiger sharks. With their catches suspended by tails at the boat harbor, the shark hunters posed for the newspapers.

On December 23 another surfer was attacked at the north shore, several miles away. His board was nearly bitten in two, but he escaped without injury.

The state had caught nine tigers in the last six months. Private fishermen were now getting into the act. Commercial fisherman Perry Dane declared that a "rogue" shark was responsible for the series of attacks, and that he was going after it. On January 1 Dane caught two large tiger sharks. The huge fish were dragged still alive behind Dane's boat for an hour after they had been shot with 44-magnum bangsticks. "They were tough to kill," Dane said.

A few days later Charlie Maxwell resigned in protest from the Task Force, charging the state was "encouraging the creation of instant 'great white hunters.' " Turning the shark hunting into a media spectacle, he said, was a double affront to Hawaiians.

The Hawaiian response was complicated, but clearly there was a cultural difference in attitude toward this animal. I asked Dan Kawai'ae'a, area manager of Pu'u Koholā National Historic Site, about his family's relationship with sharks.

Pu'u Koholā is a place of great *mana*, or spiritual power. On a small hill on the dry, rough coast of North Kona are a very old *heiau* (temple) and an enormous war *heiau* built by Kamehameha in 1790, in the midst of his ultimately successful campaign to conquer all the islands. In the murky water of a small bay beneath these two temples is a *heiau* Dan Kawai'ae'a has never seen: one dedicated to the shark gods.

Dan Kawai'ae'a, who is a burly Hawaiian-Chinese with the Hawaiian side showing, looked down toward the bay, and remembered hearing about how his grandmother swam with a shark.

It was on Maui, near the family home. His grandmother would enter the bay and join the shark, who would always be there, waiting. The shark was the family *'aumakua*, Dan said. "When there was a new baby in the family my grandmother would put the *piko* [umbilical cord] on the rocks near where the shark was.

"My father was a fisherman," he continued. "I was the bag boy. Sometimes in Hilo Bay we would catch hammerheads; we always put them back. My father told me we should respect the shark because it was our *'aumakua*. I did a lot of diving and I never saw a shark.

"I see sharks here in this bay all the time, you know...." Dan said, his voice trailing off. Then he looked at me. "But this is where the doubt comes in, for my generation ... we know the shark is *'aumakua*, but we wonder, will it recognize us?"

I didn't expect to see any sharks, but I drove around to the harbor and walked out to a point of the bay. I could look up at Pu'u Koholā now from nearly the point of view of an approaching war canoe. The huge, tiered structure was open to the sea like a hollow layer cake—an enormous geometric pile of reddish waterworn stone—all carried here by hand from a valley twelve miles away. The *heiau* glowed in the late afternoon sun. A massive pewter-colored rain cloud draped the tops of ancient cinder cones studding the mountain behind Pu'u Koholā.

I saw a fin emerge midway across the water, drifting up slowly, dreamily, like a semaphore hoisted by a somnambulist. It was a sight I had waited in trepidation for, the last several years, on a thousand swims in the ocean—that triangle shape of fin, slicing through the water. But it no longer seemed ominous. I could sense the whole animal beneath, here in this powerful landscape, where it simply belonged, with a rightness one very occasionally glimpses in the human figure as well, bending in a garden, coming over the crest of a hill. I felt as though suddenly returned to sanity after a long period of lunacy.

I knew as a member of a land culture I would never understand the relationship of ocean people—Hawaiians, Pacific islanders—to sharks. I could only reflect on my own culture; the way the bear is embedded in Western tradition, for example, even if we see only the tag-ends of the bear worship that permeated neolithic European culture in our fairy tales. The bear was a complex figure—animal messenger from the spirit world, protector of the forest, fierce warrior, great mother, circus clown. If the bear was our animal shadow, then the shark, it appears, is the animal shadow for Pacific island cultures; the mediator between human and nonhuman worlds.

In the Gilbert Islands, some chiefly clans still claim descent from the shark. In New Ireland and the Solomons shark-calling is still practiced by a dwindling few who know the old ways: the purifying rituals, the cowrie or coconut shell rattle stuck in a certain way against the canoe to attract the shark, the right way to handle the noose that will hold a wooden drag to exhaust the shark so that he can be brought alongside the canoe and killed with a heavy wooden club. Sharks were both venerated and valued highly as food.

In Tahiti sharks were messengers from the gods of the ocean, or sometimes they were possessed by the spirits of people. They would go to the rescue of their human relatives and carry them on their backs or in their jaws to land while making sympathetic sounds that mimicked the tones of the human voice. Sharks were used to test those who claimed to be heirs to chiefly positions. The aspirant would stand in the waters the shark deities frequented; if they approached him and he did not show fear, he had passed the test.

It was over a year before Kim Holland's shark-tracking program got under way, and several months before I was able to go out with the researchers when they checked their lines. In the meantime, I had seen many sharks and met a few in the water.

I was researching a book on the Northwestern Hawaiian Islands, the atolls and small coral islands at the oldest end of the archipelago. The area is a nature reserve, and wildlife abounds, including sharks. At French Frigate Shoals, we met small white-tip sharks when we snorkeled over shallow reef. We saw tiger sharks from the Boston whaler as we motored across the lagoon to band seabirds on tiny islets.

One day we came close enough to one that I was able to put on a mask, and hang over the gunwale and watch him swim leisurely along, keeping pace with our boat. I looked in awe at the huge animal, its blunt head blending into a massive body with rigidly held pectoral fins planing the water, telltale stripes running like watery ripples down its sides, the huge tail making a majestic, muscular sweep.

There is one steep pinnacle of rock still standing near the center of the lagoon, a reminder that this atoll was once a high volcanic island. We stopped there to snorkel. As I headed back to the boat, a shark appeared, swimming directly toward me, emerging, suddenly, out of a background of deep blue. It was hard to judge its size, and for a heart-stopping second I thought it was the tiger we had seen earlier. It came to within fifteen feet and then swerved into a leisurely circling. From the side I could see it was smaller—perhaps six feet—and lacking the watery stripes. I began a slow, erratic progress toward the boat, trying to keep my eye on the shark. The shark stayed right with me. I held down my terror by thinking it was herding me toward the boat. I reached the boat and levitated over the side, landing in a heap in the bottom.

I didn't begin to lose some of my fear of sharks until my time on Laysan Island. Laysan is utterly wild; we were dropped there by boat to spend six weeks studying the Hawaiian monk seal. At one end of the island, in a sandy pool nearly encircled by reef, over a dozen gray reef sharks congregated during most of the daylight hours. I would sit and watch them as they seemed to bask in the warm shoal water. Sometimes a monk seal would swim through their midst, unconcerned. I would walk out on the barely submerged reef and look down on them in their shallow enclosure, dark, graceful forms nearly at my feet, the high tailfins with the distinctive notch at the end emerging to fling drops of spray against my legs.

A few years after the death of Martha Morrell, I met the shark research crew early one morning at a Honolulu harbor. Kim Holland was absent, but Brad, Chris, Jerry Crow, a marine biologist from the Waikiki aquarium, and I sailed a half mile out in a small fishing boat, towing a Boston whaler. Baited lines had been put out the night before.

The research crew had not had an easy time. They had managed to tag twenty-five tiger sharks. Nine had been fitted with tracking devices that would send out a signal for eighteen days; one with a very expensive device that would signal for eighteen months. But the signal range was limited.

Only three sharks had been tracked successfully. In each case the researchers were surprised to find the sharks headed out to sea—"Went out and turned like getting on a freeway on-ramp," said Brad. The fishing boat was able to keep up with them until they were off the coast of Moloka'i, some thirty miles away.

"We have to do enough tracks to overcome arguments these animals are responding to stress," said Brad, "that they're going way out of their normal range because they're fleeing after being caught. But it's beginning to look to us like they're pretty migratory animals. In that case, what's the chance a shark hunt will net the animal that actually did the attack?"

On the first line the researchers pulled up, they found a Galapagos shark, moving feebly. They cut it loose. On the second there was the front of a neatly severed black-tip reef shark.

The third line held a tiger shark. He came up with fight left, jaws agape, the blunt head bashing itself against the boat. Brad and Jerry Crow climbed into the Boston whaler, holding the line. They pushed off from the fishing boat and reeled in the line.

The shark tired quickly, and they were able to bring him alongside. Brad reached out and dropped a loop of rope around the shark's tail, pulling it close to the boat. With the tail controlled, Jerry used the line hooked into its mouth to pull the shark's head up close, while Brad maneuvered another loop of rope up over the dorsal fin. Both men, tugging, were able to flip the shark on its back. The fish was suddenly still, held against the side of the boat. "They go rigid, the way a frog does if you turn it over," said Chris.

Brad took measurements—340 centimeters, over eleven feet. He noted that the shark was male and sexually mature. Jerry attached a tag by punching a hole through the edge of a pectoral fin with a leather punch.

The shark was motionless. I wondered if it was still alive.

I looked at the shark, trussed like a turkey to the side of the boat while the men moved over it, measuring and tagging. In the bottom of our boat the truncated body of the black-tip shark, its eyes open and blank, balanced on its pectoral fins as if ready to swim. I looked back to shore, at the crowded buildings of downtown Honolulu, and then down the coast to Waikiki, where I could see bright specks of color dotting the beach. Sunbathing tourists, perhaps idly staring out to sea, seeing our boat, wondering what we were fishing for. It was hard, at that moment, to feel that science would help us toward any deep understanding of these animals.

Mary Pukui, the world's foremost authority on Hawaiian traditions in our time, died less than a decade ago. She worked frantically to get the knowledge written down, before it all slipped away. She worked against the numbing sense of what was already gone. Her notes on sharks in the Bishop Museum record the names of more than fifty sharks who were recognized and fed by Hawaiian families. She tells of seeing her grandparent 'Opupele feed the shark named Pakaiea near her home.

"With the passage of time," she writes, "the departure from the old beliefs . . . the names of our finny kinfolk of the deep, the sex, coloring of skin, behavior, place of abode . . . all are forgotten." The last words in her notes are *"minamina wale"—deep regret for what has been lost.*

Ignoring the elbow-high leather gloves in his tagging kit, Jerry Crow reached out and released the hook from the shark's mouth. Brad unhitched the rope and pulled the loops slack around the shark's body.

For a minute it rolled with the ocean swell like a dead thing. "Swim," I found myself urging, silently. Then the tail made a weak sweep and the head moved down, and the shark began a slow descent. In a few seconds it was a wavering white glimmer in deep blue, and then the shark was gone.

Naomi Mattis

The wind has been blowing incessantly for five days and nights. We have a water shortage here in the New Mexico desert after a winter without snow; the dryness of my skin and the dryness of the earth feel the same. Today the first flower of spring bloomed in my garden—a red tulip. Sound of wind in thrashing branches; all else is silent. How does the flower stay on its stem in the midst of this harsh movement? Not so delicate as it looks.

When Laura died at home eighteen years ago, I was by her side, and noticed the vase of red tulips. I had never before been with someone just as they were dying, but it felt natural. Her death infused me with an urgency about the way I was living. For several years in the seventies, I had been working as a psychotherapist in a community project that was groundbreaking. The focus was on transformation; the people who came for help had been diagnosed with terminal illness. Being close to death makes what is false so noticeable. I saw that underneath my care and competence, fear was clouding my heart. I thought if only I could touch that fear, name it, release it, the simple truth would remain. After Laura's death I turned to nature, to the earth and the sky, to the trees and wild-flowers for friendship and solace.

On most weekends I left the city, my family, and work and went to a small cabin in the mountains. It was in the cabin one Sunday around mid-day that something unexpected happened. I was sitting on the couch when I saw a large white bird flying north, soaring, wings outspread. My body started to shake all over. If it wasn't for the shaking I might have missed it. I kept my attention on my body, because I know the body doesn't lie. Words appeared before my eyes—directions: "Your life as you've known it is over. Get a van. Drive north."

Six months later I left Los Angeles in my VW van with no idea where I was going, why, or if I was ever coming back. I was guided by the same voice that spoke in the cabin to places like Mt. Shasta and Heart Lake in California, Colestein valley and Williams in Oregon, Orcas Island in Washington, to places not on the map, camping alone or parking my van on the land of people I'd meet in town who would say "Come up to my land and stay awhile." What was happening I called magic from the smallest details to the sublime: When I needed matches I found them in the dirt at the door of my van. When I needed a spiritual teacher I found him sitting under a pine tree in a remote part of Oregon. After four months on the road I sensed it was time to slowly head south toward home.

On the way back I was staying on the land of someone I had just met and working in his vegetable garden. On this early Sunday morning everyone had gone to town. I was looking forward to having dinner with an old friend, but welcomed some time alone in the old frame house and a leisurely day before I would meet him in town. The simple house sat on a large piece of land surrounded by over a thousand acres of national forest. I ran water in the clawfoot bathtub, adding more hot from the stove. Rinsing my hair with the garden hose attached to the tub faucet, I thought what a luxury this was after living in my van. Naked, I went downstairs to get some clothes off the line, letting the warm sun and slight breeze continue to bathe me. What was it about this day that felt special? The lighting seemed different; it had a golden quality. I dressed in white—loose cotton pants and a short cropped V-necked T-shirt—slipped into my sandals, went to the kitchen to get the jar of corn silk tea I had prepared, and started back down the narrow dirt road. It was about a half-mile walk from the house to the garden where my van was parked.

As I turned around the bend past the barnyard I could see them walking toward me. A ram and a ewe. Moments later the ewe veered off into the riverbed and up the other side. The ram kept walking on the path. I moved to the hill side of the road to give him plenty of room to pass. The other day I had heard talk about this ram, whose horns had been removed. He didn't seem to belong to anyone and lived wild in the hills, making occasional visits to the barn. He'd been around for a few days now and was acting feisty. Approaching at a steady pace, he came to a complete stop before me. We were face-to-face, the ram and I. His eyes were dark brown and fiery, never blinking.

I attempted to walk around him and he adjusted his stance so I couldn't get by. Standing there and facing him, I felt his animal power, smelled his animal smell. All motion seemed to stop—even the breeze—as my brown eyes gazed back into those two brown vortexes of energy and all else receded into a softly luminous still life. Giant oaks were spread against a backdrop of blue sky, the rocky riverbed dry after a summer with no rain, the earth parched and dusty. A feeling of awe rushed through me. Then my mind began to move, became uneasy. I wanted to keep walking and he was blocking my way. I thought, I better do something to get past this animal.

Like an old pro I started talking to the ram. I reassured him in a voice both calm and firm. "I'm not here to harm you. If you'll please let me pass now, we can both continue on our way." No response. I tried to recall everything I knew about animals as I kept talking, explaining, and finally bargaining. He stood there as if carved in stone, but the fire in his eyes showed he was alive and alert. Then he backed up a few steps. "He's leaving," I thought, but instead he lowered his head and charged toward me with full force. His head struck me like a boulder on my upper left thigh. The jar of corn silk tea flew from my hands and broke into pieces. He kept striking as I tried to push him off. He knocked me to the ground. Springing up with my mind quick and alert I made sure to stay clear of the glass and not turn my back to the rocks of the riverbed. We faced off again.

Exhilarated by the exchange, I was at once acutely aware of all the minute sensual details around me and of abstractions, like the mythic quality of the scene and that the full moon was in Ares. Yet I wasn't thinking. I was in the dream and watching it all within a vast space. I was enlivened and humbled by the forceful presence of this animal and by the knowing that nothing less than all of me was demanded in this moment. The soul knows what it needs, like thirst knows water and hunger knows a piece of bread.

Three times I shouted, "Help!" even though I knew there was nobody around. Still, I owed it to myself to try everything. I thought about impermanence. I looked down at my hand; my finger was broken. How long would we stand here like this?

There was no time to answer. He charged again. It felt like the side of my thigh was being pulverized by the impact of his head. When I rose to my feet, I was barefoot and my clothes were no longer white. My face was grimy, my hair coated with dust. One sandal was over near the glass. "If this were a man I'd be terrified," I thought, as I realized with amazement I felt no fear. I seemed to have no preconceptions about animals. Our eyes met again and locked. Never had I seen such intense eyes. Over and over he charged. We wrestled; he threw me to the ground, I got up and would meet him again face-to-face. Still I was weakening and beginning to wonder how long I could keep this up. He of course was not suffering at all. He wore me down until I could no longer resist him. When he next charged and threw me to the ground I couldn't get up. I lay there realizing I might die here: This might be my time of death. Exhausted and hurting, I was losing my will to get up, even though I wanted to live. I prayed that if there was a way to get through this I be shown it now.

Then my body, heavy, moving itself in slow motion, lifted to its feet. I didn't move from my will this time. Instead of facing the ram, I was standing at his side, my hands going to him of their own accord, sinking into his thick matted wool, the right hand on his neck and the left on his rump, holding his wool, resting on his body, firmly, gently. My hands felt warm, permeable, and much larger than their ordinary size. Energy radiated through them in a way not known to me before. I knew right then, he was subdued. With confidence, I relaxed. My stomach softened, my heart was open. Some things you can't fight. All the ways that really work come from the heart.

> RAM, primordial wisdom fire
> Sacred act sacred fire eyes on fire blood fire
> In the cool moon full moon clear mind
> Cool detached in heat of passion
> Ram Ram Rama Rama . . .

With my hands in his fleece, the ram remained placid. Aching to find a more comfortable position for my body, I tried to lift my hands. Immediately, he became skittish, moving around to find me. He moved and I moved with him. We circled around together as I followed him so that I was always at his side and never face-to-face in the adversarial position. When I placed my hands firmly on his body he quieted down. I waited a long time and then tried again to separate from him, lifting my hands almost imperceptibly. Exhaustion demanded that I change position or at least get a moment's respite from the strain on my back. But I could not detach. The ram insisted, through agitated movements, that my hands remain on his body as with each attempt to lift them, we again danced our dance in a circle. If my feet weren't so raw I could have enjoyed this exchange.

Now it was a matter of extreme patience, waiting it out until someone came. His animal smell wouldn't let me forget my body, his body, that this was happening here now and there was no place to go. My feet were sore and bleeding. I could feel the pebbles that had lodged under my skin. Longing to lie down and rest, I stayed bent over the ram, with my hands on his back and neck making the difference between violence and pacification.

Hours passed. The sun was moving west. There was no moisture, no breeze. I desperately wanted a drink of water. After a long, long time, I heard a vehicle coming up the road. A truck parked at the green metal gate, and as they got out I recognized three women—Adele, Tuli, and Susan with their dogs. I whispered the words, "My sisters have come as witnesses." I called to them to distract the ram. They began yelling and throwing apples from a sack in the truck. The dogs participated in the commotion, barking and running around until finally the ram ran up into the hills and I painfully made my way down to the gate.

The women came, helped me into the truck and drove to the emergency hospital where a doctor cleaned the wounds in my hands and feet. He could do nothing about the deep bruising and released me.

When my friend with whom I was to have dinner saw me disheveled and injured, he became enraged. I had always known him as a peaceful person, a man of heart. Now he hated the ram. All he could talk about was wanting to kill him. He wished he had a gun; he'd blow his fucking brains out.

I was grateful the women were there. Then Susan said if she'd had a gun, she would have shot the ram in self-defense, though not in anger. Still, during the entire encounter with the ram, killing him had never occurred to me. The ram was my ally.

On the way back to the land, I saw the ram on the crest of the ridge, standing alone at dusk.

SWEET HOPE WAITING

Barbara Earl Thomas

The birds were plentiful that spring. The air thick with sparrows, starlings, low-flying crows, and fabulously fat robins. Since the vines around my porch had finally started to thicken, it seemed that the birds approached ever more closely, swirling, dipping, and then lighting to pick at invisible insects or to drink from the moisture trapped on the leaves. One morning after I turned to enter the house, after inspecting my seeding flower bed, a robin squawked as I opened the screen door. Startled, I looked up to find her aloft in the corner, perched on the edge of my hanging fuchsia basket. Amidst the foliage I could make out her profile, a solid inflated form out of which stared one piercing black eye. For some moments I stood transfixed by her. But I could see no evidence for her protest. I broke our gaze, went in, and gave it no further thought.

In the week that followed, I noticed her again and again. She squawked upon my entrance or exit. With each squawk her glare intensified. I just stared back. The longer I held her defiant gaze, the more she puffed up. I began to anticipate her presence and that annoying commotion. Like an official announcement, it heralded my comings and goings, and affirmed my presence. When she was away from the basket, I wondered, I'm here, so where are you? Come announce me, pierce me with your black eye.

I took to watching and waiting for the bird. Once I was able to pick her out from among the several in the yard, I noticed that she was not always alone. At times she was accompanied in her daily activities by another smaller robin. I watched them come and go in and out of the vine, rustling it as they went. They appeared content to have me there as long as I remained still. They never flew directly into the vine. One or the other might stop first on the telephone wire, then cautiously move to the

285

magnolia just south of the porch, then on to the rosebush and then furtively move onto the vine. They came carrying in their beaks twigs and other bits of debris. By now, I knew their secret: They were building a nest somewhere in the upper corner of my vine. I looked for it, at first casually and then with determination. For days its location eluded me until, while watering my hanging fuchsia basket, I spied an unusual formation at the base of the plant's branch structure. It was a weaving in and out, a soft scooped-out cup, a construction in progress.

After a brief moment of triumph, panic set in. What was wrong with these birds? Where were their instincts? Why did they pick this hanging basket, and not a tree, on a porch within eye and earshot of humans? I could only imagine that these birds are just like us, pushed by the pressures of an ever-speeding world until they had lost their intuition. I surmised they had picked the porch because the overhang provided protection from low-swooping crows, and the plant because it offered so much foliage and the branches formed a perfect warp for weaving a nest. But without water it would soon not be an ideal hiding space. If the nest was going to be there I had to somehow figure out how to water the plant. And furthermore, if we were all going to be out there on the porch together, the bird was going to have to stop all that squawking every time I walked in and out of the door. After all, it was my porch first.

With the construction of the nest completed, the two bird flights in and out of the vine waned, and the job of tending it fell, at last, to the one that had so abruptly caught my eye some weeks ago. If my fat bird friend, whom I had taken to calling Mama Bird, squawked when I was outside, I'd talk to her out loud. I'd say, "Hey, pipe down, no one's done anything to you yet and you've been here for weeks. And besides, you made this decision, so live with it!" This must have seemed reasonable, for she soon quieted down and just sat in motionless profile when I appeared. She even let me water the plant on the side away from the nest with my long-spouted watering can, but she always kept that one black eye trained on me.

On a day when Mama Bird happened to be away, I ventured carefully up on the ledge of the porch to peer down into the hanging basket. While I knew that the eggs would be there, I was surprised and touched to actually see them. There they were, three tiny eggs of the most delicate translucent blue I had ever seen. They glowed and in their translucence appeared to be floating just above the nest that held them. I moved quietly away and down. It was too much. I began to wish again that she had done it in a tree.

In the days that followed, Mama Bird and I fashioned a set of rules that allowed us to be on the porch together. I agreed not to bustle too near her nesting station and she came to understand the futility of her wild squawking. But that eye of hers, to which I had now grown accustomed, maintained its strict surveillance, keeping me in line lest I forget myself and somehow offend. It grew hard to imagine what a fuchsia could look like without a fat robin burrowed in amongst its branches. I began to think that hanging pots should come with birds to nest in them.

I must admit I wasn't actually looking forward to these pink-eyed, naked chicks chirping for worms. I'm a worrier. I worry about everything. I was just at the point of hyperventilation when I heard her trill, and caught sight of her circuitous approach. From treetop, to rosebush, to vine, Mama Bird traveled back with her beak full of a dark, wiggling mass. The pink ones met her return with jubilation and a bobbing-headed joy. I could see them there, all three of them with their beaks stretched open, instinctively begging. So this is how it's done. I thought I should water the lawn and even open the compost bin, that was always full of worms. Maybe I could even scoop out a few rich shovelfuls and bring them around so she wouldn't have to fly so far.

When Mama Bird was not feeding the chicks, she was sitting on top of her brood to keep them warm. They grew fast. At feeding time I could easily see their heads above the ridge of the nest. I was now in the habit of checking each morning and night to see if my fat robin was there at her station. In the evening before bed I viewed it as a good omen when I was able to make out her profile, sitting steady and solid on her nest, ready to pass the night.

On one of these nights I was awakened by the most piercing, mournful shrill I had ever heard. It was the sound of terror. It surrounded me, filling the room. It entered my bones and I bolted upright. I knew in an instant that it was the bird. She was there, just beyond my bedroom window, beating her wings furiously against the gutter, which echoed her shrieking. Like a shot I was up and out of the bed with my husband close on my heels.

In an instant I was on the porch. To my horror I found a big, yellow, thick-necked tomcat seated snugly in the middle of the fuchsia basket. He had one bird in his mouth. The two others had fallen down onto the porch floor and were there stumbling about. In shock and disbelief, I waved my arms wildly and screamed at the cat to get out! Get out! In response the cat just turned its head calmly and eyed me as if I was the most absurd creature it had ever encountered.

Seeing the predicament, my husband quickly jumped up onto the ledge and forcibly extracted the cat by the scruff of the neck, flinging him to the porch. Upon hitting the ground, the cat shook its head, dropped its prey and shot me one last confused glance before retreating into the night with baby bird on his breath.

By this time the neighbors on either side were out in their yards wondering who had been burglarized, or worse, murdered. I remember only briefly acknowledging their presence before my attention trained on the calamity at hand. Two birds were still wobbling around while the mama bird moaned somewhere not far off. The carcass of the third lay lifeless on the edge of the stair leading out to the yard. I thought I saw my husband make a motion as if he were going to pick up one of the birds. Now I was shrieking. Don't touch them! Don't touch them! Somewhere in my bungled brain I remembered hearing that parent birds wouldn't care for their young if they were touched by human hands.

My first thought was to take down the plant holding the nest to see if I might coerce the chicks to jump up into it. Upon looking again at the terrified, weary little creatures, I immediately thought better of that plan. In a flash I found myself in the kitchen, looking around for some helpful tool. What I chose was a large ladle-like soup spoon. Back out on the porch, instrument in hand, I swooped down and presented the spoon at the feet of one of the little birds. Without hesitation, to my amazement, it jumped right into the spoon as if it were the elevator it had been waiting for all of its little bird life. I lifted it quickly and carefully back up into the nest. The second baby followed suit.

I anxiously awaited Mama Bird's return the next day. I watched and worried. Several times I found myself just standing in front of the window or out on the porch, willing myself to see her familiar shape. The waiting was long and painful. It was unbearable to consider that I might have saved the chicks from the cat only to have them die of exposure and hunger. I imagined Mama Bird on some nearby branch weighing her options and watching me with those black robin eyes.

I, too, was weighing my options, none of which seemed the least bit reasonable. While not impossible, the idea of climbing up to the nest several times a day with worms had absolutely no appeal. I vacillated between being desperate and morose. When I finally could stand it no longer I went out onto the porch and called to her in a high-pitched singsong voice, chanting, Mama Birdie, Mama Birdie, over and over—willing her to take up her place once more in the fuchsia.

As the day wore on I resigned myself to the difficult task ahead and the reality of the poor prospects for my brood. I scolded myself for not having anticipated the possible dangers.

With dusk at hand, I was at the point of conceding when I heard a movement and bustle from the basket. It was too much to hope for, I thought. I feared that my wanting had finally driven me to hallucinations, a conjuring of phantom birds. But no, it was true. It was her solid robin-self, briskly surveying the damage and checking the babies. She was back!

Like a condemned man reprieved, I was filled with such joy I could barely contain myself.

This was a second chance, rarely granted, and with it I would not fail or be caught off guard by natural, or any other, predators. I staked out the porch. What we needed was a gentle but effective barrier, an early warning system, or a moat perhaps filled with water. My solution was to gather up all the available buckets and jars, fill them with water and place them all around the porch and along the ledge leading up to the nest. This obstacle course was meant to impede and confuse any predatory approach. Cats trying to make their way up to the nest would either fall into the pails, which would make them so crazy they would leave, or knock over the jars, in which case I would hear them and come running.

The next step was to move my sleeping quarters from the second to the first floor. I convinced my husband that we should sleep on the sofa bed with the front door ajar until the birds completed their nesting. After all, one could hardly maintain a vigil sleeping upstairs a floor away. The final piece of the plan called for one of us to be at the house at all times. It was too stressful to leave the house thinking I might find dead birds upon returning.

Who can guess what Mama Bird made of it all. But in truth I sensed that she went about raising the two remaining chicks with a renewed energy. Perhaps she, too, was joyously living her second chance, having escaped nature's odds. And, while she continued to keep close watch on me and all else surrounding her porch, I swear that black eye of hers had lost its opaque darkness. It had become instead a dark liquid pool that shone. It no longer nailed me or shut me out. Now, when she held my gaze, it included me in its reflection as something necessary and natural to her home on the porch.

Mama Bird chirped and sang as she flew in and out to the chicks who were no longer the pink-beige things I had spied only weeks before. They were now gawky preteen downy birds, starting to show their first signs of feathers. Although Mama Bird continued to bring food in, she seemed to do so less frequently, and at times she would sit in the little tree just across from the porch in full sight of the nest and sing to the young ones, who grew excited and implored her to feed them.

Around this time I rarely left the house. I knew that soon I would see their first flight. Now and then she would arrive without worms, and the teen birds would flap their wings and move about in great agitation. She would groom them and then fly to her perch in the tree just across from the nest. As she sat in the tree watching her brood and they watching her, I heard a distinctly different ring to her song. It was a low, resonant, melodious coo that seemed to come from some place deep inside her chest. It was cajoling, and it drew the birds up onto the edge of the nest, flapping their wings.

One and then the other would take its place at the edge of the nest. Testing for flight, they would jump up, teeter, flap their wings awkwardly, and eventually fall back into the nest, seemingly exhausted or hoping that Mama Bird would see their difficulty and just bring them their food. But she just continued her song, low and sweetly, "It is your time, it is your time, you must come, you must come."

All of this I watched for hours from my station out beyond the porch, beyond the driveway, crouched low, sitting, watching, and waiting. Each new attempt drew my silent urging in consort with Mama Bird for them to go up and out. I dared not even go to the bathroom.

Finally the bigger of the two birds made his most courageous effort. He unfolded his wings, and stretching them, he went even further than before. He pulled himself up and out as if unwrapping to become a larger bird. It was as though the timer of his instinct had just gone off, and he knew something now that only moments before he hadn't. Once more he mounted the edge of the nest. With wings in motion, he chirped to Mama Bird. She, in return, cooed low and soft, steadily imploring, imploring. In measured response, a loosened grip, an edging forward in one last tilt that almost looked like falling, the bird flew off.

Having held my breath, for how long I could not say, I gasped and lunged slightly forward. With my heart pumping the sound of oceans through my ears, time stood still, all was silent witness, and one flight stood out from among countless first flights taken.

HAND-RAISING A RHINO IN THE WILD

Anna Merz

Samia, the female black rhino who was my pride and my joy, was born ten years ago in the Ngare Sergoi Rhino Sanctuary on the western side of Lewa Downs, a 45,000-acre cattle ranch situated on the northern slopes of Mt. Kenya. I have lived all my life with animals and I have hand-raised many, but Samia was truly unique. Between us there existed a love, a trust, a reaching out for understanding unlike anything I had known in a relationship before. With her there was none of the usual relationship between man and beast. I never tried to discipline or hold her; she lived as a wild rhino. Yet of her own free will, she kept alive with me the bonds of love, trust, and friendship until her death.

Early in 1984 the sanctuary received its first rhinos, including Samia's mother, Solia. At the present time there are nineteen white and twenty-two black rhinos. Twenty calves have been born here. Not all have survived, but those that died, died of natural causes; none have been poached.

On February 15, 1985, Solia gave birth to a calf, Samia, and promptly deserted her. At that time I knew virtually nothing about rhinos, and certainly nothing about raising rhino babies, not even the proper composition of black rhino milk. Over weeks and months I battled with Samia's unending bouts of diarrhea, dehydration, and abnormal temperatures. As a tiny baby, she slept in my bed, causing matrimonial complications with the amazing messes she produced. Raising her was a series of crises, but at about six months, she started to stabilize.

Each day I walked her over ever-increasing distances to introduce her to the world of which she would be a part and its inhabitants. I remember our first encounter with a group of giraffes; long black eyelashes aflutter, they peered at us with astonishment, this strange combination of old woman, baby rhino, and black dog. Samia didn't see them until they moved and then, in terror at their size, dashed between my legs for safety. This was not a practical proposition and I sat down with a thud. Unable to get under me she compromised by sitting on my prostrate form, snorting her disapproval.

Samia learned quickly that I did not really appreciate being knocked over, even in play, and as her strength grew so her gentleness with me increased. As we walked, she would, of her own accord, offer a helping tail to pull me up the steeper trails. When I weaned her at three and a half years, I expected the bond between us to loosen, as would be only natural, but it never did. For ten years, Samia and I were companions, and even when she was mature and integrated with the wild rhinos, she usually returned to visit with me at least once a day.

During our time together, she taught me so much about the world of the rhino that I could never have learned otherwise. I also tried to teach Samia what I thought she would need to know in order to survive. But I was not always successful. To help Samia develop her sense of smell, I hid, hoping she would put her nose to the ground and search after me. Instead, she went to the garden gate, opened it to let the dogs out, then galloped after them straight to me. By no stretch of the imagination can this be described as instinctive behavior.

Rhinos are not, as reputed, solitary, bad-tempered, stupid animals. I had been warned that after my experience with chimps in Ghana, I would find them dangerous and boring. Rather the opposite. Rhino intelligence is close to that of chimps and their outstanding characteristics are curiosity and nervousness rather than aggression. Through her incredible intelligence, Samia was able to reveal a great deal about the social structure of rhino society and much of the complex methods of communication her species uses, including a wide variety of noises and the regulation of breathing to form a sort of Morse code of sound.

In the beginning of our relationship, I was the teacher and the protector. As she matured our roles reversed, and she showed herself capable of teaching and protecting me. A few weeks before the birth of Samia's own calf, she joined me, which was not unusual, when I was walking the dogs one evening. The thick tropical dusk was falling when three rhinos emerged on the track ahead of us. To avoid them I would have to make a long detour through the thorny bush in the dark. Samia, sensing both my fear and my indecision, realized my predicament and took charge of the situation. She knew these three white rhinos well and would normally have ignored them. Now, she trotted up to them, ears laid flat, huffing and hurrumphing angrily, and they retreated in astonishment at her aggressive behavior. Satisfied that they were routed, she returned to me and the dogs and escorted us safely past where they had been. When she was satisfied that we were safe, she left us to resume her own affairs.

When Samia was mated it was by the wild and violent-tempered bull Kenu. He was a small but immensely powerful rhino and many times he came near my house. On one occasion, Samia saw I was in danger and moved very quickly between us with the intention of stopping his charge. Another day Samia and Kenu visited me together. I went to the gate to greet her not realizing he was there. She stood between us and I could sense his rage and hatred of me, his desire to obliterate both me and that gate that stood between us. For forty long minutes we three stood together and I could both see and hear the breathing patterns by which they were communicating with one another. I could literally see the control that Samia was exercising over his behavior. The first time she protected me, I thought it was chance and good luck, but the second and subsequent times revealed her focus and intention. From running to me for safety, she had come to act as my protector against buffalo and her own kind, but never had I expected her to actually protect me from her own mate.

On the morning of April 11, 1995, I learned, via a radio call, that Samia had had a baby. With both joy and terror, I and a tracker crept to where I could see her, feeding quietly. Deep in the long grass near her flickered the tips of two long ears. There was no sound but that of Samia's munching. I was relieved because I knew from painful experience that baby rhinos cry only if they are in trouble. Half an hour later, the tiny creature staggered to its feet, wobbled round Samia's hind legs, thrust its wee nose into her flank, and started to suckle. Samia stopped feeding and stood quietly while it drank from first one teat and then the other. There was no doubt that she had milk, nor was there any doubt as to the baby's sex—Samia had a son.

Two days later, I was watching her with two trackers and was so absorbed that I did not notice the change in the wind. The trackers moved back but she had got my scent. Now what? These long years of observation have taught me that rhinos are fiercely protective mothers and very solitary for the first year of their baby's life. My knees were shaking so much I had to sit down. Then Samia came to me and, as she had in the past, rested her great head in my lap. While her baby stood a scarce foot away wearing a bewildered expression, I rubbed behind her ears and gently told her how clever she was and how beautiful her son was with his huge ears, blunt nose, big feet, and pearl satin skin. Obviously the bond we had created over the past ten years had withstood his birth.

When Samuel was still a few days old, Samia came to me, leaving him sleeping under a nearby bush. She was standing beside me when he awoke and cried out in fear at finding himself alone. Samia's action was swift and wholly instinctive. She swiped me sideways with her head, knocking me to the ground, and ran to him. Seeing that no harm had befallen him, she returned to me, still sitting where I had fallen. She thrust her nose at me and I assured her that I was unhurt. Then she turned and, as often in days gone by, presented me with her tail for a pull up!

I never attempted to touch her baby, but slowly he got used to my scent and his inborn fear of me lessened. Almost daily at dawn, Samia would come to visit me with him at heel. Each day would start with the knowledge that they were well and safe and that she knew how to raise and protect her child. Frequently, hand-raised animals do not.

I had worried whether Samia would appreciate the dangers surrounding her baby; there was so much I had not been able to teach her. But after some time, I realized that these fears were groundless. Samia had also always been fully aware that I only pretended to eat thornbushes and had not been able to teach her how to manipulate the thorn in her mouth. But at four months, Samuel browsed on these same thornbushes alongside his mother. It was something very beautiful to behold. I watched Samia's affection for her baby, saw how the bond between them became stronger, and felt quite ridiculously proud of her.

Because our April rains virtually failed, I started to supplement Samia's natural browse with a small quantity of alfalfa so her milk wouldn't fail. Almost daily at dawn, she came to my garden fence with her baby. As soon as she heard me open the door, she called to tell me that she was there and hopeful of being fed. The rest of the day she spent in the bush. Seeing her thus was my greatest joy.

Then tragedy struck. Samia did not come to visit me one morning. I went down the valley with Patrick, a tracker, to look for her and found her dead. She was lying on her back below the cliff from which she and her child had fallen. Her death must have been instantaneous. Her baby lay nearby, still alive. I tried to help him rise, but being unable to do so, sent Patrick with the radio to call for help. For two hours, I knelt beside little Samuel, offering what poor comfort I could. Nearby a leopard was grunting, but I could not see it. The valley was beautiful, full of birds and color, and I thought of the many happy hours and days that Samia and I had spent there.

Ian Craig, who came with ropes and other people, realized what I had not, that the baby rhino's back was broken low down near his tail. A merciful shot ended his suffering. Later, after the local Game Warden had come to remove Samia's horns, the trackers laid Samuel beside his mother and I went to say good-bye to them and to cover them with a sackful of flowers.

Samia's death has to me been a tragedy. There was real love and friendship between us and I miss her all the time. Beyond that it was my dearest hope that through her life and that of her child, awareness of and caring for her species could be awakened. In her life, she had proved beyond all doubt that there can be a meeting between two wholly disparate species.

URSA MINOR

Judith Freeman

Nobody could remember a time when there had been so many bears in the valley, not even the old-timers who had lived there all of their lives. It was early fall, and the weather was turning. We had had the worst summer of fires in many years, and endured the ninth year of drought. In the high country of Idaho the berry bushes were brown, and the streams had dried up. Hungry and facing the prospect of winter, the bears began moving down into the valleys.

They visited ranches up and down the Salmon River, rooted in garbage behind the Clayton Store, and fed in apple trees under the cover of night. Then they grew bold and were spotted even in daylight. It seemed to happen almost overnight, the bears coming into our lives and creating what the locals began calling the "bear problem."

I guess it was a problem, although when I think of it now I see it more as a gift. And I think particularly of a certain brown sow and her cub.

It all began one night when the sound of something crashing out on the porch woke my husband, Tony, and me. I stayed in bed while he went to investigate. He crept into my study where there was a door to the back porch and a switch for the outside light. When he turned on the light and looked out, he saw a bear standing on all fours next to an overturned barbecue, looking back at him through the window.

My husband called out softly, "There's a bear out here on the porch," and quickly I went to see. We huddled together, both naked (and feeling somehow more vulnerable because of that nakedness), and peered out at the bear, only a few feet away.

It was a brown bear, and she seemed in no hurry to leave. Of course she sensed us there at the window, and for a while she stared fixedly at that spot. Her snout was a honey-brown color and her coat appeared reddish in the light. Soon she began snuffling around, nosing the grill on which we had cooked salmon earlier that night. Then, after three or four minutes, she descended the steps and moved off down the garden path, disappearing slowly into the darkness.

Wolves and bears have long been regarded by humans as the beasties of the forest, the dark others, wildness incarnate. After I returned to bed that night I lay very still, thinking of the bear who was roaming about outside. I was excited by her visit. Old notions of the beast surfaced, and I thought of those creatures who terrify little girls in red coats, and hover over them as they sleep. I was also very aware of the great magical power of bears, how they have been our secret allies, our lovers in disguise.

In literature and throughout the history of art, bears have offered special relationships to women, like the bear in Edvard Munch's "Alpha and Omega," who is embraced by the first woman to emerge on land. "One day she met a bear," Munch wrote beneath his illustration of Omega kissing the beast. "Omega trembled when she felt the bear's soft fur against her body. When she placed her arm about its neck—it sunk deep in the fur."

For women, bears have figured in our fantasies and childhood stories, our fairy tales and history, and one might say that on a metaphorical level the *bear* has become part of us, and *we* are part of the bear. As Marina Warner has pointed out in her wonderful study of fairy tales, *From the Beast to the Blonde,* "The bear was called 'the beast that walks like a man.' Bears were thought to resemble humans (and thus became their perfect mythological counterparts) not only because they can walk upright on two legs, but because they are omnivorous, loving honey as well as meat."

In *Beauty and the Beast, East of the Sun and West of the Moon, Rose Red and Snow White,* as well as numerous other fables, they are our secret animal selves or our destined bridegrooms—souls waiting to be freed by the milk of kindness. And we, in turn, have been their beauties, who learn to become more fully human from our beast. As Warner concludes, "Beauty stands in need of the beast rather than vice versa. He holds up a mirror to the forces of nature within her, which she is invited to accept and to allow to grow. The animal is no longer seen as monstrous; but a means of charming the monstrous inside ourselves."

I went out early the next morning to feed the horses, and found plenty of evidence of the bear's visit. The compost heap had been dug up by powerful claws. There was a mound of scarlet scat left on the grass to one side of the house, which the dogs circled warily, raising their ruffs as they did.

The horses also seemed spooked, especially the oldest, Gillian. At thirty, Gillian was nearing the end of his life, and over the past months had grown increasingly thin and weak. Usually anxious to receive his morning grain, he stood back this morning, as did Gypsy and Nevada. None of them wanted to come into the corral. They were wary of a small enclosure. It must have been a frightening night for all three of them as they stood out in the darkened fields with the bear roaming about nearby. This morning their fear lingered, and they would flare their nostrils and snort, clearing their breath away to get an even sharper sense of smell. They stood clustered together at the end of the field, lifting their heads periodically and staring intently in the direction of the river and the thickets of willows that lined its banks. I watched them, trying to read their behavior, knowing their senses were sharper than mine. And what they told me was that the bear had not left the ranch. The bear was still down by the river.

The next night the bear came back, this time with her cub. When we turned on the porch light, we could see the cub was sitting on the porch railing. He was surprisingly small. A few feet away the sow was investigating a tennis ball left behind by one of the dogs. She held the ball in her mouth, but as the light came on she dropped it and seemed to send a quick message to her cub, who climbed up the tree growing next to the porch. In a few seconds, the sow followed, and the thin elm held two bears in its dark bower, one large and one very small.

We turned out the light, went back to bed, and lay in the dark, talking about the bears. We figured that the mother bear weighed perhaps 250 pounds. The cub probably weighed only about twenty-five. It seemed to us he should have been larger. He would have been born the winter before, in January or February, while the sow still hibernated in her den. In the black bear family, one baby usually makes up the first litter, then later come twins, occasional triplets, or, rarely, quadruplets. I figured the sow was perhaps just a young mother, struggling to feed her hungry cub.

"I wish we could give them some food," I said wistfully to my husband.

"I know. I wish we could too," he replied.

Then we fell silent, and I knew each of us was considering the rightness, or wrongness, of feeding them.

The bear and her cub returned the next night, and the following one as well, and we heard she'd also been seen down at the mouth of Malm Gulch, half a mile away. She'd raided Dick Settle's trash, and visited other houses downriver. A trap by local Fish and Game officers was set up down by the river near a grove of cottonwoods, in the hope of catching her and relocating her in a more remote area.

With a bear around, especially one with a young cub, we grew increasingly cautious, even in the way we moved about the ranch during the day. At night we tried to remember to lock the doors, especially the one nearest the pantry. We stopped taking scraps from the kitchen out to the compost heap. And we didn't barbecue again.

But the fact that the bears were so hungry troubled me. Each night when the bears visited again and I looked out and saw the small cub and his mother, something tugged at me and I thought, *feed them.*

I suppose it's a normal response to want to feed a hungry animal, especially when one has so much food to spare. And perhaps it's an even more normal response for women, who are by nature equipped to assume the role of nurturers.

Our urge to provide sustenance is strong and can lead to extraordinary acts. I came across a book not long ago called *Wild Brother*, a true story published by a photographer named William Lyman Underwood in 1921. He tells the tale of a foundling bear cub, brought back to a logging camp by a huntsman who had killed his mother while she slept in her den. The tiny cub did not even have his eyes open yet, and the problem was, what to feed him? A woman named Mrs. Underwood provided the answer. She took the cub and named him Bruno, and called her little daughter, born at the same time, Ursula, and she nursed them both at her breast. A photograph of her sitting in a rocking chair, with her dress opened and little Bruno at one breast and Ursula at the other, appears in the book. Below the photograph Mrs. Underwood has written: "Mr. Underwood took this picture of Ursula and Bruno and me with my consent, and I am glad to have him use it in this book." She signs it, "Bruno's Foster Mother."

It's an astonishing picture, shocking yet also wonderful. Better yet, the story has a happy ending: Bruno survived and, in Mrs. Underwood's words, grew up to be "a most enchanting character." Eventually, when he became too large to handle, he was returned to the wild.

The temptation I felt to feed the sow and her cub, though in quite a different league than that of Mrs. Underwood, was nonetheless terribly strong. It would have been so easy to take some of the scraps from the lamb we'd recently slaughtered and leave them down by the river at dusk. And yet I knew we shouldn't feed the bears. Some of our neighbors didn't think it was such a bad idea to shoot bears—or at least shoot at them, and more than one person was keeping a loaded gun in their house. In nearby communities a few bears had already been shot. Under those circumstances, it wasn't exactly a good idea to encourage the mother and her cub to hang around.

As it turned out, food showed up without us having to provide it. A beaver turned up dead on the banks of the irrigation canal one morning. It had been killed in a trap set by a rancher downriver whose water was being cut off by the beaver's dam—*accidently* killed, as the rancher claimed, in a trap that was only meant to contain it until it could be taken away and relocated. I never saw the dead beaver, I only heard about it from a neighbor. By the time I went to look at it the next day, the carcass was gone.

We were pretty sure the beaver had been eaten by the bear (what else could carry off a carcass of that size, leaving no evidence behind?). And as much as we hated to see the beaver killed, we were also happy to think that the bear and her cub had at least made a meal of it. Two days later, while fishing down at the river, my husband came across the beaver's remains. There among the polished rocks he found a skeleton picked clean, and a single furry paw.

The bear and her cub hung around for almost a week, visiting the porch and waking us each night. And then, just as suddenly as they had come into our lives, they disappeared. I checked with the Fish and Game officer to see if the sow and her cub had been trapped. No, they had not, he said. They were still trying to capture them.

I thought she had probably left the area and moved on.

A few days later, I awoke early one morning and let out our dogs, two Labrador–golden retriever mixes, a brother and sister named Mookie and Freda. As I turned to go back inside something dark streaked by out in the yard, and was soon followed by the dogs. Before I could take in what was happening, Mookie and Freda had chased the cub up a big elm tree. The cub reached the first branch, high enough to be out of reach, and stopped and looked down at the dogs. I called them off quickly and glanced around, anxiously looking for the sow. Where, I wondered, was the mother?

For some time we waited in the house, my husband and myself, and Mookie and Frieda, all watching the cub through the window and waiting for its mother to come. But she never came, so we called Mark, the Fish and Game officer in town whom we'd spoken with earlier.

We told him the cub was up in a tree in our yard, but we couldn't see the mother, though we had been waiting and watching for some time. And that's when he told us the sow had been killed on the highway two nights before. She was hit by a semi, he said, while crossing the highway around two in the morning, and was killed instantly when she bounded in front of the speeding truck. And yes, there had been a cub with her, the driver had reported. He had seen it in the headlights. He knew it was uninjured in the accident because he had watched it run away from its dead mother.

So, the cub was an orphan now. What he wanted to do, Mark said, was to bring a cage over and leave it in our yard, parked under the tree and baited with food. Would that be all right? he asked. He could come right away.

I hung up the phone and went back outside. The news of the sow's death left us feeling dejected. She had come down out of the mountains because she was starving, come to our ranch in search of food, and it hadn't gone well for her here, it hadn't gone well at all. I looked up at the cub in the tree. He had a pale brown snout and a white patch on his chest, and a face that could melt a heart. I cut some apple slices and I put one in the crook of the tree below him. He looked at the apple for a long time but didn't take it. Instead, he sort of smacked his jaws together and looked down at me, a tiny and beautiful little thing. So frightened, with his mother now dead. And I knew there was a good chance he soon would be too, unless we could help him.

"It isn't easy to catch bear cubs," Mark said to us an hour or so later as we unhitched the cage from his truck and the three of us dragged it by hand, moving it carefully into place near the tree. "We haven't had much luck at it," he continued. "But if we can catch him, it'll be his best chance of survival. Without his mother he won't know to hibernate, and without her to protect him and help him find food, he probably won't last long in any case."

Before Mark left he looked up at the bear cub, sitting in the crook of the tree, clasping the trunk with both paws. "That's a pretty small cub," he said softly. "He's been on his own now for two days and probably hasn't eaten much. He ought to be hungry anyway. Let me know if he comes down and takes the bait."

We went about our business that morning as we always did, taking care of the morning chores. I worked in my study. My husband fixed breakfast. But all the time we were doing these things we were also constantly watching the tree, moving about quietly in the house, hoping the cub would come down.

It took about an hour for him to finally do so. He shimmied down the tree very cautiously, stopping frequently to look around. Once on the ground, he urinated on the grass at the base of the tree, seeming to take a long time to relieve himself. The trap was only a few feet away from him. He began sniffing the air. Pork chops had been left on the floor of the cage, and more meat hung from a hook which, if disrupted, would trigger the door and make it shut.

The cub's hunger finally overpowered his fear, and warily he reached inside the cage and pulled out a pork chop and ate it on the grass. Then he took another. And then he went deeper into the cage to reach the hanging meat and, in an instant, the door clanged shut.

For the rest of that day and into the evening the little cub stayed there in the cage in our yard while calls were made to try and find him a home.

As the day wore on and calls went back and forth between us and the Fish and Game office, we discovered there were four orphaned cubs in the valley, not only "our" cub but three others whose mothers had been shot. It was depressing to think of this. Depressing, too, to think that the cubs might end up in an urban zoo, Mark's first idea for a solution.

We spent a lot of time that day, my husband and myself, visiting the little bear, going out to sit by the cage, alone or sometimes together. At first he was so frightened that whenever we approached he smacked his jaws together anxiously. Later he came to accept our presence, though I don't suppose he ever lost his fear completely.

He grew calmer as we talked to him and fed him crab apples from the tree growing nearby. The meat no longer interested him—it had led to his capture and perhaps he sensed it might cause him further trouble— but he did like the little apples we brought him. When we pushed one through the holes in the wire mesh, he would reach down and curl his little tongue around it slowly and take it into his mouth.

In many ways it was a strange day and a very long one, the day we spent with the cub, feeding him, watching him, simply sitting very quietly beside him. We didn't feel like going anywhere and leaving him alone, nor did anyone stop by to visit. There was a feeling of existing in suspended time. Once or twice the phone rang and it was always Mark calling to say that he was still trying to find the cubs a home.

What could *home* mean in this context? Was a zoo really any kind of *home* for *him*? The idea of the cub ending up in such a place hardly seemed like a satisfying solution. Yet what, we wondered, were the alternatives?

As it turned out, no zoo wanted the orphaned cub. Mark tried zoos in Boise, Salt Lake City, and other western towns, but the answer was always the same, thanks but no thanks. Apparently there were already enough bears in captivity and no one needed another one. So we fed him more apples and waited throughout a long afternoon.

Later in the day, while sitting near the cage, I experienced something extraordinary. The cub was whimpering, as he had done off and on throughout that day. It seemed to me he was crying, and why shouldn't he cry? With the death of his mother he had lost everything, and now even his freedom was gone. As he whimpered, I began humming to him, soft and low, a little made-up tune I hoped would calm him. I put everything I felt for the cub into that song—all the tenderness I felt toward him, the concern as well as my hopes for his future. And after a while he stopped whimpering and sat listening quietly to me.

It began to grow dark and still we hadn't heard anything more from Mark. As the light faded, we wondered whether the cub would just be left at our place overnight.

And then Mark called, and he had good news. He had located a man in Boise, three and a half hours way, someone who was willing to take all the orphaned cubs and feed them over the winter. This man, whose name I never learned, could keep them in a large barn where he could feed them without being seen and try to rear them with as little human contact as possible. In the spring they would be released into the wild and, with any luck, they just might survive.

An hour or so later Mark arrived and we hitched up the trailer and said goodbye to the cub. The last we saw of him he was headed up the driveway, looking back at us through the wire mesh of his cage.

The problem with humans is that we so often see animals only as extensions of our own private worlds and, in writing about the cub as I have, perhaps I, too, am guilty of this sin. After all bears are really just bears, separate entities with their own separate dignity—not lovers in fairy tales, nor the beasts of our collective psyches, nor the objects of our amusements.

But whatever happened that fall, the bears did come to us, and we did try to help them, not for any other reason than we wished to do so. What we really wanted was simply to see the bears go on being bears, wild and free.

For a long while afterward, I thought about the cub and his mother who'd been killed on the highway. Their story isn't meant to prove anything beyond an affection for its subjects. It doesn't have any moral or even a happy ending because I never knew what became of the little cub. I never heard any more about him, whether he survived the winter in captivity, let alone his release into the wild.

But I do think of him now and then, and I will always owe him a debt. Animals are good to think with, as Claude Levi-Strauss once said. Something has happened to me as a result of thinking with that little bear for the time that I did. He charmed me, and I know I will never think of bears in the same way again.

There's a photograph of my mother that I keep on my desk. It was taken in Yellowstone in the 1950s when she must have been about the same age that I am now. She's standing in a grove of trees, dangling something in the air (a strip of bacon? a piece of fruit?) and a bear is standing on his hind legs in front of her, reaching up with both paws for whatever it is that she holds. In the background are several other bears, and several small children, one of whom could be me. The bears and the little children are all close together, forming a tight little group. In the foreground, my mother looks radiant: She has the most wonderful broad smile on her face. The way she stands so close to the bear, facing him, it almost looks like they're dancing.

I keep the photograph in a prominent place because it makes me feel good when I look at it. In the years since this picture was taken, feeding bears in Yellowstone has been prohibited. We've learned it's not the *correct* thing to do. Still, there's an innocence in that old photograph that I love. It's the innocence of the children mixing so freely with the bears. It's the innocence of my mother, the woman who doesn't yet know she shouldn't feed the bear, and who stands so fearlessly, and so joyously, before him. Perhaps my mother and Mrs. Underwood understood something quite important after all.

THE MOON BY WHALE LIGHT

Diane Ackerman

This section of "Whales" takes place in Patagonia, in a protected bay where right whales stop on their way to the rich feeding grounds of Antarctica. From a cliff near camp, I have a clear view of mother and baby right whales going about their dramas.

When a whale sleeps, it slowly tumbles in an any-old-crazy, end-over-end, sideways fashion, and may even bonk its head on the bottom. Or it just lies quietly, looking like a corpse. When it rises again to breathe in the midst of its sleep, it comes up as slow as a dream, breaks the surface, breathes a few times and, without even diving, falls again slowly toward the bottom. Right whales sometimes sleep in the mornings on calm days in Argentina, and some of them seem to be head-heavy, with light tails. The result is that they fall forward and their tails rise out of the water. But the behavior of right whales is easy to study, because they're at-the-surface whales. They're so fat that they float when relaxed, and they spend a lot of time with their backs in the air. When they're asleep at the surface, their breathing rate drops tremendously, they don't close their nostrils completely between breaths, and so sometimes they snore. In fact they make marvelous, rude, after-dinner noises as they sleep. When they wake, they stretch their backs, open their mouths, and yawn. Sometimes they lift their tails up and shake them, and then they go about their business. Often, they sleep at the surface so long on calm days that their backs get sunburned; and then they peel the same way humans do, but on a big, whale-size scale. The loose skin from their backs falls into the water and becomes food for birds. Sometimes the birds don't wait for the skin to fall, but sweep down and pull it from the whales' backs.

Juan, a researcher, appeared at the edge of camp, on foot, apparently hiking in from a walk to a neighboring bay. By the time I got back to the main house, he was just arriving, wearing shorts, a T-shirt, and a knitted hat.

"Tired?" I asked with an inflection that said, *I really hope you aren't.* "Want to go find some whales?"

He grinned. "Just let me get a Coke, then *vamos.*"

I put on a leotard and tights and began crawling into a half-inch-thick wetsuit that included Farmer John overalls, a beaver-tail jacket, boots, gloves, and a hood. There was so much neoprene in the suit, trapping air, that I'd need to wear weights around my waist to keep from bobbing on the surface.

Juan tugged on a thin wetsuit and boots, and we went down to the beach and climbed into a Zodiac. Heading north along the bay, we came upon two mothers and calves, but the mothers were naturally protective of their calves and hurried them away. We wanted to find a young adult. Juan had been collecting loose skin for Judy and then going into the water to photograph the heads of the whales it came from in order to identify them. I hoped to join him. We searched for an hour but found none in the mood to be approached. Finally, we headed back toward camp and, coming around a bend, discovered Fang and her calf still playing. We cut the motor about two hundred yards from the whales. Juan and I slipped over the side of the boat and began to swim toward them, approaching as quietly as possible, so that they wouldn't construe any of our movements as aggressive. In a few minutes, we were only yards from the mother's head. Looking down, I saw the three-month-old baby beside her underwater, its callosities bright in the murky green water. Slowly, Juan and I swam all the way around them, getting closer and closer. The long wound on Fang's flank looked red and angry. When her large tail lifted out of the water, its beauty stunned me for a moment, and then I yanked Juan's hand, to draw his attention, and we pulled back. At fifty feet long, weighing about fifty tons, all she would have needed to do was hit us with a flipper to crush us, or swat us with her tail to kill us instantly. But she was moving her tail gently, slowly, without malice. It would be as if a human being, walking across a meadow, had come upon a strange new animal. Our instinct wouldn't be to kill it but to get closer and have a look, perhaps touch it. Right whales are grazers, which have balleen plates, not teeth. We did not look like lunch. She swung her head around so that her mouth was within two feet of me, then turned her head on edge to reveal a large white patch and, under that, an eye shaped much like a human eye. I looked directly into her eye, and she looked directly back at me, as we hung in the water, studying each other.

I wish you well, I thought, applying all the weight of my concentration, in case it was possible for her to sense my mood. I did not imagine she could decipher the words, but many animals can sense fear in humans. Perhaps they can also sense other emotions.

Her dark, plumlike eye fixed me and we stared deeply at one another for some time. The curve of her mouth gave her a Mona Lisa smile, but that was just a felicity of her anatomy. The only emotion I sensed was her curiosity. That shone through her watchfulness, her repeated turning toward us, her extreme passivity, her caution with flippers and tail. Apparently, she was doing what we were—swimming close to a strange, fascinating life-form, taking care not to frighten or hurt it. Perhaps, seeing us slip over the side of the Zodiac, she thought it had given birth and we were its young. In that case, she might have been thinking how little we resembled our parent. Or perhaps she understood only too well that we were intelligent beasts who lived in the strange, dangerous world of the land, where whales can get stranded, lose their bearings and equilibrium, and die. Perhaps she knew somehow that we live in that desert beyond the waves from which whales rarely return, a kingdom we rule, where we thrive. A whale's glimpse of us is almost as rare as our glimpse of a whale. They have never seen us mating, they have rarely if at all seen us feeding, they have never seen us give birth, suckle our young, die of old age. They have never observed our society, our normal habits. They would not know how to tell our sex, since we hide our reproductive organs. Perhaps they know that human males tend to have more facial hair than females, just as we know that male right whales tend to have more callosities on their faces than females. But they would still find it hard to distinguish between a clothed, short-haired, clean-shaven man and a clothed, short-haired woman.

When Fang had first seen us in the Zodiac, we were wearing large smoked plastic eyes. Now we had small eyes shaped like hers—but two on the front of the head, like a flounder or a seal, not an eye on either side, like a fish or a whale. In the water, our eyes were encased in a glass jar, our mouths stretched around a rubber tube, and our feet were flippers. Instead of diving like marine mammals, we floated on the surface. To Fang, I must have looked spastic and octopuslike, with my thin limbs dangling. Human beings possess such immense powers that few animals cause us to feel truly humble. A whale does, swimming beside you, as big as a reclining building, its eye carefully observing you. It could easily devastate you with a twitch, and yet it doesn't. Still, although it lives in a gliding, quiet, investigate-it-first realm, it is not as benign as a Zen monk. Aggression plays a big role in its life, especially during courtship. Whales have weapons that are equal in their effects to our pointing a gun at somebody, squeezing a finger, and blowing him away. When they strike each other with their flukes in battles, they hit flat, but they sometimes slash the water with the edge. That fluke edge could break a person in two instantly. But such an attack has never happened in the times people have been known to swim with whales. In many of our science-fiction stories, aliens appear on earth and terrible fights ensue, with everyone shooting weapons that burn, sting, or blow others up. To us, what is alien is treacherous and evil. Whales do not visualize aliens in that way. So although it was frightening to float beside an animal as immense and powerful as a whale, I knew that if I showed her where I was and what I was and that I meant her no harm, she would return the courtesy.

Suddenly, Juan pulled me back a few feet and, turning, I saw the calf swimming around to our side, though staying close to its mother. Big as an elephant, it still looked like a baby. Only a few months old, it was a frisky pup and rampantly curious. It swam right up, turned one eye at us, took a good look, then wheeled its head around to look at us with the other eye. When it turned, it swung its mouth right up to my chest, and I reached out to touch it, but Juan pulled my hand back. I looked at him and nodded. A touch could have startled the baby, which might not have known its own strength yet. In a reflex, its flipper or tail could have swatted us. It might not have known that if humans are held underwater—by a playful flipper, say—they can drown. Its flippers hung in the water by its sides, and its small callosities looked like a crop of fieldstones. Swimming forward, it fanned its tail, and the water suddenly felt chillier as it stirred up cold from the bottom. The mother was swimming forward to keep up with it, and we followed, hanging quietly in the water, trying to breathe slowly and kick our flippers as little as possible. Curving back around, Fang turned on her side so that she could see us, and waited as we swam up close again. Below me, her flipper hovered large as a freight elevator. Tilting it very gently in place, she appeared to be sculling; her tail, too, was barely moving. Each time she and the baby blew, a fine mist sprayed into the air, accompanied by a *whumping* sound, as of a pedal organ.

We did not have their insulation of blubber to warm us in such frigid waters and, growing cold at last after an hour of traveling slowly along the bay with them, we began to swim back toward the beach. To save energy, we rolled onto our backs and kicked with our fins. When we were a few hundred yards away from her, Fang put her head up in a spy hop. Then she dove, rolled, lifted a flipper high into the air like a black rubber sail, and waved it back and forth. The calf did the same. Juan and I laughed. They were not waving at us, only rolling and playing now that we were out of the way. But it was so human a gesture that we automatically waved our arms overhead in reply. Then we turned back onto our faces again. Spears of sunlight cut through the thick green water and disappeared into the depths, a bottom soon revealed itself as tawny brown about thirty feet below us, and then the sand grew visible, along with occasional shells, and then the riot of shells near shore, and finally the pebbles of the shallows. Taking off our fins, we stepped from one liquid realm to another, from the whale road, as the Anglo-Saxons called the ocean, back onto the land of humans.

MAZES

Ursula Le Guin

I have tried hard to use my wits and keep up my courage, but I know
now that I will not be able to withstand the torture any longer. My perceptions of time are confused, but I think it has been several days since I
realized I could no longer keep my emotions under aesthetic control, and
now the physical breakdown is also nearly complete. I cannot accomplish
any of the greater motions. I cannot speak. Breathing, in this heavy foreign air, grows more difficult. When the paralysis reaches my chest I shall
die: probably tonight.

The alien's cruelty is refined, yet irrational. If it intended all along to
starve me, why not simply withhold food? But instead of that it gave me
plenty of food, mountains of food, all the greenbud leaves I could possibly want. Only they were not fresh. They had been picked; they were
dead; the element that makes them digestible to us was gone, and one
might as well eat gravel. Yet there they were, with all the scent and shape
of greenbud, irresistible to my craving appetite. Not at first, of course. I
told myself, I am not a child, to eat picked leaves! But the belly gets the
better of the mind. After a while it seemed better to be chewing something, anything, that might still the pain and craving in the gut. So I ate,
and ate, and starved. It is a relief, now, to be so weak I cannot eat.

The same elaborately perverse cruelty marks all its behavior. And
the worst thing of all is just the one I welcomed with such relief and delight at first: the maze. I was badly disoriented at first, after the trapping,
being handled by a giant, being dropped into a prison; and this place
around the prison is disorienting, spatially disquieting, the strange, smooth,
curved wall-ceiling is of an alien substance and its lines are meaningless to
me. So when I was taken up and put down, amidst all this strangeness, in
a maze, a recognizable, even familiar maze, it was a moment of strength

and hope after great distress. It seemed pretty clear that I had been put in the maze as a kind of test or investigation, that a first approach toward communication was being attempted. I tried to cooperate in every way. But it was not possible to believe for very long that the creature's purpose was to achieve communication.

It is intelligent, highly intelligent, that is clear from a thousand evidences. We are both intelligent creatures, we are both maze-builders: surely it would be quite easy to learn to talk together! If that were what the alien wanted. But it is not. I do not know what kind of mazes it builds for itself. The ones it made for me were instruments of torture.

The mazes were, as I said, of basically familiar types, though the walls were of that foreign material much colder and smoother than packed clay. The alien left a pile of picked leaves in one extremity of each maze, I do not know why; it may be a ritual or superstition. The first maze it put me in was babyishly short and simple. Nothing expressive or even interesting could be worked out from it. The second, however, was a kind of simple version of the Ungated Affirmation, quite adequate for the reassuring, outreaching statement I wanted to make. And the last, the long maze, with seven corridors and nineteen connections, lent itself surprisingly well to the Maluvian mode, and indeed to almost all the New Expressionist techniques. Adaptations had to be made to the alien spatial understanding, but a certain quality of creativity arose precisely from the adaptations. I worked hard at the problem of that maze, planning all night long, re-imagining the lines and spaces, the feints and pauses, the erratic, unfamiliar, and yet beautiful course of the True Run. Next day when I was placed in the long maze and the alien began to observe, I performed the Eighth Maluvian in its entirety.

It was not a polished performance. I was nervous, and the spatio-temporal parameters were only approximate. But the Eighth Maluvian survives the crudest performance in the poorest maze. The evolutions in the ninth encatenation, where the "cloud" theme recurs so strangely transposed into the ancient spiraling motif, are indestructibly beautiful. I have seen them performed by a very old person, so old and stiff-jointed that he could only suggest the movements, hint at them, a shadow-gesture, a dim reflection of the themes: and all who watched were inexpressibly moved. There is no nobler statement of our being. Performing, I myself was carried away by the power of the motions and forgot that I was a prisoner, forgot the alien eyes watching me; I transcended the errors of the maze and my own weakness, and danced the Eighth Maluvian as I have never danced it before.

When it was done, the alien picked me up and set me down in the first maze—the short one, the maze for little children who have not yet learned how to talk.

Was the humiliation deliberate? Now that it is all past, I see that there is no way to know. But it remains very hard to ascribe its behavior to ignorance.

After all, it is not blind. It has eyes, recognizable eyes. They are enough like our eyes that it must see somewhat as we do. It has a mouth, four legs, can move bipedally, has grasping hands, etc.; for all its gigantism and strange looks, it seems less fundamentally different from us, physically, than a fish. And yet, fish school and dance and, in their own stupid way, communicate! The alien has never once attempted to talk with me. It has been with me, watched me, touched me, handled me, for days: but all its motions have been purposeful, not communicative. It is evidently a solitary creature, totally self-absorbed.

This would go far to explain its cruelty.

I noticed early that from time to time it would move its curious horizontal mouth in a series of fairly delicate, repetitive gestures, a little like someone eating. At first I thought it was jeering at me; then I wondered if it was trying to urge me to eat the indigestible fodder; then I wondered if it could be communicating *labially*. It seemed a limited and unhandy language for one so well provided with hands, feet, limbs, flexible spine, and all; but that would be like the creature's perversity, I thought. I studied its lip-motions and tried hard to imitate them. It did not respond. It stared at me briefly and then went away.

In fact, the only indubitable *response* I ever got from it was on a pitifully low level of interpersonal aesthetics. It was tormenting me with knob-pushing, as it did once a day. I had endured this grotesque routine pretty patiently for the first several days. If I pushed one knob I got a nasty sensation in my feet, if I pushed a second I got a nasty pellet of dried-up food, if I pushed a third I got nothing whatever. Obviously, to demonstrate my intelligence I was to push the third knob. But it appeared that my intelligence irritated my captor, because it removed the neutral knob after the second day. I could not imagine what it was trying to establish or accomplish, except the fact that I was its prisoner and a great deal smaller than it. When I tried to leave the knobs, it forced me physically to return. I must sit there pushing knobs for it, receiving punishment from one and mockery from the other. The deliberate outrageousness of the situation, the insufferable heaviness and thickness of this air, the feeling of being forever watched yet never understood, all combined to drive me into a condition for which we have no description at all. The nearest thing I can suggest is the last interlude of the Ten Gate Dream, when all the feintways are closed and the dance narrows in and in until it bursts terribly into the vertical. I cannot say what I felt, but it was a little like that. If I got my feet stung once more, or got pelted once more with a lump of rotten food, I would go vertical forever . . . I took the knobs off the wall (they came off with a sharp tug, like flowerbuds), laid them in the middle of the floor, and defecated on them.

The alien took me up at once and returned me to my prison. It had got the message, and had acted on it. But how unbelievably primitive the message had had to be! And the next day, it put me back in the knob room, and there were the knobs as good as new, and I was to choose alternate punishments for its amusement . . . Until then I had told myself that the creature was alien, therefore incomprehensible and uncomprehending, perhaps not intelligent in the same *manner* as we, and so on. But since then I have known that, though all that may remain true, it is also unmistakably and grossly cruel.

When it put me into the baby maze yesterday, I could not move. The power of speech was all but gone (I am dancing this, of course, in my mind; "the best maze is the mind," the old proverb goes) and I simply crouched there, silent. After a while it took me out again, gently enough. There is the ultimate perversity of its behavior: it has never once touched me cruelly.

It set me down in the prison, locked the gate, and filled up the trough with inedible food. Then it stood two-legged, looking at me for a while.

Its face is very mobile, but if it speaks with its face I cannot understand it, that is too foreign a language. And its body is always covered with bulky, binding mats, like an old widower who has taken the Vow of Silence. But I had become accustomed to its great size, and to the angular character of its limb-positions, which at first had seemed to be saying a steady stream of incoherent and mispronounced phrases, a horrible nonsense-dance like the motions of an imbecile, until I realized that they were strictly purposive movements. Now I saw something a little beyond that, in its position. There were no words, yet there was communication. I saw, as it stood watching me, a clear signification of angry sadness—as clear as the Sembrian Stance. There was the same lax immobility, the bentness, the assertion of defeat. Never a word came clear, and yet it told me that it was filled with resentment, pity, impatience, and frustration. It told me it was sick of torturing me, and wanted me to help it. I am sure I understood it. I tried to answer. I tried to say, "What is it you want of me? Only tell me what it is you want." But I was too weak to speak clearly, and it did not understand. It has never understood.

And now I have to die. No doubt it will come in to watch me die; but it will not understand the dance I dance in dying.

V: COME INTO ANIMAL PRESENCE

Testimonies

Sometimes we are called on as poets to speak what we have seen. Sometimes we are called to act according to what we see and what we understand. In both cases, the demand is to be ruthless in one's honesty, to look without flinching.

The necessity of the writer to speak what is meets the necessity of the animal to be itself. The story must be told with the same eloquence as that with which the animal lives its life. To come into the animal presence, much must be set aside, much risked, and it takes us down to the bone. These are testimonies. They come out of the discipline of bearing witness. And as Denise Levertov informs us, "An old joy returns in holy presence."

Denise Levertov

Come into animal presence.
No man is so guileless as
the serpent. The lonely white rabbit
on the roof is a star
twitching its ears at the rain.
The llama intricately
folding its hind legs to be seated
not disdains but mildly
disregards human approval.
What joy when the insouciant
armadillo glances at us and doesn't
quicken his trotting
across the track into the palm bush.

What is this joy? That no animal
falters, but knows what it must do?
That the snake has no blemish,
that the rabbit inspects his strange surroundings
in white star-silence? The llama
rests in dignity, the armadillo
has some intention to pursue in the palm forest.
Those who were sacred have remained so,
holiness does not dissolve, it is a presence
of bronze, only the sight that saw it
faltered and turned from it.
An old joy returns in holy presence.

Linda McCarriston

You know that they burned her horse
before her. Though it is not recorded,
you know that they burned her Percheron
first, before her eyes, because you

know that story, so old that story,
the routine story, carried to its
extreme, of the cruelty that can make
of what a woman hears *a silence*,

that can make of what a woman sees
a lie. She had no son for them to burn,
for them to take from her in the world
not of her making and put to its pyre,

so they layered a greater one in front of
where she was staked to her own—
as you have seen her pictured sometimes,
her eyes raised to the sky. But they were

not raised. This is yet one of their lies.
They were not closed. Though her hands
were bound behind her, and her feet were
bound deep in what would become fire,

she watched. Of greenwood stakes
head-high and thicker than a man's waist
they laced the narrow corral that would not
burn until flesh had burned, until

bone was burning, and laid it thick
with tinder—fatted wicks and sulphur,
kindling and logs—and ran a ramp
up to its height from where the gray horse

waited, his dapples making of his flesh
a living metal, layers of life
through which the light shone out
in places as it seems to through the flesh

of certain fish, a light she knew
as purest, coming, like that, from within.
Not flinching, not praying, she looked
the last time on the body she knew

better than the flesh of any man, or child,
or woman, having long since left the lap
of her mother—the chest with its
perfect plates of muscle, the neck

with its perfect, prow-like curve,
the hindquarters'—pistons—powerful cleft
pennoned with the silk of his tail.
Having ridden as they did together

—those places, that hard, that long—
their eyes found easiest that day
the way to each other, their bodies
wedded in a sacrament unmediated

by man. With fire they drove him
up the ramp and off into the pyre
and tossed the flame in with him.
This was the last chance they gave her

to recant her world, in which their power
came not from God. Unmoved, the Men
of God began watching him burn, and better,
watching her watch him burn, hearing

the long mad godlike trumpet of his terror,
his crashing in the wood, the groan
of stakes that held, the silverblack hide,
the pricked ears catching first

like dryest bark, and the eyes.
And she knew, by this agony, that she
might choose to live still, if she would
but make her sign on the parchment

they would lay before her, which now
would include this new truth: that it
did not happen, this death in the circle,
the rearing, plunging, raging, the splendid

armor-colored head raised one last time
above the flames before they took him
—like any game untended on the spit—into
their yellow-green, their blackening red.

HEALING THE MARE

Linda McCarriston

Just days after the vet came,
after the steroids that took
the fire out of the festering
sores—out of the flesh that in
the heat took the stings too
seriously and swelled into great
welts, wore thin and wept, calling
more loudly out to the green-
headed flies—I bathe you
and see your coat returning,
your deep force surfacing in a
new layer of hide: black wax
alive against weather and flies.

But this morning, misshapen
still, you look like an effigy,
something rudely made, something
made to be buffeted, or like
an old comforter—are they both
one in the end? So both a child

and a mother, with my sponge and
my bucket, I come to anoint, to
anneal the still weeping, to croon
to you *baby poor baby* for the sake
of the song, to polish you up,
for the sake of the touch, to a shine.

As I soothe you I surprise wounds
of my own this long time unmothered.
As you stand, scathed and scabbed,
with your head up, I swab. As you
press, I lean into my own loving
touch, for which no wound
is too ugly.

TIPPET

Linda McCarriston

For better than a week
they've dragged it around among
the three houses: the five dogs
I walk with; the diminishing
carcass of a deer. My two
are the old ones, who don't
go off without me, who can't be
running deer, so I look the other way
till my red setter, Kate, *grande*
dame bird-dog, knobby with arthritis,
presents what's left to the front lawn
framed by the big bay window.
No more denying.
So I plow out through a foot of snow
to collar her, queen of the hearth's
circle, gnawing away at the delicate
face of a doe, the balance
of which is a tippet of gray-
gold fur and a strand of flesh
—or a tendon—to the left foreleg
from the knee down, the hoof
a glossy miniature, snowpacked,
hard-packed from its running.
Because I want them not to get
even late a lust for the taste of it,
I head for the covered rubbish
with the creature in my arms, cradling

its skull and bundle of frozen hide,
without thinking, against my breast
like a pet or a child. It hardly
seems grotesque as I do it
to shift it up to my shoulder
—just so—freeing one hand
to lift the lid and slip it in.
I surprise myself, starting to cry then,
having no grave in the iron earth,
no word to lessen the waste
as I throw her away. For solace
I turn to my ignorance—human,
encyclopedic—and say
a shared animal wisdom beyond me
governed this chase. But my flesh
where her head rested
keeps faith with its rue.

THE UNIVERSE RESPONDS:
OR, HOW I LEARNED WE CAN HAVE PEACE ON EARTH

Alice Walker

A few years ago I wrote an essay called "Everything Is a Human Being," which explores to some extent the Native American view that all of creation is of one substance and therefore deserving of the same respect. I described the death of a snake that I caused and wrote of my remorse. I wrote the piece to celebrate the birth of Martin Luther King, Jr., and I read it first to a large group of college students in California. I also read it other places, so that by summer (I had written it in winter) it had been read three or four times, and because I cannot bear to repeat myself very much, I put it away.

That summer "my" land in the country crawled with snakes. There was always the large resident snake, whom my mother named "Susie," crawling about in the area that marks the entrance to my studio. But there were also lots of others wherever we looked. A black-and-white king snake appeared underneath the shower stall in the garden. A striped red-and-black one, very pretty, appeared near the pond. It now revealed the little hole in the ground in which it lived by lying half in and half out of it as it basked in the sun. Garden snakes crawled up and down the roads and paths. One day, leaving my house with a box of books in his arms, my companion literally tripped over one of these.

We spoke to all these snakes in friendly voices. They went their way. We went ours. After about a two-week bloom of snakes, we seemed to have our usual number; just Susie and a couple of her children.

A few years later, I wrote an essay about a horse called Blue. It was about how humans treat horses and other animals; how hard it is for us to see them as the suffering, fully conscious, enslaved beings they are. It also marked the beginning of my effort to become non-meat-eating (fairly successful). After reading this essay in public only once, this is what happened. A white horse came and settled herself on the land. (Her owner, a neighbor, soon came to move her.) The two horses on the ranch across the road began to run up to their fence whenever I passed, leaning over it and making what sounded to my ears like joyful noises. They had never done this before (I checked with the human beings I lived with to be sure of this), and after a few more times of greeting me as if I'd done something especially nice for them, they stopped. Now when I pass they look at me with the same reserve they did before. But there is still a spark of *recognition*.

What to make of this?

What I have noticed in my small world is that if I praise the wildflowers growing on the hill in front of my house, the following year they double in profusion and brilliance. If I admire the squirrel that swings from branch to branch outside my window, pretty soon I have three or four squirrels to admire. If I look into the eyes of a raccoon that has awakened me by noisily rummaging through the garbage at night, and acknowledge that it looks maddeningly like a mischievous person—paws on hips, masked eyes, a certain impudent stance, as it looks back at me—I soon have a family of raccoons living in a tree a few yards off my deck. (From this tree they easily forage in the orchard at night and eat, or at least take bites out of, all the apples. Which is not fun. But that is another story.)

And then, too, there are the deer, who know they need never, ever fear me.

In white-directed movies about the Indians of the Old West, you sometimes see the "Indians" doing a rain dance, a means of praying for rain. The message delivered by the moviemaker is that such dancing and praying is ridiculous, that either it will rain or it will not. All white men know this. The Indians are backward and stupid and wasting their time. But there is also that last page or so in the story of Black Elk, in which his anthropologist/friend John Neihart goes with him on a last visit to the Badlands to pray atop Harney Peak, a place sacred to the Sioux. It is a cloudless day, but the ancient Black Elk hopes that the Great Spirit, as in the real "old" days, will acknowledge his prayer for the good of his people by sending at least a few drops of rain. As he prays, in his old, tired voice, mostly of his love of the Universe and his failure to be perfect, a small cloud indeed forms. It rains, just enough to say "Yes." Then the sky clears. Even today there is the belief among many indigenous holy people that when a person of goodness dies, the Universe acknowledges the spirit's departure by sending storms and rain.

The truth is in the country, where I live much of the time, I am virtually overrun by birds and animals—raccoons, snakes, deer, horses (occasionally). During a recent court trial at which a neighbor and I both happened to find ourselves, her opening words of greeting included the information that two wild pigs she'd somehow captured had broken out and were, she feared, holed up somewhere on my land.

At least, I thought, my house in the city is safe.

But no.

One night after dinner, as some friends were leaving my house, I opened my front door, only to have a large black dog walk gratefully inside. It had obviously been waiting quietly on the stoop. It came into the hallway, sniffed my hands, and prepared to make itself at home, exactly as if it had lived in my house all its life. There was no nervousness whatsoever about being an intruder. No, no, I said, out you go! It did not want to go, but my friends and I persuaded it. It settled itself at the door and there it stayed, barking reproachfully until I went to bed. Very late that night I heard its owners calling it. George! they called. George! Here, George! They were cursing and laughing. Drunk. George made no response.

I suddenly realized that George was not lost. He had run away. He had run away from these cursing, laughing drunks who were now trying to find him. This realization meant the end of sleep for me that night as I lay awake considering my responsibility to George. (I felt none toward his owners.) For George obviously "knew" which house was at least *supposed* to be a stop on the underground railroad, and had come to it; but I, in my city house, had refused to acknowledge my house as such. If I let it in, where would I put it? Then, too, I'm not particularly fond of the restlessness of dogs. The way they groan and fart in their sleep, chase rabbits in their dreams, and flop themselves over, rattling their chains (i.e., collars and dog tags). George had run away from these drunks who "owned" him, people no doubt unfit to own anything at all that breathed. Did they beat him? Did they tie him to trees and lampposts outside pubs (as I've so often seen done) while they went inside and had drink after drink? Were all the "lost" dogs one heard about really runaways? It hit me with great force that a dog I had once had, Myshkin, had undoubtedly run away from the small enclosed backyard in which he had been kept and in which he was probably going mad, whereas I had for years indulged in the fantasy that he'd been stolen! No dog in his right mind would voluntarily leave a cushy prison run by loving humans, right?

Or suppose George was a woman, beaten or psychologically abused by her spouse. What then? Would I let her in? I would, wouldn't I? But where to put George, anyway? If I put him in the cellar, he might bark.

I hate the sound of barking. If I put him in the parlor, he might spread fleas.

Who was this dog, anyway?

George stayed at my door the whole night. In the morning I heard him bark, but by the time I was up, he was gone.

I think I am telling you that the animals of the planet are in desperate peril, and they are fully aware of this. No less than human beings are doing in all parts of the world, they are seeking sanctuary. But I am also telling you that we are connected to them at least as intimately as we are connected to trees. Without plant life human beings could not breathe. Plants produce oxygen. Without free animal life I believe we will lose the spiritual equivalent of oxygen. "Magic," intuition, sheer astonishment at the forms the Universe devises in which to express life—itself—will no longer be able to breathe in us. One day it occurred to me that if all the birds died, as they might well do, eventually, from the poisoning of their air, water, and food, it would be next to impossible to describe to our children the wonder of their flight. To most children, I think, the flight of a bird—if they've never seen one fly—would be imagined as stiff and unplayful, like the flight of an airplane.

But what I'm also sharing with you is this thought: The Universe responds. What you ask of it, it gives. The military-industrial complex and its leaders and scientists have shown more faith in this reality than have those of us who do not believe in war and who want peace. They have asked the Earth for all its deadlier substances. They have been confident in their faith in hatred and war. The Universe, ever responsive, the Earth, ever giving, has opened itself fully to their desires. Ironically, Black Elk and nuclear scientists can be viewed in much the same way: as men who received from it a sign reflective of their own hearts.

I remember when I used to dismiss the bumper sticker PRAY FOR PEACE. I realize now that I did not understand it, since I also did not understand prayer, which I now know to be the active affirmation in the physical world of our inseparableness from the divine; and everything, *especially* the physical world, is divine. War will stop when we no longer praise it, or give it any attention at all. Peace will come wherever it is sincerely invited. Love will overflow every sanctuary given it. Truth will grow where the fertilizer that nourishes it is also truth. Faith will be its own reward.

Believing this, which I learned from my experience with the animals and the wildflowers, I have found that my fear of nuclear destruction has been to a degree lessened. I know perfectly well that we may all die, and relatively soon, in a global holocaust, which was first imprinted, probably against their wishes, on the hearts of the scientist fathers of the atomic bomb, no doubt deeply wounded and frightened human beings; but I also know we have the power, as all the Earth's people, to conjure up the healing rain imprinted on Black Elk's heart. Our death is in our hands.

Knock and the door shall be opened. Ask and you shall receive.

Whatsoever you do to the least of these, you do also unto me—and to yourself. For we are one.

"God" answers prayers. Which is another way of saying, "the Universe responds."

We are *indeed* the world. Only if we have reason to fear what is in our hearts need we fear for the planet. Teach yourself peace.

Pass it on.

DANCE OF THE DEER

Erica Helm Meade

One day I took a walk near my island home. Across the road a rufous doe grazed in the meadow with her new fawn—a picture of docility. A large yellow dog sauntered down the road toward me. He was bulky and intimidating, even from a distance. He stopped at the edge of the road to watch the doe and her fawn in the meadow. The fawn went on munching grass. The doe glanced up at the big dog, and then continued grazing. As I neared the dog, the fawn moved a few feet away from its mother. The dog sized up the scene very carefully. The moment he saw a beeline between himself and the fawn, he shot toward it at lightning speed. I shouted, as if that would stop him, but my voice mattered little. For a brief second it looked as if the fawn would be done for, and then I saw the rufous doe behave as I'd never seen before. She raised up tall and filled her chest with air, magnifying her size. She swiftly positioned herself between the dog and her fawn. Then she directly faced the dog. I feared he'd go for her throat and take her down, but no. Instead he hesitated before her. Then she advanced toward him stomping like a flamenco dancer. Her sharp black hooves pummeled the earth. It was quite impressive. At this the dog retreated. I hoped that would be the end of it. He left them in the meadow and returned to the road. I shooed him and commanded, "Go home!" But he was still intrigued.

He stayed there at the road's edge, eyeing the deer, waiting for another opening. The doe seemed as casual as could be. She grazed without looking up. She allowed the fawn to wander. She could surely hear me shooing the dog, but she seemed to pay us no mind. At last the dog saw his chance. He darted across the field toward the fawn. The fawn seemed oblivious, but the doe moved more fleetly than before. In an instant she was protectively positioned to guard her fawn. She reared up to show the dog her height. Then she advanced toward him, hammering her hooves in his face, mincing the grass at her feet. He moved backward a few steps. She kept pounding. Her hooves could easily have gouged out his eye or punctured his chest. But she seemed to want to demonstrate the threat of it without actually doing the damage. He turned tail and ran several feet as he had done before. But this time she kept coming, tearing up the sod beneath her hooves as she advanced. The dog ran to the road, then turned around to watch her. She held her ground at the edge of the road. He lowered his head to threaten another advance, and she puffed up and thumped the earth again as if to say, "Just try it, Buster." It was daunting, this dance of hers. The dog wanted no more of it and skulked away down the road.

Since then I've concluded the rufous doe is a superb model for any woman. Her gentle calm is appropriate for nearly every situation, except the rare occasions when salivating jaws threaten. Then it's necessary to have a set of sharp hooves up one's sleeve and the resolve to keep stomping until the predator retreats. When people praise doe-eyed gentleness, I don't argue, but I'll never forget she can be every bit as fierce as she is soft.

Since then, when life brings me face-to-face with a predator, my knees still knock and my legs tremble. But now I know this is more than a reflex, more than just fear. It's the dance of the deer stirring inside—it's my hooves warming up—preparing to stomp.

Judith Minty

I. THE DREAM/THE NEED

White on white, it feathers
in layers,
silk folding over silk.
No detail, but the sense
of snow
exploding out of snow.

The sleeper floats within
the dream. White sound
soars from the gaping "O"
of the mouth, all motion
held beyond the outstretched arm
that rises, the cry
sinking into the pillow,
the sheet fluttering,
a cloud against bones.

Blink of yellow light, breath
suspended.
Wings falter, it falls.
The eye
opens, the head revolves,
stares into winter.

2. THE COLD/THE MOTION

This will be their hardest season.
Wind slants, beats snow in circles,
heaves drifts against the house.
She whimpers, but holds the weight and bears
witness to trees bending, to a lake
that sinks into armor. What was
descends. The surface freezes.

She spins inward in the lamplight,
spreads hands over the flame, and speaks
of flight, of something like a cloud
floating over the tundra. Her eyes slit,
round. She tells him she loves him,
though she no longer believes in words.
Tiny animals skitter, become what is hunted.

3. THE HUNT/THE PATTERN

Waiting is the backbone of winter.
Pale light from sun and moon. Cold
whips at skirts, the entrance to sleeves.
Days whirl by without shadow.
She leans into the lash, it coils around her.

Flutter of white by the river. She reels
through drifts like a derelict.
Not him, only snow on a log.
Here, dark things define themselves:
bridge, bare willows lacing the bank,
stump locked in ice near lowland.

It was a mistake to speak of poems
and white owls in a breath, foolish
to count on patterns for a cure, on feathers
that might be gathered off the snow,
ghosts of words waiting to be written.
She returns without him.

4. THE LIGHT / THE PRESENCE

He comes when she least expects him,
like a lover, out of night into morning.
When he flies by her window, she thinks she hears thunder
and claps her hands to her face. She does not see
his shadow melt into the snow.

He waits in the corner of her garden.
She trembles on the threshold, unable
to go there, to step inside his wings.

White on white, feathers like silk,
the head turns slowly. In winter
dreams hide beneath blankets, only the eyelids glow
yellow chrysanthemums. At last she sees
how fire burns from within and steps forward.
His eyes ignite, the flame rises.

DESTROYING THE CORMORANT EGGS

Judith Minty

Black, black as the plumage
of the Double-Crested Cormorant, all black
except for the orange chin pouch below its slender,
curved bill, who nests by the shore in shadow and crack
of rock along with the lighter, tan or gray or white
gulls and terns on Little Gull Island and Gravelly Island
in the middle of Lake Michigan—Black as the long shadow
of this fisherman, or madman, slipping
over these rocks, these nests, an eclipse or is it God,
something without conscience between sun and earth/water,
his staff much like a shepherd's crook, but
this time carried for balance and for the rest of it: the
choosing, knowing which eggs, only lovely pale blue,
not the gulls' and terns' brown or buff, then
to lift out, to hurl against the granite,
to punish them for fishing these waters,
to crush under boot or beat with his stick,
two thousand eggs, the cormorants now emitting faint squawks,
flapping their wings over this darkness,
the albumin and yolk, the embryos shining on dull rock,
the small pieces of sky fallen down—Black
as the night waters of a man's dream where he gropes
below the surface, groaning with the old hungers,
the luminescence of his skin covered by something
so thick his arms stroke heavy with it, the water
without end, and no island, no island in sight.

THE HUMMINGBIRD

Marsha De La O

The hummingbird's down, his wings
folded across his back, eyes bright
and beady, brought to this moment,

this dying, here on the concrete as I
am brought to this moment, walking
the strip in front of the mini-mall.

He only wants to be left alone,
no intervention; burning brightly
green over gray watered silk.

His long beak rendered immobile,
dying, seems freakish, an archaic
device, an invention for which

no use could be imagined. His eyes
saw the passersby, saw me, a monster,
Frankenstein lumbering across

the asphalt and all he wants
is some form of solitude, having landed
here in the worst possible place,

a sidewalk in front of a supermarket,
his eyes filled, still, with life,
the plumage settled around him,

and some fierce dignity there, looking
outward at the world, wary, regarding
us as he has so many times before,

weighing motion and color,
whatever comes to him of intent,
poised before the tight opening

of the flower, hovering mid-air
among all the beauty and
all the danger of the world.

I come along, my face
a shambling bearish grief.
I've seen the way they tie a bear

to a post in the village square in central
Asia and set the dogs upon him, his big paws
slapping only so many down as more mount

slashing from behind, hysterical only
for more death, and it doesn't matter whose,
and the bear knowing that things are

bad in those moments before it all
begins and ends, the spectacle, the hounds
baying. Now the children zoom around

the corner, skating closer and closer
to the helpless bird. We all come
to die somewhere, and the question is

Why here? Some disaster or miscalculation,
and you find yourself set down
in the tumult, the mortal

tumult, turning, lacking any
other means, turning what
is left to turn, your regard.

WILD MOTHERS

Eloise Klein Healey

Wild kitty sneaks up my stairs
with two wisps of tiger behind her.
Wild mothers always find me.
Red Tail who lived in my driveway
and that chew-eared thing
who grew old in my carport.
Three bowls of dry food
every day and their tribes
in proscribed circles
waiting for me.
One-legged bluejay, waiting, too.
Lost ocelot hiding in the garage,
escaped cockatoo raucous in the eucalyptus.
Sparrow nesting over my doorway.
Mockingbird in the wisteria.
They find me where the clearing meets
the trees and night and light cross.
I have needed that they weren't mine,
that they would only come that close.

CHANGE OF LIFE

Judith Collas

Her life was okay. Sometimes she wished she
were sleeping with the right man instead of with her dog,
but she never felt she was sleeping with the wrong dog.

GREAT WHITE HERON

Maía

PART ONE

The harp in the rain's
gone silent

Heron's eye inscribes
black zigzag over tobacco gold
of the pond

the head zooms in, the legs lift
slow as the hands of a clock

Wings half-open, white silk umbrella
she spies into her own shadow

hunting the kick
of amphibian, the hot yellow
gleam of carp

All morning, nothing
the bowing rushes, mist curling
off the water

In the afternoon, a few feet
from the pond—under sand willow
deep in kikuyu grass
of Anisq Oyo Park downtown—
gopher pokes a nose out
of his burrow

blinks . . . . . stiletto-beak
thrusts, seizes him!

One two three four
dance steps back to the water
she dips him in the pond, tosses him
down her pretty gullet

Wind-claws riffle
belly and breast feathers

gopher bundled neat in her
gut, slips
deeper
fishy juices solve, render
earthy puzzle of gopher

to whistling
flight

PART TWO

We are walking the streets to keep warm
and to forget hunger

and you say to me *remember
how we used to laugh because we could see
with our own eyes
God had not abandoned this world?*

and you say *now it has happened*

and I am about to answer you
about to say *yes, gone*—I look up

and the great white heron passes over us

rowing east toward the salt lagoon
where I know she still roosts, rosy light
under her wings, skinny legs stretched out
in the wake, no sound but wind

and my eyes open beneath her

and I know the sweet drone
of light crossing over, taut strings
of the senses unable to stop
ringing, ever

and I understand that after we die
we pass like the wind into the hands of strangers
the body of the one beloved

and it's heaven here on earth
an angel standing in the sun, the heron
passing over: white cloud filled with snow
belly dark with bullfrog and snail

the heron hunting
and the heron in flight, rose light
under the wings, calligraphy
of the long long legs and the shooting
arrow of the beak

I haven't answered you
how will I answer?

I could cry at a glimpse of her, cry out
through the throat of that child
who might never see the heron
except in a book or a dream, I could

dance—take a sideways step and wonder
how the leap got into me—dance
where the roads come together, dance
the merciless hunt and the orderly
unfolding of willow leaves, light

unexpected—catch it
the good news, the green flash
once every ten thousand sundowns
catch it—heron catches gopher
quick don't think!

I haven't answered you

I lift my eyes to the rising moon
and the moon rolls back past the heron's claw
and my hand slips around your waist
and you turn to me

and your eyes follow mine
straight up, then east
where the salt marsh lies

and I say to you *Look!*
She is here, She is passing, always passing
into and out of this world

CROWS

Marge Piercy

They give me a bad
reputation, those swart rowers
through the air, heavy winged
and heavy voiced, brass tipped.
Before us they lived here
in the tallest pine. Shortly
after coming I walked in
on a ceremony, the crows
were singing secretly
and beautifully a ritual.
They divebombed me. To make
peace I brought a sacrifice,
the remains of a leg
of lamb. Since then
we have had truce.
Smart, ancient, rowdy and far-
sighted, they use our land
as sanctuary for raiding
where men shoot at them.

They come down, settling like
unwieldy cargo jets, to the bird
food, scattering the
cardinals, the juncos. *God
they're big, I've never seen
them so near a house,*
the guest says. We look

at each other, the crows
and me. Outside
they allow my slow approach.
They do not touch our crops
even in the far garden
in the bottomland. I'm aware
women have been burned
for less. I stand
under the oldest white oak
whose arms coil fat as pythons
and scream at the hunters
driving them back
with black hair coarse and streaming:
Caw! Caw!

THE CHIMPANZEE AT STANFORD

Fran Peavey

One day I was walking through the Stanford University campus with a friend when I saw a crowd of people with cameras and video equipment on a little hillside. They were clustered around a pair of chimpanzees—a male running loose and a female on a chain about twenty-five feet long. It turned out the male was from Marine World and the female was being studied for something or other at Stanford. The spectators were scientists and publicity people trying to get them to mate.

The male was eager. He grunted and grabbed the female's chain and tugged. She whimpered and backed away. He pulled again. She pulled back. Watching the chimps' faces, I began to feel sympathy for the female.

Suddenly the female chimp yanked her chain out of the male's grasp. To my amazement, she walked through the crowd, straight over to me, and took my hand. Then she led me across the circle to the only other two women in the crowd, and she joined hands with one of them. The three of us stood together in a circle. I remember the feeling of that rough palm against mine. The little chimp had recognized us and reached out across all the years of evolution to form her own support group.

THE BEAR STORY

Fran Peavey

I faced the publication of my first book, *Heart Politics,* with a lot of fear. I had written the part of the truth I could find words for, but only the writer knows all the corners she cuts, all the half-truths encompassed in her telling. I dreaded readers criticizing me for all I did not tell, and for the errors that would surface in time. So I decided to go to Idaho, the land of my upbringing, to find the strength to face the publication.

I drove up the Pacific coast and across the Columbia basin into the primitive area of Idaho. I was tired from a long day's travel and decided to put my sleeping bag out in a camping site along the road. Only two sites were filled with people but since it was late I decided the considerate thing would be to pull into a quite separate site so that I would not bother any sleeping people as I set out my bedroll.

I was so tired that I did not even wash before falling asleep. This part of Idaho is so undeveloped that there is no electricity. It was a dark night with little moonlight. The stars twinkled a universal message and I fell asleep quickly and deeply. I was sleeping on my stomach with my hands on either side of my head when I felt something scratching on my left hand. I moved my hand as I awoke and a little squirrel scampered away. Looking over my left shoulder I saw a deer and a bear standing about five feet from the bottom of my sleeping bag.

I wondered if I should be afraid. Mother told me to be afraid of bears. But I don't feel afraid. If this bear were hungry wouldn't it eat the deer? A bear that hangs around with a deer can't be that bad. I finally decided to slowly turn over so I could protect myself with my hands if things turned ugly.

It seemed like a long time that we stared at each other. Probably it wasn't. Finally the bear walked on all fours over to me. I remember its paw being next to my arm—not on the arm, not hurting me, but very much next to my arm. I looked up and realized that the bear was so large that if I had raised my arm up I would not have reached the top of its shoulders. I could not tell whether it was black or brown but it was a dark bear. I was still arguing with myself about how frightened I should be when the bear licked the side of my head. Then he/she licked again. I thought, "This is how a salt lick must feel." Maybe six or seven times the bear licked me. It felt incredibly intimate and erotic. I wanted to put my arms around the bear and roll around holding it closely. But I knew my mother, long dead, would not approve.

Then Bear walked away into the woods with the deer. Finally I felt such a fright that I jumped out of my sleeping bag and scampered into the car, locking all the doors. I shivered for quite a while thinking of what could have happened, and wondering if the bear was coming back with some friends to eat such a good tasting piece of meat. I felt some shame for the deep intimacy I had felt. I wondered if this could be a dream. I felt the gooeyness on the right side of my head and thought that I would sleep on the left side of my head so that if I awoke with my hair still gooey, I would know the experience was not a dream. Finally I went back to sleep.

When I awoke the hair on the right side of my head was very different in consistency than that on my left side. It was dry but thick and stuck to my head.

In my mind I gave the experience many meanings, thought about it a lot. It was such a private affair I didn't want to talk much about it. I expected anyone who heard about it would have doubts about my sanity. I wondered if perhaps I had betrayed my species. I had never known such acceptance from such an exotic animal before.

Each time I give a book talk and feel intimidated, I say, "I wasn't afraid of Bear, why should I be afraid now?" Thank you, Bear.

THE BEAR

Fiz Harwood

A couple of years ago I drove to northern Montana to visit with some Indians. On my way back, I came through Yellowstone National Park. As I was driving out through the southern portal, I noticed there was a lot of traffic. In fact, cars were almost bumper to bumper. Just beyond the park gate a car three cars ahead of me hit a bear. I had seen her coming across the road just before I saw the car throw her clear off to the other side. She was a brown bear, about 250 pounds, and she had two cubs with her. I got out of my car, and without a second thought went right to her as she lay dying by the side of the road. I sat by her as she died. In the woods just above us were her two cubs crying. I sat close beside her, her fur brushing my knees. Encountering an animal who had that wildness in her, completely unlike a domestic animal, was an incredible experience. She died very quietly; I could see the life going out of her. Her eyes misted over and she was dead. I took a tuft of her hair and kept it for a long time. I felt graced to have been in her presence. I went back to the ranger station at the entrance of the park and told the rangers where those two cubs were, close by the side of the road. They assured me that they would take the cubs and care for them until they could be released once again into the wild. The bear's presence lingered on for weeks.

I told this story at a gathering about a year later, and the three men who were present were so upset that I had sat so close to that bear as she died. One by one they approached me privately, each expressing their astonishment that I had been so foolish. How surprising. I had thought my response to the bear completely obvious and natural.

THE DARKNESS IS LIGHT ENOUGH: FIELD JOURNAL OF A NIGHT NATURALIST

Chris Ferris

8:30 a.m. At Holmoak Lane, en route for home. Met a man I know well by sight who told me a fox was snared up on the bank there. At night, going to Ashcroft Woods, I sometimes see badgers cross the tarmac at this point to follow the up-and-over path on the bank and so under the wire. Sure enough, a fox was caught by its hindquarters in a *badger* snare. It was meant to pass over the larger animal's snout and tighten where the slender neck meets the body, but in the smaller creature it had passed straight on to the pelvis. Fortunately, it was not made from cutting wire, but insulating cord. The man returned with a pair of pincers, so whilst he set to on the wire, I kept the little vixen occupied—stroked her head and made the soft contact call. The man was, at first, anxious that the animal shouldn't bite him but I, to my own surprise, found calming this stranger fox quite easy. Gently, with one hand still stroking, I ran the other under her belly and took the strain of the cord, gradually easing her body backwards. Although she would be bruised from her earlier efforts to escape, she wasn't cut. This wire cord was meant to hold and secure, not damage the animal. How beautiful these creatures are—always very interested in foxes unknown to me. My companion remarked that he had seen this type of snare before, fixed at this part of the fence.

   At last she was free and I felt the tension on my hand relax—the man and I grinned at one another. As I gently took my hands away, the one from under her belly felt wet, and glancing down I saw milk on my palm! This was a lactating vixen with cubs to feed. Her sharp little face looked at us briefly, then off she raced—nothing much wrong with her! Halfway across the field, she turned and stared back at us, gave herself a quick shake, then casually trotted away. We scrambled back down the bank together laughing. It's a marvellous feeling, releasing an animal unharmed—and the way that vixen moved, she would soon be back feeding her cubs.

AN INTERVIEW WITH KEIKO'S TRAINERS

E. K. Caldwell

For most people, the thought of having a personal relationship with a great killer whale is the stuff of fantasy and movie magic. For two young animal trainers born and raised in Mexico City, the fantasy became reality when, five years ago, they met Keiko, who was soon to become the most famous orca in the world. These remarkable young women, Karla Corral (age twenty-four) and Renata Fernandez (age twenty-five), were Keiko's exclusive trainers for four years at Reino Aventura, a marine amusement park in Mexico City that purchased Keiko from Marineland in Ontario, Canada.

Originally captured in 1979 in the Atlantic Ocean off Iceland and taken to Saedyrasfnid, an Icelandic aquarium, Keiko was sold to Marineland in 1982 and to Reino Aventura in 1985. A decade later Warner Bros. filmed Keiko for scenes in *Free Willy*, a surprise box-office hit that inspired a new emotional loyalty to killer whales for millions of schoolchildren and adults. After *Life* magazine published a story revealing that Keiko lived in a facility inadequate for his needs, a campaign was launched (with Reino Aventura's sanction) to find a more appropriate "home" and eventually release him back into the wild.

In May 1994 the Earth Island Institute, an environmental and marine mammal advocacy group in San Francisco, determined that the Oregon Coast Aquarium met their criteria: an educational mission; access to an unlimited supply of cold, clean, natural seawater; room to accommodate a huge new pool; and no performing animals. The aquarium constructed a two-million-gallon state-of-the-art tank that was completed and filled with seawater by mid-December 1995. Renata and Karla accompanied Keiko on his historic journey to the Oregon Coast Aquarium on January 7, 1996, hoping to make his transition easier with their presence.

These two dedicated young women, interviewed in February 1996, returned to Mexico City in April. When they talk about leaving Keiko, our interview is punctuated with a visceral grief. It is not "Willy," the movie star whale (who was played almost entirely by special effects robotics) that inspired their fierce loyalty. Their love is for Keiko, their friend.

EK: Has your training been basically from observation, intuition, and trial and error?

Renata: Mostly from intuition. In other places you have a head trainer who is responsible for training new staff. Our head trainer wanted to do it all by himself and be the star of the whole show. Sometimes the guys think that they are in total charge of this aggressive huge powerful animal and they try to be tougher than it is. He thought he was the "real trainer" and we were just girls for the show. He didn't show us anything except a few signals specifically related to the show. When he left, we were put in charge of Keiko. We learned most of all by ourselves. I think we did a nice job because Keiko was very happy with us in Mexico, and he was never happy with anybody else.

EK: When you and Keiko were establishing your communication, how long did it take to go from basic recognition to a trusting and accepting relationship?

Renata: A few weeks after I was there, he came to me and got underneath me so I could be on top of him and ride him—and it was outside of session. This meant that he liked me. He was not doing it for food. He was doing it because he wanted to. He would show me affection when I was around in the pool.

Karla: I had to go there every day and sit by the pool and talk to him and tell him that I really wanted to be his friend. It took about two months. Finally, one day he let me touch him and pet him. From that day on we were good friends and our relationship is very close now.

He is the one who decides whether you can make contact with him. You just sit there and talk and hope he comes near you and after a while he will come and let you touch him and then he leaves. As each day goes by, he will stay there longer. I started telling him about myself, my life and my friends, my problems, my likes and dislikes. He would stay and listen to me talk.

He wanted to be careful and take his time. There were many trainers coming and going every two or three weeks, so he wanted to see if I was really going to stay. When he realized that I was staying, he decided, "OK, maybe I will give her a chance!"

Renata: When I started to actually work with him, our relationship changed. He got tougher. You have to earn his respect. At first working together was hard because he knows you had been giving him your affection for free. Now you won't give it to him unless he works, even if he doesn't want to. He would be lazy sometimes, just like everybody is lazy sometimes. Finally I gained his respect working-wise. Then I didn't even have to give him food because he wanted to work with me.

Sometimes the head trainer would be there and Keiko would work very well during the session because the trainer was very tough, but after the session the guy would try to touch him and Keiko would move back. He drew the line between work and friendship with this guy.

EK: Some scientists claim that these animals don't really have their own feelings and that we project our emotions onto them. Do you believe that?

Renata: We haven't heard that in Mexico. I assure you that Keiko really likes some and not others. These animals are intelligent, so how can we say they don't have feelings of their own? The larger animals like orcas don't have any facial muscles to show facial expressions. But you look in their eyes and you can see what's going on. Their eyes might get red and that can mean that they are mad or getting excited. Or the eyelids come down, "I'm ignoring you."

Karla: Why can we be the only ones who are allowed to have feelings? That's selfish and foolish. If they don't have feelings, why would they have preferences? Keiko likes children. How can he sense the children from the adults if he doesn't have feelings?

EK: In many of the Creation stories of the tribes up here, the humans are not considered the finest or smartest creations. I notice in the Creation stories of the dominant culture, Genesis for instance, the humans are first and always in charge of the animals and the Earth herself. This ties into the belief that animals don't have spirits.

Karla: In Mexico, our ancestors believed animals have feelings and spirits and we still do. It is true in our experience with animals.

Renata: In Mexico we believe that they definitely have spirits. The people who are educated in the school systems say they don't believe it anymore. They often think they have other things to worry about that are more important than nature. But those in small towns and villages know that animals have spirits. Keiko has a spirit. Sometimes I prefer not to say it, because for the people who don't believe it, they sometimes think I'm crazy. I have to learn not to care about their opinions because I know Keiko has a spirit and feelings; he shows them to us.

Karla: I think the greatest gift Keiko has given me is to understand that we are not the only ones who can think. Before working with Keiko, I loved animals, but I didn't know wild animals at all. Now they are real to me.

EK: Do you think women have an easier time communicating with animals?

Karla: Yes. Male trainers fight for power with Keiko. You are *with* the animal, you don't need to fight for power. He will cooperate with you if you cooperate, too. That is something humans do—fight about power.

Renata: It's different with women. Keiko worked for male trainers, but he worked better after the men left. In the last four years when he has been only with us, he worked better, ate better, and started to socialize more with the other animals. Even his papilloma got better. I know I am not the very best trainer because I don't have as much experience as many other people, but I think we have been the best trainers for Keiko.

EK: What do you think it is about women that helps them communicate differently?

Renata: It's the certain way we talk to animals and the touching that is our own female way. You have to praise them and I think it is easier for women to give praise.

I've read about women trainers who said they left the aquariums not because of the shows, but because men try to be tougher than the animals. Since these are big and powerful animals, the Kings of the Sea, many men think, "You're the King, but I'm in charge of you!"

Karla: Women don't care about that. We think women have a special gift for working with animals. I read *The Great Apes*, and the author [Michael Nichols] pointed out that almost all the women who work with great apes, like Jane Goodall, were exceptional with animals. He saw the special bond between women and the animals and recognized the differences from the way he saw men work with animals. I think women have a stronger and more clear connection with animals.

EK: Now, at the Oregon Coast Aquarium, men work with Keiko. How he is adjusting to that change?

Renata: These men here seem very nice and they are experienced, good trainers. Hopefully some women will be orca trainers, too. They have two women who are currently working with the sea lions and the sea otters, but I don't know if they will be working with Keiko.

Karla: I think he is enjoying working with the males here because, after all, he is a male. He likes to play rough sometimes and guys can do that. He is very aware that he can hurt Renata and me more easily.

In terms of training and understanding, I definitely think he prefers women. We like to sit and talk with him and pet him, while the guys are louder and more aggressive. We are more like mothers, and even though he is a huge animal, sometimes he needs to be babied, too.

I do think they are more open to women here, and that eventually they will give some females the opportunity to work with Keiko.

EK: Do you think Keiko will go back to the ocean? Karla, you mentioned you think he is completely institutionalized.

Karla: It is too early to determine if he will be able to survive in the wild. He's been in captivity for too long. If we were talking about a whale who had been in captivity for five years, then I know for sure he could adapt back to the ocean. But we're talking about seventeen years of captivity here, with only maybe two years in the wild. He is also too kind and mellow. Right now it is hard for me to believe that he will be a good killer whale in the wild. Keiko is not aggressive. That's my biggest concern about his release. But I would love to see him be with his family.

Renata: Right now we're trying to train Keiko to hunt food. It will take a long time, not because he isn't smart enough to do it, but he has been captive all his life.

If Keiko becomes fully recovered and goes into the sea, I would be so happy. He is the animal I love most, like a friend or a brother. My feelings for him are very strong. But the best thing is going to be whatever is best for him. It might mean being in captivity all his life. And if he goes free, then I would be very glad, but it may not happen.

EK: Would a female whale accept him to parent her baby? How about the pod she is from?

Renata: There might not be a female who will want Keiko because of the background that he has. He has not learned to socialize with whales.

EK: If he fathered a baby, would that give him a family that would accept him?

Karla: It has never happened like that. Orcas have a family structure that is very tight and it is based around the mother. Pods don't mix except to mate or hunt.

But maybe he could mate with a transient whale because their pods tend to be more loosely structured. It would be wonderful if he could join up with one of them, wouldn't it?

EK: What kinds of danger would he be in if he is released too early?

Karla: He likes to be petted and touched too much. One of the big dangers I see for him is his chasing boats so people would touch him. People don't know very much about orcas and they could be frightened and think he is coming to hurt them or take their salmon catch or something. People have a tendency to kill animals that scare them. We have to think about that.

Renata: If the other whales don't accept him, he might die. They are emotional. Sometimes they kill themselves because they are alone and unhappy.

EK: What are your feelings about public display facilities? Do you think there is a difference in those with performance aspects?

Karla: We need facilities for public display. We have to teach people to get to know whales and love them. The only way we can protect the animals is by knowing them and having some idea what they feel and think. That's why I think some animals will need to be in captivity. But not everything has to be a show. Unfortunately, the only way to teach some people about how intelligent the animals are is by performing, but hopefully rehabilitation facilities will grow.

EK: What do you think is the hardest thing about the public display facilities?

Karla: There is not enough information given to the people. People need true information about the animals, like where they come from, what they eat, how long they live, and about their family. That is much more important than doing a performance that is not real at all.

Renata: Sometimes Keiko doesn't want to work because he feels bad. People start whistling and hollering because they have paid their money and they want Keiko to perform. You are asking them to please understand that he is not a robot. He's just an animal and he feels bad just as any human can feel bad, so please understand that he is not available now and cannot work. They get angry and impatient because they paid money and they want that show now. So, you have to choose what is best for the animal or what is best for the public.

EK: Do you have any ideas about why some whales are chosen to be in captivity? Are they just unlucky to get captured? Some say they are "ambassador animals" to humans.

Karla: I think they are the chosen ones to teach the people. If all the whales were really aggressive, people would think they had to kill them.

Keiko gives a different image of killer whales. Look how kind and gentle he is. I don't know if he really wants to teach or not, but he generates love in people. He is a star because he reaches inside people to the place where there is love.

Renata: I wouldn't say they are ambassadors. We definitely have to learn about these animals and we have learned more about animals in captivity than in the wild, although people do study them in the wild.

Sometimes people give all their attention to Keiko, while in the sea there are animals who are dying every day because of pollution and because of people. There are people who throw food from boats for dolphins and these dolphins come too close to the propellers. These people act self-righteous, saying, "Well, I don't need to see animals in captivity because I go to my bay and give food to the animals in the wild." But they're making these wild animals dependent on boats and often they are killed by the propellers. I've seen a dolphin who had half of his face cut off by a boat propeller because he was trying to reach the boat for food.

Some people would do better to take care of the animals in the wild instead of just focusing on "Willy" (because you know they call Keiko "Willy" now). We are learning from Keiko and applying these studies to other whales. If an orca is sick and you want to help him, don't just take him out of the water and into captivity. Learn ways to cure him out there in the sea.

Karla: I have learned amazing things from Keiko in our time together, things that I want to talk about, but can't talk about very often because many people, especially the media, do not believe you. Maybe the women who are going to be in this book will have a better understanding of what I am saying because of their experiences. There was a time when I had to leave for one month to go on vacation. I sat with Keiko and told him all about it. I was really feeling sad and started crying. When he cries he makes this little noise and bobs his head a certain way. When I started crying, he backed up a little bit and started crying, too. I couldn't believe it! Then I said, "Enough of this crying" and he stopped crying and I stopped crying. Then he came and let me touch him again. I was shocked. That experience in my life I will never forget because I knew he was feeling what I was feeling. I went to one of the trainers and told him and he said, "No, it must have been a coincidence." It was like he tried to take it away from being what it was.

Once we were playing in the pool. Keiko was pushing me around and playing with me, but he got bored and left me. I got mad about him ignoring me, so I started playing dead in the water. He thought I was hurt and he came back really slowly, and I could hear his breathing coming closer and closer. He started pushing me. I kept playing dead. He pushed me all the way to the platform and up out of the water. And this is not like the movie, this was real life! I was so amazed when he did this that I got up and started kissing him. My mom cries every time I tell this story, but it was really something unique and showed me that he cared about me and was worried that I was hurt. I will never forget that. It will always be one of my best memories of Keiko.

EK: Considering your close relationship, how are you preparing yourself and Keiko for your return to Mexico?

Renata: I don't want to think about it. I don't want to prepare. I've had many bad things in my life already, really tough times, so I know I can handle this one. We are doing sessions with the new trainers with Keiko so he will get to know them and get used to them.

Karla: I try not to think about it because it just makes me cry. You have to realize that Keiko has been the most important part of my life and the best thing I have experienced. I left my family, my boyfriend, my friends, everything, to come and be with him here. I don't think I will ever have another experience like this, even if I work with another whale.

He is such a good friend. But I know it is the best thing for him to be here, although I want to say it is very important that he have at least one companion animal so he does not become too lonely and depressed. Orcas are very social.

EK: Will you come back to visit Keiko?

Renata: I would like to, but for me it is very expensive. But I will try.

Karla: Yes. I could never not come and visit him.

Editor's Note: In January 1996, Keiko was moved to a special pool in Newport, Oregon, where he experienced natural seawater for the first time in fourteen years. Since 1985, Keiko has not seen another whale. If his rehabilitation continues to succeed as it has so far and if the Iceland government allows him to return to his native waters, Keiko will be the first captive whale to be restored to the open sea.

MIND IN THE WATERS

Joan McIntyre

The whale rolls unseen through the water, steady, sure, alert. On the surface a small group of people drift in a rubber boat, wait for the appearance of the whale. The whale rolls like a great wheel, turning over smoothly, silently. It is night. There is nothing to see except the calm dark surface of the sea. Then the water parts, reveals the rolling back. The blowhole of the whale opens and the sound of her breathing deepens the silence. She continues her long steady motion, rolling back into the sea from where she came.

She knows more about us than we know about her. She knows exactly where we are and all our changes of direction. She relates her course to ours, changing direction as the swells carry us into her pathway. We sit silently in the rubber boat wondering why we are here, and what we have come to see. We see only the flat calm sea, the rolling back, the glassy slick as she disappears again beneath us.

The whale turns in the water, moonlight reflects off her back, phosphorescence leaves silvered trails behind her as she circles the lagoon. She is looking for her mate, answering his long deep calls. She turns seaward to meet him.

Later, lying on the warm sand of the shore of the gulf we hear their deep breathing in the distance, like hearing the sea herself breathe, the breathing of all creatures that live, the deep strong exhalations condensing sound in the night stillness. The sound of their breathing comforts us during the night; we wake to listen, then drift back into sleep, aware of the love-making of the great whales. We drift into our dreams.

As I recollect the whales, I realize how strange they are to me—these enormous, cumbersome, yet supremely graceful beings that move like monsters out of the past, beneath the surface of the sea. I envy them, envy their life and the ease of their connections. I wish to be of them, yet my thoughts, my ideas, become obstacles to the possibility of that experience.

This is the mind I have always believed existed somewhere. The deep calm mind of the ocean, connected to body, living *in* the world, not looking out at it. Surrounded by the gentle clicking of each other's sound, these creatures drift and dive, carve shining bubbled circles in the still water, move like dream ghosts out of the sea's unchanging past. Not changing the world around them—only listening, touching, eating, being. It seems enough.

VI: RESTORATION

Bringing Back the Animals

To restore a species to its rightful habitat is to return animal and human to a natural order. We humans do not have the power or knowledge to actually restore an animal, in the sense of bringing it back into existence— but we can begin to give back what we have taken away: by not hunting or casually ignoring a species slipping into extinction, by actively committing ourselves to other animals to help restore them to their proper place in our own shared habitat. The women activists and writers in this section are all participating in various restorations.

Reneé Askins devoted much of her life to bringing the wild wolf back to its natural habitat of Yellowstone National Park in 1995, where it has flourished against all odds; by the year 2000, it is hoped that the wolf in Yellowstone will no longer be an endangered species as it is all over the world. Christine Jurzykowski preserves a small Texas savannah to help restore antelopes, rhinos, giraffes, elephants, and cheetahs—living free from hunters and poachers. Gillian van Houten, who lives on an animal preserve in South Africa, moved her family to another country for more than a year so that the hand-raised lion Shingalana could join a pride of her own animal peers.

We are all born into a world lonelier than ever for animal peers. These other animals have been injured, decimated, disappeared. As women, we can say we will help to restore these animals. And by doing so, restore our bond, our shared and intimate nature.

COMING HOME

Deena Metzger

It is forbidden to cause any suffering to any living creature.
This is biblical law.

—BAVA METZIA 32B, DEUTERONOMY RABBAH 6:1[1]

I look around the small cottage where I live in Topanga, a rural area in the Santa Monica mountains, and wonder who I am and how I came to live here in this way. Animal images predominate. Bones, fetishes, totems. Mayumi Oda's Kwan Yin as the Goddess who gave names to the animals presides over my study. On another wall, there is a painting of a blue bull by Maureen Piper. Everywhere there are photographs of Timber Wolf, who lived with me for fourteen years, and Owl and Isis, the hybrid timber and arctic wolves who are my companions now.

I was not prepared for these passions and concerns. My early life followed the sorrowful trajectory that holds that human evolution requires us to separate from animals and the natural world. Still there was a hidden stream in my childhood; I wasn't always aware of it but I seem to have followed it unknowingly. It was similar to the underground stream I detect in my tradition. Now I am trying to come home. I am sixty. This is not how I had imagined my life.

How does one change? The journey toward relatedness is arduous even when some of the forms it takes are easy and pleasing. Living in a natural setting, watching jays, finches, towhees, crows streak across the land, listening to the songbirds, is joyous and reminds me that we live among each other. But I want to be more than a tourist in the natural world; I want to change my habits of Western mind. This means shattering the ego and ideas of species superiority and privilege. This means recognizing animals as other intelligent beings who may understand humans better than we understand them and who live far better than we do within the net of Indra, the shimmering ecological relationships between all things.

[1]Shlomo Pesach Toperoff, *The Animal Kingdom in Jewish Thought.*

This means creating alliances with animals, though they most likely mourn and rage against the human species for the ways our activities increasingly circumscribe, diminish, and threaten their circumstances, possibilities, and lives.

I am not alone in such an endeavor. A change of consciousness is taking hold in our culture, sustained to a great extent by the insights of indigenous peoples. Returning to appropriate and respectful relationships with the animal world has, for me, meant returning to an original but suppressed tradition of my people, stumbling on hidden truths. Even as the sacred books encourage separation from the animal world, they also contain the evidence of an early totemic, even shamanic, connection; that which is so profoundly rejected speaks to an earlier affiliation.

Change has also meant recognizing a series of betrayals I have perpetrated and learning through my grief. So much is at stake; we must be more conscious. What began as a spiritual inclination has become an ethical obligation.

For almost a year I have been doing a meditation without being conscious of it as meditation. Each day I choose an animal from among the rabbits, quail, mourning doves, turkey vultures, crows, falcons, hawks, deer, coyotes, bobcats, foxes, cougars with whom I share the land, and quietly attempt to free my mind so that I can recognize the unique and distinct intelligence as equal to mine. I am working against the assumption of human preeminence and entitlement. I try to see myself and the world through the animal's eyes while respecting the animal's subjectivity.

But I may never understand. Each of us inhabits a separate and wondrous universe whose life and vision has its own dynamic pattern and makes its own maverick sense. We are always facing the implacable presence of the animal other; we can't ever assume that we know, understand, or see the other as she or he is. Still, patient and respectful observation may bring two distinct worlds into empathetic dialogue, may move us closer to what we are willing and able to reveal to each other.

I attempt to make myself naked in the presence of the animal while refraining from seeing myself in the other. This is not only a strategy. To respect the other's subjectivity, one must allow oneself to be shaped by the other's contours and in order to do this one must get out of the way before one can see the reality that is beyond oneself.

And here is a paradox: One cannot really know an other without intimacy. Detached, objective observations alone leave a surface upon which it is too easy to project one's own image or fantasies. In intimacy, one respectfully interacts with the other, invites the penetration of the other, enters into a common effort, and then the strange and distinct contours of self and other become more apparent. Needless to say, this means putting myself in jeopardy when for the last centuries, the animal has been at risk.

Why do I ask for this connection? I ask out of desire and eros. There is within me an increasing and powerful longing to live in what I call sacred relationship, in what Buddhists might call right relationship to all beings. And because I hear a call to us from the animals and I am trying to heed this call.

The little girl I was loved animals. Love animals. How easy it is to say. But love is difficult and particular. Love implies highly nuanced, shifting, complex feelings. Love can be sweet, violent, obsessive, detached, constant or intermittent, plodding or stellar. Love can be blind or accurate as a laser. It can torture and it can redeem. Each variation is shaped by the particularities of the parties involved. And love implies relationship.

So love for the animal . . . ? Who is the animal? Captive bundles of warm, moving fur usually called dog who are willing or compelled to trade animal freedom and the exercise of animal intelligence for reliable bowls of food of our choosing served regularly at our convenience? Loving these bundles but conditionally: if they lived with us in this way but not in that way, if they were independent in these ways but not those ways, if they obeyed . . . and so on. Meanwhile smaller mammals who were not so happy to sleep under my bed, who would not refrain from scampering through the pantry, who would not come when I called and preferred to breed in the sock drawer were somehow excluded from this satisfying universal: Love animals. My elders taught me that bestowing love upon animals was a benevolent gesture from a superior being to an inferior entity and that one had to establish barriers to protect humans from animal filth and danger.

It has taken a long time to be properly humbled by the irrefutable evidence that I have been living much of my life in the presence and territory of other, distinct, awesome, mighty intelligences without having any but the most rudimentary understanding of the meaning of their individual and species lives which I have, nevertheless, so deeply violated. This cultural and historic obliviousness, which sometimes overwhelms even those traditions that hold otherwise, has now brought all of us to the brink of destruction. So even if I weren't personally compelled on this quest, even if it hadn't opened up worlds of beauty and interest, even if I weren't motivated by irrepressible passions and curiosity, it would behoove me to ask the animals: Who are you?—and to continue to adjust my life according to what I hope will be an increasing ability to understand their answers.

Several nights ago I dreamed an elephant, the sensuousness of her stride, her lustiness and passion, the glory of her sense of her own beauty, the weight of her age, her subtle and intricate relationships with her daughters, sons, grandchildren, members of her tribe, her fears for the savannah, and her humiliation and rage for her kin who had been hunted and killed during her lifetime or, as officials call it, "culled," and for those of her beloveds who have been kidnapped, enslaved, and bred in public captivity. When I awakened inside my relatively puny body, remembering the knowledge I had briefly held, I felt bereft but strangely comforted by the final image of the dream. As I was separated from her, I was confronted by a great unblinking elephant eye that transmitted everything I had experienced in a wink. And now I return to that memory. See the eye. It flickers. I receive. Now, it's gone. . . .

I have been reading about captive elephants, how these exceedingly intelligent beings who have created complex social and cultural systems have been violently separated from their own people, chained for hours, controlled through beatings and metal hooks called anises, then trained to perform inane "tricks" like stepping onto a small stool or raising their trunks on cue. These elephants are going berserk, rampaging, turning against their trainers, trying to break out of the ring. A rash of such activities recently. I'm caught again by the elephant's eye. I try to understand. We have recently discovered that elephants can communicate over long distances through the means of subsonic calls. Are elephants even more skilled and intelligent than we have been willing to imagine? Might these uprisings indicate that they are communicating with each other though separated by continents? Have we, in the arrogance of our oppositional thumb, isolated ourselves from a web of intelligence whose development and extent we cannot even begin to imagine?

The lives of most animals are threatened by human behavior. The majority of animals are enslaved or hunted, are confined to small preserves and zoos, or are exterminated as in the current tragedy of 4.5 million cows awaiting the crematorium because they suffer from mad cow disease. And what, we might ask, drives the cows mad?

One of the answers is telling: What seems to have caused the disease in cattle has been adding animal products, raw brain and spinal cord from sheep infected with scrapie to the food of these *herbivores*. Ultimately, then, the human predilection to manipulate nature is one cause of this disease in cows. Writing this in April 1996, I learn that 165,000 cows have so far been cremated. The progress is slow, a professor tells me, because there are not enough crematoriums. As he says this we both pause—the Nazis also felt themselves stymied by not having enough crematoriums.

I look back and see the long and difficult road of coming to consciousness. I have lived through my people's flight from profound and complex interchange with animals to the current global frenzy of destruction, domination, consumption, and utilization until now, finally, I find myself wearily coming home again, thankfully clearer of these imprinted habits of mind and able to see things closer to what may be possible: a community of animals, including humans, who live together as peers and sometimes companions. At the very least, I must begin by communicating my deep sorrow. Yes, I think that is a proper beginning: Let us, human and animal, human animal and nonhuman animal, woman and animal, sit down together to mourn.

Behind the history of my childhood is another history, the Judeo-Christian history that dominates the minds of most Westerners at this time. Present but transparent like shades in Hades, unacknowledged animals float through this history, mostly as symbols and images, but also as beings to which we were once connected. The sacred texts are ambiguous. Sometimes the animals are honored, sometimes despised. God sends a dove to Noah and ravens feed Elijah. Rachel is a ewe and Leah is an antelope. Lilith has little owl feet. Balaam's ass can see the angels that Balaam cannot see.

One of the first animals mentioned is Snake, who appears in the Garden of Eden in a despised form as tempter, the enemy of God. Behind this image is the early image of Lucifer, light, the beloved of God, and also the Seraphs, depicted as snakes before they were revisioned as angels. Behind these is a series of Mother goddesses and their snake familiars or in their snake manifestations including the Egyptian, Cretan, Akkadian, and Babylonian snake goddesses. Eve, Hawah, mother of all things, derives her name from *hawa* to instruct and *heywa*, serpent.

Eve and Adam were given the task of naming the animals. In the Hebrew tradition, saying The Name, Calling The Name, Naming has enormous spiritual power; is, perhaps, the supreme ritual act. It is possible that this event also refers to the invocation of the animal spirit or the God in Animal form. To imagine this as also true is to exit the myth of hierarchy and enter a myth of alliance and peership. This is the path of reparation.

As a Levite, a member of the Hebrew tribe of Levi, my ancestry has been traced back to Leviathan, the Great Serpent also referred to as "fleeing" serpent *(nahash bariah)* or "crooked" serpent *(nahash aqala-ton)*.[2] But my contemporaries do not acknowledge that we are snake clan, that Jewish medallions of the first and second centuries represented Jehovah as a serpent god, that Nehustan, a name for the God of Moses, is the Great Serpent. In Numbers xxi. 8–9, God orders Moses to erect a brazen serpent to heal those who were bitten by fiery serpents. As it says in John 3:15: And as Moses lifted up the serpent in the wilderness, even so must the Son of Man be lifted up.[3]

A rattlesnake extended itself across the threshold to my house when, as a single woman whose grown children were living elsewhere, I first moved to Topanga. I panicked. I sprained my wrist chopping off the snake's head with an ax. The wrist never fully healed but I don't lament the wound of snake; it reminds me of how I used to be. I took an ax against my totem animal—a grave transgression. I recognize the violation—and reparation.

Reading between the lines, we see the profound connection Western peoples had with animals, that they saw them as equals or greater than themselves. Once animals carried the manna of God, were manifestations of God. But as we became increasingly anthropocentric, various strategies of domination were enacted against the animal world. Where the sky gods prevailed, transcendence of earth, body, and life was frequently valorized and nature, including animals, was abhorred. The human animal insisted it was not animal. In other instances, the human was elevated far above the animal in order to undermine paganism and earth-centered religions. In all these cases, the animal, regarded as stupid, brutish, or evil, is a construction of the human imagination. This unceasing and unacknowledged war against animals is still enacted in daily cruelty and increasing violence toward animals in general. The modern response to Darwin has been a terrified lunge away from the reality of our animal natures through deriding animal attributes and then scorning the animal within ourselves. The terror of the body or sexuality are signs of this. Animals are valued in the dominant culture, if at all, not with the respect due to ancestors, but for the ways they serve humans. By virtue of our supposed superiority, intelligence, divine right, or power—our "fitness"—we use, subjugate, torture, exploit, devour the other.

Reading the Old and New Testaments can be like breaking a code. These sacred books chronicle Western disconnection from the animal world

---

[2]Robert Graves and Raphael Patai, *Hebrew Myths: The Book of Genesis.*
[3]Barbara Walker, *The Woman's Encyclopedia of Myths and Secrets.*

even as they preserve the evidence of earlier spiritual connections. The Old Testament stories of twins and brothers, as in other traditions, encode the essential unity of all the worlds. The light and the dark brother, like Jacob the smooth man and Esau the hairy man, represent the brother in this world and the brother in the other world, with the maligned Esau carrying animal nature and their kinship holding the mystery of their inseparability.

These stories echo the profound knowledge of many indigenous peoples that humans and animals participate in twinship, each human and animal having his or her brother or sister in the other realm, their fates and lives interlocked. The familiar interpretation of conflict between hunter-gatherers, pastoral people, and agriculturists offers only one understanding of the Old Testament. Cain's offering of the fruits of the field is not as acceptable as Abel's burnt offering of the ram. This may mean that the invading pastoral people are demonizing the resident matriarchal agricultural people. It may also indicate that Cain has forgotten his animal twinship.

Several years ago during the High Holidays, my husband and I were studying the Torah portion where Abraham is required to offer his son Isaac as a sacrifice to the sky God Yahweh, Jehovah, associated with the ram. When Abraham demonstrated his willingness he was given a ram, his totem animal, to substitute on the fiery altar. Esoterically, the son, Isaac, and the ram are twins and become one in God. The sacrifice is made sacred by being offered to the holy, and, accordingly, the worlds of human and animal are unified. Or the ram, the animal form of God, is substituted for Isaac the human form of the ram, and the sacrifice is a covenant of unification. Here, as in the Cain story, orthodox understandings prohibit understanding that spirit may manifest as human, animal, or animal god. The same play between the historic, the literal, and the mystical exists in the Christ story. It is one of the Mysteries that Christ *is* the lamb and that the true nature of reality is contained within the dance of human as lamb and spirit as dove.

The year that I recognized this, I protested the literal interpretation of this Torah portion by refusing to celebrate the sacrifice of the real animal for the real human. "It's time," I said to the Rebbe, "to stop sacrificing the animal for the sake of the human."

In contemporary times, the sacred itself is often sacrificed. In 1969, I came upon a Cuchulain festival in Ireland. Five high school beauty queens seated around a caged pure white mountain goat that had supposedly never seen a human being were paraded around the town square in a horse-drawn cart. Traditionally, the scapegoat, carrying the sins of the village, is to be driven back up to the mountain. This time, however, the goat became the mascot of the U.S. Navy football team. The totem was reduced to a trinket.

Returning to kinship with animals is an exercise of heart and mind. The stories that were emptied of their sacred relationships are to be filled again. But in all this we cannot forget the real animal in its real and endangered habitat who exists in this real and treacherous world. It is so easy to fall into the thrall of spirit animal and forget the real.

It is not simple, our life with animals. As we seclude ourselves in increasingly lifeless cubicles, we forget that we live among them. Human prestige increases by separating itself from other life-forms. This isolation diminishes our lives and destroys the lives of animals. It is not only that we withdraw but that we withdraw the land with us. Or we poison it. One way or another we render it useless to them. And yet we are so dependent upon them. Their lives sustain us. They instruct us as well.

When I look back I realize how much I have learned through animals, their images, and the way they live in our imagination. I was always fascinated by tales of people who spoke the languages of animals and birds and secretly hoped to become one. *The Burgess Books of Animals* expanded my ideas of possibility and interrelationships. Then *Black Beauty* taught me politics. That book was my primer on oppression and domination. But as I grew up, human language took precedence as did my concerns about human society and human suffering. Animal languages and animal suffering slipped to the background.

Of course, I retained sweet feelings for animals, real and fictional, but these figures were incorporated into the hierarchy of sovereign and subject. The deeper lessons of noninterference and coexistence were to come when as an adult I became conscious of the behavior I now grieve. Coming, finally, to see the animal as an equal, as a life valuable in itself, I am forced to review actions that were innocent then but are heinous now. Not guilt, but shame, helps me move forward with more consciousness, evaluating each future activity with this sorrowful knowledge from my past.

This is not a confessional. I list some of my misdeeds because they are common ordinary acts resulting from ignoring interdependence, from insisting that humans are superior to animals and that human life takes precedence.

I had turtles with painted backs and insanely bored goldfish who swam interminably around tiny bowls. Crying because I had spent the morning feeding the cats, kittens, dogs, puppies, mice, tarantula, tortoise, fish, and chicken that had somehow come to live with me and my sons, I flushed several tiny mice down the toilet in a paroxysm of desperation and

frustration when two mice, a gift to my sons, exploded to village propor-
tions. I lied to my sons and they also knew the truth.

I used insecticide. I drowned snails. I trapped mice and rats, breaking
their necks. I ate meat, chicken, eggs, fish without concern about the lives
the animals had lived first or the method of their captivity or death. I did
not educate myself about animal research or experimentation. I applauded
at circuses that were my favorite form of entertainment, rivaling only visits
to the zoo. I sent a dog who'd been given to me back to the animal "shelter" because she was old and didn't please me.

When I was unable to imagine keeping my son's beloved wolf,
Loba—though Timber Wolf stayed with me—once we moved away, I
gave her to an animal trainer without realizing what my son would suffer,
what Loba and Timber would suffer separated from each other, or what
Loba might endure in that environment. This was the injury that I inflicted and afterward carried within myself until the unremitting pain of
that betrayal brought me to understand what I had done and caused me
to reassess my behavior in terms of animals in general. The pain of it is
still as extreme as if I had given up for adoption one child but not another
and then, additionally, had given her to someone whose child-rearing
practices I had come to abhor.

My history with animals has been erratic, filled with moments of insight followed by moments of blindness, and yet I see that it progressed
inexorably away from what would be expected given that I was born in a
suburb of New York to traditional Jewish parents whose concerns were
not with the natural world. It was considered quite exotic that my father,
as a young man, had made a trip to the western forests and had himself
photographed standing on a redwood bridging a chasm. Coming from a
tiny Russian village, he had a longing for nature that he actively suppressed with other passions that could have no place in his American life.
The natural world permitted him was his garden, which he tended faith-
fully, and a few weekends in bungalow colonies in the Catskills, a luxury
he once or twice was able to provide for my mother.

Ironically, I gave Loba away when I moved to a rural area. My son
would be away at school and I feared I couldn't manage Loba on my
own. But was it that I could not yet imagine this life? I certainly didn't
realize Timber would be able to run free here. For the first days, I led him
with a leash about this relatively wild land and then, laughing at myself,
took the leash off. Somehow I came to see that he would negotiate the
territory, not terrorize the neighbors or their animals. There were a few
instances in which he got into trouble. Once a neighbor complained that
he was trying to break down the door of a shed where a female dog in heat
was sequestered. "I'll talk to him," I said. It must have sounded humorous

but it represented a change of consciousness. There was nothing I could do but talk with Timber because I could no longer confine him.

Another time Timber got in a tussle with a neighbor's goat. The neighbor scared him away with a shotgun. Timber stayed away from that house for several years. Then one day when furniture was being delivered, Timber followed the men into the house and pissed on the new couch.

Timber seemed to forgive me for separating him from Loba. He became my companion. I was a counselor. I watched Timber discern my patients' needs and come to them, pushing open the door from the outside, laying his head quietly in their lap, or laying down by their feet, when they experienced grief or pain too great to be met or comforted by a human. His intuition was infallible. His entrance into the room was often a sign. I began to rely on him. For almost two years, a feral woman who was living in a trailer on my property would fall asleep, wherever she was, anywhere on the land. Timber always found her, slept beside her, turning her every hour to see that she was alive. He was with her whenever she was in great pain, her constant companion until she no longer needed him. When I was at a loss for how to be with her, he was gentle and present, jostling her out of the deepest depressions.

But she was not his sole concern. He appeared, after having been gone for hours, the moment a friend finished digging a grave for his beloved dog. Timber buried the dog with his nose in the way that Isis, his companion, would years later bury him.

It is not hyperbole to say Timber was my teacher. He took me across the boundary between human and animal. He began to teach me his language. He taught me that there were more worlds and dimensions than I had dreamed or imagined. By the time he died, we all called him the Buddha wolf, and his teaching did not stop with his death.

Some years ago, Brenda Peterson took me to visit three belugas that she had befriended at the aquarium at Point Defiance Zoo in Tacoma, Washington. As circumstances prevented us from entering the pool area proper, we found ourselves alone in front of the curved glass wall of the pool in which the whales are confined. The day before we had howled for hours with the wolves at Wolf Haven, a sanctuary in Washington State. Instinctively, I placed my lips against the glass to hum to the whales. After a few minutes, two of the belugas, Shikku and Inuk, began swimming back and forth behind the glass wall. The third whale, Mauyak, was swimming morosely at the far end of the pool with the red rubber buoy she had been given as a substitute for the stillborn calf she had just delivered.

Brenda joined in the humming. The song entered the water. Once I watched two lovers from different countries in an airport permanently separated by a glass desperately running their hands alongside each other's. With the same passion to traverse the humanly constructed wall of glass, Brenda and I reached toward the belugas.

It was obvious that the sounds we were making did touch, perhaps entered, the whales in a precise and substantial communication, as if the sounds were hands. Modulating the tones, harmonizing them with our thoughts, we were touching the whales and speaking with them through our sounds. Children passing through the area stopped, fascinated. We brought the children into the humming. Soon the entire gallery area was ahum. After thirty minutes, when Brenda and I were again almost alone before the glass, the two whales began sounding back to us, and I was physically aware of the sonar entering my body.

I knew that whales, like dolphin, could "read" my body with their sonar. I did not know that I could enter their bodies with my own sound. Nor could I imagine then what Brenda meant when she declared, "Now the whales are imprinting *you* with their sonar." A few months later I found myself in a state of extreme unease after reading about proposed experiments that threaten deep-diving mammals including blue and gray whales. The Acoustic Thermometry of Ocean Climate Program [ATOC] would allegedly test global warming by transmitting loud, low-frequency rumbles for a duration of twenty minutes every four hours for ten years across the Pacific Ocean, an experiment that could seriously damage ocean ecology. The theory is that instruments would register infinitesimally small changes in the time it would take for a signal to cross a warming ocean. In the meantime, the sound waves could well disrupt the feeding, breeding, and navigation patterns of those animals who depend upon sound to negotiate their lives.

As it happened, two whales were found dead near the test area within a very short time after the commencement of testing. Officially, it was assumed that the deaths were unrelated to the tests.

My alarm was extreme and felt personal. The whales had indeed imprinted me. We were beginning to communicate with each other.

The next summer I came upon a dead squirrel, a road kill, and stopped my car to bury it. Later than afternoon as I was returning from a hike in the forest, I saw the white-frosted tail and tasseled ears of an Abert's squirrel as it climbed up a ponderosa pine to peer down at me from one of the branches. Instinctively, I called aloud, "I'm sorry about your friend, but I am glad that you are so very much alive."

As Squirrel continued to look at me as if it understood, it seemed polite to continue the conversation and so, remembering my experience with the beluga, I began to hum quite loudly. When I came to the end of my breath, I stopped. Squirrel remained fixed on the branch, eyeing me, silent. I hummed again. Squirrel seemed transfixed. I continued making the sound. When I stopped, Squirrel peered at me as if waiting for me to begin again. I did. This went on a very long time.

When I couldn't maintain this posture any longer, I began to walk away very slowly and quietly. I was afraid it would respond, of course. If it did, the world I lived in would shatter. And, also, I hoped it would.

When the tree was behind me, I heard the sound. Squirrel had come around the tree to another branch closer to me and uttered its own distinct sound, something between a bark, a yip, and a cheep. I stopped. And turned around and hummed again. And stopped. Squirrel made its sound—*chirp*. I made mine. Squirrel responded. And so we went on for another ten minutes or so. Then I eased myself down onto an earthen bank, the two of us sounding to each other.

When I changed the pitch of the hum, Squirrel responded. Squirrel seemed to prefer the higher tones. Once Squirrel made a distinctly higher tone and I followed suit. Once, I changed the tone and Squirrel followed suit. Soon, as we were chasing each other up the scales, Squirrel began to move up and down the tree.

I knew what was coming. I watched Squirrel come down the trunk, go up again, then come down to the ground. Then Squirrel sat up on its haunches and tapped its paws. Instinctively I tapped back. Squirrel bounded back up the tree, sprinting onto the one dead branch sticking out perpendicular to the trunk. We were now about ten feet from each other. Squirrel came to the tip of the limb and looked at me. Tapping, Squirrel made a new sound, deeper and rounder, hollow. *Croc croc*. I tapped my hands. Squirrel made its sound. I imitated and came closer. And so we spoke together: *tap* tap, *croc* croc, *chirp* hum, and so on.

Squirrel went up and down the tree again. Each time, Squirrel came lower and lower, swirling about the trunk, stopping to look at me at each turn. Finally Squirrel came down to the ground directly in front of me and sat up on its haunches, tapping once more. I tapped again with a distinct desire to communicate homage. For several minutes more, Squirrel stayed at the base of the tree, slipping around the tree, facing me, traversing it again, facing me for several minutes. Then, as I became aware of the light dimming, Squirrel glanced at me timidly and, as if we didn't know each other, crossed the path and disappeared into the undergrowth, wildflowers, daisies, and columbine. I looked at my watch. We had been in conversation for almost an hour. The sun had set.

On the spring equinox 1996, I was at Cook Harbor on the Big Island of Hawaii where dolphins and whales come to birth and raise their young. Each day the dolphins come and each day dozens of people climb into kayaks and follow them to the bay. I wanted to go with them and I did not know if I should. One morning I went out to the point and sat on a tree limb that was bent down into the waves. The dolphins were close by. In my mind I called out to them and within a moment I felt pangs of grief as strong as if I had been struck by lightning. I found myself sobbing with what seemed to be the pain of the dolphins who were unable to escape the constant presence, curiosity, and need of the human. During the course of the week, I also went out several times in a kayak. On one occasion, I jumped into the water and saw the dolphins swimming below me and then away. I felt the enormity of my longing to be recognized by them and climbed back into the kayak a bit ashamed. Perhaps it was not appropriate for me to swim with them. My loyalty and concern were to be enacted by staying away. This is as profound a teaching as I have ever received.

But I do not generalize from this experience. Virginia Coyle tells me that she has met a Russian physician who delivers babies underwater in a cove where dolphins gather. It is, he says, not unusual for a dolphin to midwife the birth of the human child and that afterward the child and the dolphin seem to bond for life. We have come to a time in human history when the possible interactions between humans and animals as species and as individuals are infinite.

Each animal and each species is a unique intelligence necessary to the ecologies of world and spirit. Coming to recognize the rights and necessity for animals to exist within their own lives and territories, we are being blessed by their willingness to communicate with us and to teach us, among other things, the folly of separating the realm of the sacred from the material and the human from the animal.

As I have been writing this a snake has stretched out in the screened porch adjacent to my house exactly where I killed the rattler fifteen years ago. Snake's tail is conveniently tucked under Snake's body so I cannot see if Snake is gopher or rattler. I learned about Snake's presence when my wolf, Owl, who has not wanted to be inside for months, pushed open a side door to enter the house. The snake is alongside his bed. I look at the snake and smile, learning what it means to be snake clan by finding ways to accommodate Snake's presence.

I am engaged in a continuous and ongoing rigorous journey of exploration and change. Along the way I have come across Theodore Reik's *Pagan Rites in Judaism*. When I read that the acts of wrapping oneself in a prayer shawl or wearing phylacteries, prayer boxes, were symbolic reenactments of becoming the animal, of enfolding oneself within the animal, of writing the holy name of the animal on our bodies before approaching God, I came home to knowledge that has always lived secretly within me.

Wrapping myself in the animal, I realize that the alliance of human and animal is at the base of a deep pool of consciousness, the forgotten, unacknowledged forbidden ground that is a foundation of religious and spiritual practice. In the past, this alliance has been prohibited to me. Coming to know this, I begin the descent to the depths where the required and blessed reconciliation can be made.

During the High Holy Days, after hours of ritual, prayer, and meditation, it is still the plaintive call of the animal, the raw melody of longing sounded by blowing the *shofar*, the ram's horn, which finally opens the heavens. My heart breaks apart as the ram carries me across to the Holy of Holies.

SHADES OF GRAY

Reneé Askins

Every morning I look at a photograph that hangs near my desk. It appears to be black and white except for the shock of a trail of red blood that stretches from the lower left corner to the middle of the scene. It is an early winter hillside in Yellowstone where the Beartooth Mountains melt down into the Lamar Valley. Somewhere below this hillside the Mammoth/Cook City road winds through the valley like a paved stream through paradise. The white slope in the photograph is pocked by clumps of sage and an occasional sapling. A faint trace of animal tracks crosses the snow in the upper right corner of the picture. Probably coyote. From behind the shadowy branches of a fir in the lower left corner the path of blood emerges, leading across the white snow, ending in the dark silhouette of two animals, one standing, the other prone. They look joined, and in fact are, bonded by the ancient order of predator and prey: to eat and be eaten, to live and die in the oldest rhythm of the world. It is a gray wolf feeding on an elk calf he has just killed. Four other wolves, each a different shade of gray, are caught in mid-pose below, one dropping into a scent roll, one slinking off with a hunk of hide, and the last two observing the rest. It is a freeze-frame of the mythic and mundane. It is black and white in color.

Having only had a year to contemplate the meaning of actually having wolves in Yellowstone—after fourteen years of dreaming what it would be like once they were here—my dreaming still spills over the reality of their presence like drifting snow across black pavement. Instead of pinching myself I look at this photograph every morning. It is one of the few black and white renderings of what it means to have wolves back in Yellowstone. I trust it is real because of the red. I trust the red is blood. I have learned, after fourteen years of working to bring these wolves back to Yellowstone, that nothing real is ever black and white; the meaning is always nestled, like a sleeping wolf in the wind-swept snow, somewhere in the shades that drift between the arch of unyielding black and immaculate white.

We are a nation that longs for things to be black and white. We do not like ambiguity. We do not like the uncertain, the unpredictable, the uncontrollable. We like secure borders. We like either/or, all or nothing, black or white, not gray. Wolves come in many shades of gray. In this photograph their colors range from charcoal to ash, the same colors we see as our world turns from dark to dawn—the crepuscular colors. Wolves travel in those shadows between night and day, between the cultivated and wild, between man and beast, between black and white. It is in this "gray area" that dreams find their home. We mostly know or see wolves in our dreaming, and wolves speak back to our dreaming in the ephemeral way they reveal themselves. A dark long-legged form floating along the ridge of a steaming geyser basin. Was it? Maybe not. Maybe so. The rising and fading notes of a howl that come and retreat like a tide, leaving its listener wondering. A wolf howl? Yes. No? There was a howl, wasn't there? The mirage-like glimmer of a pack through a spotting scope, ten visible and a split second later, none. It was ten right? Maybe eight. They were wolves, weren't they? Wolves play in our dreams . . . and with our dreams. We sleep better and dream deeper knowing there is a little wildness nuzzling at our door.

Wildness is an interesting word. It does not mean wilderness, or wild animals; it refers to the *quality* of the wild, of wild-ness. In a cover piece on wolves a few years ago *Newsweek* magazine misquoted Henry Thoreau, as is often done, as saying, "In Wilderness is the preservation of the World." What Thoreau actually wrote is: "In Wildness is the preservation of the World." The two are quite different. Wilderness is a place, wildness a quality. Wilderness is the violin, wildness the music. Wilderness without wildness is like a Stradivarius lying on a museum shelf . . . inert, lifeless. Wolves often exist in wilderness, but what they are and what they offer us, as few other things do, is contact with wildness. And it is that contact that heals us, that can make us whole—that might in the end, as Thoreau put it, preserve the world.

Whether or not wildness will preserve the world, in our culture it is increasingly rare, and extraordinarily difficult, to give value to things that we cannot quantify, that we can't accurately name, or to which we cannot attach a price tag. Wildness is such a thing. It is a quality, not a quantity. It is not enough to put wild animals in a zoo to preserve the wild. Caged animals are not wild, any more than a Hopi vase decorating a restaurant is sacred. As my friend Jack Turner writes in his lovely book *The Abstract*

Wild, "The wild and the sacred are not the kinds of things that can be collected. We cannot put a quality in a museum, we cannot reduce it, or compartmentalize it. There are many things that cannot be collected or catalogued ... the set of complex numbers, gravity, dreams ... love. It is the sheer essence of wildness, the autonomous and the self-willed; the vital and the free, the unpredictable and the passionate," as Turner describes them, that still call to us through our contact with creatures in the wild like the wolf. We have forgotten, in fact, many of us have never known, the reciprocity between wild nature and the wild in our selves, between knowledge of the wild and knowledge of the self. This was something that was central to primitive cultures, to their rituals, their relationships, their lives, and it is all but lost today.

We still hunger for it ... we are a culture obsessed with the native traditions. We have our sweat lodges, and our animal fetishes, our dream catchers, and our nostalgic movies. We buy exotic pets, and own wolf-hybrids, and wear T-shirts with our favorite animals painted on them ... we mount antlers and pelts and game trophies on our walls. We are grasping at things representative of the wild because we feel it slipping away. We think if we mount it or wear it or own it we can retain it. We unconsciously understand that a tame world is a dead one. A world without wildness is a world beyond its capacity to heal. Underneath our lives with their veneer of control and predictability, a deep, profound truth still resonates in us; by some grace, our souls still whisper to us, our wildness still calls to us, and it is up to us whether we listen.

Something mysterious happens to us when we hear the howl of a wolf, or look into the eyes of a wolf. Something familiar is calling back to us, or looking back at us. Ourselves? Yes, but we also see an other. We see something that is in us, and yet outside us, something we know, but perhaps lost, something we fear, but are drawn toward. We recognize wildness ... our own and an other's. The "other" is very important because it is through the presence and respect for the "other" that we recognize and heal ourselves. Intuitively we understand that the assumption and attitude of dominion that led to our efforts a hundred years ago not to just control wolves but to conquer them, is the same attitude that has driven us not to just exploit our planet, but to fill it with toxic wastes, polluted skies, sewage-filled rivers, and dying forests. Ultimately it is not a choice between wolves *or* humans, but rather a question of how our worlds meet. Collision or confluence? Can we make room? Can we allow, endure, even revel in their wildness? Can we preserve their world, and in doing so preserve our own? Instinctively we know that what we do to the wolf, we do to ourselves and what we do for the wolf, we do for ourselves.

We need not decide between black or white, the barbaric or civilized, the bad or good, the innocent or corrupted. Wolves, like so much that is wild, lead us to the bridges over the chasms of either/or. The wild can teach us the virtue of our vices and the vice in our virtues. It reminds us that the imperfect is our paradise. A fallen tree, a stream stone traverse, a daring leap—we need only follow the animals for it is we, not they, who have forgotten how to navigate the nature of the "gray areas." We are of that nature, not apart from it. We survive because of it, not in spite of it. The wild reminds us that we find life, take life, and live life in neither the barren black forest nor on the flawless white plain, but rather the tracked gray hillside where dark blood weeps into white snow and leaves a trail of red.

SHINGALANA:
THE LIONESS OF LONDOLOZI

Gillian van Houten

A few hundred miles northeast of Johannesburg, the country falls dramatically five thousand feet into a subtropical low-lying region known locally as the Lowveld, an area extending through Mozambique to the Indian Ocean in the east and the Kruger National Park to Zimbabwe in the north. At the heart of the region is a vast wilderness, similar in size to Switzerland. To the Shangaan people of the region this is the Mananga, the wilderness where the wild animals live.

The Lowveld is a mosaic of grasslands, woodlands, scrub bush, thickets, and riverine forest. It is a harsh and exacting place of great beauty, the beauty of extremes so typical of Africa. Home to rhino, elephant, buffalo, leopard, lion, it is an ecosystem throbbing with a rich diversity of life. It is a place too of dry, bitter dust for it is kept lean by a relentless cycle of drought.

Within this wilderness area is Londolozi game reserve. The name Londolozi means "the protector of living things" in the Zulu language. This is the story of Shingalana, the lioness of Londolozi.

Late August 1992, a fresh spring morning in the Lowveld: I remember feeling uneasy, strangely restless, and unable to concentrate on the elephant article I was writing. At the time I put it down to the desperation we all felt as we watched the drought take its toll on the land and the animals around us. This was the worst drought in living memory.

John Varty—we call him J.V.—was downstairs in his studio assembling a film on predators. I could hear the static crackle of the two-way radio we always monitor when the game rangers are out driving in the bush reporting the positions of the game. Then the call came through. A

lion cub had been abandoned. Within minutes Elmon—our friend and
J.V.'s right hand in the bush—joined us and we drove to the area where
the cub had been sighted. It's not unusual for a lioness to abandon a cub if
it is the only one she produces or if she is young and inexperienced. It *is*
unusual to see it happen. In a lifetime spent in the bush neither J.V. nor
Elmon had ever seen this. A cub abandoned at birth, when it weighs no
more than two pounds, is so fragile that it will barely live a few hours before succumbing to exposure or dehydration. Most likely though its cries
of distress will attract a nearby predator.

As we arrived the Sparta pride, the resident lions of the area, was
moving off. In the dry grass lay the abandoned cub. I couldn't believe
how tiny she was or that something that small could make such loud cries
of protest. It was quite certain that she had been abandoned. Under normal circumstances a lioness would never allow anything to move between
her and her cub, but as we drove up the pride continued to move off, ignoring our presence completely and without so much as a backward
glance at the cub. Lionesses produce cubs in synchrony; it's a mechanism
that makes optimum use of the collective energy of the pride. With this
pride it appeared that there were no other cubs. This single cub wouldn't
warrant the time and energy required to raise it.

We sat and watched and waited. The sun rose higher and higher in the sky
and beat down mercilessly on the little creature, until its cries became
weaker and weaker.

J.V. is a wildlife filmmaker and the drama unfolding before our eyes
would have made spectacular and rare footage, but his camera lay untouched in its case. I am a writer and photographer, but I made no notes and
took no photographs. Elmon, a naturalist whose knowledge of the bush and
the ways of the animals is unrivaled, made no comments or observations. In
fact none of us spoke at all during the time that we sat there and waited. Perhaps, just perhaps, the lioness would return.

In my memory those few hours are fused into one timeless image. A tiny
cub, no more than a scrap of fur, is valiantly trying to raise itself onto its front
legs and calling with pitiful distress for its mother. Its cries pierce the heart.

Finally J.V. and Elmon circle the area, making certain that there was
no den with other cubs nearby. In an instant I was holding the tiny creature. She was no more than a handful and I could feel her little heart
pounding furiously against her chest as she burrowed against my body
seeking warmth, protection, and nourishment, fighting for survival.

We called her Shingalana, which means "little lion" in the Shangaan language, and right from the start we knew she was a survivor. The first few days with Shingi were a blur of bottles, milk formula, cleaning, grooming, and anxious moments in the early hours, checking to see if she was still breathing. Keeping Shingi alive filled our days and nights. Every moment was critical and J.V. and I found ourselves completely caught up in the fight for her life. Shingi lacked the critical colostrum of the first feeds and so had no natural immunity. I was awestruck at the intensity of this little creature's raw and courageous struggle for survival.

Nature has a way of making all her young creatures completely captivating and Shingalana was no exception. She was funny and cute and thrived on physical warmth and contact. She slept wrapped around our necks where she could feel the reassuring throb of a pulse. We groomed her daily with a soft bristle brush to imitate the rough tongue of her mother licking her with affection, cleaning her, and stimulating her digestion. Shingi would lie on her back, round tummy in the air, eyes closed in bliss, puny back legs stuck out straight, toes pointed with delight. Cubs suckle to bond as well as for comfort and food, so our thumbs had to be a poor but adequate substitute, calming and soothing her and often sending her off to sleep. That was how we cared for Shingi, something like lions would and something like people would.

As with all newly born creatures Shingi's world was small, one of eating and sleeping, warmth and affection. She had accepted us completely as her caregivers. Her needs were few but in her asking we soon became aware that she was also offering. There was an exchange taking place; she gave us the unique opportunity to reconnect in a very tangible way with a wild part of Nature. Something would happen to people when they touched her. In making this connection with something wild, a door opened within them.

After the first few weeks were over and Shingi's condition was stable, J.V. and I sat down to put together a plan. We drew on every wildlife source we could, researching successful attempts to secrete lost or abandoned cubs back into a pride with cubs of a similar age. The question was one of timing. At about twelve weeks of age the young cubs in a pride are first taken to a kill to eat meat. If one picked a time when the pride was on a carcass, all the attention of the adults would be on the food. Amid the distractions and heightened emotions of a kill, Shingi might enter the pride unnoticed. We could take Shingi that far but the rest would be up to her. Inappropriate behavior on her part would spell death or reabandonment.

We monitored the pride that had abandoned Shingi very closely and our hopes rose when they linked up with an aunt who had produced two cubs some six weeks earlier. But these cubs were bigger and more advanced than Shingi. The risk of her being noticed was high. Shingi's chances of rejoining her family looked bleak.

When the time came we made up our minds almost without discussion. Having saved a life one becomes responsible for it. As wildlife communicators we had always kept the boundaries clear, silent observers in the dramas of nature that unfolded before us, filming, photographing, and writing about animals without other participation. But we had broken our rules when we brought Shingi home. Now what could we offer her? What if she were offering us something? How far were we prepared or able to go?

Nature works in curious ways and perhaps the most curious are those where boundaries blur or when events conspire to change our understanding of the world we know. We accepted what we'd come to see as an offer. We would keep Shingi and reintroduce her to the wild ourselves, a project that would take five years or more. It would mean moving deep into the bush with her and exposing her to the experiences that would best equip her for a life as a wild lion. We would have to walk with her, hunt with her, feed her, and protect her until she grew up. We would have to become Shingi's pride.

The success rate of such projects is low and the commitment absolute. But for me there was no choice. We'd embarked on something and we had to follow through. No matter how unorthodox the situation might be, I felt that if Shingi came to know what it was to be a wild lion and experienced love and companionship, albeit from humans, our gamble would surely have been worthwhile. For us the reward lay in the privilege of living with a wild animal. It would take courage for us to step across into Shingi's world, the kind of courage she had already shown when she stepped into ours.

One of Shingi's more famous visitors in her early cubhood was Nelson Mandela, who stayed with us at Londolozi the year he ran for president. The drought which had gripped the Lowveld broke providentially the evening he arrived when the heavens opened up and delivered the first downpour of the season. Afterward the air was fresh and vibrant, charged with the promise of new hope. When the president-to-be and his party arrived at our home to join us for dinner, Shingi was on the doorstep to meet them. With the good humor that comes of a deep respect for all life, the future president inquired what the correct protocol might be when greeting a lion. I explained and then with the great dignity that is so characteristic of him—and to the horror of his bodyguards—he went down on all fours and let Shingi rub the side of her head against his, greeting the way lions do.

When Shingi was a few months old, J.V., Elmon, Shingi, and I moved to a tented camp in a remote part of Londolozi. She needed to be in a more natural environment. We chose a campsite called the Mashabene, the place of sand, a dry riverbed that runs across the game reserve, bordered on its bank by dense riverine vegetation. Here, deep in the bush, we were to spend the next year and a half together.

The mood in Shingi's pride was tense. Shingi's father, the established male, was facing a challenge for his territory from two younger males. When the two claimants killed Shingi's aunt's two cubs we realized with a deep sense of relief that our decision not to risk reintroducing Shingi to her family had been correct. One of the first acts of a male taking over a pride is infanticide, a vital part of male reproductive strategy. The two new males were wasting no time introducing their genes to the Sparta pride. We'd already seen them mating with the females.

Lions, as gregarious pride animals, sleep closely enough together that if not actually touching one another, they are near enough to sense the presence of the group. We had to put Shingi in a boma at night, a protective enclosure made of thorns. The two young males staging a takeover made Shingi very vulnerable. A territorial male lion will kill any cub in his territory he believes he has not sired, thus retaining breeding rights and the perpetuation of his genes in the territory. Shingi stayed in the boma until her social needs made themselves evident and then Shingi did the impossible. She climbed out of the boma, sleeping with us in our tent or nearby from then on.

We took daily walks with Shingi up and down the donga, ranging farther as she grew, exposing her to random experience and the animals that shared her world. Much of what lions know is learned by watching the older and more experienced members of the pride. We did our best from what we knew of lion behavior but found we were learning as much as Shingi. Our walks were seldom without adventure and often we would find ourselves running with her in mock terror from an overly ambitious plot to stalk an elephant or sharing in the pride and satisfaction of having scattered a herd of impala.

It was interesting to see the effect Shingi had on Elmon, a Shangaan who grew up at the interface of wilderness and human settlement. As a child, he had to protect his father's livestock from marauding lions. When we picked Shingi up in August he cynically remarked that by Christmas she would bite me. Now, long beyond Christmas, he played and initiated games of hunting and stalking with Shingi with uninhibited and transparent joy.

As Shingi's world expanded, the complex creature that she was began to emerge. Of all the land animals, cats, primates, and elephants have the most sophisticated forms of communication. Getting to know Shingi became more complicated than reading her body language, the subtle gestures of ear and facial muscles, specially designed body markings, or even a sense of mood. It became a deeper sense of understanding each other, of something universal shared by us. The web of life that connects all living things is something most human beings ignore. Connecting with it was a humbling experience.

My early efforts to communicate were clumsy. Often I'd get the feeling that Shingi was indulging me, waiting until I stumbled onto some knowledge that she had and I was seeking. I read widely about human-animal relationships and learned about the Tellington Touch, a system of physical contact that can deepen connections between people and animals. Shingi and I spent long hours that summer doing communication exercises. Lions are great conservers of energy, spending up to twenty hours a day lounging. I would use these opportunities to chat idly with her, either using words or mental pictures. I reckoned that if Shingi was to understand people she should experience human conversation and perhaps she might respond by sharing with me something more of the way lions communicate. And she gave generously. Initially it was an invitation to play. With a mischievous look in her eyes, Shingi would wrap her paws around my neck and draw me close and then the rough and tumble would begin. At this early stage, our communication and knowledge of each other was developing through shared experiences.

It was during this time that I came to a fundamental realization: This encounter with Shingi was not about rescuing her or saving her life or even about her successful reintroduction to the wild. It was about our relationship, about what happened between us in the time that we shared our lives and what we could learn from each other.

We walked endlessly, mostly at sunrise and sunset. The rustle of dry leaves or the snap of a twig would freeze us as we assessed whether danger or opportunity was to present itself. Before we had been observers; now we were part of it. We became sensitive to the alarm calls of the bush: the shriek of a vervet monkey, the chattering admonishments of the bush squirrel, the go-away call of the grey loerie, which would warn us of the presence of other predators while the call of the red-billed oxpecker would alert us to a large mammal up ahead. Perhaps it would be a gentle and inquisitive giraffe blinking incredulously at our unlikely pride making its way through the bush or perhaps a malcontented old buffalo bull on his own, looking for something on which to vent his spleen. These were the dangers we all faced and shared, building as we did the communal strength of our pride, social bonds of trust and cooperation, a strength that is more than the sum of its parts.

Hunting was a critical area of Shingi's education. We fed her on wild game presented to her in whole recognizable pieces, J.V. and Elmon doing the hunting as would the senior and more experienced members of a pride. Shingi would be unable to hunt for herself until she was at least a year old. As we fed her we encouraged her to hunt. She soon became alert to our body language and the mood we tried to convey of focus and concentration.

It was in woodland on the lip of the donga that Shingi made her first real kill. She was just a year old and the impala had begun their lambing season. Shingi had caught a leguvaan previously, but it had shammed dead and then launched a counterattack, biting her on the nose and hanging on with ferocity. Shingi grunted in shock and thrashed around unable to throw it off. Her enthusiasm for hunting had taken a bit of a knock, but she soon bounced back, stalking and pouncing on everything that moved. We were out walking when Shingi made a sudden rush into the woodland. We followed, ducking and weaving through the nilotica thorns to find her mauling a young impala. Her instinct had guided her to bring down the animal, but the actual killing bite is something young lions learn by watching the more experienced hunters of the pride. Not knowing what to do Shingi continued to maul the young impala and bite it at random. Eventually, with a perplexed look on her face, she sat on it and looked to me for assistance. I tried my best to send her mental images but the whole exercise was hopeless, upset and agitated as I was, torn between pity for the mother impala staring at us incredulously from the edge of the woodland and surging pride that our young lion had moved through this rite of passage to her status as a hunter. The impala eventually died of shock, but clearly Shingi would have to learn a lot about being a lion by trial and error.

One of the things we had to learn about early on was each other's physical strength. Like all young creatures, Shingi had the urge to test her strength, and when it got the better of her she'd lie in ambush and then leap on my back, sending me sprawling. Young animals, in their play, mimic the skills they need to survive as adults, and much of what Shingi was doing had to do with bringing down prey.

Shingi was puzzled by our physical weakness, soon realizing that our teeth and claws were of very little consequence. Gradually though she came to accept using "minimum force." Along with this control she learned how to retract her claws.

If I were to behave in lion style, I would need to assert my position of dominance with physical force or the threat of it. In that way she would remain subservient and respectful of her place in the hierarchy. However, I wanted to share with Shingi as a human being, so I only used tone of voice, trust, and faith in her better judgment.

When Shingi was eighteen months old she began to range farther from the camp, often alone and often at night. It was during one of these forays that she had her first serious run-in with lions. Strangely enough the first encounter had been with her own mother during a walk down the donga. The lioness had rushed at Shingi. We were able to ward off the attack, but the episode had brought home to us the fragility of our situation. Then one night Shingi came across five young adult male lions feeding on a buffalo they had killed. These young males were nomads and had roamed into our area to test the strength of the dominant male lions holding the territory. Not knowing the correct etiquette or showing enough deference to the males, Shingi had approached to feed and they had turned on her. Her superior knowledge of the area saved her life, she managed to outmaneuver them and duck back to the camp, where her strength lay in her own pride—us.

We realized then that we could delay no longer. We'd have to find a new home for Shingi in which she could begin the critical phase of socialization and integration with the resident lions. We were unable to keep her at Londolozi, a highly developed ecotourism destination with human settlement on its borders. We needed an area free of human habitation, free from hunting or poaching with abundant prey species for her to hunt, and a resident population of wild lions.

It was a long frustrating search, for Africa is no longer a vast, untamed continent. Human expansion has reduced the wilderness areas to small pockets. Finally the National Parks of Zambia gave us permission to continue our project in a remote corner of the South Luangwa National Park, a vast wilderness area. Operating there would be a logistical nightmare for the same reason that we could continue our work there. It was a rough and inhospitable area with high humidity and temperatures well over one hundred degrees Fahrenheit. It was infested with tsetse flies and had the attendant risk of vicious and deadly strains of malaria. But we'd found a safe haven for Shingi. Now her most difficult challenge lay ahead, her socialization and integration with the wild lions.

The adjustment was difficult for all of us. Conditions were tough and there were new dangers we had to face together, the most immediate being the river itself, seething with crocodiles. We needed to draw our water supply from it and cross it if we had to go anywhere. Shingi too would need to learn about the dangers that lurked beneath the surface of the waters. Supplies were a good few hours away on rutted or nonexistent tracks, a journey we made as seldom as possible. A trip to Lusaka or Chipata took a few days. Our communication with the outside world was via VHF radio, a mass of static when conditions in the valley were adverse.

Shingi's initial tendency was to keep close to the camp to reestablish a sense of belonging. We started our daily walks so Shingi could learn every inch of this new territory and fix her landmarks, familiarity being her advantage and defense in the wild. She was growing into a magnificent lioness, bigger than the average. We put her weight at 280 pounds when we relocated her, and her neck and shoulders were still developing. We estimated her full-grown weight to be 320 pounds. Watching her chasing prey across the floodplains, sand spraying from her feet as she ran, or thrusting through the river, muscles rippling across her shoulders and chest, the suggestion of unimaginable power within her body was breathtaking. And she was always polite, good-natured, and trusting.

Shingi's education was ongoing. Discovering and chasing a puku, a new species to her, was an adventure, as the athletic antelope will take to the water, hooves flying and water spraying as it makes its getaway. The first time this happened Shingi was confused, but nothing fazed her for very long, and hardly missing a beat she was in the water bounding after it.

Across the river was a vast dambo. It was here Shingi learned the art of focusing her attention on one animal and pursuing that animal when she rushed and the herd scattered. She executed the perfect hunt one day, stalking and maneuvering herself so that when she rushed, revealed herself, and pounced, her victim had no chance of a getaway. Hunting was now a serious business.

Shingi was almost two years old now and soon she would come into estrus for the first time and attract a mate. She had no experience of the reproductive behavior of lions. She also had no experience of the general social behavior of lions in a pride with all its accompanying rituals and allegiances. These two vital phases in her development might happen at the same time, placing heavy demands on her ability to cope. Still we hoped that this would be Shingi's introduction to the world of lions, knowing as we did that she would come under the protection of the territorial male lion during this critical rite of passage. There were few options for Shingi's return to the wild and this one was the most likely. There was also a possibility that she might link up with another single female lioness, a nomad who would also be looking for an associate for hunting and defense and be friendly toward her. What has been observed is that a territory has a certain "female capacity" and should numbers fall below this, nomads may be permitted to move in.

We were aware of the presence of other lions near our camp. We heard them calling at night and during the day we saw tracks in the woodland.

We saw several wild lions while out walking but they showed no interest in us or Shingi.

It was at the peak of the dry season and Shingi was two when we noticed that she was coming into estrus and would soon be ready for mating. She began to cycle every two weeks for between two and five days; the monthly cycle was stronger and coincided with the full moon. Shingi's estrus was a difficult time for all of us. She became agitated and restless and unable to contain her physical strength. During these times she presented herself to both J.V. and Elmon but not to me. The first few cycles in a female lion are a false estrus during which time she comes into heat but does not ovulate. She will advertise her condition, calling, displaying herself from a good vantage point, scuffing the ground and leaving evidence in her urine of the hormonal changes taking place in her body. Shingi was moving into this phase and would soon be attracting the territorial male or coalition of males.

One day we were on the sandbank when before us a pride of lions emerged from cover on the far side of the river. We counted nineteen, a large pride. Shingi lay and looked at them and began rolling on the sand. There'd been lion calling the previous few nights and although she had listened attentively she had not responded. It was about the time for her estrus. She moved closer to the river and began rolling and purring again. I was terrified that the pride would charge across the river and challenge her, so I followed her nervously and hid behind a sandbank as the wild lions watched her and Shingi watched them.

It was soon after we saw the pride of nineteen that Shingi spent her first night away from the camp alone. None of us slept very well that night and as soon as the first rays of light broke the following morning we set off down the river looking for her. There were tracks everywhere, and as we approached we saw a group of lionesses scatter. Elmon identified her tracks crossing the river and he and J.V. followed them. After some hours I turned away and began walking back to the camp. In the distance I saw the outline of a lioness—it was Shingi, expressing overwhelming relief that we had come for her. She quickly plunged into the river without her usual caution for crocodiles, never moving her eyes from my face. She greeted us with a terrible desperation. Shingi had been attacked and there were bites and scratches all over her nose and hindquarters. Shingi was in a state of shock. We led her back to the camp where her last ounces of strength gave out. She retreated to the cool recesses of one of the tents to lick her wounds and then rested her head on her forearms, the saddest expression I'd ever seen in her eyes. We cleaned and treated her wounds as best we could, offered her water, and sat with her for hours reassuring her that we were still there.

Initially I was delighted that Shingi had made the contact. Naturally the females of the pride would challenge an immigrant aggressively. We hadn't expected Shingi's passage to be trouble-free. The wild lions hadn't managed to do too much damage. Now Shingi had to come to know the enormous physical power of lions and their explosive behavior. She would need to find the ferocity to defend herself.

It took Shingi some weeks to recover beyond the healing of her wounds. When lions greet they rub the sides of their heads against one another, passing each other and rubbing frequently. Greeting ceremonies with Shingi now varied from quick, courteous acknowledgment through the course of the day to long and affectionate sessions whenever we left the camp for some time and returned.

The night the territorial males visited our camp was a turning point. There were two of them in the coalition that held the territory, probably brothers or littermates. We'd been sitting up night after night, listening to the males calling and Shingi responding. Then one night there they were. Thick luxuriant blond manes in the dark, catching the light of the moon, the senior male leading and his partner holding back in deference. The power and tenacity needed to hold this territory radiated from the alpha male. Shingi had succeeded in attracting a magnificent wild mate. She was skittish, coquettishly spinning and running away as he approached her. Shingi had never seen lions mating. The female role of presenting herself to the male is active rather than passive and we weren't sure she would get it right. We were anxious too that inappropriate behavior from her might annoy him and he would either hurt her or run away. But he demonstrated touching patience with Shingi.

The following morning the male was still around the camp and Shingi trotted off at his side, a definite spring in her step. We thought they'd be away for two or three days, within which time they would mate frequently before Shingi's estrus subsided. After a few hours, though, Shingi sauntered into camp, leaping nonchalantly up onto her platform and stretching out in the morning sun. I joined her in a flash with thousands of questions. Shingi lay there grinning as only a cat can and hugged me to her big chest. We lay in the sun that morning elated.

Then came the night the wild pride attacked our camp. We'd been sitting on the platform waiting for the male to arrive when we heard a rustle of leaves, then silence. Cautiously we shone a torch and there at the edge of our camp seemed to be hundreds of yellow eyes gleaming in the darkness. It suggested such savagery, silent and primeval, that my blood ran cold. Shingi recognized the pride and to our horror got up, ran down the ladder and approached them, her posture alert and her step light. From the height of the platform we could see the alpha female maneuvering herself into position and instigating the other females to adopt theirs. And then she charged. Without hesitation we were beside Shingi. Perhaps she had been too direct with the lionesses and not shown enough acquiescence. Our role clearly was to be at Shingi's side, her best defense against the attack being a counter show of strength. Lions respect size, power, noise, and we supported Shingi with all the bluster we could summon up, firing guns into the air, kicking up sand, shouting and waving, and making ourselves as large and threatening as possible. Antagonistic behavior is often about bluff. The camp was literally seething with lions and we could not see them clearly despite our lights. At the helm was the alpha female of the group. I thought of her with compassion, imagining what hard and bitter experience she must have been through to have earned her position, and what was expected of her to maintain it. There was a single-mindedness about her, every sinew, every expression, every gesture. The females made several charges that night and each time we repelled them. Finally, after long hours, they withdrew, leaving us disheartened and exhausted and me seriously frightened.

Although her circumstances were unique, Shingi was in a way a nomad—a single lion immigrant looking for entry into a resident group of lions. About one-fifth of the total lion population is nomadic. Little is known about female nomads. However, it has been observed that there is little chance of a resident group killing a nomad outright. More likely they will intimidate the stranger and drive them out of the territory.

I woke up before dawn the following day and put on my boots with resolution, strapped my handgun to my hip, and set off up the river to where I thought the pride would be resting. I had made up my mind what I was going to do. I positioned myself against a sausage tree, making sure that the pride on the opposite bank could see me. And then I began my broadcast.

If everything, including thought, is energy, then by focusing my thoughts very strongly, I would saturate the airwaves with my ideas. Whether the pride would be receptive or not, I didn't know, but I had to try something. I sat there for many hours, broadcasting to the lions. The essence of what I told them was Shingi's story: that somewhere, somehow, human being and lion had been flung together, species had crossed and blended. Shingi had learned about us and we had learned about her. These things made her different but they made her useful. She had much to offer. Apart from her obvious reproductive ability she could hunt, she had a wonderful character, and she knew firsthand about people. They could benefit by allowing her to join them. She could tell them of a new breed of humans that had no desire to dominate but had a deep need to reestablish kinship with all living beings. I argued this way and that, keeping things simple and respectful. I spoke as a person, I spoke as a woman, I spoke as a sister, as a daughter, and as a mother, from the deepest, deepest reaches of my being where I was simply an expression of life the same as they were.

After my broadcast was over I felt completely exhausted, and I also felt utterly foolish. I was becoming hot and irritable, the tsetse flies were biting, ignoring the branch of leaves I was using to chase them off. The lions were lying very relaxed under the trees on the opposite bank. At least I hadn't antagonized them. I sat for a while open and receptive to any ideas that might have floated across. One single idea filled my mind . . . jealousy. Not being in the least gifted with extrasensory skills I doubted this information was coming from the pride, but I had to give the process a two-way chance.

Now Shingi was in estrus again and the attacks continued relentlessly, with different groups of females ambushing and charging us. Then one day the alpha female sent a singular message. We saw her lying in the shade of a winterthorn, watching the camp. Then we saw the male on the opposite bank looking for Shingi. As he crossed the river the alpha female saw him, jumped up, deliberately intercepting his path, and began to present herself to him for mating. She had intercepted the male on his way to mating with Shingi because she was protecting her breeding rights and the genes of her own pride. I had always respected the alpha female, but now I felt something closer to empathy. I hoped fervently that once the pride females had mated and conceived they would disregard Shingi. By late October the rains would come, so perhaps they'd move off and give Shingi another year to bond with the males who ranged over the territory in both wet and dry season.

I became pregnant during the dry season and at four months into the pregnancy I could no longer ignore the liability I was becoming. I couldn't run from the hippos like I used to or climb up the rope ladder. There was the ever-present threat of malaria, deadly strains of which had almost killed all of us just before the dry season. I knew that soon I would have to leave camp for a few months. I lay with Shingi on her platform or on the sandbank after splashing in the river at sunset. Lying on the sandbank we would look at the tantalizing buildup of thunderclouds, but the rains were still some time off. Would we be able to repel the females until they moved inland?

Shingi knew I was pregnant even though she had never experienced anything of pregnancy before. Her behavior was more attentive, gentler, less demanding of me, as if she understood my tiredness and hormonal disequilibrium. I thought Shingi understood that I would go off and have the baby and then return. That was simple lion behavior.

There was never any doubt in my mind that Shingi would be there when I returned to Lion camp, as we'd come to know our home in the Luangwa. Clearly she would need us close by her side for some time yet. But this was not to be. Shingi died while I was in South Africa. The rains had come late and the attacks from the wild lions had become life-threatening to everyone in the camp. J.V. made plans to relocate the camp but the move had to wait for the rains and the river to come up.

Shingi was in estrus and had gone off with the male. They were mating on the sandbank when the females found them and attacked, driving the two of them up against the wall of sand and cutting off Shingi's retreat to the safety of camp and the platforms. It was a terrible fight, an explosion of rage and jealousy. The male was under attack too, and he and Shingi were fighting alongside each other. When Elmon managed to intercept and get Shingi back to the camp, she was badly wounded. Despite all the medication and treatment J.V. could give her, nursing her night and day, willing her through, she died in his arms some days later.

DANCE WITH A GIRAFFE

Christine Jurzykowski

I grew up near Sao Paolo living in a house where the garden ended in the jungle. One of my first pets was a baby anteater whose mother had probably been shot. My father and I placed her in a small corral used for other animals. For days I sat on a hay bale observing closely her every move. Gradually she became used to me watching her. The daily routine was the same: I would sit in complete silence saying in my head, "You are my friend; you are safe here; you will be taken care of." After a while I knew it would be all right to touch her. She was standing close to the fence. I reached out my hand and ran it along the middle of her back. She didn't move. It was magical and natural at the same time.

Within a short time, the political situation in Brazil changed. My mother, who was of Jewish descent, had escaped Poland with my father, a Roman Catholic Polish nationalist, in 1939. Now, because of the junta, she was beginning to feel endangered in Brazil. We moved to Paris and later New York, while my father stayed in Brazil until his death when I was fourteen. I was twenty-eight years old and visiting a friend who lived in the town of Carmel in upstate New York, walking a property adjoining a larger forest sanctuary of hundreds of acres, when I suddenly remembered the interwoven relationships with the natural world that I had known as a child. All of a sudden I realized what I had been missing.

Leaving New York and my profession in film, I spent the next two years living on the sea. Being linked with nature in this way brought back more memories, igniting my passion for the conservation of wildlife. Long and adventurous, this journey brought me to Texas where my husband, Jim, and I assumed responsibility for a small ranch with five hundred animals in what had been dinosaur country. Fossil Rim is now home to 1,100 animals from the wilds of Africa, Asia, and South America as well as the

Southwest of the United States. Grevy zebra, white and black rhino, addax antelope, cheetah, reticulated giraffe, and Attwater's prairie birds, among others, find a sanctuary here in this small "island" of protected habitat.

When I am in direct, intimate relationship with an animal I am more able to ask questions from within the cycle of nature. Animals take me into the nature of nature. The universal dance of form and relationship—creation and destruction, of which we are all part. Being with Old Nick brought this feeling to me, especially when I was summoned to participate in his dance with death.

Old Nick was a six-year-old giraffe who came to Fossil Rim by way of Topeka, Kansas, in 1982. From birth, he never enjoyed good health. Nothing was specifically wrong, yet nothing was ever quite right. He suffered from swollen joints and was thinner and less active than the rest of the herd.

This giraffe, measuring eighteen to twenty feet tall, was fully grown at the age of three. Chestnut brown with white patches, he was part of a subspecies known as the reticulated giraffe. Giraffes sleep very little, usually twenty minutes at a time, and spend the majority of their day upright. When they do sleep, they kneel, tuck their knees under themselves, and flip their necks backward to rest on their tailbone. When giraffes "go down" horizontally, chances are they will never get up again. This is what happened to Old Nick one winter afternoon when Kelley, an animal caretaker, was cleaning his hooves.

I heard the call for assistance over the radio. When I arrived members of the animal care staff had moved Old Nick from the barn into the large room of the giraffe house. In this area, Old Nick was visible to the other giraffes yet physically separated by pipe bars. "Quick, prop up his head." The hustle began. "If blood pumps up any faster it will cause an aneurysm." We quickly set bales of hay behind Old Nick to keep the upper part of his body erect.

By late evening, the temperature had dropped significantly and it was cold in the giraffe house. The floors are concrete, the walls cinder block, and the ceilings are about twenty feet high all around. We gathered old blankets and anything else we could use to keep Old Nick's body from getting chilled.

Old Nick knew he was dying. So did we. So did the giraffes watching us from across the barn. Our primary concern was to make him as comfortable as possible and prevent further complications.

Being animal caregivers, it is our job to question how we interact and interrelate with the animals. There is an art to knowing how to help, where to intervene, and when to honor another being's rite of passage. We are members of the web of relationships that includes all living things. How we honor these relationships with nature is ultimately how we honor them within ourselves.

There was a moment of silence as we huddled around Old Nick. One question was in our collective mind: "How can we best honor this animal while loving and supporting him?" No one had an answer.

We took turns holding Old Nick's head on our knees. When it came my turn, I sat on the bale propping up Old Nick's neck, got comfortable, and placed this majestic creature's head in my lap. What a precarious yet precious feeling. My face was so close to his face, which was normally twenty feet in the air. I could caress his nose and brush his delicate eyelashes. And the weight—his head alone felt like fifty pounds of rock lying across my knees.

I felt sadness in my throat and dread in the pit of my stomach. My rational mind said the end would be soon, but I wanted to avoid this distraction, to be present. As I leaned closer to his face, I asked for courage. Part of me knew that everyone in this room had been chosen to be Old Nick's partner in his dying. I prayed that I would be guided through this, that this would serve me as a teaching for the months ahead.

After twelve hours, it occurred to me to match the rhythm of Old Nick's breathing. It took only a few minutes to let this animal set the pace and I dropped into a trance. My mind went elsewhere as kinesthetic awareness took over. For a moment I slipped away and forgot we were here to die. This breathing had a gentle calming effect. I entered into a different relationship with Old Nick. I was keenly aware of this rise and fall of the energy levels of his body. It was as if we were matched to a piece of music written in four-four time.

Periodically, Old Nick's willingness to fight affected the tempo of our breathing. I felt the energy rise, giving me hope. Then, just as quickly, his energy level dropped and I dropped with it into overwhelming despair. I wanted to turn my head and avert my eyes in hopes Old Nick wouldn't sense the sadness in my heart. He knew I knew he would die soon—I knew he knew too. This is what we shared. The knowing. We are all a part of this. This is nature.

Meanwhile, the herd had gathered on the other side of the barn. The giraffes began what looked like gestures of acknowledgment of Old Nick; arching their long necks and throwing their heads back, then dropping their heads forward. Arching back, then lunging forward. This gesture continued as they paced methodically in a circle. Then in unison, they stopped.

As we entered the early morning hours, the bull's gestures became more dramatic and pronounced. As if they were learning choreographed dance movements, the females matched the gestures of the bull exactly.

The dance became more animated and the herd moved toward frenzy. We weren't sure we could contain them, so we moved the bull to a room where Old Nick was out of his view, hoping this would restore quiet.

Alone, the bull continued his movements. The females, who could not see the bull, began moving with him. In unison and in silence they continued to bow and arch their necks, pacing themselves to the stamina of the dying giraffe. Their dance, my breathing.

We kept this vigil for twenty-four hours. Except for food and coffee breaks, I stayed with Old Nick the entire time. We kept having to move him, a difficult maneuver with a three-thousand-pound animal. The booming sound of the giraffes' hooves pacing on the cement floor reverberated around and around the large room.

So much happened during these twenty-four hours for us as caretakers, for Old Nick, for the herd. I had time to think, to hope, to despair, and to ask questions of myself, of the animals, of Fossil Rim. "Am I willing to imagine the possibility of true partnership in nature? Am I willing to engage in the mystery of a language beyond words? Will I trust what I hear? What am I being called on to remember?"

At last Old Nick left this world. Within minutes of his passing, deans of various schools of one of the major universities came to Fossil Rim for their official visit. I met the group at the giraffe barn as graciously as I could, tears in my eyes, devoid of sleep, dirty, and smelling of giraffe. They came over to where Old Nick lay, gave their advice and comments, and were off for a tour. This quick shift in focus shocked me out of my state of mind and left me to make my peace with it later when I could.

Holding this giraffe in my arms, experiencing in his body the push and pull of death, I thought of the ancestors he and each one of these giraffes carry inside them, the memory of their origins in the wild, dry, hot climate halfway around the world from Fossil Rim. Not even a dramatically different controlled environment could change their inner understandings. Part of being alive is knowing everything belongs to something else. Nothing exists in isolation.

If we are willing to be still and become aware of what we are truly made of—energy and matter—we may experience the connection to the living system called nature. In the awakening of our own cellular memories, we may remember the way we evolved in harmony with each other within the cycles of life, the nature of nature.

And those words from my childhood return so vividly: "You are my friend, you are safe here, you will be taken care of."

Terry Tempest Williams

The revolutionary question is: What about the Other? . . . It is not
enough to rail against the descending darkness of barbarity . . .
One can refuse to play the game. A holding action can be fought.
Alternatives must be kept alive. While learning the slow art of
revolutionary patience.

—BREYTEN BREYTENBACH, "TORTOISE STEPS"

Tortoise steps.
Slow steps.
Four steps like a tank with a tail dragging in the sand.

Tortoise steps—land-based, land-locked, dusty like the desert tortoise
himself, fenced in, a prisoner on his own reservation.
Teaching us the slow art of revolutionary patience.

It is Christmas. We gather in our grandparents' home: aunts, uncles,
cousins, babies—four generations wipe their feet at the holiday mat.
One by one, we open the front door, "Hello," "We're here," glass panes
iced are beginning to melt from the heat of bodies together. Our grandfather, Jack, now ninety, presides. His sons, John and Richard, walk in
dressed in tweed sport coats and Levi's, their polished boots could kill
spiders in corners. My aunt Ruth enters with her arms full of gifts. Jack's
sister, Norinne, in her eighties, sits in the living room with her hands
folded tightly, greeting each one of us with a formality we have come to
expect.
Tradition.
On this night, we know a buffet is prepared: filet mignon, marinated
carrots, asparagus, and cauliflower, a cranberry salad, warbread (a recipe
our great-grandmother Mamie Comstock Tempest improvised during the
Depression when provisions were scarce and raisins plentiful), and the
same silver serving piece is obscene with chocolates.
The Christmas tree stands in the center of the room, "the grandchildren's tree," and we remember our grandmother, Mimi, the matriarch of

this family whose last Christmas was in 1988. We remember her. We remember all of our dead.

Candles burn. I walk into the dining room, pick up a plate and circle the table.

"What's new, Terrence?" my uncle asks ribbing me.

"Not a thing, Rich," I respond. We both look up from the buffet smiling.

I take some meat with my fingers. He spears vegetables. We return to the living room and find a seat. The rest of the family gathers. Jack sits in the wing-backed chair, his hands on both arm rests. My father sits across the room from his brother.

"So how did the meeting go last week?"

"Terrible," Rich says.

"What did they decide?"

"Simple," my uncle says. "Tortoises are more important than people."

Heads turn, attention fixes on matters of the Tempest Company, the family construction business that began with our great-grandfather in the early part of the century, a company my brothers all work for, cousins, too.

"What are you talking about?" I ask.

"Where have you been?" my father asks incredulously. "We've been shut down eighteen months because of that—(he stops himself in deference to his aunt) that *stupid* Endangered Species Act."

I look at my brother Steve who nods his head who looks at our cousin Bob who looks at his sister Lynne who shakes her head as she turns to Brooke.

"I attended the public meeting where they discussed the Habitat Management Plan," Rich says to us.

"And?" Lynne asks as she walks over to her father and offers him a piece of warbread.

"They ruled in favor of the tortoise."

"Which job is this, John?" Brooke asks, who at the time was working for the governor's office of budget and planning as the liaison between environmental groups and the state.

"It's the last leg of the Information Highway," Dad says. "Seven miles of fiber optic cable running from the town of Hurricane to St. George linking rural Utah to the Wasatch Front."

"We're held up in permits," Rich explains. "A construction permit won't be issued until USWest complies with federal agencies."

"The government's gone too far," my great-aunt interjects.

"Too far?" my father says his voice rising like water ready to boil. "Too far? We've had to hire a full-time biologist at $60 an hour who does nothing but look for these imaginary animals. Every day he circles the crew singing the same song, 'Nope, haven't seen one yet.' "

"The guy's from BYU and sits in the cab of his truck most of the day reading scriptures," adds Steve, the superintendent.

"Thou shall not kill a turtle," someone mutters under his breath.

"Sixty bucks an hour," Dad reiterates. "That's twice as much as our foremen make! It would be cheaper to buy a poolside condominium for each mating pair of tortoises than to adhere to the costs of this ridiculous Act."

"The government's gone too far," my aunt restates like a delayed echo.

"And on top of that we have to conduct a 'turtle training course'—"

"Tortoise, John," his granddaughter Callie interrupts. I wink at my niece.

"A turtle training course for our men, OUR MEN, so they can learn to identify one and then remember to check under the tires and skids for tortoises looking for shade before turning on the backhoes after lunch."

Rich stands up to get some more food.

"$100,000 if we run over one," he says making himself a sandwich.

"Is that worth a hundred grand?" my father snaps.

"From the tortoise's point of view . . ." Lynne says pushing.

"What's St. George now, the fourth fastest growing community in the country?" Brooke asks.

"Not if the enviros have anything to do with it," Rich says.

"What do you kids want? To stop progress? You and your environmentalist friends have lost all credibility. One local told us, a bunch of radicals actually planted a tortoise in the parking lot of the WalMart Distribution Center just to shut it down."

"How do you know it didn't walk onto the asphalt by itself?" I ask.

"They had its stomach pumped and it was full of lettuce," Rich replies. We all roll our eyes.

Steve asks his cousin Matt who is a first-year medical student, "Have you performed an autopsy on a desert tortoise yet?"

"Not yet," Matt responds. "Just human beings."

"Can I get anyone anything?" Ruth asks holding her granddaughter Hannah on her hip. She looks around. No response. "Just checking."

"And you wonder why people are upset," my father says turning to me. "It's easy for you to sit here and tell us what animals we should protect while you write poems about them as a hobby—it's not your pocketbook that's hurting."

"And is yours?" I ask fearing I have now gone as far as my father has.

I was not aware of the background music until now, Nat King Cole singing, "Have a Merry, Merry Christmas. . . ."

"I don't know," Jack says clearing his throat, pulling himself out of his chair. "Why don't you boys tell them the real story?"

John and Richard look puzzled.

"What story?" Rich asks.

"Hardpan," Jack says.

"Never mind," my father says grinning. "Just keep that quiet."

Richard starts giggling like a little boy.

"Tell!" We beg our grandfather.

He places his hands on the back of the lounge. "We had twenty-two crews during the war, put all the piping in the airbases at Tooele, Salt Lake, Hill, and Ogden. I never went to bed for five years: 1941, 42, 43, 44, 45, just dropped dead on this lounge from exhaustion every night. We even had work in Las Vegas putting in a big waterline to the north. I was away for weeks, missing Kathryn and the boys. Then one day, I was walking along the trench when I spotted what I thought was a helmet. I bent down. It moved. I realized it was a tortoise. I picked it up, its head and feet shot back into its shell. I put him in the back of my truck and brought him home for the boys. We named him Hardpan."

He looks at his son, smiles and walks out of the room.

"Everybody else had a dog—" my father says. "German shepherds, Doberman pinschers, black Labs. We drilled a hole in his shell and tied a long cord to it and walked him around the block."

We all look at each other.

"No kidding," Rich says. "Every day we walked him."

"Hardpan?" I ask.

"You know, the desert without rain—hardpan, no give to the sand." Dad's voice is tender.

"He was reliable, old Hardpan, you have to say that about him," Rich adds.

"Until he disappeared—" Jack says returning to his chair.

Gopherus agassizii. Desert tortoise. Land turtle. An elder among us. Even among my family. For some of us he represents "land-locked" like the wild-lands before us. Designate wilderness and development is locked out. Find a tortoise and another invisible fence is erected. The tortoise's presence compromises our own. For others, tortoise is "land-based" a sovereign on earth, entitled to his own desert justice. He is seen as an extension of family—human and non-human alike—living in arid country. His presence enhances our own. The tension tortoise inspires calls for wisdom.

These animals may live beyond one hundred years. They walk for miles largely unnoticed carrying a stillness with them. Fifteen acres may be home range and they know it well. When they feel in their bodies that it is about to rain, they travel to where water pools. They wait. Clouds gather. Skies darken. It rains. They drink. It may be days, weeks, months before their beaks touch water again.

If native mythologies are true and turtles carry the world on their backs, the carapace of the desert tortoise is designed to bear the weight. It is a landscape with its own aesthetic. Three scutes or plates run down the vertebrae, hexagons, with two larger scutes on top and bottom. Four plates line either side of center. The shell is bordered by twenty-four smaller ones that seem to hold the animal in place. The plastron or bottom of the shell fits together like a twelve-tiled floor. The desert tortoise lives inside his own creation like a philosopher who is most at home in his mind.

In winter, the desert tortoise hibernates but not in the manner of bears. Hibernation for reptiles is "brumation," a time of dormancy where cold-blooded creatures retire, rock-still, with physiological changes occurring independent of their body temperatures. Much remains mysterious about this time of seasonal retreat but brumation among turtles suggests it is sparked by conditions of temperature, moisture, photoperiods, and food supply. They stir in their stone-ledged dens when temperatures rise, dens they inhabit year after year, one, two, maybe five individuals together. They leave. They forage. They mate. The females lay eggs in supple sands, two dozen eggs may be dropped in a nest. Buried. Incubated. Hatched. And then the quiet plodding of another generation of desert tortoises meets the sands.

It is a genealogy of evolutionary adaptation until *Gopherus agassizii* suddenly begins bumping into real estate developers after having the desert to himself for millenniums.

1996: a lone desert tortoise stands before a bulldozer in the Mojave.

My father and the Endangered Species Act. My father as an endangered species. The Marlboro Man without his cigarette is home on the range—I will list him as threatened by his own vulnerable nature. I will list him as threatened by my emotional nature. Who dares to write the recovery plan that regulates our own constructions? He will resist me. I will resist him. He is my father. I am his daughter. He holds my birth story. I will mourn his death. We face each other.

Hand over our hearts, in the American West united states do not exist even within our own families. "Don't Tread On Me." The snake coils. The tortoise retreats. When the dust devil clears, who remains?

My father, myself, threatened species.

I recall a statement made to me by another elder, a Mormon General Authority who feared I had chosen not to have children. Call it "Ode to the Gene Pool," a manipulation of theology, personalized, tailorized to move me toward motherhood, another bulge in the population.

"A female bird," he wrote to me, "has no options as to whether she will lay eggs or not. She must. God insists. Because if she does not a precious combination will be lost forever. One of your deepest concerns rests with endangered species. If a species dies out its gene pool will be lost forever and we are all the lesser because of the loss.... The eggs you possess over which your husband presides [are] precious genes.... You are an endangered family."

I resist. Who will follow? Must someone follow?

Clouds gather. It rains. The desert tortoise drinks where water has pooled.

Who holds the wisdom? My grandfather, the tortoise, calls for the story, then disappears.

Tortoise steps.

Tortoise tracks.

Tracks in time.

One can refuse to play the game.

Across from where I sit is a redrock ledge. We are only a stone's toss away from the city of St. George. I am hiking with my father. He has gone on ahead.

Today is the spring equinox, equal light, equal dark—a day of truce.

I have followed tortoise tracks to this place, a den. It is cold, the air stings my face, I did not dress warmly enough. Once again, the desert deceives as wind snaps over the ridge and rides down valley.

The tortoise is inside. I wish to speak to him, to her, to them about my family, my tribe of people who lose money and make money without recognizing their own threatened status, my tribe of people who keep tortoises, turtles, as pets and wonder why they walk away.

"Have you heard the news today?" I pull the clipping from the local paper out of my pocket, unfold it and read aloud:

If you're a desert tortoise living in Washington County, take this advice: Start crawling your way toward the hills north of St. George, Utah.

Come March 15, any tortoise living outside a specially designated "desert tortoise reserve" could become subject to "taking"—a biological term for the death of an animal or the destruction of its habitat.

State and federal officials on Friday signed an interlocal agreement that will set aside 61,000 acres of prime tortoise habitat as a reserve that wildlife biologists believe will secure the reptile's recovery.

On the flip side, the agreement also provides permission and means by which developers and others may "take" some 1,200 tortoises and develop more than 12,000 acres of tortoise habitat outside the reserve without violating the Endangered Species Act, under which the tortoise is listed as a "threatened species."

Friday's signing ends six years of battles over the slow-moving animal, whose presence around St. George has created headaches for land developers and local governments.

"We feel confident that we're going to be able to work together and have a permit that provides for the recovery and protection of the tortoise," said Bob Williams, assistant supervisor for the Fish and Wildlife Service.

Senator Bob Bennett, R-Utah, agreed. "This is clearly a very major step toward getting the endangered species issues resolved short of the trainwreck of the spotted owl."

.... Between 1980 and 1990, the Washington County's population increased 86% from 26,125 to 48,560. It is projected to have between 101,000 and 139,000 people by 2010.

Implementation of the Habitat Conservative Plan is scheduled to last 20 years and cost $11.5 million.

There is no movement inside the den.

"Tortoise, I have two questions for you from Neruda: 'Quien da los nombres y los numeros al inocente innumerable?' *Who assigns names and numbers to the innumerable innocent?* 'Como le digo a la tortuga que yo le gano en lentitude?' *How do I tell the turtle that I am slower than he?*"

The desert tortoise is still.

I suspect he hears my voice simply for what it is, human. The news and questions I deliver are returned to me and somehow dissipate in the silence.

It is enough
   to breathe, here, together.

Our shadows lengthen
   while the white-petaled heart of Datura
opens and closes.

We have forgotten the option of restraint.

It is no longer the survival of the fittest but the survival of compassion.

Inside the redrock ledge, the emotional endurance of the tortoise stares back at me. I blink. To take. To be taken. To die. The desert tortoise presses me on the sand, down on all fours. The shell I now find myself inhabiting is a keratinous room where my spine is attached to its ceiling. Head, hands, feet, and tail push through six doors and search for a way home.

Tortoise steps.
Land-based. Land-locked.
Land-based. Land-locked.
Learning the slow art of revolutionary patience, I listen to my family.

SITTING IN COUNCIL WITH ALL CREATURES:
A CONVERSATION WITH VIRGINIA COYLE

Deena Metzger

To heal ourselves, each other and the Earth
  —these are inseparable
To care for ourselves, each other and the Earth
  —these are inseparable
To listen and participate in co-creating
the world in which i/we want to live
  —this is our work

—GIGI COYLE

One afternoon in 1995, I met with Virginia Coyle at the Ojai Foundation, a land-based educational sanctuary for youth and adults that she has guided in various capacities for many years. Some years earlier when I had told chaos theoretician and mathematician Ralph Abraham that my work was turning in a new direction, that I was finding myself actively creating alliances with animals and the natural world, he said, "If you speak to one person it should be Gigi Coyle."

"Why?" I asked.

"Gigi is the one who freed Rosie and Joe."

Immediately I understood. Rosie and Joe were the captive research dolphins who had worked with John Lilly. The communication experiments they did for eight years and their ultimate release to the wild can be said to have inspired major changes in human understanding and relationship to other species, cetaceans in particular.

By the time I sat down with Gigi face-to-face, I knew that her work with these two dolphins and her life are pivotal to the work of many people who regard animals as peers to humans.

What follows is culled from conversations we had, and from *Beyond Boundaries*, a lecture transcript.

When we first met, she told me the following: "In an aboriginal cave painting, humans are coming out of the blowholes of dolphins. This poses a question: Who is dreaming whom?"

Immediately I wanted to know the woman who approaches animals in exactly the same way she does humans, who brings the same interactions and ways of thinking to the human and to the animal realms.

Rosie and Joe's release might be read, incorrectly, as heroic human efforts on behalf of two dolphins. What's far more noteworthy to me is the exchange possible between ourselves and the natural world, leading to new and more respectful ways of seeing, learning from, and interacting with other species. When we do something, seemingly for, or on behalf of, an animal, we humans receive so much in return. I experience it as the ultimate form of philanthropy or healing—in giving we all benefit.

Early on, I recognized a need in myself and others to develop patience and the ability to be present, if we want to have a relationship with anyone. Animals are particularly good teachers. Council—sitting in a circle, listening to what every being has to say—is an opportunity for such practice as well as a way of life. Council training is a process that provides a field in which each voice is respectfully heard and attentive listening is developed. The voice in council can be a spider weaving its web nearby, as easily as it can be any Jew, Arab, Christian, or child. The voices that I listen to attentively are not only the human voices. I train myself to listen to the voices of the earth as I extend the idea of partnership to all living things. I give thanks for the opportunity I've had to learn from and see through the eyes of others.

It isn't always clear what will happen in an encounter between a human and an animal, but it is probable that something important will occur if one is attentive. What I wish is that people walked in the world with the same sensitivity to each other and to the earth that they express when they are trying to communicate with dolphins.

Sometimes we as humans have an opportunity to assist animals in some way. Other times, we go to the animals to learn things for the sake of human relationships.

The challenge is simply to be awake to the animals, people, and stories in "the field." Community is a field to me more than a place. Within that field there are sometimes little windows of opportunity, times when a window opens and something can happen in a way that doesn't happen every day.

When I began working for the liberation of Rosie and Joe, I was acutely aware that I was working for my own life as well as for theirs; I hoped we would all be sustained by this activity.

The Joe and Rosie story began for me at a time in my life when despite good work, friends, and home, I was growing increasingly aware of an empty feeling. I moved into what some call the dark night of the soul. I felt ready to die. Knowing no other spiritual teacher than nature, I went to the desert. There, alone, I prayed for help. After a time, I ruminated on what the desert had once been—the ocean with her creatures. I made a connection with what was missing in my own life.

From the desert I flew to California—to be near the ocean and to visit Esalen Institute. It was there, after spending extended periods of time in the water and studying breath work, that I first experienced a strong connection to dolphins. It was timely; John and Toni Lilly, heads of the Human Dolphin Foundation (HDF), came to Esalen to speak and invited me to meet Joe and Rosie and swim with them.

Some months later, in 1982, I arrived at Redwood City, California, a research center where Joe and Rosie were housed. The researchers were recording all swimming experiences, human and dolphin, looking for the patterns that were emerging. This meant that I was as much a guinea pig in the experiment as Joe and Rosie, so a peership was created between us. Accordingly, I felt free to step into dolphin territory, the place that had drawn me for so long.

Blotting the concrete pool temporarily out of my mind, I entered the world of two long-lost friends. I looked in Rosie's eye; there was no distraction in her gaze. She scanned my body, resting her eye on my left leg, which I had severely injured three times. The overall sensation was healing. Then I had only to swim and move with Rosie and Joe, to wait for their approach and meld with their invitation.

I have always had to be careful because I see people very quickly—perhaps before they are ready to be seen—and this can feel intrusive or intimidating. With the dolphins, however, there were no restrictions or limitations. They were seeing through me and so I was invited to be fully aware and open.

I returned to visit Joe and Rosie many times over the following years. I read the logs and sat by the pool observing the fast-rising superstars. Many people, including financial supporters, scientists, gurus, and celebrities, were coming to swim with Joe and Rosie. Most of the staff still believed the contact was good stimulation for the dolphins and contributed insight and good data for the study. Everyone knew it left people feeling positively toward dolphins and, hopefully, prone to live their lives caring for or about this species. Even so, I began to question the whole idea of swimming with dolphins in captivity. The environment in which Joe and Rosie existed gradually became of more concern. Eventually the staff, too, became troubled as the number of people swimming with the two animals in a confined space began to take its toll.

The last time I swam with Joe and Rosie, I got out of the pool just minutes after entering. The mood of exploration and curiosity was long gone. Rosie and Joe had little choice about swimming with visitors. People were coming with so many expectations and needs; some happy and excited, some ill, angry, or fearful. I wondered how the dolphins could consistently transform poison to nectar. I wondered whether our search for the experience of interdependence had created the opposite—truly limited, dependent relationships.

During this time, I heard people talking more and more about release. I learned of a promise to return Joe and Rosie to the wild after a few years of experimentation. This promise made to release them seemed an essential part of the journey.

The Redwood City research didn't make sense to me on some level, and so I went to the wild with my questions. I carried a vision of open community where dolphins could come and go and where experiments in communication might be pursued once dolphins were befriended.

I wisely decided to visit Jim Nollman and his wife, Katie, who had created Interspecies Communication. Jim told me he had been spending summers in Northwest Canada interacting musically with larger dolphins and orca whales. He also said he was tired of being the solo guy out there, as if caught in the single male hero myth. He believed a group relationship might be more appropriate with a species that lives and moves in pods. He was interested in pod-to-pod connection. On this note, given my interest and experience in community, we formed a partnership.

Orcananda was designed to bring groups of people together with the whales for a month of exploration and interspecies community experiment. We were not to pursue the whales, nor to intrude on their territory other than placing ourselves within it. When we were on land, we encouraged everyone to make contact through music, meditation, sound, attentiveness, and ceremony. We went out in kayaks and we contacted the whales from boats, but the greater number of contacts occurred during the evening when the orcas came to us, every evening over the four years I was there. Our intention was to dialogue, to create music with the orca, playing and listening, call and response.

The people who came to Orcananda, a wide mixture of ages, occupations, and cultures, carried this experience back into their own lives. We knew that after this experience they would not limit their sense of constituency to people alone and that they would be inspired to include insights gleaned from their relationship with a species that has been here far longer. I found more joy there in that short period of time than with any group of people with whom I had worked to date. Our communication and understanding, our sense of partnership in relationship, communication and creativity was definitely enhanced in the presence of the orca.

It was on one of these trips that Alan Slifka, a benefactor of Lillys' work, HDF, brought the story of Joe and Rosie to life again. In 1985 he had realized that some of the people including John Lilly, himself, had lost interest in the original intention and research. Now there was a movement toward releasing the dolphins who had done such good work.

As a first step toward release, Joe and Rosie were transferred to the Dolphin Research Center in Florida, an open-sea facility. But a year passed and nothing happened. DRC didn't have permits from the government allowing release activity. Pursuing permits for an untried, unestablished program was risky for a dolphin center trying to establish its reputation and economic base. The days wore on and with little funding even for the dolphins' food, their future was in question. It was similar to the plight of chimpanzees who have participated in communication research experiments.

At this point, on one of the orca trips, Alan Slifka convinced me to take a look at the project and see if release was possible. I knew the complexities of the situation: Different people involved had different goals; those who had supported Joe and Rosie over the years were not likely to give more money; and there was significant opposition from the scientific community to the idea of releasing dolphins back to the wild.

Additionally, I had my own questions: Was this a valid pursuit, an appropriate use of time, funds, and energy with respect to everything that was happening with dolphins around the world? Could the project catalyze better relationships with cetaceans and other species? Was this really Joe and Rosie's destiny? Was the promise of release made with them or for them? Was release another part of their work with humans? Could Joe and Rosie, with a selected team, catalyze other opportunities for freedom? Could we learn something together?

My hope was that this project would shift all of us involved into a greater sense of collaboration and partnership. I had already seen animals bring people and nations together: Thailand, Cambodia, and Laos cooperated to preserve the ox, and Soviet submarines mobilized in efforts to save beluga and gray whales trapped in the Arctic ice. Such moments help us build confidence in our ability to ally with each other. With this in mind, I spoke with Toni Lilly, who carried the project's spirit, and HDF agreed to turn the dolphins over to us. I created ORCA [Oceanic Research Communication Alliance] and began the work.

The first task was to create a diversified team. From the beginning I involved Jim Hickman, a founder of citizen diplomacy, who had significant experience in tricky negotiations; Carol Ely, a dolphin lover and friend; and David Jessop, administrator and jack of all trades. A year later, I brought in Richard O'Barry, who, having trained all the Flippers, carried the dream of dolphin release for years, even working on his own to develop a readaptation release project. Then Abigail Alling joined us. A marine-mammal scientist, she was captain and expedition leader of the *RV Heraclitus*, an oceangoing research vessel financed by the Arizona-based research organization Space Biospheres, who had spent much of her early life in the sea islands of Georgia swimming with and observing dolphins.

We needed to train our team, determine the best place to release Joe and Rosie, and then find housing for the fourteen members of the team. We focused on the search for a place by trying to look through the eyes of the dolphins. Once we found what we thought was the best site for them, we would isolate the dolphins from the public in order to reduce their dependency upon humans, develop a live-fish feeding program, construct a "halfway house" for them, and formulate the programs that would assure the dolphins the best possible transition and release, including monitoring their progress once they had returned to the wild.

It was Abigail who suggested an island in Georgia, a wildlife refuge area that was frequented and populated by other dolphins, as ideal for Joe and Rosie's release. As it happened, Wassaw Island was only two hours from where I had spent my childhood learning to swim in the ocean. At first, the best idea seemed to return them to the Gulf of Mississippi, but the only group of people committed to working with dolphins there were the ones who had captured them, and I couldn't agree to leaving them in the hands of their captors.

With a potential site and a team of people we began writing applications for the permits that would give us permission to proceed. We did our paperwork and our research, overdoing everything with precision as we were not established or accepted scientists in the marine fisheries world. It surprised many when the National Marine Fisheries Service immediately granted us a permit to pursue the project.

We decided to build a halfway house, Joe and Rosie's transition home, in a secluded part of the marsh creek system near Wassaw. This was a structure where Rick lived as well as the dolphins; it was a place to be with them, not enclose them. The terminology was important; the halfway house put us into their environment rather than them into ours.

Immediately we began an environmental impact study to help monitor the consequences of our presence. Everything about the area seemed right, including it being a place where dolphins were commonplace.

On the spring equinox, the first day of the study, Abigail and some of her crew came across a dolphin stranded on the beach at Wassaw. She had been beached for many hours, was badly sunburned, and appeared to be in severe trauma. Unable to bring her to the mainland, we brought her into the Wassaw Island dock and with the help of a local exotic animal vet began to minister to her during what became a four day/night vigil to save "Georgia's" life. It was the first test of our network and our commitment to each other and dolphins.*

We were faced with many questions: Was it possible to save her? Should we move her to Florida? Many years earlier, Lilly had had a wild dream to capture a wild dolphin to release with Joe and Rosie to show them the ropes. Was this Georgia?

We were waiting for the blood test results when a stranding network team insisted their schedule allowed us only twenty minutes to decide whether to send a plane for Georgia immediately. I was forced to make a decision without knowing whether she would survive a flight or whether keeping her was taking away her one opportunity for medical care. We held council and I asked for everyone's opinion, but the decision was finally left to me. I walked around and around. I sat with Georgia, came back, returned to her. Twenty minutes came and went. I had no answer. Then the whistle blew, indicating a behavior change. I came out to find her thrashing; she took a couple of last breaths and died. Georgia seemed aware of the decision we were trying to make and entered into the process. We had been with her to help her passing. Perhaps the love given to her had been more important than any medicine. As in a ceremonial context, her death, in many ways, was the birth of our project. We were brought together in a unique way and this irrevocably deepened our commitment to the well-being of all dolphins.

All during the spring, the subject of birth was in the air. The creeks turned out to be a calving ground and dolphin calves were near our halfway house construction daily. Just when we were ready to move Joe and Rosie in May, when we thought we had things under control, the blood tests taken to ensure the dolphins were healthy enough for transfer indicated that Rosie was pregnant. Once again we stopped the project to evaluate the situation. Rosie was less than six months pregnant; gestation is twelve. Dolphins have been moved at this stage. Rosie had previously birthed a calf but it died from what appeared to be lack of care. This is not uncommon behavior for young mothers in captivity. In the wild they learn mothering from other dolphin "aunties." After much investigation and hours of council, we felt it was appropriate to bring Rosie to Georgia and trust she would learn in the wild.

While Rosie and Joe were demonstrating their ability to catch live fish in Florida, we were building the halfway house in Georgia. The Navy had the most knowledge on temporary structures, having built pens for

---

*Many of the people on the *Heraclitus* who had never been around dolphins before had a quick indoctrination. Abigail had been so inspired by the project that she talked the crew and her sponsors into working on site for six weeks; but after meeting Georgia and then Rosie and Joe, they stayed the entire time, ten months.

open-ocean dolphin research work. We approached them hesitantly. We didn't know how they would view our project or whether they would respond at all.

It is widely known that the Navy conducts research with dolphins. Accordingly they have extensive knowledge of dolphin behavior, how deep they dive, how far they swim, how their sonar works, etc. Dolphins have been used in a number of wartime situations for minesweeping. Some people report their participation in nighttime ambushes on enemy frogmen. There are many rumors and, personally, I think most of them are true. Still, the Navy folks we met with agreed to help us out, allowed us to share dock space with them, and finally, at project's end, celebrated the dolphins' release with us and became active members of our sighting network. When we were unable to raise the money for a commercial transport of the dolphins from Florida to Georgia, I got the Army to send two of their Chinook helicopters. It was a wild and wonderful way to get the military involved in a peacetime activity.

As with most everything else, transporting Joe and Rosie to Georgia was an ordeal relieved by cooperation and generosity from many people. Although momentarily stressed and fatigued from the flight, they adjusted quickly to their new home. A month after they arrived we began thinking about the release day. They had adapted well, feeding and getting physically fit in the pen by swimming back and forth with the tides.

We invited a few participants to the site to witness the release, including Alan Slifka and his family; Eugene Linden, who was covering this event for *Time* and *Whale Watcher* magazines; and a *National Geographic* film crew.

We spent the morning of release working on the sighting network and setting up tracking stations. Finally, after two years' work, we joined in a ceremonial farewell, entered the water, cut the ropes, dropped the gate, and waited for the dolphins to leave. Slifka's young son saw an arrow pass by—Joe's fin marking. Then Abigail excitedly spotted them at the edge of the creek. At this moment *National Geographic* indicated they had missed the release shot and asked us to simulate it again, exactly what I had stated we would never do. I was uncertain how to respond when Joe and Rosie intervened. They turned, came back into the pen, circled around a few times, and departed. This time the cameramen got the entire sequence. After all those years of starring with Hollywood actors, Joe and Rosie had learned what the film business is all about. They came back two more times, indicating they knew where they were and could return if they so desired. The third and final time they very definitely chose to exit and headed down the creek.

We followed them until sunset. For some time they frolicked in the bow waves of our boat, an activity common to wild dolphins. Soon they headed up a side creek where we watched them fish, swim, and cavort with each other. The next morning they were not at the creek and no-where to be seen. We motored about nervously. Some hours later when we returned to the *Heraclitus* we saw Rosie at the mouth of the river jumping in the midst of a large pod of wild dolphins. We couldn't tell if they were making love or playing, but it looked pretty good. The pres-ence of other dolphins was very important, representing to us and marine scientists her best chance for survival. But we were worried about Joe. Some scientists had wondered whether he would integrate with others because male dolphins, small ones in particular, are often ostracized. In the next two days, Joe was sighted twice, once swimming about and once doing acrobatics in the surf. Some other dolphins were nearby. This re-lieved our fears and fulfilled our highest hopes. By September, one month later, there had been eight sightings of them in the company of others and we surmised that Joe and Rosie had no interest in returning to the pen. We dismantled it in accordance with the permits' stipulation that we leave the marshes as we had found them. We also hoped that our efforts would lead to the establishment of permanent halfway houses in the future.

We remained in the area until the end of October. Eight sightings felt pretty good. We had never seen ourselves as their only family. It was time to go. We knew that it would be the people on the water, the boaters, the fishermen who would keep an eye out for them, and we were right.

In April we heard that a charter boat captain and naturalist, Edwin Longwater, had twice seen two dolphins with unusual markings among a pod. During one of the sightings he had seen two calves not far from Rosie and another dolphin. Perhaps it was Rosie's calf. This confirmed, at the least, that Joe and Rosie had lived through the winter. In November 1988 I met with Edwin Longwater and Katherine Curtin, who was pur-suing a population study in the area. Joe and Rosie didn't appear but it seemed every other dolphin in the area showed up and stayed a long time. Edwin touched my heart when he said, "I think they know you." And I couldn't help but wonder if Joe and Rosie had something to do with this.

I remembered a mutual promise made. Life felt better keeping an eye out for each other.

The animals had been mirrors, teachers for us once again. By creating the opportunity for choice, we each reconnected with our own call for free-dom. I think we all—including Joe and Rosie—said the same thing: "It's about time."

VENISON PIE:
FROM THE JOURNAL OF A CONTEMPORARY HYBRID

Tess Gallagher

This peninsula, which is nearly an island, has mountains with names anyone would be proud to give as their address. To the southwest is Round Mountain and next to that Blue Mountain, with a road winding to its top called Blue Mountain Road.

Saying "Blue Mountain Road" is such a pleasure that I often route my guests over the top of Blue Mountain, then up the eastern side of this neighboring mountain where, some ten years ago, I built my cabin. True, it's a long way around, but it's still the best way. Nearby are Elk Mountain and Deer Mountain, named for animals here aplenty at one time, creatures many now consider pests if they show themselves when their water or food becomes scarce.

My favorite mountain is Lost Mountain, a little to the east. I spent a lot of time as a child on the flank of this mountain with my parents, who were stump farmers, so I suppose it will always be my favorite—though naturally I am also partial to where I live, Dog Mountain. No one called the mountain this until recently. Even now it's a name I only tolerate, the way the ruby-throated hummingbird, or rufous-breasted hermit, or Anna's hummingbird might tolerate these names or, indeed, any name. This mountain's original designation, Hummingbird Mountain, derived from a legend about a woman who'd left an early settlement in the region to live on her own.

There were suppositions about how this woman came to be accompanied by a halo of hummingbirds that appeared to be feasting on the invisible energy that radiated from her. Wherever she went on the mountain, foraging for berries and mushrooms, hummingbirds moved with her.

A story began to accumulate around the woman in that time when white men were writing in their journals, just as I—a woman with the hybrid pedigree of a hobo stew—am writing now in mine. These early journal writers put down all the details, peculiarities, and misconceptions regarding Indians in this then-wild Washington Territory. A man named Lieutenant John Meares scribbled about a chief named Callicum who slept, he wrote, "with his head on a bag of human skulls every night."

It was a popular misconception in those days that practices unthinkable to white men, such as cannibalism, were enjoyed with great relish by Indians. Such crude beliefs perhaps were somehow necessary in the ongoing scheme of appropriation. This propensity for gruesome fabrications opened a great chasm of mistrust and incredulity, creating a veritable gorge of mistaken identity between Indians and whites, ongoing to this writing.

The woman of Hummingbird Mountain had witnessed the presentation of a venison pie by Captain Vancouver in 1792 to the Nootka Indians at Admiralty Inlet. I heard this story of venison pie when I was very young. It had been handed down to others by the woman who witnessed it. Later I was able to confirm the story when I read James Swan's account.

There was a lot of consternation by Vancouver and his men over what they considered the pure ignorance and wastefulness of the Indians on that occasion, for venison pie was a dish said to have been invented by French traders with the presumably wild, yet indigenous palates of Indians in mind. As Vancouver watched the venison pie float out toward the Pacific, feasted upon by seagulls, he must have puzzled greatly as to what had gone awry.

Imagine a woman standing on the shore. The woman witnesses the pie floating in the current. She moves closer to the two groups of men and sees that finally, after turning his back and showing signs of the greatest disgust, the leader of the tribe, whose name has not been recorded, begins to make plain to Vancouver that he and his men do not eat human flesh. He is eloquent, and he does not use *few words*, as accounts have misrecorded him. The gist of his response is that the white men can keep their stinking cuisine to themselves. Further, he allows they may feed such pies to their dogs. The leader then turns his back and walks an important distance away:

Only when one of Vancouver's men went back to the ship and hauled the haunch of a deer to the banquet site, in order to certify the origin of the venison pie, were the Indians at last persuaded to sit "at table" over still more venison pies and to sup peaceably with their white hosts.

The story of venison pie is one I like to tell when anyone is arrogant enough to think they can go through life without misunderstanding and, in fact, at times downright reinventing the people around them. "Let me tell you a story about venison pie," I say to them.

But I had begun to tell the legend of this witness-woman. Instead, I veered away, like a hummingbird sparring with a crow, to speak of venison pie and mistaken cannibals. But veering is courtship and, like the hummingbird with its metallic, iridescent sheen ruffling its breastbone, I face into the sun to best show plumage when I dive into a story. I lose sight of time and the world and everything in it. Perhaps this straying is, itself, a form of female ecstasy I initiate as I write.

Certainly there are occasions when I wish I had a peppery venison pie of my own to throw at certain cannibals of the real who daily infect the sacredness of the journey. It has been repugnant to me, for instance, to have anyone tell me I don't "look Indian," even when, with the utmost care, they couch it with: "But you don't *look* Native American."

It's true that my unknown amount of Cherokee, added to my one-sixteenth extinct and uncertifiable Kar-wee'wee, plus my pinch of Ojibwa, joined to or departing from Finnish blood, further mixed or assaulted by Pennsylvania Dutch, doesn't show up as much as one in my circumstances, a bearer of legends, could wish. My bloodline can and must be thrown into question. But no one is arguing about the Finns in my past. I say my ancestry must be questioned because this questioning, this veering of others toward and away is also a kind of aggressive, but necessary, courtship.

Nonetheless, I am certain, even though it is now unverifiable, that I am related, at the very least through spirit and desire, to the Kar-wee'wee woman I am speaking about here. One must have patience with obscure origins. I forgo the great pleasure of hurling a venison pie at those who wish to deny my attempts to connect or to reconnect, to gather up the shards and bits of my amalgamated unbelonging. I walk away. I turn my back when they try to become the cannibals of my authenticity, which is the authenticity of river, of mountain. It runs. It stands.

But many things can be known from the diligent study of others. For instance, female hummingbirds of a few species, such as the Annas, are able to manage more than one nest at a time, even though the male is of little help in the actual rearing of the young. The language of this knowledge is passionate in the exactness of its observations and attracts me like the nectar of azaleas:

As the nestlings become fledglings and head into flight from one downy sleeve laced with spider web, the female will be feeding a brood in another nest, and perhaps warming eggs in yet another. Each of these broods will have been fathered by a different mate. Since hummingbirds aren't particular about mating with different species, the great variety of hybrids is impressive.

I am fascinated, it's true, by any profusion of hybrids, as was the woman of Hummingbird Mountain. She felt a kinship, according to legend, with these female hummingbirds who chose not to trust the supposed security of the nest. Rather they preferred the backup nest and the backup nest to that. They also enjoyed the variety of mates they could expect each spring. They didn't waste energy worrying about any mate's fidelity, since it was expected that each male would also have been busy with at least one other female. As she admired her male consorts, she did not know that the beauty of their plumage depended as much on *refraction* and *interference* as upon pigment. She had not read the books, the journals of those who would later study hummingbirds, where it is observed that *radiance derives from the position of the feather*. She experienced only their unique fiery glow and the "something more" that the ever-stunted language of beauty can only gesture toward.

She became the protector and benefactor of all inhabitants on Hummingbird Mountain, but especially of female hummingbirds. When the local Indians heard of her, they said she had likely once been a hummingbird herself and had recently become their human slave or shadow-spirit as a result of having disgraced them in some way—as happens, for instance, when a hummingbird has sipped from forbidden flowers or taken too many mates or abandoned nests before chicks are hatched—a great invisible realm of possible wrongdoing.

Nonetheless, in her human state, she went happily about her task of being productively frenzied about everything, including the job of expelling an overabundance of arrogant male hummingbirds, who came to steal nectar within the *luk*, or mating area. She could approximate the swift diving and whirring sounds of hummingbirds unsettling the air like a deck of cards being shuffled at a distance of eighty yards. She managed this by some trick of pursing her mouth and bringing air all the way from her toes into her nasal passages, then expelling it through her nostrils with a great outward rush. As she gradually took on her new identity of Hummingbird-Bride, she made a second paradise of the open meadows and brambled riversides, clearing saplings away to let sunlight better illuminate the wildflowers—fireweed, foxglove, red currant. But she also offered the refractory powers of her spirit.

At some point, according to her legend, she passed with ease and honor into the form of a female hummingbird. There is some doubt from those who carried this story forward as to whether, in hummingbird form, she was ever quite as happy as she'd been as Hummingbird-Bride. Perhaps hers was one of those punishments that has no exit, which simply has to be tolerated and lived through in its endless succession of forms.

I have also been trying to make the best of circumstances here on Hummingbird Mountain since it became "Dog Mountain." Those who have heard my oft-recounted stories of this place can see that such a name carries not the least hint of its rich past, nor of its benefactor and protecting presence, the woman who became a hummingbird. "Dog Mountain" is a blatant slur on the steady industry and magical character of such a mountain.

Under the name Hummingbird Mountain there was the belief that the entire mountain could actually hover above earth while it stretched into the clouds, past broad wings of rain, to collect a sweetness it then gave back as still more nourishing rain. When fog rolled in from Fuca Strait (the old territorial name of these waters) and swirled the base of the mountain, it was easy for literal-minded visitors to observe that the mountain did, indeed, hover above earth. But such verification of the miraculous should not be necessary: *The mountain hovered.*

Why it should fall to me to defend this mountain's former identity, I don't know. Probably it has to do with my life on the mountain, simply being here and being able to write in my journal. For as they say in love— proximity is more than half the battle. Still, it's true I am unqualified in a way perhaps not dissimilar to Hummingbird-Bride, who was unsuited to be the bride of any human form.

I have dared to carry some small shards of my self-assumed relation to Hummingbird-Bride, but have been unable, in any case, to save this mountain from its disparagement as "Dog Mountain." It is suspected that there are rich deposits of ore inside this mountain, a tempting enough prospect for the mountain to be sold to mining interests so the proceeds can be used to build not one but two gambling casinos. (Already the muffled click of dice across the felt-covered table pulls at local brain stems.)

As the dog of Dog Mountain I realize a certain perverse stature. There is significance and a certain rightness in my having been called "dog," for just as dogs were precursors to the horse as carriers of burdens, so am I unaccountably the transport of this mountain's legends.

There exists among many peoples a great respect for the spirits of place. Accordingly, I celebrate fierce spirits in the long beaks of the hummingbirds that nest everywhere on this mountain. Can it be that because I'm here to tell its legend, the mountain recalls its hovering? Why am I so haunted by the velocity of multiple hummingbird hearts pumping 1,200 beats a minute? I am sure of one thing—that this mountain will vanish before it will allow itself to be sold for a throw of dice or the snap of an ace on a gaming table.

It is obvious that I have set my own flower-honed beak among the sword ferns. The spirit of my courtly veering is devotion. When I pass, the sight-blasted eye of crow stares down. I have been known to stand heedless in a certain waterfall that remembers a woman who became a hummingbird. I offer myself pensively, letting the water pour over and away from me, as I consider this mountain's rushing, its democratic gathering up, to which I am a kind of lumpish, undifferentiated, fleshy offering.

For those who wish to come here, I advise a route by way of Lost Mountain. There is, however, the warning that those who set out do not always arrive. Whether this is the residue of some irresolvable punishment or an adventurous advantage, I cannot say. Only that sometimes traders conveying overspiced venison pies, or the vision of a woman in a meadow haloed by hummingbirds, or the pitchy curiosity of legend disguised as history, fruitfully impedes the sojourner. This is the hazard, the bright and barbarous invitation of this Mountain.

COYOTE

Ann Daum

At night I dream of coyotes. Coats wheat-yellow or the dark of burning sage, sleek and long of leg, throats opened to the sky. Their shadows line the bare, shale bluffs of my family's South Dakota ranch, line the edges of my dreams, waiting, watching with their hungry eyes.

I now live far from those rolling hills and deep, water-slicked draws. I am swallowed in the housing developments of a Colorado city, a place no longer wild. Mountains tower west of town, and there are wild places there. But for as far as I can see, streetlights wash away the stars, and fences divide the prairie into cells.

On nights I cannot sleep I boil tea, sit for hours by the picture window, looking at the backyard fence. Sometimes I walk, crossing miles of asphalt rivers, tasting oil on the wind that shakes the trees. I whisper back my name to yard-tamed aspens and silent ponderosa pines, but they do not know me here. The coyotes look down from their perches in the rocky foothills as I search for them, but they never sing. It is the roar of semis, the late-night TV blaze from the house next door that break the silence here, and I am left to dream.

The summer I was seven, my father's hired hands shot coyotes, sometimes three or four a week. Howard and Cal trapped the ones they could not shoot. They ran others into the hard, black ground with their trucks, rolling the coyotes under the tires and spitting them back up into the air like clods of dirt. Then they strung the skins onto a length of baling wire stretched across the kitchen of an abandoned house.

I remember walking into that house in the dead of summer, smelling blood, red-hot and sour, beating flies from the corners of my eyes. The skins dried stiff and yellow, with four hollow tubes for legs, faces frozen stiff into a mask, and emptiness for eyes. I walked through that room with Dalen, who was Cal's son, and the coyotes' tails hung down to brush our faces. We closed our eyes and groped, felt the tails against our skin, reaching soft and supple from above like the limbs of willows.

We both jumped when Howard crept silently to the window and howled through his teeth, fake and long and high. We ran out of that forest of skins, laughing and scared at the same time, and did not go back.

That same summer Dalen showed me a coyote living in a stooping box of mesh and wood in Howard's yard. I wouldn't step too close so he poked her through the narrow wires. She didn't move, didn't look like the live coyotes I'd seen frozen in the headlights, or loping across the prairie pasture just after dawn. She looked dead, like the skins, except for her eyes, which were fixed on something, some hill or tree or bird outside the cage. When I looked in the same direction, though, I saw nothing. Something in that stare scared me, that and the musky stench of urine dripping from the corner of the cage into a can.

I didn't know then that Howard used her urine to lure other coyotes to his steel-toothed traps. That coyote died soon after, her coat blank and bristled from her skin, dry as an old horsehair brush, and she was no longer any use. Howard didn't even skin her. He laughed when I asked why; he was tall above me with his black hair and crooked nose and teeth and I felt small. He said she stank too much to touch.

Later that year, when I'd see a coyote frozen in knee-high summer grasses, or a half-grown coyote pup trotting down a draw, nosing at the ground like a yellow dog, I'd wonder about the coyote in the box. About the way Howard would throw bits of jerky from the window of his truck for Patches, my favorite of the ranch dogs, then tell me about the time he roped a coyote, strung his lariat to the bumper of the truck, and dragged her seven miles down a gravel road.

Sometimes I'd hear Patches howling along with the coyotes at night, and the line between tame and wild, between right and wrong, stretched thin.

This is when the dreams began. Some nights I ran across moonlit prairie, dried buffalo grass and sagewort crisping under the bare soles of my feet. The shale bluffs around me rippled with the silent forms of running coyotes and mule deer, jackrabbits, bobcats, and tiny swift foxes. A prairie fire crackled behind us, swallowing night and sky and dirt. One by one, the animals fell behind. There was smoke, the light and dark of burning flesh, and then I ran alone.

There were other dreams, dark, stinking dreams of death and glowing eyes; dreams where I chased but never caught a coyote's black-tipped tail; dreams that wailed from inside rock and wire and wood, where there is, and always will be, a coyote living in a box.

I tried to understand cruelty as something separate from myself, from our many dogs and cats and horses. Tried to believe that somehow coyotes, badgers, and foxes didn't count, didn't feel the pain of traps or leaden shot quite so keenly as Patches might or the soft-eyed rabbits in their cage, that wild was just the other side of tame, something annoying to change or kill.

When I was twelve, Cal's oldest son Danny showed me how to break a mustang colt. He'd bought the colt from Don Lyman, our wild, bearded neighbor who ran his mares out with two hundred woolly buffalo. The colt was wild too, a muddy brown with rolling eyes and rust around his nose and flank. He stood, trembling, on three legs. One hind foot was hitched up tight to his hairy belly with a loop of cotton rope. That rope snugged up across his withers in a knot, and another circled around his neck, just behind his shaggy ears.

Even hobbled, the colt was beautiful. His neck arched up from the ropes around his withers, and his eyes were wild, full of the fast-moving clouds that race along the prairie sky.

"Easy, colt, now don't you move," Danny said, his voice low and calm and running like the slow white water of our river into the mustang's ears.

"It doesn't matter what I say to him as long as I keep talking," he said in that same voice, and now he'd reached the horse-end of the rope.

The colt stood as Danny touched him, first on the sweaty neck, then down to rub his back and chest. His eyes moved though, and there was terror in the white-edged way they followed Danny's every move.

When Danny reached back for the red-wool saddle blanket he had swung up on the fence, the colt sprang suddenly, almost on top of him. All was dust and tangled mane and tail for a moment, then the colt was down and Danny was hatless and sitting on his head. He had a halter and a lead on the colt so fast I couldn't see his calloused fingers move.

When Danny got up the colt grunted and scrambled to his feet, tried to run on his three good legs. Danny pulled the halter rope hard and the colt fell. The colt jumped up again, and I saw the lather on his neck had turned to bloody foam. Once more he tried to run but the ropes pulled him down and this time he lay there, eyes wide and blank, breathing wretched, panicked whinnies through his open mouth.

Danny was gentle after this. He rubbed Furacin into the rope burns on his neck and legs.

"See how easy, Andy-Pandy?" he asked me, and cinched the saddle slowly, eased a rawhide bosal over his nose. But the mustang's eyes never changed. Months later, when we would ride out to check the calves, I'd hold that colt's reins while Danny or Cal wrote up a tag and punched it through a newborn ear. I'd rub the mustang's head, reach for an apple I'd saved for my horse Dollar, and he wouldn't even see me. His eyes were dark and hard and faraway, and the part of him that had run on twelve thousand empty acres, I never saw again.

I dream about coyotes because there is so little wild left. Soon, even the South Dakota prairie may be tamed, settled only with the hollow ghosts of sheep and cattle, the wind's lonely, predawn music strumming miles of barbed-wire fence.

The bobcats are hiding, if they still exist here at all. I have seen one tiny, black-tailed Swift fox in my fifteen years of watching, and the next day he was gone. There was rumor of a wolf shot trotting across an open field in western Minnesota. My father believes that wolf may have traveled through Dakota too. Terry Kirkdall, one of my father's temporary hands, swore he saw a wolf one morning on the wild south side of the river. He didn't get his rifle out quick enough, he said, and when he looked again, the wolf was gone.

The fire that is progress, that is hatred of the wild, has consumed these predators and spit them back to ash. Their lands are diminishing, closing down into a box. Sometimes even on the prairie the coyotes are silent, leaving just the stars and blue-black night, the rolling of the grass to meet the dawn, the shadow of a soul pursued hidden in a thousand hills.

At night, at least, the ranch is as it was when I was a child. I cannot see the river's newest crick and curve, the new calving shed humped up against the sky down on the oxbow land. I walk the narrow path out to the gravel pit and sit down in my favorite spot, a mound overlooking the silent water. When I have been there for a while, if I'm quiet, the coyotes begin to sing. One voice at first, a bark bleeding into wail, then a strange harmony of three, an octave higher than before. Though I know it's unlikely, I want to think one of those voices is Clyde, a smoke-colored coyote I often think and dream about, for she is the only one I've known by name.

She was real, my father's pet, captured as a pup and kept because of the beauty of her silver coat. This was back when my memories were forming, still as milky and hazy as a newborn foal's eyes.

I remember Clyde because of the sadness of her yellow eyes, and because I was not allowed to touch her and wanted to so much. She lived in our front yard, chained to the trunk of a massive Chinese Elm. And although she ate dog food from a plastic bowl, in her heart she was still wild. On nights when coyotes howled from the bluffs behind the house, I would sneak into the kitchen to watch Clyde writhe and dance in the moonlight, linked to earth only by the soldered length of chain.

She would lean into her collar, whining along with the music of other, wilder voices, then snarl jagged, choking cries when the singing stopped. She became smaller each night, huddling into the shallow hole she'd scratched beneath the tree, shriveling into a moonlit wraith with yellow eyes fixed on the horizon.

One night she disappeared, still wearing her collar, though the chain had been unsnapped. My dad was furious, certain that someone had snuck over during the night and set her free. I missed her, but sometimes thought I could pick her voice from the others I heard howling in the night.

Years later, my father still wonders what happened to Clyde. Whether she lived on in the wild, raising litters of smoky pups with that collar still latched around her neck, or whether she was shot or trapped soon after. I like to think she lived, that she still lives. That the silver coyote I see trotting down a gully by the trout dam may be her.

Sometimes when I'm sitting by the water, and there are stars glowing above and below me, I listen for Clyde, for all the coyotes. They are out there, watching with their yellow eyes, and they seem to know I wait. But theirs is a hidden world, and shy. All is silent and I am left alone.

My father calls one morning, excited to have seen a big dog-coyote on the front lawn at daybreak. He thinks it could be tame, looking for an easy meal, so he sets out a tub of dog food. The coyote doesn't reappear the next day or the next, but my father keeps waiting. He will watch for days, maybe have the guys throw a long-dead steer out behind the house to draw a couple more.

Now that he can't get around the snowy hills and draws to see the wildlife for himself, he feeds them shamelessly. Round bales of alfalfa for the deer set nose-down by the living-room window, a bony, black-hide carcass in the cornfield just behind the house. He waits at the bedroom window with binoculars, my mother says, to see the coyotes gather to their feast.

I have dreamed of coyotes mixing with the cattle for two nights in a row, and when he calls I tell him this. He says he does have a pair of coyotes in the calving pens, gray as dawn and shier, slinking back into the trees. But he isn't worried yet.

These coyotes have seemed content, so far, with afterbirth, milk-sweet calf manure, and the dead meat lying easy back behind the barn. As long as this is all their goal, my father will not shoot them. His friendship with the coyotes is based on that deadly handshake: They stay away from living calves and he leaves his rifle locked inside a cabinet in the house. He does not, like so many other ranchers, keep a rifle strung up inside the back window of his truck. Though this has not always been the case. Years ago my father leg-trapped bobcat, beaver, coyote, and badger. He clubbed a fearless black-footed ferret once, not knowing what it was, or how rare. He too used to shoot coyotes from the open window of his truck. But people change, and should change, and he has learned to appreciate the wild with the tame.

Last time I was home I walked about a mile past the barn to have a look at the bone pile. The coyotes had gnawed down the little mound of stillborn and pneumonia-killed calves, the bones stripped to flags of hide, red and black and gray, waving in the prairie wind. They had also begun work on the old brockle-faced cow—smooth-mouthed, dry of skin and bone, and missed at last fall's cull. I was surprised at the parts of her they'd shunned. Her throat, the bony stretch of hide along her back, the ear that's tagged, and all one length of ribs are untouched. These coyotes are not bone-cracking thin or they would have stripped her clean.

My father's ranch is now a testament to the fact that cattlemen and coyotes can live in peace. For the past twenty years, he has left the shelter belts and brambled ditches unmowed, reserved wild, tangled highways between plowed fields to support buffalo-berry patches, mice, shrews and gophers, insects, cottontails, and grouse—the coyotes' natural fare. He no longer allows coyotes to be trapped or hunted for sport on our land. And these coyotes do not eat cats or chickens, or even newborn calves. They live a wary, watchful balance, in their rightful role of predator, of cleaner of dead bones.

Their presence would not be allowed on other ranches. Coyotes have no place in a rancher's heart, and they are blamed for crimes they could not have managed. Ranchers, and sheep men in particular, bear a vicious grudge against the coyote, sometimes founded but often not. They poison, shoot, and trap them, hang nursing females from fenceposts by one hind leg as a warning to the rest. Ask any cattleman who shoots coyotes why he does so, and he'll answer, "Because they kill calves." Ask him the last time a coyote killed one of his healthy calves, and he may have to think for a while. If he does have an answer, he probably doesn't know for sure if the calf died first and then was gnawed by coyotes. And he's not about to find out.

The war against coyotes is more a crusade of values than anything.

Tame against wild, the intrinsic value of livestock over predators. Money is not the issue here. In the summer, few people skin the coyotes they kill, and the hide and all is left to rot. The skins are worthless in the summer, bring only twenty dollars or so mid-winter. And South Dakota, unlike Wyoming, no longer has a bounty on each coyote killed.

The killing of coyotes holds a respected place in South Dakota society. The teenage sons of ranchers often carry their own rifles from twelve or thirteen on. They have learned from their fathers, their grandfathers, to think of coyotes the same way they do mice in the feed room, or Russian thistle growing in the hay field. Destroying them is not cruel but necessary, and sometimes even fun. The sight of a coyote trotting down a bare shale slope or loping along the reedy bottom of a draw is a welcome bit of sport and useful entertainment in the middle of a long workday, or on the drive to town. Most of these boys are careful shots, and if the coyote makes it over the hill and out of sight one day, it may not be so lucky the next day, or week, or month. Coyotes learn to run hard, then stop just out of rifle range to look back. Sometimes a pup misjudges, and so he stops too soon, seems to wait there, curious, as he is shot.

In the winter, some boys chase coyotes on snowmobiles or from horseback. They shoot them, or club them senseless with the butts of rifles. Even the ones that get away aren't necessarily lucky, for calories spent running in deep snow may, in a time of hunger, be the last they'll ever spend. In the spring, boys' fathers may help them gas or drench and burn dens full of pups. And so this goes on through generations, both of coyotes and of men.

Coyotes survive, however, with the tenacity of the deep-rooted yuccas and short, thirsty sage. Tell a South Dakota rancher that his efforts may someday exterminate the coyote from his land and he'll laugh. "Hasn't yet," he'll say, and laugh some more.

There is a tough honor about these men. They are kind to children and orphan foals, and live off their land with as little contact with the outside world as can be managed. When it rains they pull their hat brims low, almost to their eyes, and carry on. In a blizzard, the calving heifers still get checked, and the river ice gets chopped so the animals can drink. But in this world the wild has little place or value and, eventually, must be destroyed.

Here at least, in the rolling hills and buttes of the White River valley, on my father's ranch and on some other scattered sections of this land, the fire licking at the coyote's heels, at every wild thing's heels, will be wetted.

Ever since Cal left in '85, Howard two years later, the coyotes have been coming back. They seem to know about, or maybe Clyde has told them of, this five-thousand-acre haven. They line up on the prairie hills, atop the ridges and the crumbling, blue-shale draws, and sing.

There is a place between dreaming and waking where something hides. I can squeeze my eyes shut some mornings, just after the alarm rings, and see the past, or maybe see a dream.

The image is grainy, blurred with time, of a little girl, her long chestnut hair swinging down her back, a darker shade than I have now. I watch her totter down the gravel driveway, hands burrowed in her flannel gown, eyes fixed on the coyote chained in the front yard.

I still feel the sharp-edged rocks cutting through her bare soles, shiver with her in the naked night air, and when she reaches Clyde's huddled, silver body, I help her fingers find and unclip the heavy chain. Through her eyes I watch the smoke-colored coyote slink away, slowly at first, then faster, in a crazy, hump-backed gallop. I see Clyde stop, look back once with eyes like crescent moons, then slip away to shadow.

APPRENTICESHIP TO ANIMAL PLAY

Brenda Peterson

During one of the darkest times of my life, I often found myself lying flat on my studio floor, face-to-face with my Siamese manx cat. As I wept over my many losses, Isabel would leap over me as if my prostrate grief were a posture to invite her kittenish pounces, her purring growls and tiny tiger attacks. If she were a kitten, I could have better understood her sudden playfulness, indeed, her mania for play. But Isabel had never played with me before. Why, when I was the most griefstricken, would she mistake my sorrow for high-spirited cat games of stalk and bat-the-birdie, and braid my hair with claws tenderly tucked?

As I lay snuffling on the old carpet, a desultory hand stroking this small, bobtailed cat who threw herself into dazzling cartwheels over my legs, I found myself smiling in spite of myself. And when Isabel grabbed my socks, growling as if I wore mouse houseshoes on my dragging feet, I had to laugh out loud. Soon I was checking out cat-play toys at the pet shop and bringing home a feathered fake bird contraption tethered to a small pole. With a whistling not unlike birdsong, the black, pink, and bright purple "bird" whizzed through the air around Isabel, inspiring her to acrobatic leaps and midair somersaults shocking in their grace and complete abandon.

One morning I was, as usual, lying on the carpet crying my eyes out. There were so many things that caused my pain: I'd left an eight-year relationship to live alone, my career was utterly confused, my family had all denounced me over my latest book, and a dear friend had just died. I can't remember which misery had me in its grips that day, but I had already gone through half a pack of Kleenex. As I was blowing my nose, I opened my swollen eyes and saw Isabel's slanting blue irises. Eyes oscillating, she stalked me with ferocious glee, her tail twitching and trembling in anticipation of her pounce—which she did, right onto my nose, snatching the tissue and shredding it all over my face. This flimsy foe vanquished, she turned tiny tail and hunkered down next to me, awaiting the next fabulous threat.

It was only then that I wondered if something about my grief had engaged my cat's imagination so deeply that her response was new behavior: this inspired play. Isabel's history was lost to me. I knew only that she'd been feral and homeless for the eight months my neighbors fed her where she cowered under their back porch. She'd never allowed them near until one day she had what my neighbor Pamela describes as a "kitty nervous breakdown." "That's all I can call it," Pamela explained as she pleaded with me to take Isabel into my own home, where I already had an older, much-beloved Siamese manx named Ivan and Ziggy, a burly chow-chow/Newfoundland mix park rangers called "a bear on a leash." Really no room for another animal.

Pamela continued, "This little rag-tag Siamese just sat in the middle of our driveway and screamed her head off as if to say, 'I can't take one more homeless day. I can't cower in the dark one more night. I've never let a human come near or even touch me, but please please just pick me up and put me out of my misery!'"

So they brought her to my house, where Isabel proceeded to perch on my bookshelf, watching the birds on a branch outside. She promptly claimed that tiny wooden square as her only territory. From this safe perch, she endured the other animals and at night sometimes stole into my bed; but she kept her distance. Isabel was silent, sneaky, and except for an essential sweetness to her nature, often what we humans would call "shut-down."

"It's trauma," the vet diagnosed. "Imagine what she's been through out there, lost and homeless. Who knows what she's seen, what she's survived. It may take her many months to know she's safe and sheltered." The vet stroked her matted, dull fur and clipped away another of the greasy globs of furball that knotted her body like tumors. "She may be just too traumatized to ever play again."

"So play is a sign of good health?" I asked the vet, intrigued.

"Oh, yes," he said. "Both physiological and psychological health. In any animal, it's a sure indicator not only of good health but of their chances for survival. When an animal never again engages in play, we don't hold out much hope for full recovery."

For over two years my cat Isabel had not remembered how to play, and perhaps I'd given up hope, or just decided it was not in her nature. And when her unexpected wholehearted playfulness coincided with my own wholehearted grief, it took me a few weeks to notice. But at last I recognized that, for some reason, her trauma was over, even as my own began. She was not trying to balance me, though she did. Perhaps her move from a house with two other alpha-animals into a studio alone with me as the only human set her free to claim more territory, and therefore more space within her own inner life. Perhaps she perceived my horizontal crying bouts as a delicious new game in which her human was at last on her level and therefore she could reveal her many mysterious, ingenious, gravity-defying talents. Whatever the explanation, her clowning was so serious that it literally eased my dark moods into musing, companionable play. It was a perfect exchange for which I shall always be grateful: We had slowly nurtured each other out of deadening trauma and into some daily delight in living.

Isabel's story is not new. Every day we read of some animal healing a human—the family dog awakens a child from coma or an elderly woman finds solace in the companionship of many cats. There are even animal-assisted therapy programs in nursing homes or hospitals in which animals literally bring us back to health. By the same token, there are many humans involved in saving, caretaking, or rehabilitating animals. Everyone knows that animals and humans help each other heal. But what strikes me most about Isabel's cat-rescues-human story is the element of play.

I have always placed a high value on play. Once, a friend decorated my birthday cake with the inscription: "I play, therefore I am." I've always considered my decade of studying and encountering dolphins, mostly in the wild, as an apprenticeship to play, learning the lessons of another intelligent species that spends three-quarters of their lives at play. What is it about play that is so important it has evolved into a central preoccupation for large-brained mammals, as well as other species?

In a recent *National Geographic* cover story on "Animals at Play," physician Stuart L. Brown describes his first discovery of the importance of play to animal and human behavior. In 1966, when Brown was on the faculty of the Department of Psychiatry at Baylor College of Medicine in Texas, he listened on the radio to gunshots from the infamous Texas Tower massacre. Charles Joseph Whitman, a university student, had climbed the twenty-seven-story tower and was firing randomly at passersby below. When he was finished with his insane vendetta and before he himself was fatally shot, there were thirteen people dead and thirty-one wounded.

It is a chilling commentary to note that three decades later, Whitman's random shootings are commonplace; but in the sixties his actions were so unprecedented that Governor John Connally (who himself had survived a gunshot wound during the Kennedy assassination) commissioned Dr. Brown to do a behavioral study of this mass murderer. What startled Brown was not Whitman's current persona of "Mr. Clean" nor his family history of abuse, but "the absence of a normal play pattern" in childhood. As Brown continued his psychiatric profiles of other murderers, he discovered that a striking 90 percent of the young men showed "either the absence of play as children or abnormal play like bullying, sadism, extreme teasing, or cruelty to animals." This dysfunctional play pattern was obsessed with winning at all costs; it was rooted in an inflexible, black-and-white morality; and its problem-solving possibilities allowed only two options: conquest or defeat. This research led Dr. Brown to expand his study of play to include noncriminal human populations as well as other animal species. He finally concluded that play is an indicator of psychological health. He also theorized that humans have much to learn about play from other animals.

He contacted Jane Goodall during his study and asked her about the chimpanzees she's studied since 1960 in Tanzania's Gombe National Park. Goodall has often described the chimpanzees as champions of play among nonhuman primates; she added that a sign of depression in orphaned infant chimpanzees may be that they stop playing at all. Goodall and Brown's work suggests that play for many species is an essential indicator of physical well-being, emotional balance, and even survival.

In the *National Geographic*'s companion video to its story on animal play, there is an interview with Mark and Helen Atwater, who run a baby gorilla orphanage in Brazzaville on the Congo River. Here the couple spend much of their day—in fact, up to seven hours a day—rehabilitating these orphaned gorillas with play before they return them to the wild. "Play is a real milestone," remarks Helen Atwater as she cradles a tiny gorilla named Goko.

Sometimes it takes as long as a year for these orphaned gorillas to play again. "Like Goko here," says Helen Atwater, "many of these baby gorillas have seen their mothers or their entire families murdered. They are too traumatized to play." Teaching these baby gorillas to play again is restoring a survival skill to a deeply endangered species. It is also a lesson our species can take to heart in a world where so many refugee children have been traumatized by war, poverty, and loss of homeland. The Atwaters and many other animal researchers are trying to preserve not only primates and habitat but also to remind us of what all parents know about their offspring: To play is to survive.

Play is not only a prelude to developing adult skills such as fighting, foraging for food, coordination, cooperative and communication skills; play is also about developing an imagination that is flexible and responsive to one's environment. As Joe Meeker, author of *Comedy of Survival*, says, "Play allows us to most easily cross boundaries between human and animal, between male and female, even between enemies." Joe, who teaches a graduate course in play at Seattle's Antioch University, has also worked with Stuart L. Brown on researching just what it is about human and animal play that makes it so crucial for our mutual survival. Meeker always assigns his students the homework of writing a personal history of play, which is a very revealing and often difficult task since so few of us really pay attention to play that is not goal-oriented or tangibly rewarding. But play that is timeless, pleasurable, and self-rewarding is often the very play that most nourishes and restores us to what we like to think of as our "humanness"—our best human natures. As Meeker explains, "In at least a dozen species, the ratio of play to nonplay in a day is the same as the ratio of REM sleep—and you know what happens when humans are deprived of those deep sleep rhythms of REM. We literally go crazy."

I am always struck by the fact that play among humans seems to differ along gender lines. Much has been written about boys-and-toy-guns and girls-and-dolls, the idea of boys being preoccupied with games of dominance and organized team or war sports. But these simplistic gender stereotypes can be misleading. As we study animal play more deeply, we begin to discover other patterns and ways of reading such notions as dominance and hierarchy among animals at play. For many years primatologists have concerned themselves with the study of hierarchy, particularly among males competing for reproductive superiority and powerful status. But recent research among rhesus monkeys shows us that our past views on hierarchy may need revision. In a 1995 *New York Times* article, several respected primatologists such as Barbara Smuts, Kim Wallen, and Robert M. Sapolsky declared that it is now an outdated perception that rhesus monkeys spend all their energy in a deadly serious play at power politics and dominance—all toward the goal of king-on-the-mountain and most likely to succeed at mating.

First of all, it is the females, not the males, who most determine reproductive choice by selecting with whom among all the wandering bachelor males they might mate. Female rhesus monkeys don't necessarily choose alpha males as reproductive partners; often they choose instead a male who has shown his alliance, goodwill, and companionship during the nonestrus periods, when grooming and sociability are generously offered. While the alpha male monkey might play at strutting and chest-thumping and thereby succeed at establishing his status among the lower-ranking males, this is not the male who tops the females' list of Most Desirable. Dr. Wallen comments, "The model we have of low-ranking animals striving to be high-ranking animals probably really isn't accurate. The low-ranking animals may be perfectly happy as long as they're getting mating opportunities and as long as they're getting fed."

Our human obsession with hierarchy and dominance—the "play hard, die hard," notion of animal behavior with dominant males ruling the roost—seems to have less and less basis in fact. Certainly our primate cousins are teaching us this new way of looking at ourselves. Primate play, though it differs along gender lines as does ours, is still more preoccupied with social skills, courtship strategies, and just plain high-spirited fun. Dr. Smuts even found in her research with olive baboons that a group of animals may not choose to even establish a dominance hierarchy, if they are fortunate enough to find themselves in an abundant habitat with an increasing and stable population. In this situation the males, "anticipating a long and productive life span, eschew haggling over rank and instead cultivate relationships with females or form amicable coalitions with other males who may help out in the future."

Those who study animals are also recognizing that female animals enjoy their own subtle hierarchies and reproductive play; females are not always simply centered on nurturing or what we humans might see as "playing with dolls." As more women scientists, sociologists, psychologists, and animal behaviorists enter the field, analyze research, and design behavioral studies, they are changing the way we perceive animals, as well as ourselves. For example, recent research, much of it done by women, reveals that among elephants, hyenas, cetaceans, and lions there are strong, complex, female-centered hierarchies. These stable societies of barren females, mothers, and postreproductive female elders not only look out for the survival of the next generation, vigilantly baby-sitting while the young are at play, but also indulge in very sophisticated games of shifting alliances, cooperative strategies, and profound sensual play.

As I, with the playful inspiration of my cat Isabel, at last recovered from my personal traumas, I again sought the cetacean companions who have done the most to restore my own sense of play. One of my favorite encounters with wild dolphins recently was in the Florida Keys when a friend, one of a few female "skippers," took a group of women nature writers out into the open ocean. There we hoped to meet a "nursery pod" of bottle-nosed dolphins with whom "Captain Rosie," as we dubbed her, has played over the past two decades. "When I first encountered this nursery pod, I didn't realize they were all female," Captain Rosie told us as she revved up her motorboat on a cold Florida winter day. We zoomed across turquoise seas, and though it was sunny, we were bundled under patchwork quilt comforters in what Rosie called a "Florida Keys Sleigh Ride." Captain Rosie explained, shouting above the wind gusts, "Over on the south side, you have the Swinging Singles—the bachelor pod of male bottlenose dolphins having themselves a mighty good time. But I like to spend my time with 'the girls,' even though some of these females are grandmothers now and I'm playing with their grandchildren—or grandcalves."

Captain Rosie laughed, her head thrown back, her short, dark hair styled by strong winds. Here was the wide-open sun-wrinkled face of a grandmother herself abandoned to the call of the sea and these sister creatures she believed were her own extended family. A mother of a grown son, Rosie divides her time between the sea, where she leads nature and wildlife expeditions, lending others her expertise as a marine environmental educator; and onshore, where she goes dancing almost every night. "Watch the water!" Captain Rosie called out to us as we shivered against each other and the motorboat roared flat-out like a high-speed hydroplane. Our faces were rearranged by the wind, smiles pulled taut, sunglasses and bright bandannas plastered to our heads with the gale force of our ocean flight. "The colors are like a topographic map to tell us depths and shallows. See that dark, emerald green path—that's the deep water and the turquoise is where we might run aground. So, hang on to your hats!"

What hats we had were already overboard by then. I was reduced to my scarf double-knotted beneath my chin. Several of the other women covered their bare heads with quilts. Only one of us was warm, an editor friend of mine who leaned out from the prow of the boat, arms outflung like a blissful, bare-bosomed masthead. No maiden she, this was the first time she'd been cool since she began menopause.

Suddenly Captain Rosie cut the motor and we trolled quietly along a luminous aqua stream of sun slanting on open sea. It was so bright, our eyes so bedazzled, it took some moments to focus on the distant dorsal fins arching up and down in high waves. "Listen," Captain Rosie whispered. "Dolphins love music, especially waltzes. It's the four-quarter time, like music at a skating rink, *da-dum, da-dum, da-dum, dum-dum . . .*" Captain Rosie sang in a resonant soprano and did a perfect pirouette at the helm. It didn't even rock the boat.

Then music surrounded us, a Strauss waltz, echoing under the fiberglass shell of Rosie's boat like an underwater speaker sending the graceful sound vibrations through the sea to that pod so familiar to our captain that she recognized each dolphin by her dorsal fin. We felt inside the rhythmic music, its romantic pulses resonating up through the boat's hull and into our feet, calves, our knees bent and balancing with the waves of waltz and sea. Everyone was exhilarated, laughing and swaying in perfect time to the music and rock of the boat. We had sea legs, like some hula girls, whose undulant bodies remember ancient rhythms of moon-tides and understand that this vast womb of water also ebbs and flows inside our women's undine bodies.

Moving like mermaids, we were not surprised when this nursery pod suddenly arched up to leap above our bow, inches away from our outstretched hands. Benevolent, unblinking eyes sought ours as mid-flight, the dolphins studied us: Were we to be trusted? Did we mean harm? Did we have bad taste in music? Would we make even tolerable dance partners?

In perfect sync, six dolphins dived back down to disappear and we were left bobbing there with only ourselves, like so many wallflowers awaiting an invitation. "Da-dum, da-dum, da-dum, dum-dum!" Captain Rosie sang out at the top of her lovely voice. And I remembered her telling us before we left shore that her first encounter with this wild nursery pod had left her utterly changed.

"They circled me underwater," she had said. "Careful and curious. After all, they had babies to protect and humans don't have such a great record for respecting their privacy. But I just hung out there with my scuba, trying to make quiet bubbles. One of the dolphins swam right up into my face mask and simply gazed at me for what seemed like an hour. Her sonar zinged inside my body like a tuning fork, her big eye studying me with such kindness I almost cried. Then she made her decision. I was a human she could afford to meet. And we've all known each other so long that sometimes I can't figure out if I'm baby-sitting them or they're looking out for me. All I know is that they keep inviting me to dance."

Captain Rosie changed the music to a more luxurious waltz, with violins and even a deep cello. This seemed to delight the dolphins who suddenly shot straight up out of the water flanking our boat on both sides, then splashing under the surface in exact rhythm to the waltz. They synchronized their breathing to time with the upbeat and then dove on the downbeat. Up—exhale. And down—inhale. Their open-close blowholes were like percussive instruments holding the syncopated heartbeat of the song. Wave after wave of music and dolphins rising and falling until scanning the horizon was like looking at a sheet of music, and the grace, half-, and trilling notes were sleek, leaping dolphin bodies. Signature whistles like high-frequency tones in our ears, our eyes tenderly held by other, animal eyes who looked into us with the uncanny intimacy of mammal kin. Didn't they breathe with us, didn't they nurse their young, and surrender to their elders the wise-woman task of taking us into the new territory, the next generation? Didn't these dolphins perhaps even recognize that in our own way we, too, were a female pod—sisters on the sea?

As the last waltz faded and the dolphins dove and disappeared as if the dance were over, Captain Rosie leaned over the helm and declared, "I only bring humans who I think will give the dolphins hope. I'm showing you to them today so that these dolphins will go back to their Swinging Single bachelor pods and say, 'Okay, guys, it's *your* turn to play with us. Let's make more love. Let's make more of *us!*' "

Play as procreation, play as creation—Captain Rosie's comments reminded me of the Australian petroglyphs that Gigi Coyle talks about in this book: rock pictures of humans coming out like little people-bubbles birthed from the blowholes of dolphins. Some of our indigenous myths also credit the animals with playing the world into creation. For those of us raised with the dreary story of Original Sin and a suffering god who has no daughters and asks his only son to love the world by dying and leaving the evil Earth, how very healing is another storyline: Original Play, with animals as our creators and inspiration. My own apprenticeship to animal play is not only healing my childhood among fundamentalists but also opening for me another future as well. This future looks a lot like the ancient and indigenous stories in which animals played, creating alongside us; and when they died they guided us into an afterlife that was less lonely because we were in the fine company of other animal souls.

Just as play is preparation for the challenges of later life, it is also a behavior that calls forth from us, animals and humans alike, the highest creativity and intelligence in imagining the future. Visionaries in any species are often those who play most profoundly. They look over the next hill; they find a new way of swinging from a tree to ford a river that one day might rise to a flash flood; they mate in new ways. They do not support the status quo. This play is often risky behavior for many animals, because while a dolphin is spinning, a monkey is pirouetting, a lion somersaulting or making love on the open savannah, that individual is at risk to predators—and sometimes even at risk from his or her own species. When we play, we give up our wariness and our walls and our old structures. Some scientists believe that those who play the most in any species are also those who most advance evolution. If play were not somehow essential to evolution, why would natural selection have permitted, even promoted such unabashed, unprotected play?

As our human culture becomes more "advanced," our capacity for play receives less respect. Human children are scheduled, structured, set down in front of televisions that baby-sit the developing brain by numbing it. In Japan, schoolchildren are committing suicide at an alarming rate, showing the stress of too much pressure to perform academically and not enough time to simply *be*, to play. In a recent article on how play has all but disappeared from the lives of many activity-addicted children, psychologist Ann Jernberg, who began Chicago's Therapy Institute, explains, "These children are very tense. They're like little high-powered executives." These kids on the fast track are simply burning out. If our children are forgetting or not being allowed the crucial solitary and communal art of play, then what are the chances of we adults regaining the openness for it?

A recent *New York Times* article on personal health cites two researchers who conduct play workshops to help people recover from addictions. The researchers explain that "many people who succumb to life's stresses have forgotten (or never learned) how to play." When we limit our survival strategies to only what works and don't ever play at developing new, adaptive ways of being in the world, we also limit our species' chances for evolving. And yet we cannot structure play as a means to an end; we can't teach ourselves or our children to play because it's "good for you." Play that is goal-oriented will soon become tiresome and just another kind of work.

Play, as any apprentice to animal play will affirm, is the most rewarding when it is the most fun. I do not believe that my cat Isabel was trying to lighten my mood and thereby get more food or attention when she literally played with my despair. Isabel's perception of my human solitude was an invitation to interspecies bonding; her take on my being single again was to claim new territory that she considered all hers, without the intrusion of other humans. Her fierce delight in what had seemed only painful to me caused me to reconsider through my cat's point of view just where I was and what was now possible.

Perhaps the unexplored and often undervalued territory of human and animal play is truly the final frontier that we can explore between species and within ourselves. Play is a pristine and wild preserve that begins an inward adventure and expands out into the wider world, where we include others in our imagination, our invitation to play.

These days, whenever I find myself lying on the floor of my studio trying to keep my tissues from being shredded by a playful Siamese, I look up at walls adorned with photos of dolphins, with a wooden ark carved with yellow giraffes and long-memoried elephant elders accompanying humans in the life-and-species-saving boat that will sail them all into the next world. And I ask myself questions that restore my sense of play as survival. What if, like dolphins, each of us spent three-quarters of every day at play? What if, like baby gorillas surviving their orphan-trauma, we spent seven hours a day grooming, tickling, preening, and wrapping our loving primate legs around each other? What if, like lions, we lay in the sunshine, our feline tails ticking off naptimes, while our offspring, the next generation, lay curled in a dreaming litter? And what if, like a little cat in new territory, we played with our griefs, our losses, our imaginary enemies—until just by going through the motions of play, we remembered not to take ourselves or our species so seriously. Until we sighed and let go, like people-bubbles popping out of the blowholes of dolphins as they play at making more of us, making new worlds on open seas—between species.

EPILOGUE: DIGGING UP THE ROOTS

Jane Goodall

When we lose something that was very precious to us, whatever its nature, we grieve. Our grief may be short-lived sorrow or lead to a lengthy period of mourning. The depth of our grief depends on the nature of the relationship that we had with what we have lost, not on who or what that person or thing actually was. We might grieve more for the loss of a dog or a cat than a person—it simply depends on the relative contributions made by each to our physical and spiritual well-being.

I have deeply loved several dogs and grieved correspondingly deeply when they died. Just a few weeks ago at our family home in the U.K. we lost Cider, the dog who has shared our lives for the past thirteen years. I hate the thought of walking where she and I walked together. When I sit on "her" couch I feel a lump in my throat, and when the doorbell rings, and there are no fierce barks, it is not easy to go and let the caller in. I miss her snoring beside my bed at night. I am not ashamed to weep for her, as I wept for the other dogs who gave me so much.

The nature of my relationship with the Gombe chimpanzees is very different from that with my dogs. For one thing, dogs are utterly dependent on humans; for another, they become part of the household. From them I receive comfort when sad, and I can give comfort in return. With them I can share joy and excitement. With the chimpanzees it is different. They are free and independent. It is true that I have impinged on their lives, but only as an observer. (I speak here of the wild chimpanzees—relations can be very different with captive individuals.) The wild apes tolerate my presence. But they show no pleasure when they see me after an absence—they accept my goings and comings without comment. And this is as it should be since we are trying to study their natural lives. Moreover, the chimpanzees, unlike my dogs, do not depend on me for food or comfort. My relationship with them can best be described as one of mutual trust.

Nevertheless, there have been Gombe chimpanzees whom I have most truly loved—even though they did not reciprocate that love. One of these was old Flo. I shall never forget seeing her body as it lay at the edge of the fast-flowing Kakombe stream. I stayed close by for the better part of three days, to record the reactions of the other chimps. As I sat there I thought back over the hours we had spent together, that old female and I. I thought of all I had learned from her about maternal behavior, and family relationships. I thought of her fearless, indomitable character. And I mourned her passing. Just as I grieved for old McGregor whom we had to shoot after polio paralyzed both legs and he dislocated one arm as he dragged his body up a tree. And I was devastated when little Getty died. He had been everyone's favorite, loved by humans and even, I would swear, by the chimpanzees themselves. It was a long time before I could watch other infants without resentment, without asking the meaningless question: Why did it have to be him?

Of course, I was also very close to David Greybeard, the first chimpanzee who ever let me approach. And I missed him very much when we finally realized he must have died. But we never knew exactly when this was, for we never found his body. Thus there was no sudden realization of his passing, no moment in time when grieving could begin.

Of all the Gombe chimpanzees I have known over the years, it was Melissa whose death affected me the most, for I was there at the very end. I wrote about it in my last book, *Through a Window*.

> By evening, Melissa was alone. One foot hung down from her nest and every so often her toes moved. I stayed there, sitting on the forest floor. . . . Occasionally I spoke. I don't know if she knew I was there or, if she did, whether it made any difference. But I wanted to be with her as night fell: I didn't want her to be completely alone. . . . There was a distant pant-hoot far across the valley, but Melissa was silent. Never again would I hear her distinctive hoarse call. Never again would I wander with her from one patch of food to the next, waiting, at one with life of the forest, as she rested or groomed with one of her offspring. The stars were suddenly blurred and I wept for the passing of an old friend. Even now, seven years later, when I pass the tree where she died, I pause for a moment to remember her.

The nature of the grief I feel when a loved dog dies has one component that is lacking from the sorrow caused by the death of one of my wild chimpanzee friends. Because dogs depend on us for food and comfort and help in sickness, there has always been an element of guilt in my grief for their passing. In their dog-minds, did I not let them down—however hard I tried to help? And could I, perhaps, have done more than I did? This nagging guilt, which we usually feel when a loved human companion passes away, has no place in my grieving for chimpanzee friends who have died. For they had no expectations of help.

The emotions triggered by the depth of a chimpanzee I have loved are different again from those that overwhelm me whenever I think of the vanishing wildlife of the world, of animals shot by hunters, snared by poachers, starved by the encroachment of farmers into their feeding grounds. I am angered, as well as saddened, when I think of their suffering, depressed when I think how hard it is to help them. The sight of a rhino killed for his horn is horribly distressing. It brings tears to my eyes, but the tears are part rage because we seem unable to stop the slaughter. True mourning, I believe, can only follow the death of an individual we have known and loved, whose life for a while has been linked with ours.

I have always had a great passion for trees, for woods and forests. Often I lay my hand on the trunk of a tree, feeling the texture of its bark and imagining the sap coursing up the trunk, taking life to the leaves far above. Some trees seem to have characters of their own: the slim and elegant individual, rustling soft songs in the breeze; the helpful one, with wide branches and dense foliage, providing shade; and the strong and comforting tree with a friendly overhanging trunk to protect one from the rain. When I was a child I used sometimes to lie looking up at the blue sky through the leaves of a birch tree in the garden. I specially loved that tree in the moonlight, when the white trunk was bright and ghostly and the leaves were black with glinting silver where the soft light caught them. And when it died, like so many other birch trees in the drought of 1977, when no leaves burst out in the spring, I felt great sadness, and also a sense of nostalgia. In sorrowing for the tree, was I also grieving for my lost youth?

A little while ago I drove along a road in Tanzania that once ran through miles of forest. Twenty years ago there were lions and elephants, leopards and wild dogs, and a myriad of birds. But now the trees are gone and the road guided us relentlessly, mile after mile, through hot, dusty country, where crops were withered under the glare of the sun and there was no shade. I felt a great melancholy, and also anger. This anger was not directed against the poor farmers who were trying to eke out a livelihood from the now inhospitable land, but against mankind in general. We multiply and we destroy, chopping and killing. Now, in this desecrated area, the women searching for firewood must dig up the roots of the trees they have long since cut down to make space for crops.

Gombe National Park is, today, like an island of forest and wildlife set in a desert of human habitation. During a recent visit I climbed to the top of the rift escarpment and looked to the east, the north, the south. In 1980 I could look out from the same place, and there was chimpanzee habitat stretched as far as I could see. Now the steep slopes are bare of trees and have become increasingly barren and rocky, more and more of the precious top soil washed away with every heavy rain. And the chimpanzees, along with most of the other wild animals, have gone. But at least the little oasis of the park is safe, and in its ancient forests I can for a while take refuge from the problems of the world outside. If Gombe was destroyed I should know inconsolable grief. For Gombe, with all its vivid and unique chimpanzee characters, with all its tumbling memories, has been an integral part of my life for more than thirty years. It is, I have always said, paradise on earth. And who would not mourn expulsion from paradise?

Diane Ackerman is a poet, writer, and naturalist whose fourteen books, including *The Moon by Whale Light* and *A Natural History of the Senses*, have reached a wide audience of readers passionately interested in the lives of animals and the natural world. Her latest books are *Rarest of the Rare* and *A Slender Thread*.

Ellery Akers is a writer, naturalist, and artist living in Port Reyes Station, California. Her book of poems, *Knocking on the Earth*, was published by Wesleyan University Press.

Natalie Angier, a science writer for *The New York Times*, has won the Pulitzer Prize, the Lewis Thomas Award, and the American Association for the Advancement of Science Award.

Susan Arkeketa is chair of the Humanities and Fine Arts Department at Haskell Indian Nations University, Lawrence, Kansas. She is the mother of Cody Elizabeth and Jessica Margaret. Susan traveled the United States as Miss Indian America XXV and graduated from the University of Oklahoma with an M.A. in Communications.

Reneé Askins lives in Moose, Wyoming, and is currently at work on a book about our relationship with animals and the wild, to be published by Doubleday.

Flor Fernandez Barrios, Ph.D., is a transpersonal psychotherapist in private practice in Seattle. Born in Cuba, she is a ritualist and writer. She is an active member of Los Nortenos, a Latin group of writers dedicated to promoting cultural awareness through storytelling. She is working on a collection of essays about her spiritual journey as a Cuban exile.

Susan F. Boucher has an M.A. in Creative Writing from the University of Colorado. She currently teaches writing to community college students in Melbourne, Florida, and riding to handicapped children and adults. Anders, the horse in Boucher's selection "Partnering Pegasus," continues to teach her.

Diane Boyd-Heger is a wildlife biologist who has studied wolves for the past twenty years, focusing on wolf recolonization in the Rocky Mountains.

Beth Brant, a Bay of Quinte Mohawk, is the author of *Mohawk Trail, Food & Spirits*, and *Writing as Witness*. She is also the editor of *A Gathering of Spirit* and *I'll Sing Till the Day I Die*.

E. K. Caldwell (Tsalabi/Shawnee/Celtic/German) was a poet/writer whose work was widely anthologized in Canada and the United States. She was a regular contributor to *News from Indian Country* and was the 1996 Native American Journalist Association Award recipient for Best Feature Story. She served on the National Caucus of Wordcraft Circle of Native Writers and Storytellers. E. K. Caldwell died during the production of this book.

Susan Cerulean has worked on behalf of wildlife conservation in Florida for seventeen years. She is a nature writer and is currently at work on her second book, *Looking After God's Birds,* from which this essay is excerpted.

Judith Collas, at the age of fiftysomething, found happiness with an American Staffordshire terrier. Judith supports her garden, dog, and writing by working behind the scenes at UCLA.

Ann Daum grew up in the White River Valley of Western South Dakota. She now shares the family ranch with five cats, seventeen horses, and five hundred mother cows. When she's not in the barn, she's working on her first book, a collection of personal essays.

Marsha De La O is the author of *Black Hope*, which won the New Issues Poetry Prize for 1997.

Gretel Ehrlich first went to Wyoming as a documentary filmmaker but began to write full-time in 1979. She has also worked on ranches—lambing, branding, herding sheep, and calving. Her prose pieces have appeared in *The New York Times*, *The Atlantic*, *Harper's*, and *New Age Journal*. She has published two books of poetry, a story collection, and a collection of essays and has received awards from the National Endowment for the Arts and the Wyoming Council for the Arts.

Chris Ferris is the author of *The Darkness Is Light Enough: The Field Journal of a Night Naturalist.*

Mary Anne Fleetwood is a nationally certified massage therapist with a practice in Rehoboth Beach, Delaware. She is also a professional writer who enjoys writing about massage therapy. She earned a B.A. in English at Hood College, an M.A. in English at Trinity College (Hartford, Connecticut), and graduated from the Baltimore School of Massage. She shares a home with two companion cats.

Dian Fossey spent thirteen years in the remote African rain forests with the greatest of the great apes, the endangered mountain gorilla. Although Dr. Fossey's work ended tragically with her murder, her book *Gorillas in the Mist* remains an enthralling testament to one of the longest field studies of primates and reveals Fossey's remarkable efforts to ensure a future for the African rain forest and the few hundred gorillas that remain there.

Judith Freeman, author of three novels and a collection of short stories, was awarded a John Simon Guggenheim Fellowship in fiction for 1997. She lives in Los Angeles and Idaho.

Pamela Frierson is the author of *The Burning Island* and other writings on nature and culture. She lives on the slopes of Mauna Loa volcano and is working on a book on the Northwestern Hawaiian Islands.

Toni Frohoff currently works as a scientific consultant and research biologist for nonprofit and government agencies on a variety of wildlife issues. She has studied and published numerous papers on the behavior of wild animals, with an emphasis on the effects of human activities on marine mammals in captivity and in the wild. Dr. Frohoff has a Ph.D. in Behavioral Biology and an M.S. in Wildlife and Fisheries Sciences.

Birute M. F. Galdikas was born in Germany and raised in Canada. She is a professor at Simon Fraser University in Burnaby, B.C. and the Universitas Nasional in Jakarta, Indonesia. She holds a Ph.D. in Anthropology from UCLA and is president of the Orangutan Foundation International in Los Angeles. She divides her time between Borneo, Vancouver, and Los Angeles.

Tess Gallagher, best known as a poet, recently completed her second book of short stories, *At the Owl Woman Saloon* (Scribner, 1997). She is the author of eight books of poetry and a book of essays. Her fascination with and love of hummingbirds, as well as her portrait, surrounded by hummingbirds, painted by Seattle painter Alfredo Arreguin, were the inspirations for her story "Venison Pie."

Jane Goodall continues to study and write about primate behavior. She has founded the Gombe Stream Research Center in Gombe National Park, Tanzania, and the Jane Goodall Institute for Wildlife Research, Education, and Conservation, which has its headquarters in Tucson, Arizona. Jane Goodall has won numerous conservation awards.

Wendy Gordon has worked at the Gorilla Foundation in Woodside, California, since 1990 as a research assistant, working regularly with the gorillas; before that she spent four years as a zoo volunteer, educating the public about gorillas. The Gorilla Foundation is currently working to establish a preserve in Hawaii where gorillas will be able to live semi-free in a protected, natural environment.

Temple Grandin, Ph.D., is a gifted animal scientist who has designed one-third of all the livestock-handling facilities in the United States. She is the author of two memoirs, *Emergence: Labeled Autistic* and *Thinking in Pictures*.

Susan Griffin is the author of several critically acclaimed books, including *Women and Nature* and *Pornography and Silence*. She is the recipient of numerous grants and awards. Her book *A Chorus of Stones* was the winner of the Bay Area Reviewers Association for Nonfiction and was a finalist for the Pulitzer Prize for Nonfiction and the National Book Critics Circle Award for Criticism.

Joy Harjo is an enrolled member of the Muscoggee Tribe and the author of several books of poetry, including *She Had Some Horses* and *The Woman Who Fell from the Sky*. Harjo edited, with Gloria Bird, the anthology of Native American women's work, *Reinventing the Enemy's Language*. Joy Harjo is also a musician with her band Poetic Justice; they have produced a CD based on Harjo's poetry and combining jazz and Native American prayer and song.

Frances (Fiz) Harwood, Ph.D., is a cultural anthropologist, bioregionalist, and permaculture designer. She currently lives off the grid in Northern New Mexico.

Eloise Klein Healey has published four books of poetry. She is the chair of the MFA in Creative Writing Program at Antioch University Los Angeles and associate editor/poetry editor of the *Lesbian Review of Books*. Her most recent collection of poems, *Artemis in Echo Park*, deals with animal life in the city.

Vicki Hearne has been training animals for more than twenty-five years. The author of two volumes of poetry, a novel, and the widely praised

Bandit and *Animal Happiness*, she received a 1992 award for outstanding literary achievement from the American Academy and Institute of Arts and Letters.

Denise Herzing, Ph.D, is Research Director of The Wild Dolphin Project and on the faculty at Florida Atlantic University's Biological Science Department. She has been studying Atlantic spotted dolphins in the wild since 1985.

Linda Hogan, a Chickasaw poet, essayist, and novelist, worked as a volunteer in wildlife and raptor rehabilitation. In 1995 she organized a conference for tribal elders on endangered species and was part of a working group for Native input into the reauthorization of the Endangered Species Act. Her lifelong area of interest has been the traditional relationship between indigenous peoples and animals. Her books include *Dwellings: A Spiritual History of the Living World*, *Book of Medicines*, and *Solar Storms*.

Gillian van Houten is a writer and photographer on the Londolozoi Productions wildlife film team in South Africa. Her special interest is exploring new ways of relating to the natural world, especially animals.

Christine Jurzykowski is co-steward of Fossil Rim Wildlife Center, a 2,700-acre wildlife preserve open to the public in Glenn Rose, Texas. Her work is dedicated to catalyzing a global realization that recognizes the interdependence of all living things.

Barbara Kingsolver is the author of *Pigs in Heaven*, *Animal Dreams*, *Homeland and Other Stories*, and *The Bean Trees*. She has also written two nonfiction books, *High Tide in Tucson: Essays from Now and Never* and *Holding the Line: Women in the Great Arizona Mine Strike of 1983*. She grew up in Eastern Kentucky and now lives with her husband and two daughters near Tucson, Arizona.

Ursula K. Le Guin is the author of more than thirty books, including *The Lathe of Heaven*, *The Left Hand of Darkness*, *Dancing at the Edge of the World*, and her recent version of the *Lao Tzu: Tao Te Ching: A Book About the Way and the Power of the Way*.

Denise Levertov frequently writes poetry celebrating nature from a feminine perspective, although she does not define herself as a nature poet or feminist. She is an activist in the peace movement while teaching at several universities. Born in London in 1923, she was educated mostly at home, worked as a nurse during World War II, and became an American citizen in 1955. She has published more than a dozen volumes of poetry.

Mary Lockwood is from the Inupiaq village of Unalakleet, Alaska.

Trish Maharam lives in Seattle, Washington. She continues to write, mother, garden, and nurture horses while maintaining a career as a magazine editor.

Maía is a poet/fiction writer living in Southern California. Recently she completed a manuscript of poems, *Kafka's Angel*.

Naomi Mattis lives in Santa Fe, New Mexico, and Crestone, Colorado. As a Buddhist teacher and psychotherapist, she works with groups and individuals and offers retreats.

Linda McCarriston is a poet and novelist living in Alaska. Her books include *Eva Mary* and *Talking Soft Dutch*.

Susan Chernak McElroy is the author of *Animals as Teachers and Healers: True Stories and Reflections* (Ballantine, 1997). Her vision is to transform the current, "dominion-based" relationship between humans and animals into one of respect and communion. Her books, articles, and audiotapes all speak to spiritual and healing aspects of the human-animal partnership. She lives in Jackson, Wyoming.

Joan McIntyre wrote and edited the groundbreaking anthology *Mind in the Waters: Celebrating the Consciousness of Whales and Dolphins*. She has also authored *The Gentle Art of Whale Watching*.

Erica Helm Meade is a storyteller, therapist, and author of *Tell It by Heart, Women and the Healing Power of Story*, published by Open Court. Her poems, articles, and stories have appeared in numerous journals and anthologies. She gives presentations and workshops at conferences, festivals, and universities in the United States and abroad.

Rigoberta Menchú is a respected Guatamalan activist whose recent book is *I, Rigoberta Menchú: An Indian Woman in Guatamala*.

Anna Merz was born in the United Kingdom. She received her degree from Nottingham University in Politics, Philosophy, and Economic History and read for the Bar. She went to Ghana in 1958 where she ran an engineering company and a racing stable. She was an Hon. Game Warden in Ghana and Kenya. She founded Ngare Sergoi Rhino Sanctuary in 1983 and is director of the Lewa Wildlife Conservancy in Kenya. She is the author of *Rhino: At the Brink of Extinction*.

Deena Metzger has lived with wolves for twenty years, writing about them from her home in the Santa Monica mountains. As poet, writer, and lay analyst, she has devoted her writing and working life to ecological and environmental concerns. Her books include *Tree*, *What Dinah Thought*, *The Woman Who Slept with Men to Take the War Out of Them*, and *Writing for Your Life*. She is currently working on a book entitled *The Broken Treaty: A Meditation on Animal Intelligence*.

Judith Minty is the author of four full-length collections of poetry and three chapbooks. Her first book, *Lake Songs and Other Fears*, was recipient of the United States Award of the International Poetry Forum in 1973. Minty presently lives along the Lake Michigan shoreline with her husband and her dog, River, and spends part of the year hermitizing at a remote area in Michigan's Upper Peninsula.

Alexandra B. Morton, born in Connecticut in 1957, began studying whales in 1978. She is the author of two books, *Siwiti: A Whale's Story* and *In the Company of Whales*, both published in Canada. She continues her research and protection of the whales' habitat.

Cynthia Moss, born and educated in the United States, moved to Africa in 1968, where she has spent the past twenty-five years studying elephants and working for their conservation. In 1972 she started the Amboseli Elephant Research Project, which she continues to direct. She is also a senior associate for the African Wildlife Foundation and the author of the highly acclaimed *Portraits in the Wild* and *Elephant Memories*. She lives in Kenya.

Francine Patterson, president of the Gorilla Foundation in Woodside, California, has been communicating with gorillas Koko, Michael, and Ndume. She began to study communication with Koko by means of sign language in 1972.

Katherine Payne, of the Laboratory of Ornithology, Cornell University, has studied the song of humpback whales for fifteen years and the southern right whales for another eleven years. She is also an expert on elephant communication and the author of the children's book, *Elephants Calling*, as well as articles in *National Geographic*.

Fran Peavey is the author of *Heart Politics*, *A Shallow Pool of Tears*, and *By Life's Grace*. A writer, environmental activist, and peacemaker, she has been honored for her significant efforts in cleaning up the Ganges and in assisting women in war-torn Bosnia and Croatia.

Brenda Peterson is author of *Nature and Other Mothers*, *Living by Water*, and *Sister Stories*, as well as three novels. She is also an environmental writer and journalist. For the past twelve years she has been studying and encountering dolphins and other whales in the wild. Since 1993 she has covered the wild wolf—from its slaughter in Alaska to its reintroduction in Yellowstone and Olympic National Park. She has written, with Linda

Hogan, a series of articles against proposed whaling in the Northwest for *The Seattle Times.*

Marge Piercy is the author of twelve novels, including *He, She and It,* for which she won the prestigious Arthur C. Clarke Award in Great Britain. Her twelve collections of poetry include *The Moon Is Always Female, Circles on the Water, My Mother's Body, Available Light,* and, most recently, *Mars and Her Children.*

Pattiann Rogers' most recent books are *Firekeeper, New and Selected Poems* (1994), and *Eating Bread and Honey* (1997), both from Milkweed Editions. She has received a Guggenheim Fellowship and a Lannan Poetry Fellowship.

Eva Saulitis has spent her summers for the past eight years on Prince William Sound, where she is engaged in long-term studies of killer whales. She bases her research boat, the *Whale II,* in Cordova. In 1993 she received her Master of Science degree in wildlife biology from the University of Alaska. Her thesis documented the natural history of the northern Pacific killer whale and explored the effects of the *Exxon Valdez* oil spill on the species.

Leslie Marmon Silko was born in Albuquerque of mixed ancestry—Laguna Pueblo, Mexican, and white. She grew up in the Laguna Pueblo Reservation and lives there today with her husband and two children. She is the author of the novel *Almanac of the Dead,* and her stories have appeared in many magazines and collections, including *Writers of the Purple Sage.* She is the recipient of a five-year MacArthur Foundation Grant.

Helena Symends has studied orcas for the past seventeen years, along with her husband, Dr. Paul Spang. Their famous Orca Lab is on a remote island in British Columbia.

Mary Tall Mountain was a Koyukon Athabascan elder and author of *Raven Tells Stories* and *Green March Moon.*

Linda Tellington-Jones is an animal activist and healer. Her revolutionary book *The Tellington Touch* describes her interspecies physical therapy techniques with wild animals all over the world.

Terry Tempest Williams is the author of *Refuge: An Unnatural History of a Natural Place, An Unspoken Hunger,* and *Desert Quartet.* Williams is Naturalist-in-Residence at the Utah Museum of Natural History and has lobbied for the preservation of wildlife and wilderness throughout her native Utah and the West.

Barbara Earl Thomas, a nationally noted artist, writes and paints in Seattle. *Storm Watch,* a book of her painting and writing, is forthcoming from the University of Washington Press in 1998.

Haunani-Kay Trask is the author of a book of poetry, *Light in the Crevice Never Seen,* a book of essays, *From a Native Daughter,* and a book of feminist theory, *Eros and Power.* She is professor of Hawaiian Studies, University of Hawaii-Manoa.

Paula Underwood wrote *Who Speaks for Wolf* as a gift for all Earth's children. An oral historian, her lifelong training in ancient Native American methodology has uniquely prepared her to share these histories with us. Underwood won the Thomas Jefferson Cup for quality writing and is director of *The Past Is Prologue* Educational Program, which was granted "Exemplary Education Program" status by the U.S. Department of Education. She was born in Los Angeles and, after thirty-five years in Washington, D.C., now lives near San Francisco.

Alice Walker is an acclaimed novelist *(The Color Purple)* and essayist; her novel *Possessing the Secret of Joy* concerns her international work on the sexual binding of women. Her most recent book is *Anything We Love Can Be Saved.*

Charlotte Zoë Walker is the author of *Condor and Hummingbird,* a novel (Wild Trees Press, 1986, and The Women's Press, 1987), and the editor of *Sharp Eyes: John Burroughs and American Nature Writing* (Peter Lang, 1997). She is a professor of English and Women's Studies at State University of New York, College at Oneonta.

Elizabeth Woody is the author of three books of poetry. She received an American Book Award in 1990 and the DNBA's William Stafford Memorial Award for Poetry in 1994 for best book of poetry.

Stacy Young and her husband, Vaughn, are the directors of West Seattle Cat Rescue (WSCR), a no-kill shelter and foster network which has found homes for hundreds of homeless and abandoned cats in Seattle. Through their nonprofit Friends of the Animals Foundation, they are raising the funds to establish a sanctuary for abused and abandoned animals in the Seattle area.

Dian Fossey, "Decimation by Poachers" (excerpts) from *Gorillas in the Mist.* Copyright © 1983 by Dian Fossey. Reprinted with the permission of Houghton Mifflin Company and Russell & Volkening, Inc. All rights reserved.

Birute M. F. Galdikas, "Akmad" from *Reflections of Eden: My Years with the Orangutans of Borneo.* Copyright © 1995 by Birute M. F. Galdikas. Reprinted with the permission of Little, Brown and Company.

Tess Gallagher, "Venison Pie." A slightly different version was published in *Indiana Review* (Spring 1996) and collected in Tess Gallagher's story collection, *At the Owl Woman Saloon* (New York: Scribner, September 1997). Reprinted with the permission of the author.

Jane Goodall, "I Acknowledge Mine" from *Visions of Caliban.* Copyright © 1993 by Dale Peterson and Jane Goodall. Reprinted with the permission of Houghton Mifflin Company and Sterling Lord Literistic, Inc. All rights reserved. "Digging Up the Roots" from *Orion* (Winter 1994). Reprinted with the permission of *Orion*, 195 Main Street, Great Barrington, MA 01230.

Susan Griffin, "His Power: He Tames What Is Wild" from *Woman and Nature: The Roaring Inside Her.* Copyright © 1978 by Susan Griffin. Reprinted with the permission of HarperCollins Publishers, Inc. and the author.

Joy Harjo, "She Had Some Horses" from *She Had Some Horses* (New York: Thunder's Mouth Press, 1983). Copyright © 1983 by Joy Harjo. Reprinted with the permission of Thunder's Mouth Press.

Eloise Klein Healey, "Wild Mothers" from *Artemis in Echo Park.* Copyright © 1991 by Eloise Klein Healey. Reprinted with the permission of Firebrand Books, 141 The Commons, Ithaca, NY 14850.

Vicki Hearne, "Justice in Venice Beach" from *Animal Happiness.* Copyright © 1994 by Vicki Hearne. Reprinted with the permission of HarperCollins Publishers, Inc. and the Robert Cornfield Literary Agency.

Denise Herzing, "Underwater Overtures" from *BBC Magazine.* Reprinted with the permission of the author.

Barbara Kingsolver, "Making Peace" from *High Tide in Tucson: Essays from Now or Never* (New York: HarperCollins Publishers, 1995). Copyright © 1995 by Barbara Kingsolver. Reprinted with the permission of the author.

Ursula K. Le Guin, "Mazes" from *Buffalo Gals and Other Animal Presences* (Santa Barbara: Capra Press, 1987). Originally appeared in *Epoch*.